C000180425

ACCA

Applied Skills

Financial Reporting (FR)

Practice & Revision Kit

For exams in September 2022, December 2022, March 2023 and June 2023

First edition 2008
Sixteenth edition February 2022

ISBN 9781 5097 4757 3
Previous ISBN 9781 5097 3805 2
eISBN 9781 5097 4463 3

British Library Cataloguing-in-Publication Data
A catalogue record for this book is available from the British
Library

Published by

BPP Learning Media Ltd
BPP House, Aldine Place
142-144 Uxbridge Road
London W12 8AA

www.bpp.com/learningmedia

Printed in the United Kingdom

Your learning materials, published by BPP Learning Media
Ltd, are printed on paper obtained from traceable,
sustainable sources.

Contents

Question index

The headings in this checklist/index indicate the main topics of questions, but many questions cover several different topics.

Past exam questions are designated with the date of the exam in which they featured, although some have been amended to reflect subsequent changes to the syllabus or in the format of the exam. There are four exam sittings per year, but ACCA only publish two exams' worth of questions per year. These releases are compiled from questions selected from the preceding sessions. These compilation exams are denoted as 'Mar/Jun' and 'Sept/Dec' in the index below.

Mock exam 1 (ACCA Practice Exam 1 CBE)
Mock exam 2 (ACCA Specimen CBE)
Mock exam 3 (ACCA Practice Exam 2 CBE)
Mock exam 4 (Section C is the ACCA Sept/Dec 21 exam)

BPP
LEARNING
MEDIA

The Financial Reporting (FR) exam

Applied Skills exams are all computer-based exams (CBE).

The examination lasts three hours and all questions are compulsory.

The exam will comprise three exam sections:

Section	Style of question type	Description	Proportion of exam, %
A	Objective test (OT) question	15 questions × 2 marks	30
B	Objective test (OT) case question	3 questions × 10 marks Each question will contain 5 subparts, each worth 2 marks	30
C	Constructed response (long questions)	2 questions × 20 marks	40
Total			100

All questions are compulsory.

Sections A and B account for 60% of the total marks available in the exam. The use of OT questions in Sections A and B give the examining team scope to examine the whole of the syllabus and bring in topics that do not feature in the longer questions. It is really not possible to pass this exam by only revising certain topics.

Section C will contain one accounts preparation question and one interpretation question. The accounts preparation question could be a group accounting question which may require the preparation of a statement of financial position or statement of profit or loss or extracts thereof, and it may include the disposal of a subsidiary. You must revise all the consolidation workings, and you must know how to account for an associate.

A single company accounts preparation question allows the examining team to bring in more complex IFRS Standards. Make sure you can deal with the more complex areas of leases, revenue recognition, deferred tax, calculating finance costs using the effective interest rate, prior period adjustments and discontinued operations.

The interpretation question may be based on a single company or group scenario. You may be asked to calculate specific ratios and provide reasons for their movement based on information within the scenario. You may also be asked to critically analyse the information you have been provided with by management by considering the validity of the information in the context of the ratios calculated. You must ensure that you use the scenario provided when discussing the movement in ratios and do not provide generic statements.

Question practice

Question practice is a core part of learning new topic areas. When you practice questions, you should focus on improving the Exam success skills – personal to your needs – by obtaining feedback or through a process of self-assessment.

Practicing as many exam-style questions as possible in the ACCA CBE practice platform will be the key to passing this exam. You should attempt questions under timed conditions and ensure you produce full answers to the discussion parts as well as doing the calculations. Also ensure that you attempt all mock exams under exam conditions.

ACCA have launched a free on-demand resource designed to mirror the live exam experience helping you to become more familiar with the exam format. You can access the platform via the Study Support Resources section of the ACCA website navigating to the CBE question practice section and logging in with your myACCA credentials.

Passing the FR exam

If you covered the technical content in the workbook and attempted a sufficient number of questions, then you should go into the exam feeling confident that you can pass this exam. What you must do is remain calm and tackle it in a professional manner. There are a number of points which you should bear in mind:

- You must read the question properly. Students often fail to read the question properly and miss some of the information. Time spent reading the question a second time would be time well spent. Make yourself do this, don't just rush into an answer.

- Workings in Section C must be clear and cross-referenced. If the marker can read and understand your workings, they can give you credit for using the right method, even if your answer is wrong. If your answer is wrong and there are no workings, or they are incomprehensible, you will get no marks for that part of the question. Many candidates simply provide the final answer in the CBE spreadsheet response area and do not provide workings or formula, which makes it very difficult to score marks. You can use the formula available within the spreadsheet response area which will help to avoid having to write out your calculations. If you use the calculator function, you need to type your workings into the response area, as the markers cannot see what has been entered on the calculator.

- Stick to the timings and answer all questions. Do not spend too long on one question at the expense of others. The number of extra marks you will gain on that question will be minimal, and you could have at least obtained the easy marks on the next question.

- Make sure you get the easy marks. If an accounts preparation question contains something that you are unable to do, just ignore it and do the rest. You will probably only lose a few marks and if you start trying to puzzle it out you might waste a lot of minutes.

- Answer the question. In a discussion-type question, such as an interpretation question, you may be tempted to just write down everything you know about the topic. This will do you no good. The marking parameters for these questions are quite precise. You will only get marks for making points that answer the question exactly as it has been set. So don't waste your time waffling – you could be scoring marks somewhere else.

Avoiding weaknesses

- There is no choice in this exam – all questions have to be answered. You must therefore study the entire syllabus – there are no short-cuts.

- Ability to answer OT questions and case question improves with practice. Try to get as much practice with these questions as you can.

- The longer questions will be based on scenarios and answers must be focused and specific to the information provided in the scenario.

Exam technique tips

Section A Objective test (OT) questions

Some OT questions are easier than others. Answer those that you feel fairly confident about as quickly as you can. Come back later to those you find more difficult. This could be a way of making use of the time in the examination most efficiently and effectively. Some questions are more time-consuming than others.

The first more time-consuming OT question will involve doing a computation. You will probably need to jot down a quick proforma to answer a computational question. If the OT question is a multiple choice question, remember that the wrong answers will usually involve common errors, so don't assume that because you have the same answer as one of the options that your answer is necessarily correct! Double check to make sure you haven't made any silly mistakes. If you haven't got the same answer as any of the options, rework your computation, thinking carefully about what errors you could have made. If you still haven't got one of the options, choose the one which is nearest to your answer.

The second more time-consuming OT question is one in which you are asked to consider a number of statements and identify which one (or more) of them is correct. Make sure that you read each statement at least twice before making your selection. Be careful to follow the requirements of the OT question exactly – for example, if you are asked to identify **two** correct statements. Make sure that you understand the wording of 'written' OT questions before selecting your answer.

Section B Case OT questions

The general advice for Section A OT questions stands for the OT case question in Section B. Additional advice is to make sure that you read the whole case scenario. Make a note of any specific instructions or assumptions, such as 'Ignore the calculation of depreciation' for a non-current asset question. Then skim through the requirements of the five questions. The questions are independent of each other and can be answered in any order.

Calculations in Section C questions

There will be some relatively straightforward calculations in the question and some will be more difficult. Always do the bits you can and don't be tempted to write off a whole question just because some bits are difficult. If you get stuck, make an assumption, state it and move on. Do not miss out on easy marks by not learning your proformas properly. Always remember to show your workings.

Discussions in Section C questions

Interpretations should be focused on the specific organisation and events described in the question and you should use the information provided to provide analysis that is relevant to the organisation you are faced with. This will gain more marks than regurgitation of knowledge. Read the question carefully and more than once, to ensure you are actually answering the specific requirements.

Pick out key words such as 'describe', 'evaluate' and 'discuss'. These all mean something specific.

- 'Describe' means to communicate the key features of
- 'Evaluate' means to assess the value of
- 'Discuss' means to examine in detail by argument

Clearly label the points you make in discussions so that the marker can identify them all rather than getting lost in the detail.

Provide answers in the format requested. Many interpretation questions now include a pre-formatted response area that you should use to give your answer structure.

Exam information

Computer-based exams

Applied Skills exams are all computer-based exams.

Format of the exam

As was noted above, the exam format will comprise three exam sections:

Section	Style of question type	Description	Proportion of exam, %
A	Objective test (OT) questions	15 questions × 2 marks	30
B	Objective test (OT) case questions	3 questions × 10 marks Each question will contain 5 subparts, each worth 2 marks	30
C	Constructed Response (long questions)	2 questions × 20 marks	40
Total			100

Section A and B questions will be selected from the entire syllabus and will contain a variety of question types. The responses to each question or subpart in the case of OT case questions are marked automatically as either correct or incorrect by computer.

Section C questions will mainly focus on the following syllabus areas but a minority of marks can be drawn from any other area of the syllabus

- Interpretation of financial statements of a single entity or groups (syllabus area C)
- Preparation of financial statements of a single entity or groups (syllabus area D)

The responses to these questions are human marked.

Additional information

The Study Guide provides more detailed guidance on the syllabus and can be found by visiting the exam resource finder on the ACCA website.

Useful websites

The websites below provide additional sources of information of relevance to your studies for *Financial Reporting*.

- www.accaglobal.com

   ACCA's website. The students' section of the website is invaluable for detailed information about the qualification, past issues of *Student Accountant* (including technical articles) and a free downloadable Student Planner App.

- www.bpp.com

   Our website provides information about BPP products and services, with a link to the ACCA website.

Helping you with your revision

BPP Learning Media – ACCA Approved Content Provider

As an ACCA **Approved Content Partner**, BPP Learning Media gives you the opportunity to use revision materials reviewed by the ACCA examining team. By incorporating the examining team comments and suggestions regarding the depth and breadth of syllabus coverage, the BPP Learning Media Practice & Revision Kit provides excellent, **ACCA-approved** support for your revision.

These materials are reviewed by the ACCA examining team. The objective of the review is to ensure that the material properly covers the syllabus and study guide outcomes, used by the examining team in setting the exams, in the appropriate breadth and depth. The review does not ensure that every eventuality, combination or application of examinable topics is addressed by the ACCA Approved Content. Nor does the review comprise a detailed technical check of the content as the Approved Content Provider has its own quality assurance processes in place in this respect.

BPP Learning Media do everything possible to ensure the material is accurate and up to date when sending to print. In the event that any errors are found after the print date, they are uploaded to the following website: www.bpp.com/learningmedia/Errata.

The structure of this Practice and Revision Kit

Using feedback obtained from ACCA examining team review:

- We look at the dos and don'ts of revising for, and taking, ACCA exams

- We focus on Financial Reporting (FR); we discuss revising the syllabus, what to do (and what not to do) in the exam, how to approach different types of question and ways of obtaining easy marks

- There are also four mock exams which provide you the opportunity to refine your knowledge and skills as part of your final exam preparations.

Selecting questions

We provide a full **question index** to help you plan your revision.

Making the most of question practice

At BPP Learning Media we realise that you need more than just questions and model answers to get the most from your question practice.

- Our **top tips** included for certain questions provide essential advice on tackling questions, presenting answers and the key points that answers need to include.

- We show you how you can pick up **easy marks** on some questions, as we know that picking up all readily available marks often can make the difference between passing and failing.

- We include **marking guides** to show you what the examining team rewards.

- We include **comments from the examining team** to show you where students struggled or performed well in the actual exam.

- We refer to the **2022 BPP Workbook** (for exams in September 2022, December 2022, March 2023 and June 2023) for detailed coverage of the topics covered in questions.

Attempting mock exams

There are four mock exams that provide practice at coping with the pressures of the exam day. We strongly recommend that you attempt them under exam conditions. **Mock exam 1** is the ACCA CBE Practice Exam 1. **Mock exam 2** is the ACCA CBE Specimen. **Mock exam 3** is the ACCA CBE Practice Exam 2. **Mock exam 4** has been formed from a mixture of exam standard questions. Sections A and B contain questions which come from various recent past exams. Section C is from the Sep/Dec 2021 CBE.

Essential skills areas to be successful in Financial Reporting

We think there are three areas you should develop in order to achieve exam success in Financial Reporting (FR).

(1)   Knowledge application

(2)   Specific FR skills

(3)   Exam success skills

These are shown in the diagram below:

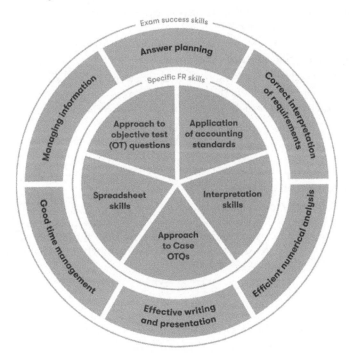

BPP
LEARNING
MEDIA

Specific FR skills

These are the skills specific to FR that we think you need to develop in order to pass the exam.

In the BPP Workbook for FR there are five **Skills Checkpoints** which define each skill and show how it is applied in answering a question. A brief summary of each skill is given below.

Skill 1: Approach to OT questions

As 60% of your marks will be gained by correctly answering OT questions, you need to ensure that you are familiar with the different types of OT question and the best approach to tackling them in the exam.

A step-by-step technique for ensuring that you approach the OT questions in the most efficient and effective way is outlined below:

> **STEP 1: Answer the questions you know first.**
> If you're having difficulty answering a question, move on and come back to tackle it once you've answered all the questions you know.
> It is often quicker to answer discursive style OT questions first, leaving more time for calculations.

> **STEP 2: Answer all questions.**
> There is no penalty for an incorrect answer in ACCA exams; there is nothing to be gained by leaving an OT question unanswered. If you are stuck on a question, as a last resort, it is worth selecting the option you consider most likely to be correct and moving on. Flag the question, so if you have time after you have answered the rest of the questions, you can revisit it.

> **STEP 3: Read the requirement first!**
> The requirement will be stated in bold text in the exam. Identify what you are being asked to do, any technical knowledge required and **what type of OT question** you are dealing with. Look for key words in the requirement such as "Which **TWO** of the following," or "Which of the following is **NOT**".

> **STEP 4: Apply your technical knowledge to the data presented in the question.**
> Work through calculations taking your time and read through each answer option with care. OT questions are designed so that each answer option is plausible. Work through each response option and eliminate those you know are incorrect

Skills Checkpoint 1 covers this technique in detail through application to a series of exam-standard questions.

Skill 2: Approach to objective test (OT) case style questions

In the exam, you will have three OT Case style questions, each worth 10 marks each. They are OT style questions, however, they will be linked along a common theme, such as recognising revenue (including government grants) or accounting for non-current asset acquisitions and resulting deferred tax adjustments. This allows the Examining Team to ask questions on specific areas in greater detail than just one OT question will permit.

Therefore, it is imperative that you are familiar with the OT style of question and recognise the style of a case question.

A case question will be scenario based, so there will be a short description together with some financial information, and five questions will be asked about the information. There will be a combination of narrative and numerical questions.

Key steps in developing and applying this skill are outlined below:

> ### STEP 1: Read the scenario carefully
> Read the introduction to the question carefully, ensuring you understand what the questions are asking you to do. Skimming the questions requirement will help you to identify whether the questions are narrative or numerical in style.

> ### STEP 2: Start with narrative questions
> Attempt the narrative questions first as this will allow you to use any remaining time to focus on the numerical and calculation questions. The case is usually split into three narrative questions with two further, calculation based questions.

> ### STEP 3: Work through numerical questions methodically
> Apply your technical knowledge to the data presented in the question.
> Work through calculations taking your time and read through each answer option with care. OT questions are designed so that each answer option is plausible. Work through each response option and eliminate those you know are incorrect.

> ### STEP 4: Be aware of time
> Stick to your time carefully, as each question is worth two marks, so spending more than the allocated time of 18 minutes on each case question is an inefficient use of your time, as you will need to move onto the Section C questions. If you are running out of time, or you cannot answer any of the questions, guess the answer from the options provided. You do not lose marks for incorrect answers.

Skills Checkpoint 2 covers this technique in detail through application to an exam-standard question.

Skill 3: Using spreadsheets effectively

Section C will require the use of the spreadsheet functionality in the exam, so you need to be familiar with the software and what the FR examining team is expecting to see in terms of presentation.

The Section C question which requires you to prepare extracts from the financial statements (this may be for a single entity or for a group, and it may be any of the primary financial statements) should be attempted using the spreadsheet software.

A step-by-step technique for using spreadsheets in the exam is outlined below.

STEP 1: Understanding the data in the question

Where a question includes a significant amount of data, read the requirements carefully to make sure that you **understand clearly what the question is asking you to do.** You can use the highlighting function to pull out important data from the question. Use the data provided to think about what formula you will need to use. For example, if the company calculates the allowance for receivables as a percentage of the balance, use the percentage function.

STEP 2: Use a standard proforma working.

You will be asked to prepare an extract or a set of financial statements. Set out your statement of profit or loss or the statement of financial position before you start to work through the question. This will give you the basic structure from where you can enter the data in the question.

Format your cells to ensure the workings look consistent, for example, using the comma function to mark the thousands in numerical answers.

STEP 3: Use spreadsheet ~~formulae~~ to perform basic calculations.

Ensure you are showing your workings by using the spreadsheet formula for simple calculations, for example, the cost of sale figure will be made up of different balances, so add them together using the formula. Cross refer any more detailed workings, and link workings into your main answer.

Step 4: Include the results of workings in the proforma

You must ensure that you include your workings form in the proforma and complete your final answer. Remember to show how you have included your workings by cross referencing to the relevant working and by using the formula within the cell to add/subtract the balance.

Skills Checkpoint 3 covers this technique in detail through application to an exam-standard question.

Skill 4: Application of IFRS standards

Knowledge of the IFRS standards will be required in all sections of the FR exam. You are unlikely to be asked to explain the requirements of an IFRS Standard in a narrative question, but may be asked questions about the application or impact of accounting standards in an OT question, or it may be relevant in the interpretation of an entity's performance and position in Section C.

A step-by-step technique for applying your knowledge of accounting standards is outlined below.

> **STEP 1: Overview of key standards**
>
> Ensure you have a high-level overview of the key standards covered in the FR exam. Use the summary diagrams at the end of the chapters in the Workbook to act as your summaries. These are a useful way of remembering the key points.

> **STEP 2: Numerical question practice**
>
> Practice the numerical questions in the Workbook and in the Practice & Revision Kit. These will test your knowledge of the mechanics of the accounting standards. Often there can be a difference between understanding what the standard does and how it applies to a specific scenario. Practice OTQs as well as longer, Section C questions to consolidate your knowledge.

> **STEP 3: Narrative question practice**
>
> Practice the narrative questions which test your understanding of how the standard can affect the financial statements. This will help you to revise your understanding of why the accounting standard is important in a scenario. For example, what are the key tests for impairment of assets and why would this be important for the financial statements?

Skills Checkpoint 4 covers this technique in detail through application to an exam-standard question.

Skill 5: Interpretation skills

Section C of the FR exam will contain two questions. One of these will require you to interpret the financial statements of a single entity or group or extracts from a set of financial statements. The interpretation will require the calculation of ratios, but your focus should be on the interpretation of those ratios to explain the performance and position of the single entity or group you are presented with.

Given that the interpretation of financial statements will feature in Section C of every exam, it is essential that you master the appropriate technique for analysing and interpreting information and drawing relevant conclusions in order to maximise your chance of passing the FR exam.

> **STEP 1: Read and analyse the requirement.**
> Read the requirement carefully to see what calculations are required and how many marks are set for the calculation and how many for the commentary.
> Work out how many minutes you have to answer each sub-requirement.

> **STEP 2: Read and analyse the scenario.**
> Identify the type of company you are dealing with and how the financial topics in the requirement relate to that type of company. As you go through the scenario, you should be highlighting key information which you think will play a key role in answering the specific requirements.

> **STEP 3: Plan your answer.**
> You will have calculated the ratios and understand the performance and position of the company. You must now plan the points you will make in interpreting the ratios. Read through the information in the scenario and identify the points that help you to explain the movement in ratios. Using each ratio as a heading, create a bullet point list of the relevant points.

> **STEP 4: Type your answer.**
> You should now take the bullet point list created at the planning stage and expand the points, remembering to use information given in the scenario and to avoid generic explanations.
> As you write your answer, explain what you mean – in one (or two) sentence(s) – and then explain **why this matters in the given scenario**. This should result in a series of short paragraphs that address the specific context of the scenario.

Skills Checkpoint 5 covers this technique in detail through application to an exam-standard question.

Exam success skills

Passing the FR exam requires more than applying syllabus knowledge and demonstrating the specific FR skills; it also requires the development of excellent exam technique through question practice.

We consider the following six skills to be vital for exam success. The Skills Checkpoints show how each of these skills can be applied in the exam.

Exam success skill 1

Managing information

Questions in the exam will present you with a lot of information. The skill is how you handle this information to make the best use of your time. The key is determining how you will approach the exam and then actively reading the questions.

Advice on developing Managing information

Approach

The exam is three hours long. There is no designated 'reading' time at the start of the exam.

Once you feel familiar with the exam, consider the order in which you will attempt the questions; always attempt them in your order of preference. For example, you may want to leave til last the question you consider to be the most difficult.

If you do take this approach, remember to adjust the time available for each question appropriately – see Exam success skill 6: Good time management.

If you find that this approach doesn't work for you, don't worry – you can develop your own technique.

Active reading

You must take an active approach to reading each question. Focus on the requirement first, underlining key verbs such as 'evaluate', 'analyse', 'explain', 'discuss', to ensure you answer the question properly. Then read the rest of the question, underlining and annotating important and relevant information, and making notes of any relevant technical information you think you will need.

Exam success skill 2

Correct interpretation of the requirements

The active verb used often dictates the approach that written answers should take (eg 'explain', 'discuss', 'evaluate'). It is important you identify and use the verb to define your approach. The **correct interpretation of the requirements** skill means correctly producing only what is being asked for by a requirement. Anything not required will not earn marks.

Advice on developing the Correct interpretation of the requirements

This skill can be developed by analysing question requirements and applying this process:

Step 1   Read the requirement

Firstly, read the requirement a couple of times slowly and carefully and highlight the active verbs. Use the active verbs to define what you plan to do. Make sure you identify any sub-requirements.

Step 2   Read the rest of the question

By reading the requirement first, you will have an idea of what you are looking out for as you read through the case overview and exhibits. This is a great time saver and means you don't end up having to read the whole question in full twice. You should do this in an active way – see Exam success skill 1: Managing Information.

Step 3   Read the requirement again

Read the requirement again to remind yourself of the exact wording before starting your written answer. This will capture any misinterpretation of the requirements or any missed requirements entirely. This should become a habit in your approach and, with repeated practice, you will find the focus, relevance and depth of your answer plan will improve.

Exam success skill 3

Answer planning: Priorities, structure and logic

This skill requires the planning of the key aspects of an answer which accurately and completely responds to the requirement.

Advice on developing Answer planning: Priorities, structure and logic

Everyone will have a preferred style for an answer plan. For example, it may be a mind map, bullet-pointed lists or creating short notes using the scratch pad within the CBE software. Choose the approach that you feel most comfortable with, or, if you are not sure, try out different approaches for different questions until you have found your preferred style.

For a discussion question, short notes is likely to be insufficient. It would be better to draw up a separate answer plan in the format of your choosing (eg a mind map or bullet-pointed lists).

Exam success skill 4

Efficient numerical analysis

This skill aims to maximise the marks awarded by making clear to the marker the process of arriving at your answer in Section C. This is achieved by laying out an answer such that, even if you make a few errors, you can still score subsequent marks for follow-on calculations. It is vital that you do not lose marks purely because the marker cannot follow what you have done.

Advice on developing Efficient numerical analysis

This skill can be developed by applying the following process:

Step 1   **Use a standard proforma working where relevant**

If answers can be laid out in a standard proforma then always plan to do so. This will help the marker to understand your working and allocate the marks easily. It will also help you to work through the figures in a methodical and time-efficient way.

Step 2   **Show your workings**

Keep your workings as clear and simple as possible and ensure they are cross-referenced to the main part of your answer. Where it helps, provide brief narrative explanations to help the marker understand the steps in the calculation. This means that if a mistake is made you do not lose any subsequent marks for follow-on calculations.

Step 3   **Keep moving!**

It is important to remember that, in an exam situation, it can sometimes be difficult to get every number 100% correct. The key is therefore ensuring you do not spend too long on any single calculation. If you are struggling with a solution then make a sensible assumption, state it and move on.

Exam success skill 5

Effective writing and presentation

Written answers should be presented so that the marker can clearly see the points you are making, presented in the format specified in the question. The skill is to provide efficient written answers with sufficient breadth of points that answer the question, in the right depth, in the time available.

Advice on developing Effective writing and presentation

Step 1   **Use headings**

Using the headings and sub-headings from your answer plan will give your answer structure, order and logic. This will ensure your answer links back to the requirement and is clearly signposted, making it easier for the marker to understand the different points you are making. Underlining your headings will also help the marker.

Step 2   **Write your answer in short, but full, sentences**

Use short, punchy sentences with the aim that every sentence should say something different and generate marks. Write in full sentences, ensuring your style is professional.

Step 3   **Do your calculations first and explanation second**

Questions often ask for an explanation with suitable calculations. The best approach is to prepare the calculation first but present it on the bottom half of the page of your answer, or on the next page. Then add the explanation before the calculation. Performing the calculation first should enable you to explain what you have done.

Exam success skill 6

Good time management

This skill means planning your time across all the requirements so that all tasks have been attempted at the end of the 3 hours available and actively checking on time during your exam. This is so that you can flex your approach and prioritise requirements which, in your judgement, will generate the maximum marks in the available time remaining.

Advice on developing Good time management

The exam is 3 hours long, which translates to 1.8 minutes per mark. Therefore a 10-mark requirement should be allocated a maximum of 18 minutes to complete your answer before you move on to the next task. At the beginning of a question, work out the amount of time you should be spending on each requirement and note the finishing time in your answer space or in the scratch pad.

Keep an eye on the clock

Aim to attempt all requirements, but be ready to be ruthless and move on if your answer is not going as planned. The challenge for many is sticking to planned timings. Be aware this is difficult to achieve in the early stages of your studies and be ready to let this skill develop over time.

If you find yourself running short on time and know that a full answer is not possible in the time you have, consider recreating your plan in overview form and then add key terms and details as time allows. Remember, some marks may be available, for example, simply stating a conclusion which you don't have time to justify in full.

Questions

PART A THE CONCEPTUAL AND REGULATORY FRAMEWORK FOR FINANCIAL REPORTING

Questions 1-8 cover the *Conceptual Framework*. Questions 9-18 cover the regulatory framework, including the impact of the measurement basis applied to assets on the financial performance of the company. Questions 1-18 are objective test (OT) questions in the style of Section A of the exam.

The Section B Questions 19-23 cover the *Conceptual Framework* and the regulatory framework.

Section A

Conceptual framework

1   **How does the *Conceptual Framework* define an asset?**

   ○   A present economic resource, which is a right that has the potential to produce economic benefits, owned by an entity as a result of past events

   ○   A present economic resource over which an entity has legal rights. An economic resource is a right that has the potential to produce economic benefits

   ○   A present economic resource controlled by an entity as a result of past events. An economic resource is a right that has the potential to produce economic benefits

   ○   A present economic resource to which an entity has a future commitment as a result of past events. An economic resource is a right that has the potential to produce economic benefits   **(2 marks)**

2   **Which of the following would meet the *Conceptual Framework* definition of a liability?**

   ○   Dexter's business manufactures a product under licence. In 12 months' time the licence expires and Dexter will have to pay $50,000 for it to be renewed

   ○   Reckless purchased an investment 9 months ago for $120,000. The market for these investments has now fallen and Reckless's investment is valued at $90,000

   ○   Carter has estimated the tax charge on its profits for the year just ended as $165,000

   ○   Expansion is planning to invest in new machinery and has been quoted a price of $570,000   **(2 marks)**

3   **Which of the following would correctly describe the value in use of a two-year old asset?**

   ○   The original cost of the asset less two years' depreciation

   ○   The amount that could be obtained from selling the asset, less any costs of disposal

   ○   The cost of an equivalent new asset less two years' depreciation

   ○   The present value of the future cash flows obtainable from the continued use of the asset and its ultimate disposal   **(2 marks)**

4   The *Conceptual Framework* identifies which of the following as an underlying assumption in preparing financial statements?

O   Going concern

O   Materiality

O   Substance over form

O   Accrual accounting   (2 marks)

5   The *Conceptual Framework* identifies four enhancing qualitative characteristics of financial information.

Which ONE of the following is NOT an enhancing qualitative characteristic?

O   Verifiability

O   Timeliness

O   Consistency

O   Understandability   (2 marks)

6   **Which TWO of the following are purposes of the *Conceptual Framework*?**

☐   To assist preparers to develop consistent accounting policies when no Standard applies to a particular event

☐   To issue rules regarding the accounting treatment of elements in the financial statements

☐   To assist in determining the treatment of items not covered by an existing IFRS Standard

☐   To be authoritative where a specific IFRS Standard conflicts with the *Conceptual Framework*   (2 marks)

7   Recognition is the process of including within the financial statements items which meet the definition of an element according to the *Conceptual Framework*.

Which of the following items should be recognised as an asset in the statement of financial position of a company?

(i)   A secret formula for the manufacture of a best-selling sauce. The recipe is kept secure at the company premises and known only by the company directors

(ii)   A highly lucrative contract signed during the year which is due to commence shortly after the year end

(iii) Items that are to be sold via a third-party agent which the company can no longer control and cannot be returned to the company of they are unsold

(iv)   A receivable from a customer which has been sold (factored) to a finance company. The finance company has full recourse to the company for any losses

O   (i) and (iii)

O   (iii) and (iv)

O   (i) and (iv)

O   (ii), (iii) and (iv)   (2 marks)

8   In accordance with the *Conceptual Framework* which of the following is/are true in relation to the enhancing characteristic of comparability?

(1)   Permitting alternative accounting treatments for the same economic phenomenon enhances comparability

(2)   Comparability requires uniformity

○   Both 1 and 2

○   Neither 1 nor 2

○   1 only

○   2 only   (2 marks)

(ACCA, Examiners Report 2017)

Regulatory framework

9   The process for developing an IFRS Standard involves a number of stages. Following receipt and review of comments on a Discussion Paper, what will be the next step undertaken by the IASB?

○   Publication of an Exposure Draft

○   Establishment of an Advisory Committee

○   Consultation with the Advisory Committee

○   Issue of a final IFRS Standard   (2 marks)

10   Which **TWO** of the following statements would be an advantage of adopting IFRS Standards?

☐   It would be easier for investors to compare the financial statements of companies with those of foreign competitors

☐   Cross-border listing would be facilitated

☐   Accountants and auditors would have more defence in case of litigation

☐   The IFRS Standards can be more easily tailored to reflect the industries of the territory adopting them   (2 marks)

11   Which **TWO** of the following statements regarding systems of regulation of accounting are true?

☐   A principles-based system will require more detailed regulations than a rules-based system

☐   A rules-based system will tend to give rise to a larger number of IFRS Standards than a principles-based system

☐   A principles-based system seeks to cover every eventuality

☐   A principles-based system requires the exercise of more judgement in application than a rules-based system   (2 marks)

12 The process for developing an IFRS Standard involves a number of stages. During the early stages of a project, the IASB will undertake consultation on the key issues.

Which of the following is correct regarding the early stages of the process:

○ In the early stages of the project, the IASB will issue a Discussion Paper to obtain views from the public

○ In the early stages of the project, the IASB will consult with the Advisory Committee and IFRS Advisory Council to seek out the key issues

○ In the early stages of the project, the IASB will issue a Discussion Paper then consult with the Advisory Committee

○ In the early stages of the project, the IASB will issue an Exposure Draft to obtain views from the public   (2 marks)

---

13 Historical cost accounting remains in use because of its practical advantages.

Which of the following is NOT an advantage of historical cost accounting?

○ Amounts of transactions are reliable and can be verified

○ Amounts in the statement of financial position can be matched to amounts in the statement of cash flows

○ It avoids the overstatement of profit which can arise during periods of inflation

○ It provides fewer opportunities for creative accounting than systems of current value accounting   (2 marks)

---

14 **Which of the following measurement bases may NOT be applied to liabilities?**

○ Fair value

○ Historical cost

○ Value in use

○ Fulfilment value   (2 marks)

---

15 Drexler acquired an item of plant on 1 October 20X2 at a cost of $500,000. It has a useful life of five years (straight-line depreciation) and an estimated residual value of 10% of its historical cost or current cost as appropriate. As at 30 September 20X4, the manufacturer of the plant still makes the same item of plant and its current price is $600,000.

What is the correct carrying amount to be shown in the statement of financial position of Drexler as at 30 September 20X4 under historical cost and current cost?

	Historical cost $	Current cost $
○	320,000	600,000
○	320,000	384,000
○	300,000	600,000
○	300,000	384,000

(2 marks)

16   **Under the current value measurement basis, what is the definition of fulfilment value?**

    ○   The amount of consideration received to incur the liability, less transaction costs

    ○   The price that would be paid to settle the liability at the measurement date

    ○   The consideration that would be received for incurring an equivalent liability at the measurement date

    ○   The present value of the estimated cash flows needed to fulfil a liability   **(2 marks)**

17   **Which of the following statements is an advantage of using the value in use measurement basis?**

    ○   It assists a user to assess the future prospects of the business

    ○   Amounts used are objective and free from bias

    ○   It is an easily understood system of valuation

    ○   Amounts are reliable and can be verified to invoices and documents   **(2 marks)**

18   **Under the current cost measurement basis, what is the definition of the value in use measurement method?**

    ○   Costs incurred at the time of acquisition

    ○   Present value of future cash flows, less costs of disposal

    ○   Open market value of the asset

    ○   Open market value of the asset, less the present value of the future cash outflows

    (2 marks)

Section B

Lisbon Co case

18 mins

Information relevant to Questions 19–23

The accountant of Lisbon is considering a number of transactions and events and how they should be treated in accordance with the concepts and qualitative characteristics of financial information as set out in the *Conceptual Framework*.

During the year ended 31 March 20X6, Lisbon experienced the following transactions or events:

(i)   Lisbon sold an asset to a finance company and immediately leased it back for the remainder of its useful life. The transaction met the criteria to be recognised as a sale under IFRS 15 *Revenue from Contracts with Customers*. The accountant determined that the transaction should be treated as a sale and leaseback in accordance with IFRS 16 *Leases* and has accounted for it accordingly.

(ii)   The company's statement of profit or loss, prepared using historical costs, showed a loss from operating its shops. Lisbon is aware that the increase in the value of its properties during the period far outweighs the operating loss.

(iii) Inventory has historically been valued using the FIFO method but the accountant is considering changing to the weighted average method for the year to 31 March 20X6.

19   The accountant is aware that some members of the board of Lisbon have little understanding of accounting and is worried about presenting the financial statements at the board meeting.

In accordance with the *Conceptual Framework*, how should the accountant deal with this situation?

   O   In doing the presentation the accountant should omit any complex issues, so that everybody can understand what they are saying

   O   The accountant should open the presentation with the advice that some of them may not understand all of it

   O   The accountant should classify, characterise and present the information clearly and precisely

   O   The accountant should deliver their presentation just to those who are financially qualified

20   **Which concept or qualitative characteristic has influenced the decision in (i) above?**

   O   Faithful representation

   O   Verifiability

   O   Accruals

   O   Comparability

21   In looking at issue (ii) above, the accountant decides that the properties should be revalued.

Which concept or qualitative characteristic has been applied in making this decision?

O   Materiality

O   Going concern

O   Relevance

O   Timeliness

22   **Because of the loss arising from operating the shops, the accountant is considering whether Lisbon is a going concern. If it was decided that Lisbon was no longer a going concern at 31 March 20X6, which of the following is correct in accordance with the *Conceptual Framework?***

O   Financial statements do not need to be prepared

O   All the assets should be liquidated

O   The financial statements should be prepared on a different basis

O   The financial statements should be prepared as normal and the going concern status disclosed in the notes

23   **In applying the enhancing qualitative characteristic of comparability, how should the change of inventory valuation basis be accounted for?**

O   The change should be disclosed only

O   The financial statements for 31 March 20X6 should show both methods

O   The notes should show what the profit would have been if the change had not taken place

O   The financial statements for the prior period as shown at 31 March 20X6 should be restated using the weighted average basis

(10 marks)

BPP
LEARNING
MEDIA

Section A

Tangible non-current assets

24   Foster Co has built a new factory incurring the following costs:

	$'000
Land	1,200
Materials	2,400
Labour	3,000
Architect's fees	25
Surveyor's fees	15
Site overheads	300
Apportioned administrative overheads	150
Testing of fire alarms	10
Business rates for first year	12
	7,112

What will be the total amount capitalised in respect of the factory?

○ $6,640,000

○ $6,950,000

○ $7,112,000

○ $7,100,000

(2 marks)

---

25   Carriageways Co had the following bank loans outstanding during the whole of 20X8 which form the company's general borrowings for the year:

	$m
9% loan repayable 20X9	15
11% loan repayable 20Y2	24

Carriageways Co began construction of a qualifying asset on 1 April 20X8 and withdrew funds of $6 million on that date to fund the construction. On 1 August 20X8 an additional $2 million was withdrawn for the same purpose.

Calculate the borrowing costs which can be capitalised in respect of this project for the year ended 31 December 20X8.

○ $549,333

○ $480,000

○ $824,000

○ $533,333   (2 marks)

---

26   Leclerc Co has borrowed $2.4 million to finance the building of a factory. Construction is expected to take two years. The loan was drawn down on 1 January 20X9 and work began on 1 March 20X9. $1 million of the loan was not utilised until 1 July 20X9 so Leclerc was able to invest it until needed.

Leclerc Co is paying 8% on the loan and can invest surplus funds at 6%.

Calculate the borrowing costs to be capitalised for the year ended 31 December 20X9 in respect of this project.

○ $140,000

○ $192,000

○ $100,000

○ $162,000   (2 marks)

---

27   **Which of the following statements is correct regarding investment properties in accordance with IAS 40 *Investment Property*?**

(1)   Transfers of IAS 16 property to or from an IAS 40 investment property should only be made when there is a change in their use.

(2)   Transfers from an IAS 40 investment property to an IAS 16 property must be made at the fair value of the investment property at the date of the transfer.

(3)   An entity should treat any difference between the measurement of an IAS 16 property and the measurement of an IAS 40 investment property at the date of transfer as an expense to the profit or loss.

○   Statement 1 only

○   Both statements 1 and 2

○   Both statements 2 and 3

○   Both statements 1 and 3   (2 marks)

---

28 Identify whether each of the following statements is true or false in accordance with IAS 40 *Investment Property*?

Following initial recognition, investment property can be held at either cost or fair value	True	False
If an investment property is held at fair value, this must be applied to all of the entity's investment properties	True	False
An investment property is initially measured at cost, including transaction costs	True	False
A gain or loss arising from a change in the fair value of an investment property should be recognised in the revaluation surplus	True	False

(2 marks)

29 Fido Feed Co has the following loans in place throughout the year ended 31 December 20X8 which constitute its general borrowings for the period.

	$m
10% bank loan	140
8% bank loan	200

On 1 July 20X8, $50 million was drawn down for the construction of a qualifying asset which was completed during 20X9.

What amount should be capitalised as borrowing costs at 31 December 20X8 in respect of this asset?

O $2.0 million

O $2.25 million

O $4.4 million

O $2.2 million   (2 marks)

30 Wetherby Co purchased a machine on 1 July 20X7 for $500,000. It is being depreciated on a straight-line basis over its useful life of ten years. Residual value is estimated at $20,000. On 1 January 20X8, following a change in legislation, Wetherby Co fitted a safety guard to the machine. The safety guard cost $25,000 and has a useful life of five years with no residual value.

What amount will be charged to profit or loss for the year ended 31 March 20X8 in respect of depreciation on this machine? (Enter your answer to the nearest whole $.)

$ [ ]   (2 marks)

31 Auckland Co purchased a machine for $60,000 on 1 January 20X7 and assigned it a useful life of 15 years. On 31 March 20X9 it was revalued to $64,000 with no change in useful life.

What will be depreciation charge in relation to this machine in the financial statements of Auckland Co for the year ending 31 December 20X9? (Enter your answer to the nearest whole $.)

$ [ ]   (2 marks)

32. Carter Co vacated its head office building and let it out to a third party on 30 June 20X8. The building had an original cost of $900,000 on 1 January 20X0 and was being depreciated on a straight-line basis over 50 years. It was judged to have a fair value on 30 June 20X8 of $950,000. At the year-end date of 31 December 20X8 the fair value of the building was estimated at $1.2 million.

Carter Co uses the fair value model for investment property.

What amount will be shown in revaluation surplus at 31 December 20X8 in respect of this building? (Enter your answer to the nearest whole $.)

$ [   ]   (2 marks)

Intangible non-current assets

33. Geek Co is developing a new product and expects to be able to capitalise the costs.

Which of the following would mean the costs cannot be capitalised?

○   Development of the product is not yet complete

○   No patent has yet been registered in respect of the product

○   No sales contracts have yet been signed in relation to the product

○   It has not been possible to reliably allocate costs to development of the product

(2 marks)

34. Assoria Co had $20 million of capitalised development expenditure at cost brought forward at 1 October 20X7 in respect of products currently in production and a new project began on the same date.

The research stage of the new project lasted until 31 December 20X7 and incurred $1.4 million of costs. From that date the project incurred development costs of $800,000 per month. On 1 April 20X8 the directors of Assoria Co became confident that the project would be successful and yield a profit well in excess of costs. The project was still in development at 30 September 20X8. Capitalised development expenditure is amortised at 20% per annum using the straight-line method.

What amount will be charged to profit or loss for the year ended 30 September 20X8 in respect of research and development costs?

○ $8,280,000

○ $6,880,000

○ $7,800,000

○ $3,800,000   (2 marks)

35 **Identify whether the following internally generated items are eligible or ineligible to be recognised as intangible assets in accordance with IAS 38 *Intangible Assets*?** (Ignore the effect of business combinations.)

A customer list built up over the last ten years of trading updated for the customer's current preferences	Eligible	Ineligible
Specialised tooling for a new product developed by the business	Eligible	Ineligible
A working version of a new machine that uses new technology used for testing of the prototype apparatus	Eligible	Ineligible
The title heading, font and design of the front page of a major broadsheet newspaper	Eligible	Ineligible

(2 marks)

36 At 30 September 20X9, Sandown Co's trial balance showed a brand at cost of $30 million, less accumulated amortisation brought forward at 1 October 20X8 of $9 million. Amortisation is based on a 10-year useful life. An impairment review on 1 April 20X9 concluded that the brand had a value in use of $12 million and a remaining useful life of three years. However, on the same date Sandown Co received an offer to purchase the brand for $15 million.

What should be the carrying amount of the brand in the statement of financial position of Sandown Co as at 30 September 20X9? (Enter your answer to the nearest $'000.)

$ [   ] 000

(2 marks)

37 Dempsey Co's year end is 30 September 20X5. Dempsey Co commenced the development stage of a project to produce a new pharmaceutical drug on 1 January 20X5. Expenditure of $40,000 per month was incurred until the project was completed on 30 June 20X5 when the drug went into immediate production. The directors became confident of the project's success on 1 March 20X5. The drug is expected to generate benefits for five years.

What is the carrying amount of any intangible asset recognised in respect of the project at 30 September 20X5 and what is the total amount Dempsey Co will charge to profit or loss for the year ended 30 September 20X5?

Select your answers from the options below and place them in the blank boxes.

Carrying amount of intangible asset at 30 September 20X5	Amount charged to profit or loss for period ending 30 September 20X5
$228,000	$240,000
$152,000	$141,333
$98,667	$88,000
$0	$0

(2 marks)

Impairment of assets

38   A cash-generating unit comprises the following assets:

	$'000
Building	700
Plant and equipment	200
Goodwill	90
Current assets	20
	1,010

Following an impairment review, it was discovered that an item of plant, carried at $40,000, is damaged and will have to be scrapped. The recoverable amount of the cash-generating unit is estimated at $750,000.

What will be the carrying amount of the building after the impairment loss has been recognised?

(to the nearest $'000)

O $597

O $577

O $594

O $548   (2 marks)

---

39   **Complete the statement using the options provided:**

The **recoverable amount** of an asset is the higher of

[   ] and [   ] under

IAS 36 *Impairment of Assets*.

Select your answers from the options below and place them in the blank boxes.

Fair value

Fair value less costs of disposal

Market value

Value in use

(2 marks)

---

40   Lichen Co owns a machine that has a carrying amount of $85,000 at the year end of 31 March 20X9. Its market value is $78,000 and costs of disposal are estimated at $2,500. A new machine would cost $150,000. Lichen Co expects it to produce net cash flows of $30,000 per annum for the next three years. The cost of capital of Lichen Co is 8%.

What is the impairment loss on the machine to be recognised in the financial statements at 31 March 20X9? (Enter your answer to the nearest whole $.)

$ [   ]   (2 marks)

---

41 IAS 36 *Impairment of Assets* suggests potential indicators of impairment.

Which TWO of the following would be EXTERNAL INDICATORS that one or more of an entity's assets may be impaired?

☐ An unusually significant fall in the market value of one or more assets

☐ Evidence of obsolescence of one or more assets

☐ A decline in the economic performance of one or more assets

☐ An increase in market interest rates used to calculate value in use of the assets

(2 marks)

---

42 The following information relates to an item of plant owned by Bazaar Co:

(i) Its carrying amount in the statement of the financial position is $3 million.

(ii) Bazaar Co has received an offer of $2.7 million from a company in Japan interested in buying the plant.

(iii) The present value of the estimated cash flows from continued use of the plant is $2.6 million.

(iv) The estimated cost of shipping the plant to Japan is $50,000.

What is the amount of the impairment loss that should be recognised in respect of the plant? (Enter your answer to the nearest whole $.)

$ [   ]   (2 marks)

---

43 A business which comprises a single cash-generating unit has the following assets:

	$m
Goodwill	3
Patent	5
Property	10
Plant and equipment	15
Net current assets	2
	35

Following an impairment review it is estimated that the value of the patent is $2 million and the recoverable amount of the business is $24 million.

What is the carrying amount of the property following the impairment review?

○ $8 million

○ $10 million

○ $7.5 million

○ $5 million   (2 marks)

44   Riley Co acquired a non-current asset on 1 October 20W9 (ten years before 20X9) at a
      cost of $100,000 which had a useful life of ten years and a nil residual value. The asset had
      been correctly depreciated up to 30 September 20X4. At that date the asset was damaged
      and an impairment review was performed. On 30 September 20X4, the fair value of the
      asset less costs of disposal was $30,000 and the expected future cash flows were $8,500
      per annum for the next five years. The current cost of capital is 10% and a five-year annuity
      of $1 per annum at 10% would have a present value of $3.79.

      **What amount would be charged to profit or loss for the impairment of this asset for the
      year ended 30 September 20X4?**

      O $17,785

      O $20,000

      O $30,000

      O $32,215   (2 marks)

---

45   The net assets of Fyngle Co, a cash-generating unit (CGU), are:

	$
Property, plant and equipment	200,000
Allocated goodwill	50,000
Product patent	20,000
Net current assets (at net realisable value)	30,000
	300,000

      An impairment review was carried out following adverse publicity received. The impairment
      review indicates that Fyngle Co has a recoverable amount of $200,000.

      **What would be the carrying amount of Fyngle Co's property, plant and equipment after the
      allocation of the impairment loss?**

      O $154,545

      O $170,000

      O $160,000

      O $133,333   (2 marks)

---

46   **Select whether each of the following statements is an indicator of impairment or is not an
      indicator of impairment under IAS 36** *Impairment of Assets.*

Advances in the technological environment in which an asset is employed has an adverse impact on its future use	Indicator of impairment	Not an indicator of impairment
An increase in interest rates which increases the discount rate an entity uses	Indicator of impairment	Not an indicator of impairment
The carrying amount of an entity's net assets is lower than the entity's number of shares in issue multiplied by its share price	Indicator of impairment	Not an indicator of impairment
The estimated net realisable value of inventory has been reduced due to fire damage although this value is greater than its carrying amount	Indicator of impairment	Not an indicator of impairment

                                                                                      (2 marks)

Plethora plc case

18 mins

Information relevant to questions 47–51

The draft financial statements of Plethora plc for the year to 31 December 20X9 are being prepared and the accountant has requested your advice on dealing with the following issues.

(i) Plethora plc has an administration building which it no longer needs. On 1 July 20X9, Plethora plc entered into an agreement to lease the building out to another company. The building cost $600,000 on 1 January 20X0 and is being depreciated over 50 years, based on the IAS 16 *Property, Plant and Equipment* cost model. Plethora plc applies the fair value model under IAS 40 *Investment Property* and the fair value of the building was assessed as $800,000 on 1 July 20X9. This valuation had not changed at 31 December 20X9.

(ii) Plethora plc owns another building which has been leased out for a number of years. It had a fair value of $550,000 at 31 December 20X8 and $740,000 at 31 December 20X9.

(iii) Plethora plc owns a retail business, which is considered a separate cash-generating unit, which suffered a difficult trading period in the previous year and was subject to an impairment review at 31 December 20X8. At that date, an impairment loss of $160,000 was recognised. The directors of Plethora plc believe the indicators of impairment have reversed by 31 December 20X9 and wish to reverse the previous impairment loss to the maximum extent possible.

Relevant financial information in respect of the retail business is as follows:

Asset	Carrying amount at 31 December 20X8 before impairment	Impairment loss at 31 December 20X8	Estimated value at 31 December 20X9	Carrying amount at 31 December 20X9 had no impairment occurred
Building	900	100	925	875
Plant and equipment	300	20	310	290
Goodwill	40	40	60	40

An impairment review has been carried out as at 31 December 20X9 and the recoverable amount of the cash-generating unit is estimated at $1.3 million.

47 **What is the amount of the revaluation surplus that will be recognised in respect of the building in (i)? (Enter your answer to the nearest whole $.)**

$ [_____]

48 **In respect of the building in (ii), how will the increase in value from $550,000 to $740,000 be accounted for?**

- ○ Credited to profit or loss
- ○ Credited to the revaluation surplus
- ○ Credited to retained earnings
- ○ Credited to an investment property reserve

49 Using the pull-down list provided, select the amount at which an impaired asset is measured when an impairment has taken place?

[▼]

Pull-down list:

Fair value
Value in use
Recoverable amount
Carrying amount

---

50 Which **TWO** of the following statements regarding the reversal of impairment losses are correct?

☐ The reversal of goodwill impairment should be recognised in other comprehensive income

☐ The reversal of impairment losses on revalued assets should be recognised in other comprehensive income

☐ An impairment loss can only be reversed if there is a change in the estimates used to determine the recoverable amount of the impaired assets

☐ Only impairment losses on non-current assets can be reversed

---

51 What will be the amount credited to the statement of profit or loss in respect of the reversal of the impairment loss in the year ended 31 December 20X9?

○ $215,000

○ $155,000

○ $125,000

○ $85,000

(10 marks)

Linetti Co case (Mar/Jun 2019)   18 mins

Information relevant to questions 52–56

During the year ended 31 December 20X8, Linetti Co built an extension to its head office. The costs associated with the head office extension are as follows:

	$m
Land acquisition	10.0
Fees for environmental certifications and building permits	0.5
Architect and engineer fees	1.0
Construction material and labour costs (including unused materials)	6.6

At 30 September 20X8, the date when the head office extension became available for use, the cost of unused materials on site amounted to $0.5 million. At that date, the total borrowing costs incurred on a loan which was used specifically to finance the head office extension amounted to $0.8 million.

Linetti Co also acquired 100% of a subsidiary, Scully Co, on 1 January 20X8. The carrying amount of the assets of Scully Co in the consolidated financial statements of the Linetti Group at 31 December 20X8, immediately before an impairment review, were as follows:

	$m
Goodwill	1.4
Brand name	2.0
Property, plant and equipment	6.0
Current assets (at recoverable amount)	2.4
	11.8

The recoverable amount of Scully Co was estimated at $9.6 million at 31 December 20X8 and the impairment of the investment in Scully Co was deemed to be $2.2 million.

52   **For the year end 31 December 20X8, how much should be capitalised in respect of the construction of the extension to the head office building?**

   ○ $18.4 million

   ○ $17.6 million

   ○ $18.9 million

   ○ $18.1 million

53   Linetti Co incurred further expenditure on the head extension after it had been completed

   Which of the following would qualify as capital expenditure?

   ○   Property insurance premiums incurred

   ○   Installation of new office fixtures and fittings

   ○   Marketing costs telling the public that the head office extension is operational

   ○   Maintenance and relocation of computers and related office equipment

54   At 31 December 20X9, the directors of Linetti Co decide to adopt the revaluation model of IAS 16 *Property, Plant and Equipment* for Linetti Co's property.

   In accordance with IAS 16, which of the following statements is NOT true?

   ○   In subsequent years, the depreciation will be based on the revalued amount of the head office building as opposed to its cost

   ○   Any revaluation gain on the head office building is recognised in other comprehensive income and any revaluation loss is recognised in profit or loss

   ○   The original head office building and the new extension are revalued separately

   ○   The residual value and the useful life of the head office building must be reviewed each year

55   **Assuming Scully Co represents a cash generating unit, what is the carrying amount of the brand at 31 December 20X8 following impairment review?**

   ○ $1.2 million

   ○ $1.45 million

   ○ $1.73 million

   ○ $1.8 million

56   **Which, if any, of the following statements regarding impairment reviews is/are correct?**

(1)   At the end of each reporting period, an entity should assess if there is any indication that assets have been impaired

(2)   Annual impairment reviews are required on all intangible assets with indefinite lives

○   1 only

○   2 only

○   Both 1 and 2

○   Neither 1 nor 2

(10 marks)

Elite Leisure Co case

18 mins

The following scenario relates to questions 57–61.

Elite Leisure Co is a private limited liability company that operates a single cruise ship. The ship was acquired on 1 October 20W6 (ten years before 20X6). Details of the cost of the ship's components and the basis on which they are depreciated is as follows:

Component	Original cost $m	Depreciation basis
Ship's fabric (hull, decks etc)	300	25 years straight-line
Cabins and entertainment area fittings	150	12 years straight-line
Propulsion system	100	Useful life of 40,000 hours

At 30 September 20X4 no further capital expenditure had been incurred on the ship.

The propulsion system has been used for 30,000 hours at 30 September 20X4. Due to the unreliability of the engines, a decision was taken in early October 20X4 to replace the whole of the propulsion system at a cost of $140 million. The useful life of the new propulsion system was 50,000 hours and, in the year, ended 30 September 20X5 the ship had used the system for 5,000 hours.

At the same time as the propulsion system replacement, Elite Leisure Co took the opportunity to do a limited upgrade to the facilities at a cost of $60 million and repaint the ship's fabric at a cost of $20 million. After the upgrade of the facilities it was estimated that their remaining useful life was five years (from the date of the upgrade). For the purpose of calculating depreciation, all the work on the ship can be assumed to have been completed on 1 October 20X4. All residual values can be taken as nil.

57   **At 30 September 20X4 the ship is eight years old. What is the carrying amount of the ship at that date?**

○ $279 million

○ $275 million

○ $229 million

○ $254 million

---

58   **What is the amount of depreciation that should be charged in respect of the propulsion system for the year ended 30 September 20X5? (Enter your answer to the nearest $m.)**

$ [　　　　　　] m

---

59   Ignoring depreciation, what is the charge to profit or loss for the year ended
      30 September 20X5? (Enter your answer to the nearest whole $.)

      $ [   ]

---

60   Elite Leisure Co's ship has to have a safety check carried out every five years at a cost of
      $50,000 in order to be licensed to operate. How should this be accounted for?

      O   Set up a provision for the discounted present value and unwind over five years

      O   Accrue the cost of the check over five years until it takes place

      O   Charge $50,000 to profit or loss when incurred

      O   Capitalise the cost when incurred and amortise over five years

---

61   Elite Leisure Co is being sued for $250,000 by a passenger who slipped on one of the
      gangways and twisted an ankle. The company's lawyer estimates that there is a 55%
      chance that it will lose the case. Legal costs for Elite Leisure Co will be $40,000.

      **Using the pull-down list provided, select the amount at which Elite Leisure Co provide in
      respect of this case.**

      [▼]

      Pull-down list:

      $290,000
      $250,000
      $159,500
      $137,500

(10 marks)

Dexterity Co case   **18 mins**

Information relevant to questions 62–66

Dexterity Co is a public listed company. It has been considering the accounting treatment of its
intangible assets and how the matters below should be treated in its financial statements for the
year to 31 March 20X4.

1   On 1 October 20X3, Dexterity Co acquired Temerity Co, a small company that specialises
     in pharmaceutical drug research and development. The purchase consideration was by
     way of a share exchange and valued at $35 million. The fair value of Temerity Co's net
     assets was $15 million (excluding any items referred to below). Temerity Co owns a patent
     for an established successful drug that has a remaining life of eight years. A firm of
     specialist advisors, Leadbrand Co, has estimated the current value of this patent to be
     $10 million, however the company is awaiting the outcome of clinical trials where the drug
     has been tested to treat a different illness. If the trials are successful, the value of the drug
     is then estimated to be $15 million. Also included in the company's statement of financial
     position is $2 million for medical research that has been conducted on behalf of a client.

2   Dexterity Co has developed and patented a new drug which has been approved for clinical
     use. The costs of developing the drug were $12 million. Based on early assessments of its
     sales success, Leadbrand Co have estimated its market value at $20 million, which can be
     taken as a reliable measurement.

3   Dexterity Co's manufacturing facilities have recently received a favourable inspection by government medical scientists. As a result of this the company has been granted an exclusive five-year licence to manufacture and distribute a new vaccine. Although the licence had no direct cost to Dexterity Co, its directors feel its granting is a reflection of the company's standing and have asked Leadbrand Co to value the licence. Accordingly, they have placed a value of $10 million on it.

4   In the current accounting period, Dexterity Co has spent $3 million sending its staff on specialist training courses. While these courses have been expensive, they have led to a marked improvement in production quality and staff now need less supervision. This in turn has led to an increase in revenue and cost reductions. The directors of Dexterity Co believe these benefits will continue for at least three years and wish to treat the training costs as an asset.

62   **Identify whether each of the following items should be capitalised as an intangible asset or recognised as an expense.**

Patent for the new drug	Capitalise	Expense
Licence for the new vaccine	Capitalise	Expense
Specialist training courses undertaken by Dexterity staff	Capitalise	Expense
Temerity Co's patent on the existing drug currently licenced for use	Capitalise	Expense

63   **Select which TWO of the following are required if Dexterity Co adopts the revaluation model for the measurement of its intangible assets.**

Select your answers from the options below and place them in the blank boxes.

Required if Dexterity Co adopts the revaluation model

The entire class of intangible assets must be revalued at the same time

Valid active market for the asset

Can be used at initial recognition of the asset if there is an active market

The asset may include costs of prepaid marketing expenses and training costs

64   IAS 38 *Intangible Assets* gives examples of activities that would be regarded as research and therefore not eligible for recognition as an intangible asset.

Which of the following would be an example of research activities?

○   The design and construction of chosen alternative products or processes

○   The design of pre-production prototypes and models

○   The design of possible new or improved product or process alternatives

○   The design, construction and operation of a pilot plant

65 At what amount should the patent acquired from Temerity Co be valued at 31 March 20X4?

- O $10,000,000
- O $9,375,000
- O $15,000,000
- O Nil

66 How should Dexterity Co treat the goodwill arising on its acquisition of Temerity Co?

- O It should be capitalised and amortised over 20 years
- O It should be capitalised and reviewed for impairment every year
- O It should be capitalised and reviewed for impairment every five years
- O It should be written off to retained earnings

(10 marks)

Advent Co case   18 mins

The following scenario relates to questions 67–71.

Advent Co is a publicly listed company. Details of Advent Co's non-current assets at 1 October 20X8 were:

	Land and building $m	Plant $m	Telecommunications licence $m	Total $m
Cost/valuation	280	150	300	730
Accumulated depreciation/amortisation	(40)	(103)	(30)	(175)
Carrying amount	240	45	270	555

The following information is relevant:

(i) The land and building were revalued on 1 October 20X3 with $80 million attributable to the land and $200 million to the building. At that date the estimated remaining life of the building was 25 years. A further revaluation was not needed until 1 October 20X8 when the land and building were valued at $85 million and $180 million respectively. The remaining estimated life of the building at this date was 20 years.

(ii) Plant is depreciated at 20% per annum on cost with time apportionment where appropriate. On 1 April 20X9, new plant costing $45 million was acquired. In addition, this plant cost $5 million to install and commission. No plant is more than four years old.

(iii) The telecommunications licence was bought from the government on 1 October 20X7 and has a ten-year life. It is amortised on a straight-line basis. In September 20X9, a review of the sales of the products related to the licence showed them to be very disappointing. As a result of this review the estimated recoverable amount of the licence at 30 September 20X9 was estimated at only $100 million.

There were no disposals of non-current assets during the year to 30 September 20X9.

67 What is the carrying amount of the land and buildings at 30 September 20X9?

- O $256 million
- O $265 million
- O $240 million
- O $258 million

68   What is the depreciation charge on the plant for the year ended 30 September 20X9?

   ○ $30 million

   ○ $25 million

   ○ $20 million

   ○ $35 million

69   Having revalued its property Advent Co is required to make certain disclosures in respect of the revaluation.

Identify whether the following disclosures are, or are not required, in respect of revaluation.

The effective date of revaluation	Required	Not required
Professional qualifications of the valuer	Required	Not required
The basis used to revalue the assets	Required	Not required
The carrying amount of assets if no revaluation had taken place	Required	Not required

70   What is the amount of the impairment loss on the licence? Select your answer from the pull-down list options below.

$ [▼]

Pull-down list:

$100 million
$140 million
$170 million
$240 million

71   Advent Co's licence is now carried at its recoverable amount.

Complete the statement using the options provided.

The **recoverable amount** of an asset of an asset is the higher of

[   ] and [   ]

Fair value less costs of disposal

Carrying amount less costs of disposal

Carrying amount

Value in use

(10 marks)

Systria Co case

The following information is relevant to questions 72–76.

Systria Co is preparing its financial statements for the year ended 31 December 20X7 and has a number of issues to deal with regarding non-current assets.

(i)   Systria Co has suffered an impairment loss of $90,000 relating to one of its cash-generating units. The carrying amounts of the assets in the cash-generating unit prior to adjusting for impairment are:

	$'000
Goodwill	50
Patent	10
Land and buildings	100
Plant and machinery	50
Net current assets	10

The patent is now estimated to have no value.

(ii)   During the year to 31 December 20X7 Systria Co acquired Dominica for $10 million, its tangible assets being valued at $7 million and goodwill on acquisition being $3 million. Assets with a carrying amount of $2.5 million were subsequently destroyed. Systria Co has carried out an impairment review and has established that Dominica Co could be sold for $6 million, while its value in use is $5.5 million.

(iii)   A freehold property originally costing $100,000 with a 50-year life has accumulated depreciation to date of $20,000. The asset is to be revalued to $130,000 at 31 December 20X7.

72   **What is the post-impairment carrying amount of plant and machinery in (i) above? (Enter your answer to the nearest whole $.)**

$ [   ]

73   **The finance director has been asked to report to the board on the reasons for the impairment review on the cash-generating unit. Which TWO of the following would be an internal indicator of impairment of an asset under IAS 36 *Impairment of Assets*?**

☐   The market value of the asset has fallen significantly

☐   There are adverse changes to the use to which the asset is put

☐   The asset is fully depreciated

☐   The operating performance of the asset has declined

74   **What is the carrying amount of the goodwill in (ii) following the impairment review? Select your answer from the pull-down list options below.**

$ [▼]

Pull-down list:

$1.5 million
$2 million
$2.5 million
$3 million

75   Using the drag and drop options below, select the correct amounts to complete the double entry required to record the revaluation in (iii).

	Debit	Credit
Accumulated depreciation		
Property at cost		
Revaluation surplus		

$20,000

$30,000

$50,000

76   What will be the depreciation charge relating to the asset in (iii) for the year ended 31 December 20X8?

○ $2,000

○ $2,600

○ $3,250

○ $2,750

(10 marks)

Section A

Revenue

77   Carraway Co entered into a contract on 1 January 20X5 to construct a factory for Seed Co.

The total contract price was $2.8 million which is expected to generate a profit for Carraway Co. Seed Co obtains control of the factory as the asset is constructed.

Carraway Co has an enforceable right for payment in respect of the construction completed to date. The contract states that the performance obligations are measured according to certificates issued by the surveyor.

Carraway Co measures satisfaction of the performance obligations under the contract by reference to the value of work certified as complete. At 31 December 20X5, the contract was certified by the surveyor as 35% complete.

$800,000 has been invoiced to the customer but not yet paid.

Identify, by selecting the correct options below, whether a contract asset or contract liability will be recognised as at 31 December 20X5 and what the carrying amount will be in the statement of financial position as at that date.

Asset or liability	Carrying amount
Contract asset	$180,000
Contract liability	$240,000

(2 marks)

---

78   America Co prepares its financial statement to 31 October each year. During the current year, America Co secured and received a government grant totalling $720,000 to support the digital upskilling of its workforce. $120,000 of the grant relates to investment in new IT equipment and the remainder is to support training across a two-year period from 1 April 20X5 to 31 March 20X7. The grant was received on 30 June 20X5. America Co fully intends to comply with the conditions of the grant. It purchased the new IT equipment on 1 April 20X5 as required and commenced training with immediate effect.

What amount should be included in non-current liabilities of America Co at the year end 31 October 20X5?

O $125,000

O $720,000

O $425,000

O $300,000   (2 marks)

---

79   On 1 October 20X2, Pricewell Co entered into a contract to construct a bridge. The total contract price was $50 million and construction is expected to be completed on 30 September 20X4. The contract is expected to generate a profit for Pricewell Co. The customer obtains control of the bridge as construction takes place. Costs to date are:

	$m
Materials, labour and overheads	12
Depreciation of specialist plant and machinery	3

The value of the work completed at 31 March 20X3 has been agreed at $22 million and the estimated cost to complete is $10 million. Pricewell Co recognises satisfaction of performance obligations determined by the value of work completed to date.

What is the profit recognised in respect of the contract at 31 March 20X3?

O $15,400,000

O $7,000,000

O $25,000,000

O $Nil   (2 marks)

---

80 The company recognises revenue on the basis of the costs incurred to date as a proportion of the total expected costs. The client gains the use of the asset during its construction.

The following details apply to a contract where performance obligations are satisfied over time at 31 December 20X5.

	$
Total contract revenue	120,000
Costs to date	48,000
Estimated costs to completion	48,000
Amounts invoiced	50,400
Amounts received from customers	40,000

What amount should be recognised as a contract asset in the statement of financial position as at 31 December 20X5?

O $9,600

O $12,000

O $14,400

O $50,400

(2 marks)

81 Broom Co successfully receives a government grant of $1,500,000 on 1 July 20X5 allowing it to purchase machinery which also costs $1,500,000 on 1 July 20X5. The machinery is depreciated on a straight-line basis over its ten-year useful life. As Broom Co has incurred the expenditure on the asset, the accountant has recognised the full amount of the grant received as other income in the year to 31 December 20X5. Company policy is to account for all grants received as deferred income.

Identify the adjustment required to correctly account for the government grant at 31 December 20X5.

	Account	Amount
DEBIT		
CREDIT		

Deferred income
Accrued income
Other income
Machinery cost

$1,500,000
$150,000
$75,000
$Nil
$1,425,000

(2 marks)

82   Batty Co has received a government grant of $400,000 on 1 January 20X5 to cover 50% of the cost of a new item of machinery. The grant was correctly recorded at that date.

The machinery will be depreciated over five years and the residual value is estimated to be $25,000. Batty Co are expecting to meet all the performance obligations of the grant.

Using the drag and drop options below, select the double entries required to record the subsequent treatment of the grant in the financial statements of Batty Co during the year ended 31 December 20X5 and the depreciation charge for the year in relation to the machinery. The options may be used more than once.

	Debit	Credit
Other income		
Deferred income		
Depreciation expense		
Accumulated depreciation		

$75,000

$80,000

$155,000

$160,000

(2 marks)

---

83   On 25 June 20X9 Cambridge Co received an order from a new customer, Circus Co, for products with a sales value of $900,000. Circus Co enclosed a deposit with the order of $90,000.

On 30 June Cambridge Co had not completed credit checks on Circus Co and had not despatched any goods.

According to IFRS 15 *Revenue from Contracts with Customers*, how should Cambridge Co record this transaction in its financial statements for the year ended 30 June 20X9?

Select your answers from the options available (options may be used more than once and all three amount boxes must be completed)

	Amount ($)	
Revenue		900,000
Current liability		810,000
Trade receivables		90,000
		nil

(2 marks)

---

84   Repro Co, a company which sells photocopying equipment, has prepared its draft financial statements for the year ended 30 September 20X4. It has included the following transactions in revenue at the stated amounts below.

Which of these has been correctly included in revenue according to IFRS 15 *Revenue from Contracts with Customers*?

○   Agency sales of $250,000 on which Repro Co is entitled to a commission.

○   Sale proceeds of $20,000 for motor vehicles which were no longer required by Repro Co.

○   Sales of $150,000 on 30 September 20X4. The amount invoiced to and received from the customer was $180,000, which included $30,000 for ongoing servicing work to be done by Repro Co over the next two years.

○   Sales of $200,000 on 1 October 20X3 to an established customer which, (with the agreement of Repro Co), will be paid in full on 30 September 20X5. Repro Co has a cost of capital of 10%.   **(2 marks)**

85   Yling Co entered into a contract which is expected to last 24 months on 1 January 20X4. The. The fixed price which has been agreed for the contract is $5 million. At 30 September 20X4 the costs incurred on the contract were $1.6 million and the estimated remaining costs to complete were $2.4 million. Yling Co measures satisfaction of the performance obligations under the contract based on the percentage of the project certified as completed. At 30 September 20X4, the percentage certified as completed to date was 38%.

On 20 September 20X4 Yling Co received a payment from the customer of $1.74 million which was equal to the total of the amounts invoiced to date.

What amount would be reported as a contract asset in Yling Co's statement of financial position as at 30 September 20X4?

○   Nil

○ $160,000

○ $1,000,000

○ $300,000   **(2 marks)**

86   Consignment inventory is an arrangement whereby inventory is held by one party but owned by another party. It is common in the motor trade.

Which TWO of the following indicate that the inventory in question is consignment inventory?

☐   Manufacturer can require dealer to return the inventory

☐   Dealer has no right of return of the inventory

☐   Manufacturer bears obsolescence risk

☐   Dealer bears slow movement risk   **(2 marks)**

87   Zayn Co spent $500,000 sending key staff on a one-day training course which took place on 1 January 20X6. Zayn Co is expected to benefit from this training for the next two years.

This training course was partly funded by a government scheme and Zayn Co received $50,000 from the government before the training commenced. The remaining balance of $50,000 is due to be received on 31 December 20X7. Current circumstances indicate that the receipt of the second instalment is virtually certain.

Selecting your answer from the pull-down list below, what amount should be charged to Zayn Co's statement of profit or loss for the year ended 31 December 20X6 to reflect the above transactions?

Pull-down list:

$150,000
$200,000
$400,000
$450,000

(2 marks)

(ACCA, Examiners Report June 2019)

---

88   Newmarket Co's revenue as shown in its draft statement of profit or loss for the year ended 31 December 20X9 is $27 million. This includes $8 million for a consignment of goods sold on 31 December 20X9 on which Newmarket Co will incur ongoing service and support costs for two years after the sale.

The supply of the goods and the provision of service and support are separate performance obligations under the terms of IFRS 15 *Revenue from Contracts with Customers*.

The cost of providing service and support is estimated at $800,000 per annum. Newmarket Co applies a 30% mark-up to all service costs.

At what amount should revenue be recognised in the statement of profit or loss of Newmarket Co for the year ended 31 December 20X9? (Ignore the effects of the time value of money and enter your answer to the nearest whole $.)

$ _____

(2 marks)

---

89   On 31 December 20X1 AB entered into a transaction to sell legal title to inventories which would take time to mature. The cost of the inventories at that date was $450,000. The inventories were sold to a financial institution for $420,000 with an option which allows AB to repurchase them on 31 December 20X3 for $463,050. At that date the selling price of the inventories would be approximately $540,000 and it was expected that AB would exercise the option.

How should the above transaction be accounted for in AB's financial statements for the year ended 31 December 20X1?

O   The inventory cost of $450,000 should be recognised in cost of sales and revenue of $420,000 should be recognised.

O   The inventories should be recorded in the statement of financial position at $420,000 and the $420,000 received should be reported as a liability. An inventory write-down of $30,000 should be reported in profit or loss.

O   The inventories should be recorded in the statement of financial position at $450,000 and the $420,000 received should be reported as a liability. There is no profit or loss effect.

O   The inventories should be recorded in the statement of financial position at $450,000 and the $420,000 received should be reported as a liability. Interest expense of $43,050 using the effective interest method should be reported in profit or loss.

(2 marks)

Introduction to groups

90   On what basis may a subsidiary be excluded from consolidation in accordance with IFRS 10 *Consolidated Financial Statements*?

  ○   The activities of the subsidiary are dissimilar to the activities of the rest of the group

  ○   The subsidiary was acquired with the intention of reselling it after a short period of time

  ○   The subsidiary is based in a country with strict exchange controls which make it difficult for it to transfer funds to the parent

  ○   There is no basis on which a subsidiary may be excluded from consolidation

  (2 marks)

---

91   When a bargain purchase arises, IFRS 3 *Business Combinations* requires that the amounts involved in computing the bargain purchase should first be reassessed.

  When the amount of the bargain purchase has been confirmed, how should it be accounted for?

  ○   Charged as an expense in profit or loss

  ○   Capitalised and presented under non-current assets

  ○   Credited to profit or loss

  ○   Shown as a deduction from non-current assets   (2 marks)

---

92   **Which of the following is the criterion for the treatment of an investment as an associate?**

  ○   Ownership of a majority of the equity shares

  ○   Ability to exercise control

  ○   Existence of significant influence

  ○   Exposure to variable returns from involvement with the investee   (2 marks)

---

93   **Which TWO of the following statements are correct when preparing consolidated financial statements?**

  ☐   A subsidiary cannot be consolidated unless it prepares financial statements to the same reporting date as the parent

  ☐   A subsidiary with a different reporting date may prepare additional statements up to the group reporting date for consolidation purposes

  ☐   A subsidiary's financial statements can be included in the consolidation if the gap between the parent and subsidiary reporting dates is five months or less

  ☐   Where a subsidiary's financial statements are drawn up to a different reporting date from those of the parent, adjustments should be made for significant transactions or events occurring between the two reporting dates   (2 marks)

94   IFRS 3 *Business Combinations* requires an acquirer to measure the assets and liabilities of the acquiree at the date of consolidation at fair value. IFRS 13 *Fair Value Measurement* provides guidance on how fair value should be established.

Identify whether the following factors are relevant or not relevant considerations when arriving at the fair value of a non-financial asset according to IFRS 13?

The characteristics of the asset	Relevant	Not relevant
The price paid to acquire the asset	Relevant	Not relevant
The principal or most advantageous market for the asset	Relevant	Not relevant
The highest and best use of the asset	Relevant	Not relevant

(2 marks)

95   An investor company assesses control to determine whether or not it is the parent of an investee company.

According to IFRS 10 *Consolidated Financial Statements*, which THREE of the following are required to determine whether an investor has control of an investee?

☐   The ability to use its power over the investee to affect the amount of the investor's returns

☐   Exposure to, or rights to, variable returns from its involvement with the investee

☐   Acquisition of 50% or more of the share capital

☐   Power over the investee
(2 marks)
(ACCA, Examiners Report June 2019)

96   Petre Co owns 100% of the share capital of the following companies. The directors are unsure of whether the investments should be consolidated.

In which of the following circumstances would the investment NOT be consolidated?

○   Petre Co has decided to sell its investment in Alpha Co as it is loss-making; the directors believe its exclusion from consolidation would assist users in predicting the group's future profits

○   Beta Co is a bank and its activity is so different from the engineering activities of the rest of the group that it would be meaningless to consolidate it

○   Delta Co is located in a country where local accounting standards are compulsory and these are not compatible with IFRS Standards used by the rest of the group

○   Gamma Co is located in a country where a military coup has taken place and Petre Co has lost control of the investment for the foreseeable future   (2 marks)

Financial instruments

97   An 8% $30 million convertible loan note was issued on 1 April 20X5 at par. Interest is payable in arrears on 31 March each year. The loan note is redeemable at par on 31 March 20X8 or convertible into equity shares at the option of the loan note holders on the basis of 30 shares for each $100 of loan. A similar instrument without the conversion option would have an interest rate of 10% per annum.

The present values of $1 receivable at the end of each year based on discount rates of 8% and 10% are:

		8%	10%
End of year	1	0.93	0.91
	2	0.86	0.83
	3	0.79	0.75
	Cumulative	2.58	2.49

What amount will be credited to equity on 1 April 20X5 in respect of this financial instrument?

O $5,976,000

O $1,524,000

O $28,476,000

O $30,000,000   (2 marks)

---

98   A 5% loan note was issued on 1 April 20X0 at its face value of $20 million. Direct costs of the issue were $500,000. The loan note will be redeemed on 31 March 20X3 at a substantial premium. The effective interest rate applicable is 10% per annum.

At what amount will the loan note appear in the statement of financial position as at 31 March 20X2?

O $21,000,000

O $20,450,000

O $22,100,000

O $21,495,000   (2 marks)

---

99   Using the drag and drop options below, complete the statement to show how IFRS 9 *Financial Instruments* require investments in equity instruments to be measured and accounted for (in the absence of any election at initial recognition)?

	with changes going through	
Fair value		profit or loss
Amortised cost		other comprehensive income

(2 marks)

100 On 1 January 20X1, Penfold Co purchased a debt instrument at its fair value of $500,000. It had a principal amount of $550,000 and was due to mature in five years. The debt instrument carries fixed interest of 6% paid annually in arrears and has an effective interest rate of 8%. It is held at amortised cost.

At what amount will the debt instrument be shown in the statement of financial position of Penfold Co as at 31 December 20X2?

○ $514,560

○ $566,000

○ $564,560

○ $520,800   (2 marks)

---

101 **Which of the following is NOT classified as a financial instrument under IAS 32 *Financial Instruments: Presentation*?**

○ Share options

○ Intangible assets

○ Trade receivables

○ Redeemable preference shares   (2 marks)

---

102 Dexon Co's draft statement of financial position as at 31 March 20X8 shows financial assets at fair value through profit or loss with a carrying amount of $12.5 million as at 1 April 20X7.

These financial assets are held in a fund whose value changes directly in proportion to a specified market index. At 1 April 20X7 the relevant index was 1,200 and at 31 March 20X8 it was 1,296.

What amount of gain or loss should be recognised at 31 March 20X8 in respect of these assets? (Enter your answer to the nearest whole $.)

$ [   ]   (2 marks)

---

103 On 1 January 20X8, Zeeper Co purchased 40,000 $1 listed equity shares at a price of $3 per share. An irrevocable election was made to recognise the shares at fair value through other comprehensive income. Transaction costs were $3,000. At the year end of 31 December 20X8 the shares were trading at $6 per share.

What amount in respect of these shares will be shown under 'investments in equity instruments' in the statement of financial position of Zeeper Co as at 31 December 20X8? (Enter your answer to the nearest whole $.)

$ [   ]   (2 marks)

Lease accounting

104   On 1 January 20X6, Fellini Co entered into a contract for the right to use a machine for a four year period. The contract meets the definition of a lease under IFRS 16 *Leases*. Fellini Co paid a deposit of $700,000 on the commencement of the lease on 1 January 20X6 and a further 3 instalments of $700,000 are payable annually in advance. The present value of the future lease payments was $1,871,100 on commencement of the lease. The interest rate implicit in the lease is 6%.

What amount will appear under non-current liabilities in respect of this lease in the statement of financial position of Fellini Co at 31 December 20X6?

    ○ $700,000

    ○ $1,983,366

    ○ $1,283,366

    ○ $1,871,100   (2 marks)

---

105   **Identify whether each of the following statements indicates or does not indicate that a contract contains a lease under IFRS 16 *Leases*?**

The lessee obtains substantially all of the economic benefits from use of the asset	Indicates that the contract contains a lease	Does not indicate that the contract contains a lease
Ownership in the asset is transferred at the end of the lease term	Indicates that the contract contains a lease	Does not indicate that the contract contains a lease
The contract relates to an identified asset	Indicates that the contract contains a lease	Does not indicate that the contract contains a lease
If it suits them to do so, the lessor can substitute an identical asset	Indicates that the contract contains a lease	Does not indicate that the contract contains a lease

                                                                    (2 marks)

---

106   Pebworth Co entered into a contract to acquire the right to use an item of plant for a period of three years from 1 April 20X7. The contract meets the definition of a lease under IFRS 16 *Leases*. The present value of the future lease payments on commencement of the lease was $15,462,000, which is also the initial carrying amount of the right-of-use asset. Pebworth Co will also make three rental payments of $6 million per annum which are due to be paid in arrears on 31 March each year. The useful life of the plant is deemed to be five years. There is no option to buy the asset at the end of the lease term.

The interest rate implicit in the lease is 8% per annum.

What is the total charge to profit or loss in respect of this lease at 31 March 20X8?

    ○ $1,236,900

    ○ $4,329,300

    ○ $6,000,000

    ○ $6,390,900   (2 marks)

---

107 **At what amount does IFRS 16 _Leases_ require a lessee to measure a right-of-use asset acquired under a lease?**

○ Lease liability + other direct costs + incentives received

○ Lease liability – other direct costs – amounts paid before or on commencement of the lease

○ Lease liability + other direct costs + amounts paid before or on commencement of the lease – incentives received

○ Lease liability – other direct costs – amounts paid before or on commencement of the lease + incentives received (2 marks)

---

108 On 1 October 20X3, Fresco Co acquired the right to use an item of plant under a five-year contract. The contract meets the definition of a lease under IFRS 16 _Leases_. The terms of the contract required an immediate deposit of $2 million with five payments of $6 million paid annually in arrears commencing on 30 September 20X4. The present value of the future lease payments is $22,745,000 on commencement of the lease. The rate of interest implicit in the lease is 10% per annum.

What is the carrying amount of the lease current liability in Fresco Co's statement of financial position as at 30 September 20X4?

○ $1,901,950

○ $4,098,050

○ $6,000,000

○ $2,274,500 (2 marks)

---

109 The objective of IFRS 16 _Leases_ is to prescribe the appropriate accounting treatment and required disclosures in relation to leases.

Which TWO of the following are among the criteria set out in IFRS 16 for an arrangement to be classified as a lease?

☐ The lessee has the right to substantially all of the economic benefits from use of the asset

☐ The lease term is for substantially all of the estimated useful life of the asset

☐ The agreement concerns an identified asset which cannot be substituted

☐ The lessor has the right to direct the use of the asset (2 marks)

---

110 Cornet Co has entered into an agreement for the right to use an asset for a period of eight years on 1 July 20X4. The useful life of the asset at that date is ten years. The lease requires annual payments of $750,000 in arrears. The present value of the future lease on commencement of the lease is $4,657,500. The interest rate implicit in the lease is 6%. Additionally, Cornet Co paid directly attributable costs of $37,500 on 1 July 20X4.

Select the total charge to the statement of profit or loss for the year ended 30 June 20X5 in respect of the right-of-use asset using the options in the pull-down list.

[▼]

Pull-down list:

$586,875
$866,325
$279,450
$1,029,450 (2 marks)

(ACCA, Examiners Report Dec 2018 (amended))

111 A sale and leaseback transaction involves the sale of an asset and the leasing back of the same asset.

If the arrangement meets the IFRS 15 *Revenue from Contracts with Customers* criteria to be recognised as a sale, how should any 'profit' on the sale be treated?

O   Recognise whole amount of profit immediately in profit or loss

O   Defer profit and amortise over the lease term

O   Recognise proportion relating to right-of-use retained

O   Recognise proportion relating to right-of-use transferred   (2 marks)

---

112 During the year ended 30 September 20X4 Hyper Co entered into the following transactions:

On 1 October 20X3, Hyper Co entered into a contract to obtain the right to use an asset for a five year period. The contract meets the definition of a lease under IFRS 16 *Leases*. An initial payment of $90,000 was made on commencement of the lease, being the first of five equal annual payments. The present value of the future lease payments on commencement of the lease was $250,000. The right-of-use asset has a five-year useful life. The lease has an implicit interest rate of 16%.

On 1 August 20X4, Hyper Co made a payment of $18,000 for a nine-month lease of an item of excavation equipment. Hyper wishes to utilise the exceptions available under IFRS 16 *Leases*.

What amount in total would be charged to Hyper Co's statement of profit or loss for the year ended 30 September 20X4 in respect of the above transactions? (Enter your answer to the nearest whole $.)

$ [   ]   (2 marks)

---

113 On 1 January 20X6, Platinum Co sold its head office property, which had a carrying amount of $7,000,000, to a financial institution for a total of $8,000,000 which was its fair value on that date. The transaction constituted a sale in accordance with IFRS 15 *Revenue from Contracts with Customers*. The accountant of Platinum Co recognised the profit of $1,000,000 in other income. Platinum Co immediately entered into an agreement for the right to use the head office for a period of five years. Under the terms of the agreement, Platinum Co must make payments of $600,000 per annum payable annually in arrears. The present value of the future lease payments was $2,162,850 on commencement of the lease and the rate of interest implicit in the lease is 12%.

What will be the adjustment required to account for the gain on sale in profit or loss for the year ended 31 December 20X6? (Enter your answer to the nearest whole $.)

$ [   ]   (2 marks)

---

114   On 1 April 20X5, Pennyroyal Co sold its property to a financial institution for $20,000,000 which was the fair value of the property at that date. The transaction constitutes a sale in accordance with IFRS 15 *Revenue from Contracts with Customers*. The property had a carrying amount of $18,000,000 and had an estimated remaining useful life of 10 years at the date of sale. Under the terms of the sale, Pennyroyal Co has the right to use the property for a four-year period commencing 1 April 20X5. The present value of the future payments under the lease have been correctly calculated as $7,092,000.

What is the amount of the gain that can be recognised in the statement of profit or loss in respect of this transaction for the year ended 31 March 20X6?

○ $709,200

○ $1,290,800

○ $2,000,000

○ $Nil   (2 marks)

115   Jetsam Co entered into an agreement for the right to use an item of plant for a period of ten years from 1 April 20X0. The agreement required payments of $15,000 to be made annually in arrears. The present value of the future lease payments was estimated to be $100,650 at the inception of the lease and the rate of interest implicit in the lease was 8%. Both the lease term and the plant's estimated useful life was ten years.

Selecting your answer from the options below, what is the total charge to appear in the statement of profit or loss in respect of the lease for the year ended 31 December 20X0?

Pull-down list:

$11,250

$6,039

$7,549

$13,588   (2 marks)

(ACCA, Examiners Report Sep 2017, amended)

Provisions and events after the reporting period

116   Candel Co is being sued by a customer for $2 million for breach of contract over a cancelled order. Candel Co has obtained legal opinion that there is a 20% chance that Candel Co will lose the case. Accordingly, Candel Co has provided $400,000 ($2 million × 20%) in respect of the claim. The unrecoverable legal costs of defending the action are estimated at $100,000. These have not been provided for as the case will not go to court until next year.

What is the amount of the provision that should be made by Candel Co in accordance with IAS 37 *Provisions, Contingent Liabilities and Contingent Assets*?

$ [   ]   (2 marks)

117   During the year Peterlee Co acquired an iron ore mine at a cost of $6 million. In addition, when all the ore has been extracted (estimated ten years' time) the company will face estimated costs for landscaping the area affected by the mining that have a present value of $2 million. These costs would still have to be incurred even if no further ore was extracted.

How should this $2 million future cost be recognised in the financial statements?

   ○   Provision $2 million and $2 million capitalised as part of cost of mine

   ○   Provision $2 million and $2 million charged to operating costs

   ○   Accrual $200,000 per annum for next ten years

   ○   Should not be recognised as no cost has yet arisen   **(2 marks)**

(ACCA, Examiners Report June 2019)

---

118   **Select whether a provision is required or is not required in the financial statements of the following companies.**

Aston Co has a company policy of cleaning up any environmental contamination caused by its operations, even though it is not legally obliged to do so	Provision required	No provision required
Brum Co has a fixed price contract to supply widgets to Erdington Co. Brum Co has calculated that it will cost more to manufacture the widgets than budgeted, which is more than the revenue agreed from Erdington Co	Provision required	No provision required
Coleshill Co is closing down a division. The board has prepared detailed closure plans which have not yet been communicated to customers and employees	Provision required	No provision required
Dudley Co has acquired a machine which requires the staff to be retrained on its safe operation. The staff training will occur in the next financial period	Provision required	No provision required

(2 marks)

---

119   Flute Co undertakes drilling activities and has a widely publicised environmental policy stating that it will incur costs to restore land to its original condition once drilling activities have been completed.

Drilling commenced on a particular piece of land on 1 July 20X8. At this time, Flute Co estimated that it would cost $3 million to restore the land when drilling was completed in five years' time. Flute Co's cost of capital is 7% and the appropriate present value factor is 0.713.

At what amount will the provision for restoration costs be measured in Flute Co's statement of financial position as at 31 December 20X8?

   ○ $2.4 million

   ○ $3.0 million

   ○ $2.29 million

   ○ $2.21 million   **(2 marks)**

(ACCA, Examiners Report June 2019)

120 Identify whether the following statements are true or false in accordance with IAS 37 *Provisions, Contingent Liabilities and Contingent Assets.*

Provisions should be made for both constructive and legal obligations	True	False
Discounting may be used when estimating the amount of a provision	True	False
A restructuring provision must include the estimated costs of retraining or relocating continuing staff	True	False
A restructuring provision may only be made when a company has a detailed plan for the restructuring and has communicated to interested parties a firm intention to carry it out	True	False

(2 marks)

121 Eilish Co had a provision of $100,000 in its financial statements at 31 December 20X4 in relation to an ongoing court case. On 10 February 20X5, Eilish Co settled this case for $120,000.

What is the accounting entry required by Eilish Co on 10 February 20X5 in relation to this provision?

○ Debit Provision $100,000, Debit Profit or loss $20,000; Credit Cash $120,000

○ Debit Cash $120,000; Credit Provision $100,000, Credit Profit or loss $20,000

○ Debit Expense $120,000; Credit Provision $120,000

○ Debit Provision $120,000: Credit Expense $120,000   (2 marks)

122 On 1 October 20X3, Xplorer Co commenced drilling for oil from an undersea oilfield. The extraction of oil causes damage to the seabed which has a restorative cost (ignore discounting) of $10,000 per million barrels of oil extracted. Xplorer Co extracted 250 million barrels in the year ended 30 September 20X4.

Xplorer Co is also required to dismantle the drilling equipment at the end of its five-year licence. This has an estimated cost of $30 million on 30 September 20X8. Xplorer Co's cost of capital is 8% per annum and $1 has a present value of 68 cents in five years' time.

What is the total provision (extraction plus dismantling) which Xplorer Co would report in its statement of financial position as at 30 September 20X4 in respect of its oil operations? (Enter your answer to the nearest whole $.)

$ [   ]   (2 marks)

123 Hopewell Co sells a line of goods under a six-month warranty. Any defect arising during that period is repaired free of charge. Hopewell Co has calculated that if all the goods sold in the last six months of the year required repairs the cost would be $2 million. If all of these goods had more serious faults and had to be replaced the cost would be $6 million.

The normal pattern is that 80% of goods sold will be fault-free, 15% will require repairs and 5% will have to be replaced.

Using the pull-down list options, select what is the amount of the provision required.

[▼]

Pull-down list:

$0.6 million
$0.8 million
$1.6 million
$2 million   (2 marks)

---

124 **Which TWO of the following events which occur after the reporting date of a company but before the financial statements are authorised for issue are classified as ADJUSTING events in accordance with IAS 10 *Events After the Reporting Period*?**

☐ A change in tax rate announced after the reporting date, but affecting the current tax liability

☐ The discovery of a fraud which had occurred during the year

☐ The determination of the sale proceeds of an item of plant sold before the year end

☐ The destruction of a factory by fire   (2 marks)

---

125 Coleridge Co is a manufacturing company.

The financial accountant of Coleridge Co is considering whether any of the events, which took place in April 20X5, require adjustment in the financial statements for the year ended 31 March 20X5

Which TWO of the following events require adjusting in the financial statements for the year ended 31 March 20X5, as required by IAS 10 *Events After the Reporting Period*?

☐ Thomas Co, a customer of Coleridge Co, which owes the company $200,000 at 31 March 20X5, entered insolvency on 3 April 20X5

☐ An employee has commenced legal proceedings against Coleridge Co following an industrial accident on 10 April 20X5. The company is expected to lose the case and estimates that damages of $350,000 will be paid to the employee

☐ Inventory that was held at cost of $200,000 on 31 March 20X5 was sold on 21 April 20X5 for $150,000

☐ The company had agreed the sale of the Wordsworth division at a board meeting on 25 March 20X5. The public announcement was made on 1 April 20X5   (2 marks)

Inventories and biological assets

126 Caminas Co has the following products in inventory at the year end.

Product	Quantity	Cost	Selling price	Selling cost
A	1,000	$40	$55	$8
B	2,500	$15	$25	$4
C	800	$23	$27	$5

At what amount should total inventory be stated in the statement of financial position? Select your answers from the pull-down list provided.

[▼]

Pull-down list:

$95,900
$95,100
$103,100
$105,100

(2 marks)

127 At 31 December 20X4, Litch Co had, in inventory, 100 items of work in progress which had cost $14,900 to produce. It estimated that the work in progress would cost $13 per unit to complete, and that each unit would then sell for $166.

Direct selling costs are estimated at 2% of revenue.

In accordance with IAS 2 *Inventories*, what is the correct value of Litch Co's inventory as at 31 December 20X4?

O $14,900

O $16,268

O $16,200

O $14,968

(2 marks)

(ACCA Examiner's Report September/December 2020)

128 At what amount is a biological asset measured on initial recognition in accordance with IAS 41 *Agriculture*?

O   Production cost

O   Fair value

O   Cost less estimated costs to sell

O   Fair value less estimated costs to sell

(2 marks)

129 Which of the following is NOT the outcome of a biological transformation according to IAS 41 *Agriculture*?

O   Growth

O   Harvest

O   Procreation

O   Degeneration

(2 marks)

130 **How is a gain or loss arising on a biological asset recognised in accordance with IAS 41 *Agriculture*?**

   ○   Included in profit or loss for the year

   ○   Adjusted in retained earnings

   ○   Shown under 'other comprehensive income'

   ○   Deferred and recognised over the life of the biological asset   **(2 marks)**

---

131 **Identify whether the following statements about IAS 2 *Inventories* are correct or incorrect:**

Production overheads should be included in cost on the basis of a company's actual level of activity in the period	Correct	Incorrect
In arriving at the net realisable value of inventories, settlement discounts must be deducted from the expected selling price	Correct	Incorrect
In arriving at the cost of inventories, FIFO, LIFO and weighted average cost formulas are acceptable	Correct	Incorrect
It is permitted to value finished goods inventories at materials plus labour cost only, without adding production overheads	Correct	Incorrect

(2 marks)

---

132 Isaac Co is a company which buys agricultural produce from wholesale suppliers for retail to the general public. It is preparing its financial statements for the year ending 30 September 20X4 and is considering its closing inventory.

In addition to IAS 2 *Inventories*, which of the following accounting standards may be relevant to determining the figure to be included in its financial statements for closing inventories?

   ○   IAS 10 *Events After the Reporting Period*

   ○   IAS 38 *Intangible Assets*

   ○   IAS 16 *Property, Plant and Equipment*

   ○   IAS 41 *Agriculture*   **(2 marks)**

---

133 In preparing financial statements for the year ended 31 March 20X6, the inventory count was carried out on 4 April 20X6. The value of inventory counted was $36 million. Between 31 March and 4 April goods with a cost of $2.7 million were received into inventory and sales of $7.8 million were made at a mark-up on cost of 30%.

Using the pull-down list provided, select at what amount inventory should be stated in the statement of financial position as at 31 March 20X6?

[▼]

Pull-down list:

$39.3 million
$36.0 million
$33.3 million
$41.1 million   **(2 marks)**

---

134 At 31 March 20X7 Tentacle Co had 12,000 units of product W32 in inventory, included at cost of $6 per unit. During April and May 20X7 units of W32 were being sold at a price of $5.40 each, with sales staff receiving a 15% commission on the sales price of the product. The financial statements of Tentacle Co were approved by the Board on 14 July 20X7.

At what amount should inventory of product W32 be recognised in the financial statements of Tentacle Co as at 31 March 20X7? (Enter your answer to the nearest whole $.)

$ [_____]   (2 marks)

Accounting for taxation

135 Ullington Co's trial balance shows a debit balance of $2.1 million brought forward on current tax and a credit balance of $5.4 million brought forward on deferred tax. The tax charge for the current year is estimated at $16.2 million. The carrying amounts of net assets are $13 million in excess of their tax base, which includes a $3 million revaluation surplus on the first-time revaluation of buildings. The income tax and deferred tax rate is 30%.

What is the amount of income tax recognised in the statement of profit or loss of Ullington Co for the year?

O $15.6 million

O $15.9 million

O $16.8 million

O $18.3 million   (2 marks)

136 Jasper Orange Co's trial balance at 31 December 20X3 shows a debit balance of $700,000 on current tax and a credit balance of $8,400,000 on deferred tax. The directors have estimated the provision for income tax for the year at $4.5 million and the required deferred tax provision is $5.6 million, $1.2 million of which relates to a property revaluation.

What is the amount of income tax amount recognised in Jasper Orange Co's statement of profit or loss for the year ended 31 December 20X3?

O $1 million

O $2.4 million

O $1.2 million

O $3.6 million   (2 marks)

137 The following information relates to an entity:

(i)   At 1 January 20X8 the carrying amount of non-current assets exceeded their tax written down value by $850,000.

(ii)   For the year to 31 December 20X8 the entity claimed depreciation for tax purposes of $500,000 and charged depreciation of $450,000 in the financial statements.

(iii) During the year ended 31 December 20X8 the entity revalued a property. The revaluation surplus was $250,000. There are no current plans to sell the property.

(iv)   The tax rate was 30% throughout the year.

What is the provision for deferred tax required by IAS 12 *Income Taxes* at 31 December 20X8?

- ○ $240,000
- ○ $270,000
- ○ $315,000
- ○ $345,000
(2 marks)

---

138   The statements of financial position of Nedburg Co include the following extracts:

Statements of financial position as at 30 September

	20X2 $m	20X1 $m
Non-current liabilities		
Deferred tax	310	140
Current liabilities		
Taxation	130	160

The tax charge in the statement of profit or loss for the year ended 30 September 20X2 is $270 million.

What amount of tax was paid during the year to 30 September 20X2?

$ [   ] million
(2 marks)

---

139   The trial balance of Highwood Co at 31 March 20X6 showed credit balances of $800,000 on current tax and $2.6 million on deferred tax. A property was revalued during the year giving rise to deferred tax of $3.75 million. This has been included in the deferred tax provision of $6.75 million at 31 March 20X6.

The income tax liability for the year ended 31 March 20X6 is estimated at $19.4 million.

What is the amount of the income tax charge in the statement of profit or loss of Highwood at 31 March 20X6?

$ [   ] million
(2 marks)

---

140   Astral Co purchased an item of plant for $40,000 on 1 September 20X1. The plant has an estimated useful life of five years and an estimated residual value of $5,000. The plant is depreciated on a straight-line basis. Local tax law does not allow depreciation as an expense, but a tax allowance of 60% of the cost of the asset can be claimed in the year of purchase and 20% per annum on a reducing balance basis in the following years. The rate of income tax is 30%.

What charge or credit for deferred taxation should be recorded in Astral Co's statement of profit or loss for the year to 31 August 20X2?

- ○ $17,000 charge
- ○ $5,100 charge
- ○ $5,100 credit
- ○ $17,000 credit
(2 marks)

(ACCA, Examiners Report June 2018)

---

141   Isaac & Joseph Co purchased new machinery on 1 January 20X5 for $1,000,000. It has
       a residual value of $200,000, with the useful life deemed to be 8 years. The plant is
       depreciated on a straight-line basis.

       Tax allowances of 50% of the cost of the asset can be claimed in the year of purchase, as
       depreciation is not allowed for tax purposes. The rate of income tax is 30%.

       **Identify by selecting the options provided below, whether a deferred tax asset or liability
       should be recognised at 31 December 20X5 and at what amount?**

Deferred tax asset or liability	Amount ($)
Asset	60,000
Liability	82,500
	120,000

(2 marks)

Section B

Derringdo Co case

Information relevant to questions 142-146

Derringdo Co is a broadband provider which receives government assistance to provide broadband to remote areas. Derringdo Co invested in a new server at a cost of $800,000 on 1 October 20X2. The server has an estimated useful life of ten years with a residual value equal to 15% of its cost. Derringdo Co uses straight-line depreciation on a time apportioned basis.

The company received a government grant of 30% of its cost price of the server at the time of purchase. The terms of the grant are that if the company retains the asset for four years or more, then no repayment liability will be incurred. Derringdo Co has no intention of disposing of the server within the first four years. Derringdo Co's accounting policy for capital-based government grants is to treat them as deferred income and release them to income over the life of the asset to which they relate.

142   What is the net amount that will be charged to operating expenses in respect of the server for the year ended 31 March 20X3?

    ○ $10,000

    ○ $28,000

    ○ $22,000

    ○ $34,000

143   What amount will be presented under non-current liabilities at 31 March 20X3 in respect of the grant?

    ○ $228,000

    ○ $216,000

    ○ $240,000

    ○ $204,000

144   Derringdo Co sells a package which gives customers a free laptop when they sign a two-year contract for the provision of broadband services. The laptop has a stand-alone price of $200 and the broadband contract is for $30 per month.

    In accordance with IFRS 15 *Revenue from Contracts with Customers*, what amount will be recognised as revenue on each package in the first year?

    Select the correct answer from the options below.

    [▼]

    Pull-down list:

    $439

    $281

    $461

    $158

145 Determining the amount to be recognised in the first year is an example of which stage in the process of applying IFRS 15 *Revenue from Contracts with Customers*?

    ○   Determining the transaction price

    ○   Recognising revenue when a performance obligation is satisfied

    ○   Identifying the separate performance obligations

    ○   Allocating the transaction price to the performance obligations

146 Derringdo Co is carrying out a transaction on behalf of another entity and the finance director is unsure whether Derringdo Co should be regarded as an agent or a principal in respect of this transaction.

Which of the following would indicate that Derringdo Co is acting as an agent?

    ○   Derringdo Co is primarily responsible for fulfilling the contract

    ○   Derringdo Co is not exposed to credit risk for the amount due from the customer

    ○   Derringdo Co is responsible for negotiating the price for the contract

    ○   Derringdo Co will not be paid in the form of commission

(10 marks)

Campbell Co case (ACCA Examiner's Report September/December 2020) 18 mins

Information relevant to questions 147-151.

The following details relate to three of Campbell Co's contracts:

Contract 1 has a total price of $9 million and commenced in 20X7. Total costs are expected to be $7 million. The progress towards completion is assessed at 90% at 31 December 20X8. Progress was measured at 20% for the year ended 31 December 20X7.

Contract 2 commenced in December 20X8 and is expected to generate a profit of $3 million. It is too early in the contract to assess progress towards completion. Campbell Co has spent $0.2 million so far, all of which is expected to be recoverable from the customer when Campbell Co sends its first invoice in 20X9.

Contract 3 relates to the sale of equipment to a customer for $2.36 million on 1 July 20X8. The sale included $0.4 million for installation of the equipment and $0.2 million relating to 12 months after-sales support. The equipment was installed on 1 July 20X8.

147 **Identify whether the following statements are correct or incorrect in respect of how revenue should be recognised in accordance with IFRS 15 *Revenue from Contracts with Customers*?**

Revenue should be recognised as an entity satisfies a performance obligation	CORRECT	INCORRECT
Progress towards completion on a contract should be measured solely on an input basis	CORRECT	INCORRECT

148 What amount of revenue should be recognised in respect of Contract 1 in Campbell Co's statement of profit or loss for the year ended 31 December 20X8? (Enter your answer to the nearest whole $.)

$ [   ]

---

149 Which of the following items would **NOT** be recorded in the financial statements for 20X8 of Campbell Co in respect of Contract 2?

○   Revenue $0.2m

○   Cost of sales $0.2m

○   Contract asset $0.2m

○   Contract liability $0.2m

---

150 What amount of revenue should be recognised in respect of Contract 3 in Campbell Co's statement of profit or loss for the year ended 31 December 20X8?

○ $2.06m

○ $2.16m

○ $2.26m

○ $2.36m

---

151 Campbell Co offers its customers an accessory for the equipment that it sells in Contract 3. Campbell Co does not manufacture the accessory itself, but has an agreement with the manufacturer to sell the accessory on the manufacturer's behalf.

Campbell Co places the order with the manufacturer and the manufacturer delivers the accessory direct to the customer. The customer pays Campbell Co for the accessory and Campbell Co then deducts 3% commission before paying the manufacturer.

An accessory is delivered to one of Campbell Co's customers on 10 December 20X8, which the customer has accepted and will pay $50,000.

Which of the following correctly describes how Campbell Co should recognise this transaction?

○ $50,000 should be recognised as revenue by Campbell Co when the accessory has been delivered and accepted by the customer

○ $1,500 should be recognised as revenue by Campbell Co when the accessory has been paid for by the customer

○ $1,500 should be recognised as revenue by Campbell Co when the accessory has been delivered and accepted by the customer

○ $50,000 should be recognised as revenue by Campbell Co when the accessory has been paid for by the customer

---

(10 marks)

Apex Co case

The following scenario relates to questions 152–156.

Apex Co is a publicly listed supermarket chain. During the current year it started the building of a new store. The directors are aware that in accordance with IAS 23 *Borrowing Costs* certain borrowing costs have to be capitalised.

Details relating to construction of Apex Co's new store:

Apex Co issued a $10 million unsecured loan with a coupon (nominal) interest rate of 6% on 1 April 20X8. The loan is redeemable at a premium which means the loan has an effective finance cost of 7.5% per annum. The loan was specifically issued to finance the building of the new store which meets the definition of a qualifying asset in IAS 23. Construction of the store commenced on 1 May 20X8 and it was completed and ready for use on 28 February 20X9, but did not open for trading until 1 April 20X9.

152   Apex Co's new store meets the definition of a qualifying asset under IAS 23.

Which of the following is the correct description of a qualifying asset under IAS 23?

    ○   An asset that is ready for use or sale when purchased

    ○   An asset that takes a substantial period of time to get ready for its intended use or sale

    ○   An asset that is intended for use rather than sale

    ○   An asset that has been financed using a specific loan

---

153   **Apex Co issued the loan stock on 1 April 20X8. Three events or transactions must be taking place for capitalisation of borrowing costs to commence in accordance with IAS 23. Which of the following is NOT one of these?**

    ○   Expenditure on the asset is being incurred

    ○   Borrowing costs are being incurred

    ○   Physical construction of the asset is nearing completion

    ○   Necessary activities are in progress to prepare the asset for use or sale

---

154   **What is the total of the finance costs which can be capitalised in respect of Apex Co's new store? (Enter your answer to the nearest whole $.)**

$ _____

---

155   Rather than take out a loan specifically for the new store Apex Co could have funded the store from existing borrowings which are:

(i)   10% bank loan $50 million

(ii)   8% bank loan $30 million

In this case it would have applied a 'capitalisation rate' to the expenditure on the asset. What would that rate have been?

    ○   10%

    ○   8.75%

    ○   9%

    ○   9.25%

156 If Apex Co had been able to temporarily invest the proceeds of the loan from 1 April to 1 May when construction began, how would the proceeds be accounted for?

    ○   Deducted from finance costs

    ○   Deducted from the cost of the asset

    ○   Recognised as investment income in the statement of profit or loss

    ○   Deducted from administrative expenses in the statement of profit or loss

(10 marks)

Bertrand Co case   **18 mins**

Information relevant to questions 157–161

Bertrand Co issued $10 million convertible loan notes on 1 October 20X0 that carry a nominal interest (coupon) rate of 5% per annum. They are redeemable on 30 September 20X3 at par for cash or can be exchanged for equity shares in Bertrand Co on the basis of 20 shares for each $100 of loan. A similar loan note, without the conversion option, would have required Bertrand Co to pay an interest rate of 8%.

The present value of $1 receivable at the end of each year, based on discount rates of 5% and 8%, can be taken as:

		5%	8%
End of year	1	0.95	0.93
	2	0.91	0.86
	3	0.86	0.79
	cumulative	2.72	2.58

157 How should the convertible loan notes be accounted for?

    ○   As debt

    ○   As debt and equity

    ○   As equity

    ○   As debt until conversion, then as equity

158 What is the amount that will be recognised as finance costs for the year ended 30 September 20X1? (Enter your answer to the nearest whole $.)

$ [   ]

159 What is the amount that should be shown under liabilities at 30 September 20X1?

    ○ $9,425,000

    ○ $9,925,000

    ○ $9,690,000

    ○   Nil

160 **If Bertrand Co had incurred transaction costs in issuing these loan notes, how would these have been accounted for?**

○ Added to the proceeds of the loan notes

○ Deducted from the proceeds of the loan notes

○ Amortised over the life of the loan notes

○ Charged to finance costs

161 Bertrand Co also purchased a debt instrument which will mature in five years' time. Bertrand Co intends to hold the debt instrument to maturity to collect interest payments.

Complete the following statement using the options below.

This debt instrument will be measured as a financial ▭

at ▭ in the financial statements of Bertrand Co.

asset	amortised cost

liability	fair value

	fair value through profit or loss

(10 marks)

Fino Co case   **18 mins**

Information relevant to questions 162–166

On 1 April 20X7, Fino Co entered into an agreement to gain the right to use plant for a period of three years. The agreement meets the definition of a lease in accordance with IFRS 16 *Leases*.

An initial payment of $100,000 was made on 1 April 20X7 and the present value of the future lease payments at that date is $173,500. Payments in respect of the lease are made in advance and are $100,000 per annum, commencing on 1 April 20X8. The rate of interest implicit in the lease is 10%. The lease does not transfer ownership of the plant to Fino Co by the end of the lease term and there is no purchase option available. Fino Co incurred initial direct costs of $20,000 to set up the lease and received lease incentives from the manufacturer totalling $7,000.

162 **Over what period should Fino Co depreciate a right-of-use asset, according to IFRS 16 *Leases*?**

○ From the commencement of the lease to the end of the lease term

○ From the commencement of the lease to the end of the useful life of the plant

○ From the commencement of the lease to the longer of the end of the lease term and the end of the useful life of the plant

○ From the commencement of the lease to the shorter of the end of the lease term and the end of the useful life of the plant

163   What is the initial cost of the right-of-use asset as at 1 April 20X7?

      ○ $293,500

      ○ $186,500

      ○ $313,000

      ○ $286,500

164   The operations director has questioned why the lease payments cannot be simply charged to profit or loss.

      In which TWO of the following situations would charging lease payments to profit or loss be the correct accounting treatment, assuming Fino Co takes advantage of any optional recognition exemptions available under IFRS 16 *Leases*? Select your answers from the drag and drop options provided.

      Correct accounting treatment

	Ownership is transferred at the end of the lease term
	The lease is for less than 12 months
	The leased asset has a low underlying value
	The leased asset has been specially adapted for the use of the lessee

165   **Selecting your answer from the options provided, what is the carrying amount of the lease liability at 31 March 20X8?**

      [▼]

      Pull-down list:

      $190,850
      $173,500
      $200,000
      $90,850

166   On 1 October 20X7, Fino Co entered into a different lease agreement on another piece of equipment. The lease runs for ten months and payments of $1,000 per month are payable in arrears. As an incentive to enter into the lease, Fino received the first month rent free. Fino wishes to take advantage of the optional recognition exemptions under IFRS 16.

      What amount should be recognised as payments under short-term leases in the year ended 31 March 20X8?

      ○ $5,000

      ○ $6,000

      ○ $4,500

      ○ $5,400

                                                                        (10 marks)

Jeffers Co case (Mar/Jun 2019)

18 mins

The following scenario relates to questions 167–171.

Jeffers Co prepares financial statements for the year ended 31 December 20X8. The financial statements are expected to be authorised for issue on 15 March 20X9.

The following three events have occurred in January 20X9:

(1) **Health and safety fine**

A health and safety investigation of an incident which occurred in 20X8 was concluded in January 20X9, resulting in a $1.5m fine for Jeffers Co. A provision for $1m had been recognised in Jeffers Co's financial statements for the year ended 31 December 20X8.

(2) **Customer ceased trading**

Notice was received on 10 January 20X9 that a customer owing $1.2m at 31 December 20X8 had ceased trading. It is unlikely that the debt will be recovered in full.

(3) **Acquisition of a competitor**

The acquisition of a competitor was finalised on 10 January 20X9, being the date Jeffers Co obtained control over the competitor. Negotiations in respect of the acquisition commenced in May 20X8.

In addition to this, there is an outstanding court case at 31 December 20X8 relating to faulty goods supplied by Jeffers Co. Legal advice states that there is a small chance that they will have to pay out $6m, but the most likely outcome is believed to be a payout of $5m. Either way, Jeffers Co will have to pay legal fees of $0·2m. All payments are expected to be made on 31 December 20X9.

Jeffers Co has a cost of capital of 10% (discount factor 0.909).

Jeffers Co believes the fault lies with the supplier, and is pursuing a counter-claim. Legal advice states that it is possible, but not likely, that this action will succeed.

167 **Which, if any, of the following statements regarding IAS 10 *Events after the Reporting Period* is/are correct?**

(1) 'Events after the reporting period' are deemed to be all events from the date the financial statements are authorised for issue up until the date of the annual meeting with the shareholders

(2) Non-adjusting events do not need to be reflected in any part of an entity's financial statements or annual report

O 1 only

O 2 only

O Both 1 and 2

O Neither 1 nor 2

168 **Select whether each of the following events, which occurred in January 20X9, would be classified as adjusting or non-adjusting events in accordance with IAS 10, by selecting the relevant answer option.**

Health and safety fine	Adjusting event	Non-adjusting event
Customer ceased trading	Adjusting event	Non-adjusting event
Acquisition of a competitor	Adjusting event	Non-adjusting event

169　Selecting your answer from the pull-down list provided, what amount should be recorded as a provision in respect of the outstanding court case against Jeffers Co as at 31 December 20X8 (to the nearest hundred thousand)?

[　　　　　　▼]

Pull-down list:

$5.6m
$5.5m
$4.7m
$4.5m

170　**At 31 December 20X8, which of the following represents the correct accounting treatment of the counter-claim made by Jeffers Co against the supplier?**

○　Nothing is recognised or disclosed in the financial statements

○　Disclose as a contingent asset

○　Recognise a receivable from the supplier

○　Net the possible counter-claim proceeds from the supplier against the provision for legal claim

---

171　In February 20X9, a major fire broke out in Jeffers Co's property and warehouse. Jeffers Co has no insurance, and now the management of the company believes it is unable to continue trading.

How should this be reflected in Jeffers Co's financial statements for the year ended 31 December 20X8?

○　No adjustment should be made to the figures in the financial statements, however, this event must be disclosed in the notes

○　The financial statements can no longer be prepared on a going concern basis

○　No disclosure is required in the financial statements; however, this event must be reflected in the financial statements for the year ended 31 December 20X9

○　The financial statements should continue to be prepared using the going concern basis, with an impairment loss recognised against the non-current assets

---

(10 marks)

Julian Co case

Information relevant to questions 172–176

The carrying amount of Julian Co's property, plant and equipment at 31 December 20X3 was $310,000 and the tax written down value was $230,000.

The following data relates to the year ended 31 December 20X4:

(i)   At the end of the year the carrying amount of property, plant and equipment was $460,000 and the tax written down value was $270,000. During the year some items were revalued upwards by $90,000. No items had previously required revaluation. In the tax jurisdiction in which Julian Co operates revaluations of assets do not affect the tax base of an asset or taxable profit. Gains due to revaluations are taxable on sale.

(ii)   Julian Co began development of a new product during the year and capitalised $60,000 in accordance with IAS 38 *Intangible Assets*. The expenditure was deducted for tax purposes as it was incurred. None of the expenditure had been amortised by the year end.

The corporate income tax rate is 30%. The current tax charge was calculated for the year as $45,000.

172   **Julian Co's accountant is confused by the term 'tax base'. What is meant by 'tax base'?**

○   The amount of tax payable in a future period

○   The tax regime under which an entity is assessed for tax

○   The amount attributed to an asset or liability for tax purposes

○   The amount of tax deductible in a future period

173   **Using the drag and drop options below, show the taxable temporary difference to be accounted for at 31 December 20X4 in relation to property, plant and equipment and development expenditure.**

Property, plant and equipment	Development expenditure
Nil	
$60,000	
$190,000	
$270,000	

174   **What is the carrying amount of the revaluation surplus at 31 December 20X4?**

○ $63,000

○ $90,000

○ $30,000

○ $27,000

175   Selecting your answer from the options below, what amount will be shown as tax payable in the statement of financial position of Julian Co at 31 December 20X4?

[▼]

Pull-down list:

$45,000
$72,000
$63,000
$75,000

176   Deferred tax assets and liabilities arise from taxable and deductible temporary differences.

Which of the following is NOT a circumstance giving rise to a temporary difference?

○   Depreciation accelerated for tax purposes

○   Development costs amortised in profit or loss but tax was deductible in full when incurred

○   Accrued expenses which have already been deducted for tax purposes

○   Revenue included in accounting profit when invoiced but only liable for tax when the cash is received

(10 marks)

Section A

Reporting financial performance

177   Which of the following would be treated as a change of accounting policy under IAS 8 *Accounting Policies, Changes in Accounting Estimates and Errors*?

    ○   A change in valuation of inventory from a weighted average to a FIFO basis

    ○   A change of depreciation method from straight line to reducing balance

    ○   Adoption of the revaluation model for non-current assets previously held at cost

    ○   Capitalisation of borrowing costs which have arisen for the first time   **(2 marks)**

178   For an asset to be classified as 'held for sale' under IFRS 5 *Non-current Assets Held for Sale and Discontinued Operations* its sale must be 'highly probable'. Which of the following is **NOT** a requirement if the sale is to be regarded as highly probable?

    ○   Management must be committed to a plan to sell the asset

    ○   A buyer must have been located for the asset

    ○   The asset must be marketed at a reasonable price

    ○   The sale should be expected to take place within one year from the date of classification   **(2 marks)**

179 **Complete the statement using the options provided.**

An asset classified as 'held for sale' should be measured at the lower of

▮▮▮▮▮▮▮▮	and	▮▮▮▮▮▮▮▮

Carrying amount less costs of disposal

Fair value less costs of disposal

Carrying amount

Value in use

(2 marks)

---

180 **Which of the following would be a change in accounting policy in accordance with IAS 8** *Accounting Policies, Changes in Accounting Estimates and Errors*?

○   Adjusting the financial statements of a subsidiary prior to consolidation as its accounting policies differ from those of its parent

○   A change in reporting depreciation charges as cost of sales rather than as administrative expenses

○   Depreciation charged on reducing balance method rather than straight line

○   Reducing the value of inventory from cost to net realisable value due to a valid adjusting event after the reporting period   (2 marks)

---

181 **Which of the following items is a change of accounting policy under IAS 8** *Accounting Policies, Changes in Accounting Estimates and Errors*?

○   Classifying commission earned as revenue in the statement of profit or loss, having previously classified it as other operating income

○   Switching to purchasing plant using leases from a previous policy of purchasing plant for cash

○   Changing the value of a subsidiary's inventory in line with the group policy for inventory valuation when preparing the consolidated financial statements

○   Revising the remaining useful life of a depreciable asset   (2 marks)

---

182   As at 30 September 20X3 Dune Co's property in its statement of financial position was:

Property at cost (useful life 15 years) $45 million
Accumulated depreciation $6 million

On 1 April 20X4, Dune Co decided to sell the property. The property is being marketed by a property agent at a price of $42 million, which was considered a reasonably achievable price at that date. The expected costs to sell have been agreed at $1 million. Recent market transactions suggest that actual selling prices achieved for this type of property in the current market conditions are 10% less than the price at which they are marketed.

At 30 September 20X4 the property has not been sold.

At what amount should the property be reported in Dune Co's statement of financial position as at 30 September 20X4?

- ○ $36 million
- ○ $37.5 million
- ○ $36.8 million
- ○ $42 million

(2 marks)

---

183   Steeplechase Co sold a machine to a Greek company which it agreed to invoice in €. The sale was made on 1 October 20X6 for €250,000. €125,000 was received on 1 November 20X6 and the balance is due on 1 January 20X7.

The exchange rate moved as follows:

1 October 20X6 – €0.91 to $1
1 November 20X6 – €0.95 to $1
31 December 20X6 – €0.85 to $1

At what amount will the receivable be shown in the financial statements at 31 December 20X6? (Enter your answer to the nearest whole $.)

$ [   ]

(2 marks)

---

184   IAS 21 *The Effects of Changes in Foreign Exchange Rates* sets out how entities that carry out transactions in a foreign currency should measure the results of these transactions at the year end.

Using the pull-down list options provided, select which exchange rate should non-monetary items carried at historical cost be measured?

[▼]

Pull-down list:

Closing rate
Average rate
Rate at date of transaction
Rate at beginning of the year

(2 marks)

---

185   Miston Co buys goods priced at €50,000 from a Dutch company on 1 November 20X8. The invoice is due for settlement in two equal instalments on 1 December 20X8 and 1 January 20X9.

The exchange rate moved as follows:

1 November 20X8 – €1.63 to $1
1 December 20X8 – €1.61 to $1
31 December 20X8 – €1.64 to $1

What will be the net exchange gain or loss to be reported in the financial statements of Miston Co at 31 December 20X8? (Enter your answer to the nearest whole $.)

$ [   ] gain/(loss)

(2 marks)

---

186   Coppola Co has a factory with a carrying amount of $1.8 million as at 30 November 20X6. Management have agreed the sale of the factory to Francis Co, which is due to complete on 14 January 20X7. The sales contract was agreed and the decision to sell the factory announced on 1 December 20X6. Relevant information relating to the factory, which is correct both at 1 December 20X6 and 31 December 20X6 is as follows:

Fair value $2.4 million
Value in use $2.2 million
Costs to sell $0.3 million

Depreciation for the factory in December 20X6 is calculated to be $0.2 million.

What is the carrying amount of the factory for inclusion in the financial statements of Coppola Co as at 31 December 20X6?

- O $1.6 million
- O $1.8 million
- O $1.9 million
- O $2.1 million   (2 marks)

---

187 **According to IAS 8 *Accounting Policies, Changes in Accounting Estimates and Errors*, which is the correct accounting treatment to be adopted by a company reporting under IFRS Standards?**

- O Changes in accounting estimates and errors should both be accounted for retrospectively
- O Changes in accounting estimates and errors should both be accounted for prospectively
- O Changes in accounting estimates should be accounted for retrospectively and errors accounted for prospectively
- O Changes in accounting estimates should be accounted for prospectively and errors accounted for retrospectively   (2 marks)

---

188 During 20X7, Greetex Co discovered that $2.1 million of inventory recognised in the financial statements at 31 December 20X6 had in fact been sold before the year end. The following extracts from the financial statements for 20X6 (as reported) and 20X7 (draft) are available.

	20X6	20X7 (draft)
	$'000	$'000
Revenue	80,000	75,000
Cost of sales	(64,600)	(62,000)
Gross profit	15,400	13,000

The cost of sales for 20X7 includes the $2.1 million error in opening inventory.

What would be the revised cost of sales figures for Greetex Co as at 31 December 20X6 and 20X7?

Using the options below, click and drag the correct response for the cost of sales figures to be included in the financial statements as at 31 December 20X7.

	31 Dec 20X6 $	31 Dec 20X7 $
Cost of sales		

31 Dec 20X6	31 Dec 20X7
62,500	59,900
64,600	62,000
66,700	64,100

(2 marks)

Earnings per share

189   Barwell Co had 10 million ordinary shares in issue throughout the year ended 30 June 20X3. On 1 July 20X2, it had issued $2 million of 6% convertible loan stock, each $5 of loan stock convertible into 4 ordinary shares on 1 July 20X6 at the option of the holder.

Barwell Co had profit for the year ended 30 June 20X3 of $1,850,000. It pays tax on profits at 30%.

What was diluted earnings per share for the year?

- ○ $0.167
- ○ $0.185
- ○ $0.161
- ○ $0.17   **(2 marks)**

---

190   At 30 September 20X2 the trial balance of Cavern Co includes the following balances:

	$'000
Equity shares of 20c each	50,000
Share premium	15,000

Cavern Co has accounted for a fully subscribed rights issue of equity shares made on 1 April 20X2 of one new share for every four in issue at 42 cents each. This was the only share issue made during the year.

Using the drag and drop options below, show the balances on the share capital and share premium accounts at 30 September 20X1.

Share capital $'000   Share premium $'000

- 4,000
- 11,250
- 37,500
- 40,000

                                                   (2 marks)

---

191   Aqua Co has correctly calculated its basic earnings per share (EPS) for the current year.

Which TWO of the following items need to be additionally considered when calculating the diluted EPS of Aqua Co for the year?

- ☐   A 1 for 5 rights issue of equity shares during the year at $1.20 when the market price of the equity shares was $2.00
- ☐   The issue during the year of a convertible (to equity shares) loan note
- ☐   The granting during the year of directors' share options exercisable in three years' time
- ☐   Equity shares issued during the year as the purchase consideration for the acquisition of a new subsidiary company   **(2 marks)**

---

192   Many commentators believe that the trend of earnings per share (EPS) is a more reliable indicator of underlying performance than the trend of net profit for the year.

Which of the following statements supports this view?

○   Net profit can be manipulated by the choice of accounting policies but EPS cannot be manipulated in this way

○   EPS takes into account the additional resources made available to earn profit when new shares are issued for cash, whereas net profit does not

○   The disclosure of a diluted EPS figure is a forecast of the future trend of profit

○   The comparative EPS is restated where a change of accounting policy affects the previous year's profits   **(2 marks)**

---

193   At 1 January 20X8 Artichoke Co had 5 million $1 equity shares in issue. On 1 June 20X8, it made a 1 for 5 rights issue at a price of $1.50. The market price of the shares on the last day of quotation with rights was $1.80.

Total earnings for the year ended 31 December 20X8 was $7.6 million.

What was the earnings per share for the year?

○ $1.35

○ $1.36

○ $1.27

○ $1.06   **(2 marks)**

---

194   The weighted average number of ordinary shares that Fogarty Co has in issue for the year to 31 December 20X7 is 5,000,000.

On 1 January, Fogarty Co issued 500,000 share options to purchase one $1 ordinary share at $2.80 per share. These options are exercisable between 1 January 20X9 and 31 December 20Y0. The average market value of each $1 ordinary share of Fogarty Co during the year ended 31 December 20X7 is $3.50.

What is the weighted average number of shares to be used in the calculation of diluted earnings per share for the year ended 31 December 20X7?

○   4.9 million

○   5.1 million

○   5.4 million

○   5.5 million   **(2 marks)**

---

195   Plumstead Co had 4 million equity shares in issue throughout the year ended 31 March 20X7. On 30 September 20X7 it made a 1 for 4 bonus issue. Profit for the year ended 31 March 20X8 was $3.6 million, out of which an equity dividend of 20c per share was paid. The financial statements for the year ended 31 March 20X7 showed earnings per share (EPS) of $0.70.

What is the EPS for the year ended 31 March 20X8 and the restated EPS for the year ended 31 March 20X7? (Enter your answer to two decimal places.)

20X8 $ [   ]

20X7 $ [   ]   **(2 marks)**

---

196   Bollingbrook Co has earnings of $313,000 and 100,000 ordinary $1 shares in issue during 20X5. The company also has in issue $100,000 10% convertible loan stock which is convertible in one years' time at a rate of 3 ordinary shares for every $10 of stock. The tax rate is 30%.

What is the diluted earnings per share?

- ○ $2.41
- ○ $2.46
- ○ $2.48
- ○ $3.13   **(2 marks)**

Section B

Tunshill Co (Dec 2010 amended) case

18 mins

Information relevant to questions 197–201

The directors of Tunshill Co are disappointed by the draft profit for the year ended 30 September 20X3. The company's assistant accountant has suggested two areas where she believes the reported profit may be improved:

(i) A major item of plant that cost $20 million to purchase and install on 1 October 20X0 is being depreciated on a straight-line basis over a five-year period (assuming no residual value). The plant is wearing well and at the beginning of the current year (1 October 20X2) the production manager believed that the plant was likely to last eight years in total (ie from the date of its purchase). The assistant accountant has calculated that, based on an eight-year life (and no residual value) the accumulated depreciation of the plant at 30 September 20X3 would be $7.5 million ($20 million / 8 years × 3). In the financial statements for the year ended 30 September 20X2, the accumulated depreciation was $8 million ($20 million / 5 years × 2). Therefore, by adopting an eight-year life, Tunshill Co can avoid a depreciation charge in the current year and instead credit $0.5 million ($8 million – $7.5 million) to profit or loss in the current year to improve the reported profit.

(ii) Most of Tunshill Co's competitors value their inventory using the average cost (AVCO) basis, whereas Tunshill Co uses the first in first out (FIFO) basis. The value of Tunshill Co's inventory at 30 September 20X3 on the FIFO basis, is $20 million, however on the AVCO basis it would be valued at $18 million. By adopting the same method (AVCO) as its competitors, the assistant accountant says the company would improve its profit for the year ended 30 September 20X3 by $2 million. Tunshill Co's inventory at 30 September 20X2 was reported as $15 million, however on the AVCO basis it would have been reported as $13.4 million.

197 **What is the nature of the change being proposed by the assistant accountant in (i) and how should it be applied?**

   ○   Change of accounting policy: Retrospective application

   ○   Change of accounting policy: Prospective application

   ○   Change of accounting estimate: Retrospective application

   ○   Change of accounting estimate: Prospective application

198 **Adjusting for the change of useful life, what will be the carrying amount of the plant at 30 September 20X3? (Enter your answer to the nearest whole $.)**

$ [＿＿＿＿＿＿＿]

199 **Which of the following would be treated as a change of accounting policy?**

   ○   Tunshill Co has received its first government grant and is applying the deferred income method

   ○   Tunshill Co has changed the rate of depreciation used for its office equipment from 25% to 20% straight line basis

   ○   Tunshill Co has reclassified development costs from other operating expenses to cost of sales

   ○   Tunshill Co has increased its irrecoverable debt allowance from 10% to 12%

200 **What will be the effect of the change in (ii) on profits for the year ended 30 September 20X3?**

- O Increased by $400,000
- O Reduced by $400,000
- O Increased by $1,600,000
- O Reduced by $1,600,000

---

201 **Using the drag and drop options below, select the correct account to show the accounting entry for the change in inventory value for the year ended 30 September 20X3?**

		Account
Debit		Cost of sales
Credit		Inventory
		Revenue

(10 marks)

Hemlock Co case **18 mins**

The directors of Hemlock Co are preparing the financial statements for the year ended 30 September 20X3. Hemlock Co is a publicly listed company.

(i) Most of Hemlock Co's competitors value their inventory using the average cost (AVCO) basis, whereas Hemlock Co uses the first in first out (FIFO) basis. The value of Hemlock Co's inventory at 30 September 20X3 on the FIFO basis, is $40 million, however on the AVCO basis it would be valued at $36 million. By adopting the same method (AVCO) as its competitors, the assistant accountant says the company would improve its profit for the year ended 30 September 20X3 by $4 million. Hemlock Co's inventory at 30 September 20X2 was reported as $30 million, however on the AVCO basis it would have been reported as $26.8 million.

(ii) Hemlock Co sold a machine to Poisson SA, a French company which it agreed to invoice in €. The sale was made on 1 October 20X6 for €250,000. €155,000 was received on 1 November 20X6 and the balance is due on 1 January 20X7.

The exchange rate moved as follows:

1 October 20X6 – €0.85 to $1

1 November 20X6 – €0.84 to $1

31 December 20X6 – €0.79 to $1

(iii) After correctly accounting for the information in (i) and (ii), Hemlock Co has earnings of $9,160,000. It had 2,000,000 ordinary $1 shares in issue during the year to 30 September 20X3. Hemlock Co has an additional 1,000,000 shares under option at the year end. The fair value of the shares at that date is $12.00 per share and the exercise price for the options is $10.00 each.

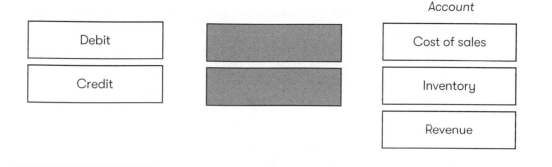

202 At what amount will the receivable of €155,000 be shown in the financial statements at 31 December 20X6?

- ○ $130,200
- ○ $196,203
- ○ $183,253
- ○ $184,524

---

203 Which of the following would be treated as a change of accounting policy?

- ○ Hemlock Co is adopting the revaluation policy for the first time for its tangible non-current assets
- ○ Hemlock Co has changed the rate of depreciation used for its office equipment from 30% to 20% straight-line basis
- ○ Hemlock Co has reclassified head office administration costs from cost of sales to other operating expenses
- ○ Hemlock Co has increased its allowance for irrecoverable debts from 10% to 12%

---

204 What would be the effect on profits for the year ended 30 September 20X3 if Hemlock Co were to adopt the AVCO method of inventory valuation?

- ○ Increased by $800,000
- ○ Reduced by $800,000
- ○ Increased by $3,200,000
- ○ Reduced by $3,200,000

---

205 The auditors of Hemlock Co have discovered a fundamental error in the prior year financial statements. The directors of Hemlock Co have agreed to correct the prior period error.

Which of the following are the disclosures which the directors should present in the financial statements?

(1)   The nature of the error

(2)   The amount of the correction for each item of the financial statements affected by the error and correction

- ○ Statement (1) only
- ○ Statement (2) only
- ○ Neither statement (1) or (2)
- ○ Both statements (1) and (2)

---

206 Calculate the diluted earnings per shares for Hemlock Co for the year ended 30 September 20X3. (Enter your answer to two decimal places.)

$ [   ]

(10 marks)

PART C: ANALYSING AND INTERPRETING THE FINANCIAL STATEMENTS OF SINGLE ENTITIES AND GROUPS

Analysing and interpreting financial statements is about more than simply calculating ratios. It is more important that you understand what the ratio tells you about the company or group and how different transactions and accounting policies can impact ratios.

One of the Section C questions will require the interpretation of the financial statements of single entities or groups. These questions will require the calculation of ratios and analysis of the performance and/or position of a company or group based on the ratios calculated and the information provided. It is essential that your discussion is relevant to the question as generic points are unlikely to score credit.

Section A questions

Questions 207–212: Interpretation of financial statements (Chapter 20)
Questions 213-220: Limitations of financial statements and interpretation techniques (Chapter 21)
Questions 221–228: Specialised, not-for-profit and public sector entities (Chapter 23)

Section B questions on these topics are in Questions 229–233

Section C questions are the longer, written questions worth 20 marks. Where the Examining Team's feedback is available (the question coming from a former exam), this feedback is given, together with top tips and easy marks.

Question 234 Woodbank Co
Question 235 Hassle Co
Question 236 Funject Co
Question 237 Pastry Co
Question 238 Quartile Co
Question 239 Mowair Co
Question 240 Perkins Co
Question 241 Pirlo Co
Question 242 Karl Co
Question 243 Kostner Co

Section A

Interpretation of accounting ratios and trends

207   Charlton Co has an average operating profit margin of 23% of which depreciation of plant and machinery accounts for 33% of the operating costs, as well as including 78% of the salaries cost within cost of sales. It has an average asset turnover of 0.8, which is similar to the averages for the industry.

The entity is most likely to be:

O   An architectural practice

O   A supermarket

O   An estate agent

O   A manufacturer   (2 marks)

 BPP LEARNING MEDIA

Questions   **71**

208 Using the pull-down list provided, select the correct option to complete the following statement.

Reducing the [▼] will increase the length of a company's operating cycle?

Pull-down list:

receivables collection period
inventory holding period
payables payment period
time taken to produce goods

(2 marks)

209 In the year to 31 December 20X9 Weston Co pays an interim equity dividend of 3.4c per share and declares a final equity dividend of 11.1c. It has 5 million $1 shares in issue and the ex div share price is $3.50.

What is the dividend yield?

O   4%

O   24%

O   3.2%

O   4.1%   (2 marks)

210 Analysis of the financial statements of Capricorn Co at 31 December 20X8 yields the following information:

Gross profit margin	30%
Current ratio	2.14
Return on capital employed (ROCE)	16.3%
Asset turnover	4.19
Inventory turnover	13.9

What is the net profit margin?

O   3.9%

O   7.6%

O   16.1%

O   7.1%   (2 marks)

211 Camargue Co is a listed company with four million 50c ordinary shares in issue. The following extract is from its financial statements for the year ended 30 September 20X4.

STATEMENT OF PROFIT OR LOSS

	$'000
Profit before tax	900
Income tax expense	(100)
Profit for the year	800

At 30 September 20X4 the market price of Camargue Co's shares was $1.50. What was the P/E ratio on that date?

[ ]

(2 marks)

212   Extracts from the financial statements of Perseus Co are as follows:

STATEMENT OF PROFIT OR LOSS		STATEMENT OF FINANCIAL POSITION	
	$'000		$'000
Operating profit	230	Ordinary shares	2,000
Finance costs	(15)	Revaluation surplus	300
Profit before tax	215	Retained earnings	1,200
Income tax	(15)		3,500
Profit for the year	200	10% loan notes	1,000
		Current liabilities	100
		Total equity and liabilities	4,600

What is the return on capital employed (ROCE)?

[   ]

(2 marks)

Limitations of financial statements and interpretation techniques

213   Cyan Co carries its property at revalued amount. Property values have fallen during the current period and an impairment loss has been recognised on the property, however its carrying amount is still higher than its depreciated historical cost.

Complete the statement using the pull-down list below, showing the effect of the impairment on the return on capital employed (ROCE) and gearing ratios of Cyan Co.

The effect of this impairment will [▼] the ROCE of Cyan Co, and

[▼] its gearing ratio.

Pull-down list:

Decrease
Increase

(2 marks)

214   **Magenta Ltd has a current ratio of 1.5, a quick ratio of 0.4 and a positive cash balance. If it purchases inventory on credit, what is the effect on these ratios?**

	Current ratio	Quick ratio
○	Decrease	Decrease
○	Decrease	Increase
○	Increase	Decrease
○	Increase	Increase

(2 marks)

215   Fritwel Co has an asset turnover of 2.0 and an operating profit margin of 10%. It is launching a new product which is expected to generate additional sales of $1.6 million and additional profit of $120,000. It will require additional assets of $500,000.

Assuming there are no other changes to current operations, how will the new product affect these ratios?

Select the impact on the ratios below using the drag and drop options

Operating profit margin

[   ]

ROCE

[   ]

| Decrease |
| Increase |
| No change |

(2 marks)

---

216   **Which of the following is a possible reason why a company's inventory holding period increases from one year to the next?**

○   An increase in demand for its products

○   A reduction in selling prices

○   Obsolete inventory lines

○   Seasonal fluctuations in orders   (2 marks)

---

217   Use of historical cost accounting means asset values can be reliably verified but it has a number of shortcomings which need to be considered when analysing financial statements.

Which of these is a possible result of the use of historical cost accounting during a period of inflation?

○   Overstatement of non-current asset values

○   Overstatement of profits

○   Understatement of interest costs

○   Understatement of return on capital employed (ROCE)   (2 marks)

---

218   Creative accounting measures are often aimed at reducing gearing.

Identify whether the following measures will increase, reduce or have no effect on gearing.

Renegotiating a loan to secure a lower interest rate	Increase	Reduce	No effect
Applying the options recognition exemption to a lease contract under IFRS 16 *Leases*	Increase	Reduce	No effect
Repaying a loan just before the year end and taking it out again at the beginning of the next year	Increase	Reduce	No effect
'Selling' an asset under a sale and leaseback agreement	Increase	Reduce	No effect

(2 marks)

---

219 **If a company wished to maintain the carrying amount in the financial statements of its non-current assets, which of the following would it be unlikely to do?**

    ○   Enter into a sale and short-term leaseback, the terms of which meet the requirements to use the optional recognition exemption under IFRS 16 *Leases*.

    ○   Account for asset-based government grants using the deferral method

    ○   Revalue its properties

    ○   Change the depreciation method for new asset acquisitions from 25% reducing balance to ten years straight line   **(2 marks)**

---

220 Trent uses the formula: (trade receivables at year end/revenue for the year) × 365 to calculate how long on average (in days) its customers take to pay.

Which of the following would NOT affect the correctness of the above calculation of the average number of days a customer takes to pay?

    ○   Trent experiences considerable seasonal trading

    ○   Trent makes a number of cash sales through retail outlets

    ○   Reported revenue does not include a 15% sales tax whereas the receivables do include the tax

    ○   Trent factors with recourse the receivable of its largest customer   **(2 marks)**

Specialised, not-for-profit and public sector entities

221 **Which of the following are unlikely to be stakeholders in a charity?**

    ○   Taxpayers

    ○   Financial supporters

    ○   Shareholders

    ○   Government   **(2 marks)**

---

222 The International Public Sector Accounting Standards Board regulates public sector entities and is developing a set of accounting standards which closely mirror IFRS Standards.

Which of these is the main concept which needs to be introduced into public sector accounting?

    ○   Materiality

    ○   Accruals

    ○   Relevance

    ○   Faithful representation   **(2 marks)**

223 Public sector entities have performance measures laid down by government, based on Key Performance Indicators (KPIs). Which **THREE** of the following are likely to be financial KPIs for a local council?

☐ Rent receipts outstanding

☐ Interest cover

☐ Dividend cover

☐ Financial actuals against budget

☐ Return on capital employed   (2 marks)

224 Which **TWO** of the ratios are **NOT** relevant for Yellow, a charity which operates from high street stores?

☐ Operating profit margin

☐ Inventory holding period

☐ Current ratio

☐ Earnings per share   (2 marks)

225 Which of the following is the main aspect in which public sector bodies differ from charities?

○ Importance of budgeting

○ Funded by government

○ Performance measured by key performance indicators

○ No requirement to earn a return on assets   (2 marks)

226 Although the objectives and purposes of not-for-profit entities are different from those of commercial entities, the accounting requirements of not-for-profit entities are moving closer to those entities to which IFRS standards apply.

Which of the following IFRS requirements would **NOT** be relevant to a not-for-profit entity?

○ Preparation of a statement of cash flows

○ Requirement to capitalise a leased asset

○ Disclosure of dividends per share

○ Disclosure of non-adjusting events after the reporting date   (2 marks)

227 Which **TWO** of the following statements about a not-for-profit entity are valid?

☐ There is no requirement to calculate an earnings per share figure as it is not likely to have shareholders who need to assess its earnings performance

☐ The revaluation of its property, plant and equipment is not relevant as it is not a commercial entity

☐ It prioritises non-financial KPIs over financial targets

☐ Its financial statements will not be closely scrutinised as it does not have any investors   (2 marks)

228 Cyan is a charity which operates high street charity shops. Its goods for sale comprise donations from the public and inventories purchased from suppliers on credit. It makes sales in its stores in cash only.

Which TWO of the following ratios are relevant for Cyan?

☐ Inventory holding period

☐ Return on capital employed

☐ Receivables collection period

☐ Payables payment period   (2 marks)

Section B

Sandbag plc case

18 mins

The following scenario relates to questions 229–233.

Sandbag plc is a listed manufacturing company. Its summarised statement of financial position is given below.

STATEMENT OF FINANCIAL POSITION AS AT 31 DECEMBER 20X4

	$m
Non-current assets	610
Inventories	96
Trade receivables	29
Current asset investments	5
Cash and cash equivalents	3
	133
	743
Equity and liabilities	
$1 ordinary shares	400
Retained earnings	190
	590
Non-current liabilities – loans	50
Trade and other payables	103
	743

229 **What is Sandbag plc's current ratio at 31 December 20X4?**

○ 0.37

○ 1.29

○ 0.87

○ 1.26

---

230 The finance director of Sandbag plc is worried about its current ratio. He is considering a number of actions that he hopes will improve Sandbag plc's current ratio.

Which of the following would increase Sandbag plc's current ratio?

○ Offer a settlement discount to customers

○ Make a bonus issue of ordinary shares

○ Make a rights issue of ordinary shares

○ Sell current asset investments at the carrying amount

---

231 **What is Sandbag plc's acid test (quick) ratio at 31 December 20X4? (Enter your answer to two decimal places)**

[   ]

---

232 The finance director of Sandbag plc knows that the acid test ratio is below 1. He is planning two changes:

Proposal 1: Offering a 2% early settlement discount to credit customers
Proposal 2: Delaying payment to all trade payables by one extra month

Using the options below, match the effect the proposals would have on the acid test ratio (tokens can used more than once).

Proposal 1	*Proposal 2*

Increase ratio
Decrease ratio

233 **Sandbag plc is a manufacturing company. Which of the following ratios would best assess the efficiency of Sandbag plc?**

○ Price/earnings ratio

○ Gearing ratio

○ Non-current asset turnover

○ Current ratio

(10 marks)

Section C

234 Woodbank Co (Jun 2014 amended)   36 mins

Shown below are the financial statements of Woodbank Co for its most recent two years:

STATEMENTS OF PROFIT OR LOSS FOR THE YEAR ENDED 31 MARCH:

	20X4 $'000	20X3 $'000
Revenue	150,000	110,000
Cost of sales	117,000	(85,800)
Gross profit	33,000	24,200
Distribution costs	(6,000)	(5,000)
Administrative expenses	(9,000)	(9,200)
Finance costs – loan note interest	(1,750)	(500)
Profit before tax	16,250	9,500
Income tax expense	(5,750)	(3,000)
Profit for the year	10,500	6,500

STATEMENTS OF FINANCIAL POSITION AS AT 31 MARCH

	20X4 $'000	20X3 $'000
ASSETS		
Non-current assets		
Property, plant and equipment	118,000	85,000
Goodwill	30,000	–
	148,000	85,000
Current assets		
Inventories	15,500	12,000
Trade receivables	11,000	8,000
Cash and cash equivalents	500	5,000
	27,000	25,000
Total assets	175,000	110,000
EQUITY AND LIABILITIES		
Equity		
Equity shares of $1 each	80,000	80,000
Retained earnings	15,000	10,000
	95,000	90,000
Non-current liabilities		
10% loan notes	55,000	5,000
Current liabilities		
Trade payables	21,000	13,000
Current tax payable	4,000	2,000
	25,000	15,000
Total equity and liabilities	175,000	110,000

The following information is available:

(i)   On 1 January 20X4, Woodbank Co acquired a controlling interest in Shaw Co for
        $50 million. It paid for the acquisition through the issue of additional 10% loan notes and by
        using some of its cash reserves. Shaw Co was an unincorporated entity and its results (for
        three months from 1 January 20X4 to 31 March 20X4) and net assets (including goodwill
        not subject to any impairment) are included in Woodbank Co's financial statements for the
        year ended 31 March 20X4. There were no other purchases or sales of non-current assets
        during the year ended 31 March 20X4.

(ii) Extracts of the results (for three months) of the previously separate business of Shaw Co, which are included in Woodbank Co's statement of profit or loss for the year ended 31 March 20X4, are:

	$'000
Revenue	30,000
Cost of sales	(21,000)
Gross profit	9,000
Distribution costs	(2,000)
Administrative expenses	(2,000)

Required

Using the preformatted table provided below:

(a) Calculate the equivalent ratios for Woodbank Co for the year ended 31 March 20X4.

(5 marks)

(b) Calculate , as far as the information permits, the equivalent ratios for Woodbank Co for the year ended 31 March 20X4 **excluding** the effects of the purchase of Shaw Co.

(3 marks)

(c) Assess the comparative financial performance and position of Woodbank Co for the year ended 31 March 20X4. Your answer should refer to the effects of the purchase of Shaw Co.

(12 marks)

(Total = 20 marks)

Pre-formatted response table

Ratio	Woodbank Co 20X3	Working	Woodbank Co 20X4	Working	Woodbank Co 20X4 excluding Shaw
Return on capital employed	10.5%				
Gross profit margin	22%				
Profit before interest and tax margin	9.1%				
Current ratio	1.7:1				
Gearing (debt/(debt + equity))	5.3%				

235 Hassle Co

Hassle Co is a large public company that would like to acquire (100% of) a suitable private company. It has obtained the following draft financial statements for two companies, Astral Co and Breakout Co. They operate in the same industry, which is clothing manufacturing within the fashion sector. Both companies compete in the younger, high turnover, discount fashion markets.

STATEMENTS OF PROFIT OR LOSS FOR THE YEAR ENDED 30 SEPTEMBER 20X8

	Astral Co $'000	Breakout Co $'000
Revenue	12,000	20,500
Cost of sales	(10,500)	(18,000)
Gross profit	1,500	2,500
Operating expenses	(240)	(500)
Finance costs – loan	(210)	(300)
– overdraft	–	(10)
– lease	–	(290)
Profit before tax	1,050	1,400
Income tax expense	(150)	(400)
Profit for the year	900	1,000
Note. Dividends were paid during the year	250	700

STATEMENTS OF FINANCIAL POSITION AS AT 30 SEPTEMBER 20X8

	Astral Co $'000	Breakout Co $'000
Assets		
Non-current assets		
Freehold factory (Note 1)	4,400	–
Owned plant (Note 2)	5,000	2,200
Leased plant (Note 2)	–	5,300
	9,400	7,500
Current assets		
Inventory	2,000	3,600
Trade receivables	2,400	3,700
Bank	600	–
	5,000	7,300
Total assets	14,400	14,800
Equity and liabilities		
Equity shares of $1 each	2,000	2,000
Revaluation surplus	900	–
Retained earnings	2,600	800
	3,500	800
	5,500	2,800
Non-current liabilities		
Lease liabilities (Note 3)	–	3,200
7% loan notes	3,000	–
10% loan notes	–	3,000
Deferred tax	600	100
Government grants	1,200	–
	4,800	6,300

	Astral Co $'000	Breakout Co $'000
Current liabilities		
Bank overdraft	–	1,200
Trade payables	3,100	3,800
Government grants	400	–
Lease liabilities (Note 3)	–	500
Taxation	600	200
	4,100	5,700
Total equity and liabilities	14,400	14,800

Notes

1   Both companies operate from similar premises.

2   Additional details of the two companies' plant are:

	Astral Co $'000	Breakout Co $'000
Owned plant – cost	8,000	10,000
Right-of-use asset – Leased plant – original fair value	–	7,500

There were no disposals of plant during the year by either company.

3   The interest rate implicit within Breakout Co's leases is 7.5% per annum. For the purpose of calculating ROCE and gearing, all lease liabilities are treated as long-term interest bearing borrowings.

4   The following ratios have been calculated for Astral Co and can be taken to be correct:

Return on year end capital employed (ROCE)	14.8%
(capital employed taken as shareholders' funds plus long-term interest- bearing borrowings – see Note 3 above)	
Pre-tax return on equity (ROE)	19.1%
Net asset (total assets less current liabilities) turnover	1.2 times
Gross profit margin	12.5%
Operating profit margin	10.5%
Current ratio	1.2:1
Closing inventory holding period	70 days
Trade receivables' collection period	73 days
Trade payables' payment period (using cost of sales)	108 days
Gearing (see Note 3 above)	35.3%
Interest cover	6 times
Dividend cover	3.6 times

Required

(a)   Calculate for Breakout Co the ratios equivalent to all those given for Astral Co above.

                                                          (8 marks)

(b)   Assess the relative performance and financial position of Astral Co and Breakout Co for the year ended 30 September 20X8 to inform the directors of Hassle Co in their acquisition decision.   **(12 marks)**

                                                          (Total = 20 marks)

236 Funject Co (Mar/Jun 2017)   36 mins

Funject Co has identified Aspect Co as a possible acquisition within the same industry. Aspect Co is currently owned by the Gamilton Group and the following are extracts from the financial statements of Aspect Co:

EXTRACT FROM THE STATEMENT OF PROFIT OR LOSS FOR THE YEAR ENDED 31 DECEMBER 20X4

	$'000
Revenue	54,200
Cost of sales	21,500
Gross profit	32,700
Operating expenses	11,700
Operating profit	21,000

STATEMENT OF FINANCIAL POSITION AS AT 31 DECEMBER 20X4

	$'000	$'000
Assets		
Non-current assets		24,400
Current assets		
Inventories	4,900	
Receivables	5,700	
Cash and cash equivalents	2,300	12,900
Total assets		37,300
Equity and liabilities		
Equity		
Equity shares		1,000
Retained earnings		8,000
		9,000
Liabilities		
Non-current liabilities		
Loan		16,700
Current liabilities		
Trade payables	5,400	
Current tax payable	6,200	11,600
Total equity and liabilities		37,300

Additional information:

(i) On 1 April 20X4, Aspect Co decided to focus on its core business and so disposed of a non-core division. The disposal generated a loss of $1.5m which is included within operating expenses. The following extracts show the results of the non-core division for the period prior to disposal which were included in Aspect Co's results for 20X4:

	$'000
Revenue	2,100
Cost of sales	(1,200)
Gross profit	900
Operating expenses	(700)
Operating profit	200

(ii) At present Aspect Co pays a management charge of 1% of revenue to the Gamilton Group which is included in operating expenses. Funject Co imposes a management charge of 10% of gross profit on all of its subsidiaries.

(iii) Aspect Co's administration offices are currently located within a building owned by the Gamilton Group. If Aspect Co were acquired, the company would need to seek alternative premises. Aspect Co paid rent of $46,000 in 20X4. Commercial rents for equivalent office space would cost $120,000.

Required

(a) Redraft Aspect Co's statement of profit or loss for 20X4 to adjust for the disposal of the non-core division in note (i) and the management and rent charges which would be imposed per notes (ii) and (iii) if Aspect Co was acquired by Funject Co. **(4 marks)**

(b) Using the preformatted table provided below, calculate the equivalent 20X4 ratios for Aspect Co based on the restated financial information calculated in part (a).

Note: You should assume that any increase or decrease in profit as a result of your adjustments in part (a) will also increase or decrease cash. **(6 marks)**

Pre-formatted table

	Industry KPIs 20X4	Working	Aspect Co 20X4
Gross profit margin	45%		
Operating profit margin	28%		
Receivables collection period	41 days		
Current ratio	1.6:1		
Acid test (quick) ratio	1.4:1		
Gearing (debt/equity)	240%		

(c) Using the ratios calculated in part (b), comment on Aspect Co's 20X4 performance and financial position compared to the industry average KPIs provided in the pre-formatted table. **(10 marks)**

(Total = 20 marks)

237 Pastry Co (ACCA March/June 2021)   36 mins

Pastry Co is considering the acquisition of a subsidiary in the catering industry. Two companies have been identified as potential acquisitions and extracts from the financial statements of Cook Co and Dough Co have been reproduced below:

STATEMENTS OF PROFIT OR LOSS FOR THE YEAR ENDED 30 SEPTEMBER 20X7:

	Cook Co $'000	Dough Co $'000
Revenue	21,500	16,300
Cost of sales	(14,545)	(8,350)
Gross profit	6,955	7,950
Operating expenses	(1,940)	(4,725)
Finance costs	(650)	(200)
Profit before tax	4,365	3,025
Income tax	(1,320)	(780)
Profit for the year	3,045	2,245

EXTRACTS FROM THE STATEMENTS OF FINANCIAL POSITION AS AT 30 SEPTEMBER 20X7:

	Cook Co $'000	Dough Co $'000
Non-current assets		
Property	22,250	68,500
Equity		
Equity shares of $1 each	1,000	1,000
Revaluation surplus	–	30,000
Retained earnings	18,310	2,600
Non-current liabilities		
Loan notes	7,300	5,200

Notes

1   Both companies are owner-managed. Dough Co operates from expensive city centre premises, selling to local businesses and the public. Cook Co is a large wholesaler, selling to chains of coffee shops. Cook Co operates from a number of low-cost production facilities.

2   On 1 October 20X6, Dough Co revalued its properties for the first time, resulting in a gain of $30 million. The properties had a remaining useful life of 30 years at 1 October 20X6. Dough Co does not make a transfer from the revaluation surplus in respect of excess depreciation. Cook Co uses the cost model to account for its properties. Dough Co and Cook Co charge all depreciation expenses to operating expenses.

3   Cook Co charges the amortisation of its research and development to cost of sales, whereas Dough Co charges the same costs to operating expenses. These costs amounted to $1.2 million for Cook Co and $2.5 million for Dough Co.

4   The notes to the financial statements show that Cook Co paid its directors total salaries of $110,000 whereas Dough Co paid its directors total salaries of $560,000.

5   The following ratios have been correctly calculated in respect of Cook Co and Dough Co for the year ended 30 September 20X7:

	Cook Co	Dough Co
Gross profit margin	32.3%	48.8%
Operating profit margin	23.3%	19.8%
Return on capital employed	18.8%	8.3%

Required

(a)   Adjust the relevant extracts fron Dough Co's financial statements to apply the same accounting policies as Cook Co and re-calculate Dough Co's ratios provided in note (5).

(6 marks)

(b)   Based on these adjusted accounting ratios, compare the performance of the two companies. Your answer should comment on the difficulties of making a purchase decision based solely on the extracts of the financial statements and the information provided in notes (1) to (5).

(14 marks)

(Total = 20 marks)

238 Quartile Co (Dec 2012 amended)   36 mins

Quartile Co sells jewellery through stores in retail shopping centres throughout the country. Over the last two years it has experienced declining profitability and is wondering if this is related to the sector as a whole. It has recently subscribed to an agency that produces average ratios across many businesses. Below are the ratios that have been provided by the agency for Quartile Co's business sector based on a year end of 30 June 20X2.

The financial statements of Quartile Co for the year ended 30 September 20X2 are:

STATEMENT OF PROFIT OR LOSS

	$'000	$'000
Revenue		56,000
Opening inventory	8,300	
Purchases	43,900	
Closing inventory	(10,200)	
Cost of sales		(42,000)
Gross profit		14,000
Operating costs		(9,800)
Finance costs		(800)
Profit before tax		3,400
Income tax expense		(1,000)
Profit for the year		2,400

STATEMENT OF FINANCIAL POSITION

	$'000
ASSETS	
Non-current assets	
Property and shop fittings	25,600
Development expenditure	5,000
	30,600
Current assets	
Inventories	10,200
Cash and cash equivalents	1,000
	11,200
Total assets	41,800
EQUITY AND LIABILITIES	
Equity	
Equity shares of $1 each	15,000
Revaluation surplus	3,000
Retained earnings	8,600
	26,600
Non-current liabilities	
10% loan notes	8,000
Current liabilities	
Trade payables	5,400
Current tax payable	1,800
	7,200
Total equity and liabilities	41,800

Notes

1 The directors of Quartile Co regularly hold 'all stock must go' sales to increase sales and make space to bring new inventory into the stores. These sales are very popular with customers and generate strong sales.

2 Quartile revalued its retail stores for the first time on 30 September 20X2 which resulted in the revaluation surplus shown.

3 The 10% loan notes were issued in 20X1 and are due to be repaid in 20X4. A dividend of $1.5 million was paid in the current year.

4 The development expenditure relates to an investment in a process to manufacture artificial precious gems for future sale by Quartile Co in the retail jewellery market.

 BPP LEARNING MEDIA

Questions 87

Required

(a) Using the preformatted table below, calculate the equivalent ratios for Quartile Co for 20X2. (8 marks)

Pre-formatted table

	Sector average	Working	Quartile Co
Return on year-end capital employed (ROCE)	16.8%		
Net asset turnover	1.4 times		
Gross profit margin	35%		
Operating profit margin	12%		
Current ratio	1.25:1		
Average inventory turnover	3 times		
Trade payables' payment period	64 days		
Gearing	38%		

(b) Assess the financial and operating performance of Quartile Co in comparison to its sector averages. (12 marks)

(Total = 20 marks)

239 Mowair Co (Sept/Dec 17)   36 mins

Mowair Co is an international airline which flies to destinations all over the world. Mowair Co experienced strong initial growth but in recent periods the company has been criticised for under-investing in its non-current assets.

Extracts from Mowair Co's financial statements are provided below.

Statements of financial position as at 30 June:

	20X7 $'000	20X6 $'000
Assets		
Non-current assets		
Property, plant and equipment	317,000	174,000
Intangible assets (note ii)	20,000	16,000
	337,000	190,000
Current assets		
Inventories	580	490
Trade and other receivables	6,100	6,300
Cash and cash equivalents	9,300	22,100
Total current assets	15,980	28,890
Total assets	352,980	218,890
Equity and liabilities		
Equity		
Equity shares	3,000	3,000
Retained earnings	44,100	41,800
Revaluation surplus	145,000	Nil
Total equity	192,100	44,800
Liabilities		
Non-current liabilities		
6% loan notes	130,960	150,400
Current liabilities		
Trade and other payables	10,480	4,250

	20X7 $'000	20X6 $'000
6% loan notes	19,440	19,440
Total current liabilities	29,920	23,690
Total equity and liabilities	352,980	218,890

Other EXTRACTS from Mowair Co's financial statements for the years ended 30 June:

	20X7 $'000	20X6 $'000
Revenue	154,000	159,000
Profit from operations	12,300	18,600
Finance costs	(9,200)	(10,200)
Cash generated from operations	18,480	24,310

The following information is also relevant:

(i)   Mowair Co had exactly the same flight schedule in 20X7 as in 20X6, with the overall number of flights and destinations being the same in both years.

(ii)   In April 20X7, Mowair Co had to renegotiate its licences with five major airports, which led to an increase in the prices Mowair Co had to pay for the right to operate flights there. The licences with ten more major airports are due to expire in December 20X7, and Mowair Co is currently in negotiation with these airports.

Required

(a)   Using the preformatted table provided below, calculate the required ratios for Mowair Co for the years ended 30 June 20X6 and 20X7:

Pre-formatted table

	20X7	Working	20X6	Working
Operating profit margin				
Return on capital employed				
Net asset turnover				
Current ratio				
Interest cover				
Gearing				

Note. For calculation purposes, all loan notes should be treated as debt.   **(6 marks)**

(b)   Comment on the performance and position of Mowair Co for the year ended 30 June 20X7.

Note. Your answer should highlight any issues which Mowair Co should be considering in the near future.   **(14 marks)**

(Total = 20 marks)

240 Perkins Co (Mar/Jun 18)   36 mins

Below are extracts from the statements of profit or loss for the Perkins Group and Perkins Co for the years ending 31 December 20X7 and 20X6 respectively.

	20X7 (Consolidated) $'000	20X6 (Perkins Co individual) $'000
Revenue	46,220	35,714
Cost of sales	(23,980)	(19,714)
Gross profit	22,240	16,000
Operating expenses	(3,300)	(10,000)
Profit from operations	18,940	6,000
Finance costs	(960)	(1,700)
Profit before tax	17,980	4,300

The following information is relevant:

On 1 September 20X7, Perkins Co sold all of its shares in Swanson Co, its only subsidiary, for $28.64 million. At this date, Swanson Co had net assets of $26.1 million. Perkins Co originally acquired 80% of Swanson Co for $19.2 million, when Swanson Co had net assets of $19.8 million. Perkins Co uses the fair value method for valuing the non-controlling interest, which was measured at $4.9 million at the date of acquisition. Goodwill in Swanson Co has not been impaired since acquisition.

In order to compare Perkin Co's results for the years ended 20X6 and 20X7, the results of Swanson Co need to be eliminated from the above consolidated statements of profit or loss for 20X7. Although Swanson Co was correctly accounted for in the group financial statements for the year ended 31 December 20X7, a gain on disposal of Swanson Co of $9.44 million is currently included in operating expenses. This reflects the gain which should have been shown in Perkins Co's individual financial statements.

In the year ended 31 December 20X7, Swanson Co had the following results:

	$m
Revenue	13.50
Cost of sales	6.60
Operating expenses	2.51
Finance costs	1.20

During the period from 1 January 20X7 to 1 September 20X7, Perkins Co sold $1 million of goods to Swanson Co at a margin of 30%. Swanson Co had sold all of these goods on to third parties by 1 September 20X7.

Swanson Co previously used space in Perkins Co's properties, which Perkins Co did not charge Swanson Co for. Since the disposal of Swanson Co, Perkins Co has rented that space to a new tenant, recording the rental income in operating expenses.

The following ratios have been correctly calculated based on the above financial statements:

	20X7 (Consolidated)	20X6 (Perkins Co individual)
Gross profit margin	48.1%	44.8%
Operating margin	41%	16.8%
Interest cover	19.7 times	3.5 times

Required

(a) Calculate the gain on disposal which should have been shown in the consolidated statement of profit or loss for the Perkins group for the year ended 31 December 20X7.

(5 marks)

(b) Remove the results of Swanson Co and the gain on disposal of the subsidiary to prepare a revised statement of profit or loss for the year ended 31 December 20X7 for Perkins Co only. **(4 marks)**

(c) Calculate the equivalent ratios to those given for Perkins Co for 20X7 based on the revised figures in part (b) of your answer. **(2 marks)**

(d) Using the ratios calculated in part (c) and those provided in the question, comment on the performance of Perkins Co for the years ended 31 December 20X6 and 20X7. **(9 marks)**

(Total = 20 marks)

241 Pirlo Co (Mar/Jun 2019 amended)   36 mins

The consolidated statements of profit or loss for the Pirlo group for the years ended 31 December 20X9 and 20X8 are shown below.

	20X9 $'000	20X8 $'000
Revenue	213,480	216,820
Cost of sales	(115,620)	(119,510)
Gross profit	97,860	97,310
Operating expenses	(72,360)	(68,140)
Profit from operations	25,500	29,170
Finance costs	(17,800)	(16,200)
Investment income	2,200	2,450
Profit before tax	9,900	15,420
Share of profit of associate	4,620	3,160
Tax expense	(2,730)	(3,940)
Profit for the year	11,790	14,640
Attributable to:		
Shareholders of Pirlo Co	8,930	12,810
Non-controlling interest	2,860	1,830

The following information is relevant:

(i) On 31 December 20X9, the Pirlo group disposed of its entire 80% holding in Samba Co, a software development company, for $300m. The Samba Co results have been fully consolidated into the consolidated financial statements above. Samba Co does not represent a discontinued operation.

(ii) The proceeds from the disposal of Samba Co have been credited to a suspense account and no gain/loss has been recorded in the financial statements above.

(iii) Pirlo Co originally acquired the shares in Samba Co for $210m. At this date, goodwill was calculated at $70m. Goodwill has not been impaired since acquisition, and external advisers estimate that the goodwill arising in Samba Co has a value of $110m at 31 December 20X9.

(iv) On 31 December 20X9, Samba Co had net assets with a carrying amount of $260m. In addition to this, Samba Co's brand name was valued at $50m at acquisition in the consolidated financial statements. This is not reflected in Samba Co's individual financial statements, and the value is assessed to be the same at 31 December 20X9.

(v) Samba Co is the only subsidiary in which the Pirlo group owned less than 100% of the equity. The Pirlo group uses the fair value method to value the non-controlling interest. At 31 December 20X9, the non-controlling interest in Samba Co is deemed to be $66m.

(vi)   Until December 20X8, Pirlo Co rented space in its property to a third party. This arrangement ended and, on 1 January 20X9, Samba Co's administrative department moved into Pirlo Co's property. Pirlo Co charged Samba Co a reduced rent. Samba Co's properties were sold in April 20X9 at a profit of $2m which is included in administrative expenses.

(vii) On 31 December 20X9, the employment of the two founding directors of Samba Co was transferred to Pirlo Co. From the date of disposal, Pirlo Co will go into direct competition with Samba Co. As part of this move, the directors did not take their annual bonus of $1m each from Samba Co. Instead, they received a similar 'joining fee' from Pirlo Co, which was paid to them on 31 December 20X9. These individuals have excellent relationships with the largest customers of Samba Co, and are central to Pirlo Co's future plans.

(viii) Samba Co's revenue remained consistent at $26m in both 20X9 and 20X8 and Samba Co has high levels of debt. Key ratios from the Samba Co financial statements are shown below:

	20X9	20X8
Gross profit margin	81%	80%
Operating profit margin	66%	41%
Interest cover	1.2 times	1.1 times

Required

(a)   Calculate the gain/loss on the disposal of Samba Co which will be recorded in:

- The individual financial statements of Pirlo Co; and
- The consolidated financial statements of the Pirlo group.   (4 marks)

(b)   Calculate ratios equivalent to those provided in note (viii) for the Pirlo group for the years ended 31 December 20X9 and 20X8. No adjustment is required for the gain/loss on disposal from (a).   (3 marks)

(c)   Briefly explain the conditions that the directors of Pirlo would have considered in determining whether Samba Co was a discontinued operation and briefly explain the impact on the group financial statements if they had determined that Samba Co was a discontinued operation.   (3 marks)

(d)   Comment on the performance and interest cover of the Pirlo group for the years ended 31 December 20X9 and 20X8. Your answer should comment on:

- The overall performance of the Pirlo group;

- How, once accounted for, the disposal of Samba Co will impact on your analysis; and

- The implications of the disposal of Samba Co for the future results of the Pirlo group.
                    (10 marks)

                    (Total = 20 marks)

242 Karl Co (ACCA September/December 2020)   36 mins

At 1 January 20X8, the Karl group consisted of the parent, Karl Co, and two wholly-owned subsidiaries. There were no intra-group transactions during the year.

The sale of one of the subsidiaries, Sinker Co, was completed on 31 December 20X8 when Karl Co sold its entire holding for $20 million cash. Sinker Co had net assets of $29 million at the date of disposal. The sale does not meet the definition of a discontinued operation and has been correctly accounted for in the consolidated financial statements. The gain/loss on disposal of Sinker Co is included in administrative expenses.

Karl Co had originally purchased Sinker Co on 1 January 20X2 for $35 million. The fair value and carrying amount of net assets of Sinker Co at the date of acquisition were $28 million. Goodwill was considered to be impaired by 70% at 31 December 20X8.

Extracts from the consolidated financial statements for the years ended 31 December 20X8 and 20X7 are shown below:

EXTRACTS FROM THE STATEMENTS OF PROFIT OR LOSS FOR THE YEAR ENDED 31 DECEMBER:

	Consolidated 20X8 $m	Consolidated 20X7 $m
Revenue	289	272
Cost of sales	(165)	(140)
Gross profit	**124**	**132**
Administrative expenses	(45)	(23)
Distribution costs	(15)	(13)
Operating profit / (loss)	64	96

EXTRACTS FROM THE STATEMENTS OF FINANCIAL POSITION AS AT 31 DECEMBER:

	Consolidated 20X8 $m	Consolidated 20X7 $m
Current assets	112	125
Equity	621	578
Non-current liabilities	100	150
Current liabilities	36	161

The following information is also relevant:

(i) The majority of non-current liabilities is comprised of bank loans.

(ii) Sales of Sinker Co represented 14% of the total group sales for 20X8, however, in March 20X8, Sinker Co lost a significant customer contract resulting in a number of redundancies. These redundancy costs amounted to $15 million and are included in administrative expenses. Overall, Sinker Co made an operating loss of $17 million.

(iii) The Karl group manufactures food packaging. The inventory included in the above consolidated statement of financial position is:

Group inventory at:

	$m
31 December 20X8	65
31 December 20X7	78

(iv) At 31 December 20X8, Sinker Co had inventory of $42 million.

Required

(a) Calculate the gain/loss arising on the disposal of Sinker Co in the consolidated financial statements of the Karl group. (4 marks)

(b) Based on the financial statements provided, calculate the following ratios and comment on the financial performance and position of the Karl group for the years ended 31 December 20X8 and 20X7:

    (i) Gross profit margin;
    (ii) Operating profit margin;
    (iii) Return on capital employed;
    (iv) Current ratio; and
    (v) Gearing ratio (debt/debt + equity)).

    Note. A maximum of 5 marks is available for the calculation of ratios. (13 marks)

(c) Comment on how the sale of Sinker Co will affect the comparability of the consolidated financial statements for the years ended 31 December 20X7 and 20X8. (3 marks)

(Total = 20 marks)

BPP
LEARNING
MEDIA

243 Kostner Co

Statement of cash flows for Kostner Co for the year ended 31 December 20X8

	$'000	$'000
Cash flows from operating activities		
Profit before taxation	350	
Adjustments for:		
Depreciation	600	
Profit on disposal of PPE	(3,000)	
Interest expense	270	
	(1,810)	
(Increase) decrease in inventories	(838)	
(Increase) decrease in trade & other receivables	(722)	
Increase (decrease) in provisions	50	
Increase (decrease) in trade payables	710	
Cash used in operations	(2,610)	
Interest paid	(300)	
Income taxes paid	(472)	
Net cash from operating activities		(3,382)
Cash flows from investing activities		
Interest received	40	
Proceeds from disposal of property	9,900	
Purchase of property, plant and equipment	(800)	
Net cash from investing activities		9,140
Cash flows from financing activities		
Proceeds from long term borrowings	1,100	
Proceeds from issue of share capital	1,500	
Payments under leases	(2,440)	
Net cash from financing activities		160
Net increase in cash and cash equivalents		5,918
Cash and cash equivalents at beginning of period		(2,500)
Cash and cash equivalents at end of period		3,418

Extract of the statement of profit or loss for the year ended 31 December 20X8

	31 December 20X8 $'000	31 December 20X7 $'000
Revenue	3,206	3,107
Cost of sales	(807)	(745)
Gross profit	2,399	2,362
Administration costs	(379)	(350)
Other operating expenses	(1,470)	(920)
Operating profit	550	1,092
Interest paid	(270)	(20)
Interest received	40	39
Profit before taxation	320	1,111

Kostner Co runs a small number of gym and leisure facilities in the south west of England.

The following information is also provided regarding the company:

- Inventories held by the gyms are mainly consumables such as towels, drinks and snacks which are all available for purchase by the clients. During December, Kostner purchased a new range of high protein recovery drinks, ProBizz. Marty Grosman, the Purchases Manager, helped Kostner obtain a 'great margin' on the drinks by buying in bulk. Revenue from consumables has remained relatively static year on year.

- Gym members pay an annual subscription by monthly direct debit. New members must pay a non-refundable joining fee which is recognised immediately in the financial statements.

- Other revenue comes from Kostner licensing out its brand of bespoke fitness classes, the 'TotemPower', based on a core strength workout using poles. The licence is capitalised and reviewed for impairment on an annual basis.

- During September, it was decided to rent out some of the unused studio space for freelance gym instructors to use to put on specialist group classes such as Pump Strength, Hi-Intensity Workout, PilaYoga and Free Dance. This has proved very popular, with the freelancers being invoiced in arrears. This amount was outstanding at year end as the credit controller had been on long term sick leave.

- There was an inaugural fitness festival to attract clients to the gyms in the new year which was held at the South Kimble gym in December, income of $325,000 from this event is currently outstanding from the organisers. This debt is expected to be recovered in full.

- There is a provision in the accounts for a legal claim made against Kostner from a client who injured herself on a faulty piece of equipment. The provision in the accounts recognises that the claim is likely to succeed and is close to settlement at the year end.

Breakdown of the revenue

	20X8 $000	20X7 $000
Fitness festival	325	–
TotemPower	280	260
Rental of rooms	300	–
Membership & sundries	2,301	2,847
Total revenue	3,206	3,107

Required

(a) Interpret the profitability and cash flow of Kostner Co using the information provided. Highlight any areas of concern for the management team supporting your answer with relevant evidence. (15 marks)

(b) Compare the usefulness of information from the statement of cash flows with that obtained from the statement of profit or loss extract. (5 marks)

(Total = 20 marks)

Section C of the exam will include a question on the preparation of financial statements for single entities or groups. You may be asked to prepare a single entity or consolidated statement of profit or loss and/or consolidated statement of financial position. You may be asked to prepare a statement of changes in equity for a single entity. In respect of the statement of cash flows, you may be asked to prepare *extracts* for a single entity only.

Section A questions

Section A

Consolidated statement of financial position

244   Witch Co acquired 70% of the 200,000 equity shares of Wizard, its only subsidiary, on 1 April 20X8 when the retained earnings of Wizard Co were $450,000. The carrying amounts of Wizard Co's net assets at the date of acquisition were equal to their fair values.

Witch Co measures non-controlling interest at fair value, based on share price. The market value of Wizard Co shares at the date of acquisition was $1.75.

At 31 March 20X9 the retained earnings of Wizard Co were $750,000. At what amount should the non-controlling interest appear in the consolidated statement of financial position of Witch Co at 31 March 20X9?

$ [   ]   (2 marks)

245   Cloud Co obtained a 60% holding in the 100,000 $1 shares of Mist Co on 1 January 20X8. Cloud Co paid $250,000 cash immediately with an additional $400,000 payable on 1 January 20X9 and one share in Cloud Co for each two shares acquired. Cloud Co has a cost of capital of 8% and the market value of its shares on 1 January 20X8 was $2.30.

What was the total consideration paid for Cloud Co's share of Mist Co?

O $689,370
O $719,000
O $758,370
O $788,000   (2 marks)

246   On 1 June 20X1, Premier Co acquired 80% of the equity share capital of Sandford Co. At the date of acquisition the fair values of Sandford Co's net assets were equal to their carrying amounts with the exception of its property. This had a fair value of $1.2 million **BELOW** its carrying amount. The property had a remaining useful life of eight years.

What effect will any adjustment required in respect of the property have on group retained earnings at 30 September 20X1?

$ [   ] Increase/decrease   (2 marks)

247 On 1 August 20X7, Patronic Co purchased 18 million of the 24 million $1 equity shares of Sardonic Co. The acquisition was through a share exchange of two shares in Patronic Co for every three shares in Sardonic Co. The market price of a share in Patronic Co at 1 August 20X7 was $5.75. Patronic Co will also pay in cash on 31 July 20X9 (two years after acquisition) $2.42 per acquired share of Sardonic Co. Patronic Co's cost of capital is 10% per annum.

What is the amount of the consideration attributable to Patronic Co for the acquisition of Sardonic Co?

- ○ $105 million
- ○ $139.5 million
- ○ $108.2 million
- ○ $103.8 million

(2 marks)

248 On 1 April 20X0, Picant Co acquired 75% of Sander Co's equity shares by means of a share exchange and an additional amount payable on 1 April 20X1 that was contingent upon the post-acquisition performance of Sander Co. At the date of acquisition Picant Co assessed the fair value of this contingent consideration at $4.2 million but by 31 March 20X1 it was clear that the amount to be paid would be only $2.7 million.

Using the drag and drop options below, demonstrate how Picant Co would account for this $1.5 million adjustment in its financial statements as at 31 March 20X1?

Account

Debit	Account	Current liabilities
Credit	Account	Goodwill
		Retained earnings

(2 marks)

249 Crash Co acquired 80% of Bang Co's 100,000 $1 ordinary shares for $800,000 when the retained earnings of Bang Co were $570,000.

Bang Co also has an internally developed customer list which has been independently valued at $90,000.

The directors of Crash Co are deciding whether to recognise non-controlling interest at fair value or at its share of the net assets of Bang Co at the date of acquisition. The fair value of the non-controlling interest in Bang Co was judged to be $220,000 at the date of acquisition.

What was the goodwill arising on the acquisition of Bang Co if the NCI is measured at fair value or as a proportionate share of the net assets at acquisition?

Fair value	Share of net assets
$260,000	
$350,000	
$192,000	
$264,000	

(2 marks)

250 Tazer Co, a parent company, acquired Lowdown Co, an unincorporated entity, for $2.8 million. A fair value exercise performed on Lowdown Co's net assets at the date of purchase showed:

	$'000
Property, plant and equipment	3,000
Identifiable intangible asset	500
Inventories	300
Trade receivables less payables	200
	4,000

How should the purchase of Lowdown be reflected in Tazer Co's consolidated statement of financial position?

○ Record the net assets at the carrying amounts shown above and credit profit or loss with $1.2 million

○ Record the net assets at the carrying amounts shown above and credit Tazer Co's consolidated goodwill with $1.2 million

○ Derecognise the identifiable intangible asset, record the remaining net assets at the carrying amounts shown above and credit profit or loss with $700,000

○ Record the purchase as a financial asset investment at $2.8 million   (2 marks)

251 On 1 January 20X5, Pratt Co acquired 80% of the equity shares of Sam Co. Pratt Co values non-controlling interests at fair value and, at the date of acquisition, goodwill was valued at $20,000. At December 20X5, the goodwill was fully impaired.

In reviewing the fair value of Sam Co's net assets at acquisition, Pratt Co concluded that property, plant and equipment, with a remaining life of five years, had a fair value of $5,000 in excess of its carrying amount.

Sam Co has not incorporated any of these adjustments into its individual financial statements.

What is the total charged to group retained earnings at 31 December 20X5 as a result of these consolidation adjustments?

○ $16,800

○ $21,000

○ $17,000

○ $20,800   (2 marks)

---

252 Platt Co has owned 60% of the issued equity share capital of Serpi Co for many years. At 31 October 20X7, the individual statements of financial position included the following:

	Platt Co $	Serpi Co $
Current assets	700,000	500,000
Current liabilities	300,000	200,000

Neither had a bank overdraft at 31 October 20X7.

During the year ended 31 October 20X7, Platt Co made $100,000 sales on credit to Serpi Co. Serpi Co had one-quarter of these goods in inventory at 31 October 20X7. Platt Co makes a 20% gross profit margin on all sales.

On 31 October 20X7, Serpi Co sent a cheque for $50,000 to pay all of the outstanding balance due to Platt Co. Platt Co did not receive this cheque until 2 November 20X7.

Platt Co's policy for in-transit items is to adjust for them in the parent company.

In respect of current assets and current liabilities, what amounts will be reported in Platt Co's consolidated statement of financial position at 31 October 20X7?

○ Current assets $1.197 million and current liabilities $0.5 million

○ Current assets $1.145 million and current liabilities $0.45 million

○ Current assets $1.195 million and current liabilities $0.45 million

○ Current assets $1.195 million and current liabilities $0.5 million   (2 marks)

---

253 Boat Co acquired 60% of Anchor Co on 1 January 20X4. At the date of acquisition, the carrying amount of Anchor Co's net assets were the same as their fair values, with the exception of an item of machinery which had a carrying amount of $90,000, a fair value of $160,000 and a remaining useful life of five years. Non-controlling interests are valued at fair value.

What is the journal entry required to reflect this fair value adjustment in the consolidated statement of financial position of Boat Co as at 31 December 20X6?

			$	$
○	Debit	Retained earnings	25,200	
	Debit	Non-controlling interest	16,800	
	Debit	Property, plant and equipment	28,000	
	Credit	Goodwill		70,000
○	Debit	Retained earnings	8,400	
	Debit	Non-controlling interest	5,600	
	Debit	Property, plant and equipment	56,000	
	Credit	Goodwill		70,000
○	Debit	Retained earnings	57,600	
	Debit	Non-controlling interest	38,400	
	Debit	Property, plant and equipment	64,000	
	Credit	Goodwill		160,000
○	Debit	Retained earnings	42,000	
	Debit	Property, plant and equipment	28,000	
	Credit	Goodwill		70,000

(2 marks)

254 On 1 July 20X5, Pull Co acquired 80% of the equity of Sat Co. At the date of acquisition, goodwill was calculated as $10,000 and the non-controlling interest was measured at fair value. In conducting the fair value exercise on Sat Co's net assets at acquisition, Pull Co concluded that property, plant and equipment with a remaining life of ten years had a fair value of $300,000 in excess of its carrying amount. Sat Co had not incorporated this fair value adjustment into its individual financial statements.

At the reporting date of 31 December 20X5, the goodwill was fully impaired. For the year ended 31 December 20X5, Sat Co reported a profit for the year of $200,000.

What is the Pull Group profit for the year ended 31 December 20X5 that is attributable to non-controlling interests?

○ $16,000

○ $12,000

○ $35,000

○ $15,000   (2 marks)

---

255 Zebra Co acquired 75% of the 2 million issued $1 ordinary shares of Penguin Co on 1 January 20X2 for $3,700,000 when Penguin Co's retained earnings were $1,770,000. Zebra Co has no other subsidiaries.

Zebra Co elected to measure non-controlling interests in Penguin Co at their fair value of $1,140,000 at the acquisition date.

An impairment review performed on 31 December 20X3 indicated that goodwill on the acquisition of Penguin Co had been impaired by $100,000. No impairment was recognised in the year ended 31 December 20X2.

Which THREE of the following statements are true in respect of the non-controlling interest to be included in the consolidated statement of financial position of the Zebra group for the year ended 31 December 20X3?

☐   Non-controlling interest would be higher if the proportionate method was used

☐   It will be included at its fair value on acquisition plus share of post-acquisition earnings of Penguin Co.

☐   It will be included as a separate component of equity.

☐   25% of the impairment in the goodwill arising on acquisition will be debited to it.

☐   It will be included in the non-current liabilities of the Zebra group.   (2 marks)

---

256 Platinum Co acquired 80% of the ordinary share capital of Palladium Co on 1 April 20X0 by means of cash and contingent consideration. At this date, Platinum Co assessed the fair value of contingent consideration at $250,000. Platinum Co measures non-controlling interest at fair value at the date of acquisition, which was estimated to be $100,000 the goodwill arising on acquisition was $300,000.

The following figures for Palladium Co are relevant:

	$'000
Ordinary shares of $1 each at acquisition	500
Retained earnings/(losses) at 1 January 20X0	(300)
Profit for the year ended 31 December 20X0	120

The profits for Palladium Co have accrued evenly throughout the year.

What was the cash consideration paid by Platinum Co for the investment in Palladium Co?

$ [ ]   (2 marks)

(ACCA Financial Reporting March/June 2021 Examiner's report www.accaglobal.com)

257 Indicate, by selecting the relevant boxes in the table, whether the following statements are true or false in relation to accounting for the acquisition of a subsidiary.

	TRUE	FALSE
Where a parent company is satisfied that there has been a gain on a bargain purchase (negative goodwill), it should be recognised in the consolidated statement of profit or loss immediately	TRUE	FALSE
If the liabilities of the acquired entity are overstated, then goodwill will also be overstated	TRUE	FALSE

                                                                         (2 marks)

(ACCA Financial Reporting March/June 2021 Examiner's report www.accaglobal.com)

Consolidated statement of profit or loss and other comprehensive income

258 Paprika Co purchased 75% of the equity share capital of Salt Co on 30 April 20X4. Non-controlling interests are measured at fair value.

The cost of sales of both companies for the year ended 30 April 20X6 are as follows:

	Paprika $	Salt $
Cost of sales	60,000	100,000

The following information is provided:

(1) Salt Co had machinery included in its net assets at acquisition with a carrying amount of $120,000 but a fair value of $200,000. The machinery had a remaining useful life of eight years at the date of acquisition. All depreciation is charged to cost of sales.

(2) During the year, Salt Co sold some goods to Paprika Co for $32,000 at a margin of 25%. Three quarters of these goods remained in inventory at year end.

What is the cost of sales in Paprika Co's consolidated statement of profit or loss for the year ended 30 April 20X6?

O $144,000

O $132,000

O $176,000

O $140,000   (2 marks)

259 Hillusion Co acquired 80% of Skeptik Co on 1 July 20X2. In the post-acquisition period Hillusion Co sold goods to Skeptik Co at a price of $12 million. These goods had cost Hillusion Co $9 million. During the year to 31 March 20X3 Skeptik Co had sold $10 million (at cost to Skeptik Co) of these goods for $15 million.

How will this affect group cost of sales in the consolidated statement of profit or loss of Hillusion Co for the year ended 31 March 20X3?

- ○ Increase by $11.5 million
- ○ Increase by $9.6 million
- ○ Decrease by $11.5 million
- ○ Decrease by $9.6 million   (2 marks)

---

260 On 1 July 20X7, Spider Co acquired 60% of the equity share capital of Fly Co and on that date made a $10 million loan to Fly Co at a rate of 8% per annum.

What will be the effect on group retained earnings at the year-end date of 31 December 20X7 when this intragroup transaction is cancelled?

- ○ Group retained earnings will increase by $400,000
- ○ Group retained earnings will be reduced by $240,000
- ○ Group retained earnings will be reduced by $160,000
- ○ There will be no effect on group retained earnings   (2 marks)

---

261 Wiley Co acquired 80% of Coyote Co on 1 January 20X8. At the date of acquisition Coyote Co had a building which had a fair value $22 million and a carrying amount of $20 million. The remaining useful life of the building was 20 years.

Coyote Co's profit for the year to 30 June 20X8 was $1.6 million which accrued evenly throughout the year.

Wiley Co measures non-controlling interest at fair value. At 30 June 20X8 it estimated that goodwill in Coyote Co was impaired by $500,000.

What is the total comprehensive income attributable to the non-controlling interest at 30 June 20X8?

- ○ $40,000
- ○ $50,000
- ○ $187,500
- ○ $150,000   (2 marks)

---

262 Basil Co acquired 60% of Parsley Co on 1 March 20X9. In September 20X9 Basil Co sold $46,000 worth of goods to Parsley Co. Basil Co applies a 30% mark-up to all its sales. 25% of these goods were still held in inventory by Parsley Co at the end of the year.

An extract from the draft statements of profit or loss of Basil Co and Parsley Co at 31 December 20X9 is:

	Basil Co	Parsley Co
	$	$
Revenue	955,000	421,500
Cost of sales	(407,300)	(214,600)
Gross profit	547,700	206,900

All revenue and costs arise evenly throughout the year.

What will be shown as gross profit in the consolidated statement of profit or loss of Basil Co for the year ended 31 December 20X9?

$ [   ] (2 marks)

263 Premier Co acquired 80% of Sanford Co on 1 June 20X1. Sales from Sanford Co to Premier Co throughout the year ended 30 September 20X1 were consistently $1 million per month. Sanford Co made a mark-up on cost of 25% on these sales. At 30 September 20X1 Premier Co was holding $2 million inventory that had been supplied by Sanford Co in the post-acquisition period.

By how much will the unrealised profit decrease the profit attributable to the non-controlling interest for the year ended 30 September 20X1?

$ [   ] (2 marks)

264 Brigham Co has owned 70% of Dorset Co for many years. It also holds a $5 million 8% loan note from Dorset Co. One of Dorset Co's non-current assets has suffered an impairment of $50,000 during the year. There is a balance in the revaluation surplus of Dorset Co of $30,000 in respect of this asset. The impairment loss has not yet been recorded.

The entity financial statements of Dorset Co show a profit for the year of $1.3 million.

What is the amount attributable to the non-controlling interests in the consolidated statement of profit or loss?

$ [   ] (2 marks)

Disposals of subsidiaries

265 On 1 January 20X3, Westbridge Co acquired all of Brookfield Co's 100,000 $1 shares for $300,000. The goodwill acquired in the business combination was $40,000, of which 50% had been written off as impaired by 31 December 20X5. On 31 December 20X5 Westbridge Co sold all of Brookfield Co's shares for $450,000 when Brookfield Co had retained earnings of $185,000.

Using the pull-down list provided, select which is the correct answer for the profit on disposal that should be included in the consolidated financial statements of Westbridge Co?

[▼]

Pull-down list:

$145,000
$165,000
$245,000
$330,000 (2 marks)

266 On 1 January 20X8, Lentil Co acquired all of Chickpea Co's 100,000 $1 shares for $400,000. The goodwill acquired in the business combination was $60,000, of which 40% had been written off as impaired by 31 December 20X8. On 31 December 20X5 Lentil Co sold all of Chickpea Co's shares for $680,000 when Chickpea Co had retained earnings of $215,000.

What is the profit on disposal that should be included in the individual entity financial statements of Lentil Co?

$ [   ]   (2 marks)

267   Alderminster Co acquired a 70% holding in Bidford Co on 1 January 20X4 for $600,000. At that date the fair value of the net assets of Bidford Co was $700,000. Alderminster Co measures non-controlling interest at its share of net assets.

On 31 December 20X6 Alderminster Co sold all its shares in Bidford Co for $950,000. At that date the fair value of Bidford Co's net assets was $850,000. Goodwill was not impaired.

What was the profit or loss on disposal to be recognised in the consolidated financial statements of Alderminster Co?

[▼] profit/loss

Pull-down list:
$135,000
$200,000
$245,000
$355,000   (2 marks)

268   Jalapeno Co is preparing its consolidated financial statements for the year ended 31 December 20X7. Jalapeno Co acquired a 75% holding in Habanero Co on 1 January 20X4 for consideration of $580,000. The fair value of the net assets of Habanero Co was $640,000 at that date. The goodwill of Habanero Co was impaired by 20% in the current year; it was not previously impaired. Jalapeno Co also acquired a holding of 70% of the shares in Bonnet Co on 1 January 20X5 with goodwill of $50,000 arising on acquisition. The goodwill in Bonnet Co has not been impaired. Jalapeno Co sold its entire holding of Bonnet Co on 31 December 20X7.

Jalapeno Co measures non-controlling interests at acquisition as a share of net assets.

What is the carrying amount of goodwill to be recognised in the consolidated financial statements of Jalapeno Co at 31 December 20X7?

$ [   ]   (2 marks)

269   At 1 January 20X2, the Dug Group consisted of Dug Co, the parent company, and its two wholly-owned subsidiaries Russel Co and Karl Co. There were no intra-group transactions during the year to 31 December 20X2.

Dug Co sold its entire holding of Russel Co for cash consideration of $50 million on 31 December 20X2. Dug Co had net assets of $39 million at the date of disposal. Dug Co had originally purchased Russel Co on 1 January 20X1 for consideration of $28 million when the net assets of Russel Co were $22 million. The goodwill was impaired by 50% in the year to 31 December 20X2.

What is the profit or loss recognised in the consolidated statement of profit or loss on the disposal of Russel Co? (You should enter a loss as a negative number.)

$ [   ]   (2 marks)

Accounting for associates

270 On 1 October 20X8, Pacemaker Co acquired 30 million of Vardine Co's 100 million shares in exchange for 75 million of its own shares. The fair value of Pacemaker Co's shares at the date of this share exchange was $1.60 each.

Vardine Co's profit is subject to seasonal variation. Its profit for the year ended 31 March 20X9 was $100 million. $20 million of this profit was made from 1 April 20X8 to 30 September 20X8.

Pacemaker Co has one subsidiary and no other investments apart from Vardine Co.

What amount will be shown as 'investment in associate' in the consolidated statement of financial position of Pacemaker Co as at 31 March 20X9?

○ $144 million

○ $150 million

○ $78 million

○ $126 million (2 marks)

---

271 Jarvis Co owns 30% of McLintock Co. During the year to 31 December 20X4 McLintock Co sold $2 million of goods to Jarvis Co, of which 40% were still held in inventory by Jarvis at the year end. McLintock Co applies a mark-up of 25% on all goods sold.

What effect would the above transactions have on group inventory at 31 December 20X4?

○ Debit group inventory $48,000

○ Debit group inventory $160,000

○ Credit group inventory $48,000

○ No effect on group inventory (2 marks)

---

272 Ulysses Co owns 25% of Grant Co, which it purchased on 1 May 20X8 for $5 million. At that date Grant Co had retained earnings of $7.4 million. At the year-end date of 31 October 20X8 Grant Co had retained earnings of $8.5 million after paying out a dividend of $1 million. On 30 September 20X8, Grant Co sold $600,000 of goods to Ulysses Co, on which it made 30% profit. Ulysses Co had not resold these goods by 31 October.

At what amount will Ulysses Co report its investment in Grant Co in its consolidated statement of financial position at 31 October 20X8?

○ $5,000,000

○ $5,275,000

○ $5,230,000

○ $4,855,000 (2 marks)

---

273 On 1 February 20X3, Pinot Co acquired 30% of the equity shares of Noir Co, its only associate, for $10 million in cash. The profit for the year of Noir Co for the year to 30 September 20X3 was $6 million. Profits accrued evenly throughout the year. Noir Co made a dividend payment of $1 million on 1 September 20X3. At 30 September 20X3 Pinot Co decided that an impairment loss of $700,000 should be recognised on its investment in Noir Co.

What amount will be shown as 'investment in associate' in the statement of financial position of Pinot Co as at 30 September 20X3?

$ [   ] (2 marks)

---

274 Ruby Co owns 30% of Emerald Co and exercises significant influence over it. Emerald Co reports a profit of $1,980,000 in its individual financial statements for the year ended 30 September 20X7. During the year, Emerald Co sold goods to Ruby Co for $160,000. Emerald Co applies a one-third mark-up on cost. Ruby Co still had 25% of these goods in inventory at the year end.

What amount should be recognised as the share of profit from the associate in the consolidated statement of profit or loss of Ruby Co for the year ended 30 September 20X7?

$ [   ]   (2 marks)

---

275 Chloe Co owns 40% of Amy Co and exercises significant influence over it. During the year, Chloe Co sold goods to Amy Co, earning a margin of 30% on the sale. Amy Co still had half of these goods in inventory at the year end.

Identify the correct adjustments to eliminate the unrealised profit in inventories.

Cost of sales

Investment in associate

Share of profit of associate

Inventories

Dr

Cr

[   ]

[   ]

(2 marks)

---

276 **Identify TWO associate companies of Zuckal Co (identify one from each group).**

Group 1

Acquisition of 10% of Artles Co. Zuckal Co has no representation on the board or Artles Co. All decisions are made at board level.

Acquisition of 40% of Bandoka Co. Due to an agreement with other shareholders, Zuckal Co effectively holds 52% of the voting rights.

Acquisition of 50% of Castur Co. Zuckal Co has appointed two of the five board members.

Associate

Associate 1

Group 2

Acquisition of 21% of Dunnatonn Co. The other 79% of Dunnatonn Co is owned by Yentee Co, a company with no links to Zuckal Co.

Acquisition of 70% of Eahnn Co. Zuckal Co has been able to direct the operating activities of Eahnn Co for many years, and has exercised that right.

Acquisition of 15% of Furnitt Co. Zuckal Co can appoint one of Furnitt Co's five board members. No party can appoint more than two.

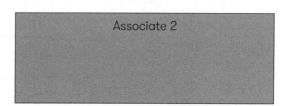

(2 marks)

(ACCA Examiner's Report, September/December 2020)

Presentation of published financial statements

277   Which of the following would not **NECESSARILY** lead to a liability being classified as a current liability?

○   The liability is expected to be settled in the course of the entity's normal operating cycle

○   The liability has arisen during the current accounting period

○   The liability is held primarily for the purpose of trading

○   The liability is due to be settled within 12 months after the end of the reporting period
(2 marks)

278   Which of the following would be shown in the 'other comprehensive income' section of the statement of profit or loss and other comprehensive income?

○   An increase in valuation on an investment property

○   Profit on sale of an investment

○   Receipt of a government grant

○   A revaluation surplus of a factory building
(2 marks)

279   Using the pull-down list provided which of the following are **NOT** items required by IAS 1 *Presentation of Financial Statements* to be shown on the face of the statement of financial position?

Pull-down list:

Inventories
Provisions
Government grants
Intangible assets
(2 marks)

280 How does IAS 1 *Presentation of Financial Statements* define the 'operating cycle' of an entity?

○ The time between acquisition of assets for processing and delivery of finished goods to customers

○ The time between delivery of finished goods and receipt of cash from customers

○ The time between acquisition of assets for processing and payment of cash to suppliers

○ The time between acquisition of assets for processing and receipt of cash from customers   (2 marks)

281 Where are equity dividends paid presented in the financial statements?

○ As a deduction from retained earnings in the statement of changes in equity

○ As a liability in the statement of financial position

○ As an expense in profit or loss

○ As a loss in 'other comprehensive income'   (2 marks)

Statement of cash flows

282 Extracts from the statements of financial position of Nedburg Co are as follows:

Statements of financial position as at 30 September:

	20X2	20X1
	$m	$m
Equity		
Ordinary shares of $0.50 each	750	500
Share premium	350	100
Retained earnings	1,980	1,740

On 1 October 20X1, a bonus issue of one new share for every ten held was made, financed from share premium. This was followed by a further issue for cash.

The statement of profit or loss of Nedburg Co shows a profit for the year of $480,000.

Using the pull-down list available, what amount will appear under 'cash flows from financing activities' in the statement of cash flows of Nedburg Co for the year ended 30 September 20X2 in respect of share issues?

Pull-down list:

$500 million
$660 million
$160 million
$210 million   (2 marks)

283 The statement of financial position of Pinto Co at 31 March 20X7 showed property, plant and equipment with a carrying amount of $1,860,000. At 31 March 20X8 it had increased to $2,880,000.

During the year to 31 March 20X8, plant with a carrying amount of $240,000 was sold at a loss of $90,000, depreciation of $280,000 was charged and $100,000 was added to the revaluation surplus in respect of property, plant and equipment.

What amount should appear under 'investing activities' in the statement of cash flows of Pinto Co for the year ended 31 March 20X8 as cash paid to acquire property, plant and equipment?

○ $1,640,000

○ $1,440,000

○ $1,260,000

○ $1,350,000 (2 marks)

---

284 The following information is available for the property, plant and equipment of Fry Co as at 30 September:

	20X4	20X3
	$'000	$'000
Carrying amounts	23,400	14,400

The following items were recorded during the year ended 30 September 20X4:

(i) Depreciation charge of $2.5 million

(ii) An item of plant with a carrying amount of $3 million was sold for $1.8 million

(iii) A property was revalued upwards by $2 million

(iv) Environmental provisions of $4 million relating to property, plant and equipment were capitalised during the year

What amount would be shown in Fry Co's statement of cash flows for purchase of property, plant and equipment for the year ended 30 September 20X4?

○ $8.5 million

○ $12.5 million

○ $7.3 million

○ $10.5 million (2 marks)

---

285 The carrying amount of property, plant and equipment was $410 million at 31 March 20X1 and $680 million at 31 March 20X2. Right of use assets are included within property, plant and equipment.

During the year, property with a carrying amount of $210 million was revalued to $290 million. The company entered into lease arrangements during the year. The lease liability was initially measured as $12 million. Direct costs of $1 million were paid to arrange the lease and a deposit of $5 million was paid to secure the lease. The total depreciation charge for the year was $115 million. There were no disposals.

What amount will appear in the statement of cash flows for the year ended 31 March 20X2 in respect of purchases of property, plant and equipment?

$ [ ] (2 marks)

---

286 Extracts from Deltoid Co's statements of financial position are as follows:

STATEMENT OF FINANCIAL POSITION AS AT 31 MARCH

	20X1 $'000	20X0 $'000
Non-current assets		
Property, plant and equipment		
Right-of-use asset	6,500	2,500
Non-current liabilities		
Lease liability	4,800	2,000
Current liabilities		
Lease liability	1,700	800

Right-of-use assets are initially measured equal to the initial amount of the lease liability, other than to correctly account for direct costs of $50,000 which were incurred on the arrangement of new lease contracts. During the year to 31 March 20X1 depreciation charged on right-of-use assets was $1,800,000.

What amount will be shown in the statement of cash flows of Deltoid Co for the year ended 31 March 20X1 in respect of payments made under leases?

$ ☐ (2 marks)

Section B

Root Co and Branch Co case   **18 mins**

Information relevant to questions 287–291

On 1 April 20X7, Root Co acquired 116 million of Branch Co's 145 million ordinary shares for an immediate cash payment of $210 million and issued at par one 10% $100 loan note for every 200 shares acquired.

At the date of acquisition Branch Co owned a recently built property that was carried at its depreciated construction cost of $62 million. The fair value of this property at the date of acquisition was $82 million and it had an estimated remaining useful life of 20 years.

Branch Co also had an internally developed brand which was valued at the acquisition date at $25 million with a remaining life of 10 years.

The inventory of Branch Co at 31 March 20X9 includes goods supplied by Root Co for a sale price of $56 million. Root adds a mark-up of 40% on cost to all sales.

287   **What is the total amount of the consideration transferred by Root Co to acquire the investment in Branch Co? (Give your answer in millions).**

$ [   ] million

288   **What will be the amount of the adjustment to group retained earnings at 31 March 20X9 in respect of the movement on the fair value adjustments?**

    ○ $7 million

    ○ $3.5 million

    ○ $5.6 million

    ○ $2.8 million

289   **What is the amount of the unrealised profit arising from intragroup trading? (Give your answer in millions).**

$ [   ] million

290   **Using the drag and drop options available, show how should the unrealised profit be posted?**

Account

Debit		Cost of sales
Credit		Inventories
		Non-controlling interest
		Non-current assets

291 Branch Co has recently lost some large contracts and the directors of Root Co are wondering if Branch Co can be excluded from consolidation next year.

Which of the following situations would allow a subsidiary to be excluded from consolidation?

○ The activities of the subsidiary are significantly different to the activities of the rest of the group

○ Control of the subsidiary has been lost

○ Control of the subsidiary is only intended to be temporary

○ The subsidiary operates under long-term restrictions which prevent it from transferring funds to the parent

(10 marks)

Port Co and Alfred Co case

18 mins

Information relevant to questions 292–296

On 1 November 20X4, Port Co purchased 75% of the equity of Alfred Co for $650,000. The consideration was 35,000 $1 equity shares in Port Co with a fair value of $650,000.

Noted below are extracts from the draft statements of profit or loss for Port Co and its subsidiary Alfred Co for the year ending 31 December 20X4 along with the draft statements of financial position as at 31 December 20X4.

The profits of Alfred Co have been earned evenly throughout the year.

DRAFT STATEMENTS OF PROFIT OR LOSS FOR THE YEAR ENDING 31 DECEMBER 20X4 (extract)

	Port Co $'000	Alfred Co $'000
Gross profit	364	240
Profit for the year	330	96

DRAFT STATEMENTS OF FINANCIAL POSITION AS AT 31 DECEMBER 20X4 (extracts)

	Port $'000	Alfred $'000
Equity		
$1 Equity shares	200	100
Share premium	500	85
Retained earnings	2,900	331
Revaluation surplus	30	–
	3,630	516

Port Co has not accounted for the issue of its own shares or for the acquisition of the investment in Alfred Co.

292 **Using the drag and drop options below, show the balances on the share capital and share premium accounts at 31 December 20X4.**

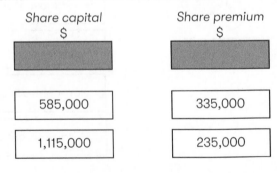

293   What are the net assets of Alfred Co at acquisition?

$ [   ]

294   The accountant of Port Co is finalising the consolidated financial statements. Which **TWO** of the following statements are true regarding consolidated financial statements?

☐   The non-controlling interest share of profit is part of the consolidated statement of profit or loss

☐   Goodwill on acquisition should be amortised over a period not exceeding 20 years

☐   If a subsidiary is acquired during the year, its results are apportioned over the year of acquisition

☐   Only the group share of the subsidiary's non-current assets is shown in the statement of financial position

295   What is the amount of group gross profit for the year ended 31 December 20X4?

$ [   ]

296   What is group retained earnings at 31 December 20X4?

O $2,912,000

O $2,916,000

O $2,972,000

O $2,996,000

(10 marks)

Polestar Co case

18 mins

The following scenario relates to questions 297–301.

On 1 April 20X3, Polestar Co acquired 75% of the 12 million 50 cent equity shares of Southstar Co. Polestar Co made an immediate cash payment of $1.50 per share. The statements of profit or loss for the year ended 30 September 20X3 show revenue for Polestar Co and Southstar Co as $110 million and $66 million respectively. Revenue accrued evenly over the year.

Additional information:

(i)   At the date of acquisition, the fair values of Southstar Co's assets were equal to their carrying amounts with the exception of right-of-use property held under a lease agreement. This had a fair value of $2 million above its carrying amount and a remaining lease term of ten years at that date. All depreciation is included in cost of sales.

(ii)   Contingent consideration was estimated to be $1.8 million at 1 April 20X3, but by 30 September 20X3 due to continuing losses, its value was estimated at only $1.5 million. The contingent consideration has not been recorded by Polestar Co and the directors expect the acquisition to be a bargain purchase.

(iii) Polestar sold materials at their cost of $4 million to Southstar Co in June 20X3. Southstar Co processed all of these materials at an additional cost of $1.4 million and sold them back to Polestar Co in August 20X3 for $9 million. At 30 September 20X3 Polestar Co had $1.5 million of these goods still in inventory. There were no other intragroup sales.

(iv)   Polestar Co's policy is to value the non-controlling interest at fair value at the date of acquisition. Southstar Co's share price of $1.20 per share at that date can be deemed to be representative of the fair value of the shares held by the non-controlling interest. The retained earnings of Southstar at the acquisition date were $14.3 million.

297   **What was the fair value of Southstar Co's net assets at the acquisition date? Submit your answer to one decimal place.**

$ [   ] million

---

298   **What is consolidated revenue for the year ended 30 September 20X3?**

- ○ $130 million
- ○ $143 million
- ○ $163 million
- ○ $156 million

---

299   Due to lower than expected profits of the acquired company, Southstar Co, the estimated value of the contingent consideration has fallen from $1.8 million to $1.5 million.

Using the drag and drop options below, show how this be accounted for in Polestar Co.

Account

Debit	[ ]	Goodwill
Credit	[ ]	Liability
		Profit or loss

---

300   **What is the amount of the adjustment to profit attributable to the non-controlling interest in respect of unrealised profit?**

$ [   ]

---

301   **Polestar Co measures the non-controlling interest in Southstar Co at fair value. Which of the following applies when non-controlling interest is measured at fair value?**

- ○   The non-controlling interest will be allocated its share of any negative goodwill
- ○   The non-controlling interest will be allocated the whole of the pre-acquisition profits
- ○   The non-controlling interest will be allocated its share of any goodwill impairment
- ○   If the subsidiary's share price falls, the non-controlling interest will be adjusted

(10 marks)

Plateau Co case

The following information relates to questions 302–306.

On 1 October 20X6, Plateau Co acquired the following non-current investments:

- Three million equity shares in Savannah Co by an exchange of one share in Plateau Co for every two shares in Savannah Co plus $1.25 per acquired Savannah Co share in cash. The market price of each Plateau Co share at the date of acquisition was $6 and the market price of each Savannah Co share at the date of acquisition was $3.25.

- 30% of the equity shares of Axle Co at a cost of $7.50 per share in cash.

Only the cash consideration of the above investments has been recorded by Plateau Co.

Extracts from the summarised draft statements of financial position of the three companies at 30 September 20X7 are:

	Plateau Co $'000	Savannah Co $'000	Axle Co $'000
Equity shares of $1 each	10,000	4,000	4,000
Retained earnings			
– at 30 September 20X6	16,000	6,000	11,000
– for year ended 30 September 20X7	9,250	2,900	5,000
	35,250	12,900	20,000

The following information is relevant:

(i) At the date of acquisition Savannah Co had five years remaining of an agreement to supply goods to one of its major customers. The agreement has been consistently renewed when it expires. The directors of Plateau Co estimate that the value of this customer-based contract has a fair value of $1 million and an indefinite life and has not suffered any impairment.

(ii) During the year ended 30 September 20X7 Savannah Co sold goods to Plateau Co for $2.7 million. Savannah Co had marked up these goods by 50% on cost. Plateau Co had a third of the goods still in its inventory at 30 September 20X7. There were no intragroup payables/receivables at 30 September 20X7.

(iii) It is the group policy to value non-controlling interest at acquisition at full (or fair) value. For this purpose the share price of Savannah Co at the acquisition date should be used.

302 **What is the total of the consideration paid by Plateau Co for Savannah Co?**

- ○ $3,750,000
- ○ $9,750,000
- ○ $12,750,000
- ○ $21,750,000

---

303 **How should the customer contract in note (i) be accounted for?**

- ○ Should not be recognised as item is internally generated
- ○ Group share of 75% should be recognised and not amortised
- ○ Should be recognised at $1 million and not amortised
- ○ Should be recognised at $1 million and amortised over five years

---

304 **What amount will be shown as non-controlling interest in the consolidated statement of financial position at 30 September 20X7?**

○ $3,900,000

○ $3,250,000

○ $3,225,000

○ $3,975,000

---

305 **What amount will be shown in the consolidated statement of financial position at 30 September 20X7 in respect of the investment in Axle Co?**

$ [   ]

---

306 Plateau Co is negotiating a contract to supply goods to Axle Co in the coming year (ended 30 September 20X8) at 20% profit.

How will the unrealised profit on the sale of these goods be eliminated from the consolidated financial statements for the year ended 30 September 20X8? Select your answers from the drag and drop options provided.

Account

| Debit | | Group inventory |

| Credit | | Investment in associate |

Share of profit of associate

Cost of sales

(10 marks)

Pinto Co case   **18 mins**

The following scenario relates to questions 307–311.

Pinto Co is a publicly listed company. The following financial statements of Pinto Co are available:

STATEMENT OF PROFIT OR LOSS AND OTHER COMPREHENSIVE INCOME FOR YEAR ENDED 31 MARCH 20X8 (extract)

	$'000
Profit before tax	440
Income tax expense	(160)
Profit for the year	280
Other comprehensive income	
Gains on property revaluation	100
Total comprehensive income	380

STATEMENTS OF FINANCIAL POSITION (extracts) AS AT

	31 March 20X8		31 March 20X7	
	$'000	$'000	$'000	$'000
Non-current assets (note (i))				
Property, plant and equipment		2,880		1,860
Investment property		420		400
		3,300		2,260
Equity				
Retained earnings		990		860
Non-current liabilities				
Deferred tax	50	50	30	430
Current liabilities				
Trade payables	1,610		1,270	
Current tax payable	150		–	

The following supporting information is available:

(i) An item of plant with a carrying amount of $240,000 was sold at a loss of $90,000 during the year. Depreciation of $280,000 was charged (to cost of sales) for property, plant and equipment in the year ended 31 March 20X8.

(ii) Pinto Co uses the fair value model in IAS 40 *Investment Property*. Pinto Co sold investment property for $160,000 on 1 February 20X8. Its fair value at 1 April 20X7 was $140,000. Other movements in the carrying amount of investment property were due to fair value adjustments.

You are preparing a statement of cash flows for Pinto Co for the year to 31 March 20X8.

307 **What is the amount of tax that Pinto Co either received or paid during the year?**

○ $60,000 paid

○ $60,000 received

○ $10,000 paid

○ $10,000 received

---

308 **What is the net cash used in investing activities?**

$ ☐

---

309 **What was the amount of the dividend paid in the year?**

○ $150,000

○ $250,000

○ $50,000

○ $310,000

BPP
LEARNING
MEDIA

310 Under which **TWO** classification(s) can dividends paid be shown in the statement of cash flows?

☐ Investing activities

☐ Financing activities

☐ Operating activities

☐ Movement in payables

311 Which of the following items will **NOT** be adjusted against Pinto Co's profit before tax in arriving at net cash from operating activities?

○ The increase in trade payables

○ The proceeds from sale of plant

○ The increase in the warranty provision

○ The investment income

(10 marks)

Woolf Co case   18 mins

The following scenario relates to questions 312–316.

The following extracts are from the draft financial statements of Woolf Co for the year ended 31 December 20X7:

	31 Dec 20X6 $'000	31 Dec 20X7 $'000
Current liabilities		
Government grants	400	600
Lease liabilities	800	900
Non-current liabilities		
Government grants	900	1,400
Lease liabilities	1,700	2,000

	$000
Interest received	40
Profit before taxation	50

The following supporting information is available:

(i) Woolf Co initially measured right-of-use assets acquired under lease contracts arranged during the year at $1,540,000. The amount was calculated as the initial measurement of the lease liability adjusted to take account of direct costs incurred of $40,000.

(ii) Woolf Co purchased a factory during the year which qualified the company to receive government grants of $950,000, which was included within liabilities on receipt. Total depreciation recognised in profit before taxation was $2,200,000.

(iii) The net movement in working capital balances resulted in an outflow of $100,000 over the course of the year.

312 Using the pull-down list provided, select the correct amount paid in respect of lease liabilities for the year ended 31 December 20X7

[_____ ▼]

Pull-down list:

$400,000
$1,100,000
$1,140,000
$1,900,000

---

313 Insofar as the information allows, what is the cash from operations figure for inclusion in the statement of cash flows for Woolf Co at 31 December 20X7?

○ Cash inflow of $1,860,000

○ Cash inflow of $2,110,000

○ Cash inflow of $2,360,000

○ Cash inflow of $3,060,000

---

314 Which of the following statements provides a plausible reason for the movement in the working capital balances of Woolf Co during the year?

(i) A decrease in inventories due to a successful year end warehouse sale

(ii) A decrease in trade receivables due to the recruitment of an experienced credit controller

(iii) A decrease in trade payables due to Woolf Co seeking prompt payment discounts instead of utilising the full credit period terms

○ Option (i) only

○ Option (ii) only

○ Option (i) and (ii)

○ Option (iii) only

---

315 Which of the following cash flows would NOT be included under cash flows from financing activities?

○ Cash proceeds from issuing ordinary share capital

○ Cash proceeds from repayments of lease liabilities

○ Cash proceeds from the sale of a factory

○ Cash payments from the issue of debentures by the company

BPP
LEARNING
MEDIA

316 IAS 20 *Government Grants and Disclosure of Government Assistance* allows two choices for the presentation of government grants relating to assets.

Which of the following accounting treatments would be valid options for Woolf Co to adopt in respect of the grant received for the factory unit?

(i)   Recognise the income from the grant as deferred income

(ii)   Deduct the grant in arriving at the carrying amount of the asset acquired

(iii)   Present the whole grant as a separate credit in the statement of profit or loss within 'other income'

O   Option (i) only

O   Option (ii) only

O   Options (i) and (ii)

O   Option (iii)

(10 marks)

Section C

317 Pedantic Co (Dec 2008 amended)   36 mins

On 1 April 20X8, Pedantic Co acquired 60% of the equity share capital of Sophistic Co in a share exchange of two shares in Pedantic Co for three shares in Sophistic Co. At that date the retained earnings of Sophistic Co were $5 million. The issue of shares has not yet been recorded by Pedantic Co. At the date of acquisition shares in Pedantic Co had a market value of $6 each. Below are the summarised draft statements of financial position of both companies.

STATEMENTS OF FINANCIAL POSITION AS AT 30 SEPTEMBER 20X8

	Pedantic Co $'000	Sophistic Co $'000
Assets		
Non-current assets		
Property, plant and equipment	40,600	12,600
Current assets	16,000	6,600
Total assets	56,600	19,200
Equity and liabilities		
Equity shares of $1 each	10,000	4,000
Retained earnings	35,400	6,500
	45,400	10,500
Non-current liabilities		
10% loan notes	3,000	4,000
Current liabilities	8,200	4,700
Total equity and liabilities	56,600	19,200

The following information is relevant:

(i)   At the date of acquisition, the fair values of Sophistic's assets were equal to their carrying amounts with the exception of an item of plant, which had a fair value of $2 million in excess of its carrying amount. It had a remaining life of five years at that date (straight-line depreciation is used). Sophistic Co has not adjusted the carrying amount of its plant as a result of the fair value exercise.

(ii)   Sales from Sophistic Co to Pedantic Co in the post-acquisition period were $8 million. Sophistic Co applied a mark-up on cost of 40% on these sales. Pedantic Co had sold $5.2 million (at cost to Pedantic Co) of these goods by 30 September 20X8.

(iii)   Sophistic Co's trade receivables at 30 September 20X8 include $600,000 due from Pedantic Co which did not agree with Pedantic Co's corresponding trade payable. This was due to cash in transit of $200,000 from Pedantic Co to Sophistic Co. Both companies have positive bank balances.

(iv)   Pedantic Co has a policy of accounting for any non-controlling interest at full fair value. The fair value of the non-controlling interest in Sophistic Co at the date of acquisition was estimated to be $5.9 million. Consolidated goodwill was not impaired at 30 September 20X8.

Required

(a)   Prepare the consolidated statement of financial position for Pedantic Co as at 30 September 20X8.   (16 marks)

(b)   Pedantic Co has been approached by a potential new customer, Trilby Co, to supply it with a substantial quantity of goods on three-month credit terms. Pedantic Co is concerned at the risk that such a large order represents in the current difficult economic climate, especially as Pedantic Co's normal credit terms are only one month's credit. To support its application for credit, Trilby has sent Pedantic Co a copy of Tradhat Co's most recent audited consolidated financial statements. Trilby Co is a wholly owned subsidiary within the Tradhat Co group. Tradhat Co's consolidated financial statements show a strong statement of financial position including healthy liquidity ratios.

Comment on the importance that Pedantic Co should attach to Tradhat Co's consolidated financial statements when deciding on whether to grant credit terms to Trilby Co.

(4 marks)

(Total = 20 marks)

318 Gold Co (March/June 2021)   36 mins

On 1 January 20X2, Gold Co acquired 90% of the 16 million $1 equity share capital of Silver Co. Gold Co issued three new shares in exchange for every five shares it acquired in Silver Co. Additionally Gold Co will pay further consideration on 31 December 20X2 of $2.42 per share acquired. Gold Co's cost of capital is 10% per annum and the discount factor at 10% for one year is 0.9091. At the date of acquisition, shares in Gold Co and Silver Co had fair values of $8.00 and $3.50 respectively.

Statement of profit or loss for the year ended 30 September 20X2:

	Gold	Silver
	$'000	$'000
Revenue	103,360	60,800
Cost of sales	(81,920)	(41,600)
Gross profit	21,440	19,200
Distribution costs	(2,560)	(2,980)
Administrative expenses	(6,080)	(3,740)
Investment income	800	–
Finance costs	(672)	–
Profit before tax	12,928	12,480
Income tax expense	(4,480)	(2,560)
Profit for the year	8,448	9,920

The following information is relevant:

(1)   At 1 October 20X1, the retained earnings of Silver Co were $56 million.

(2)   At the date of acquisition, the fair value of Silver Co's assets were equal to their carrying amounts with the exception of two items:

- An item of plant had a fair value of $2.6 million above its carrying amount. The remaining life of the plant at the date of acquisition was three years. Depreciation is charged to cost of sales.

- Silver Co had a contingent liability which Gold Co estimated to have a fair value of $850,000. This has not changed as at 30 September 20X2.

Silver Co has not incorporated these fair value changes into its financial statements.

(3)   Gold Co's policy is to value the non-controlling interest at fair value at the date of acquisition. For this purpose, Silver Co's share price at that date can be deemed to be representative of the fair value of the shares held by the non-controlling interest.

(4)   Sales from Gold Co to Silver Co in the post-acquisition period had consistently been $600,000 per month. Gold Co made a mark-up on cost of 25% on these sales. Silver Co had $1.2 million of these goods in inventory as at 30 September 20X2.

(5)   Gold Co's investment income is a dividend received from its investment in a 40% owned associate which it has held for several years. The associate made a profit of $3 million for the year ended 30 September 20X2.

(6)   On 1 October 20X1 Gold Co issued 100,000 $100 6% convertible loan notes at par value, with interest payable annually in arrears over a five-year term. The equivalent rate for non-convertible loan notes was 8%. Gold Co has recorded the loan notes as a liability at par value and charged the annual 6% interest to finance costs.

Discount factors in year 5:	Annuity factors for 5 years:
6% 0.747	6% 4.212
8% 0.681	8% 3.993

(7)   At 30 September 20X2 no impairment to goodwill is required.

(8)   Profits accrue evenly throughout the year unless otherwise stated.

Required

(a)   Calculate the goodwill arising on the acquisition of Silver Co.   **(6 marks)**

(b)   Prepare the consolidated statement of profit or loss for Gold Co for the year ended 30 September 20X2.

Note. All workings should be done to the nearest $'000.

(14 marks)

(Total = 20 marks)

319 Paradigm Co (Dec 2011 amended)   36 mins

On 1 October 20X2, Paradigm Co acquired 75% of Strata Co's equity shares by means of a share exchange of two new shares in Paradigm Co for every five acquired shares in Strata Co. In addition, Paradigm Co issued to the shareholders of Strata Co a $100 10% loan note for every 1,000 shares it acquired in Strata Co. Paradigm Co has not recorded any of the purchase consideration, although it does have other 10% loan notes already in issue.

The market value of Paradigm Co's shares at 1 October 20X2 was $2 each.

The summarised statements of financial position of the two companies at 31 March 20X3 are:

	Paradigm Co $'000	Strata Co $'000
ASSETS		
Non-current assets		
Property, plant and equipment	47,400	25,500
Financial asset: equity investments (note (i))	7,500	3,200
	54,900	28,700
Current assets		
Inventories (note (ii))	17,400	8,400
Trade receivables (note (iii))	14,800	9,000
Bank	5,100	–
Total assets	92,200	46,100
EQUITY AND LIABILITIES		
Equity		
Equity shares of $1 each	40,000	20,000
Retained earnings/(losses) – at 1 April 20X2	19,200	(4,000)
– for year ended 31 March 20X3	7,400	8,000
	66,600	24,000
Non-current liabilities		
10% loan notes	8,000	–

	Paradigm Co $'000	Strata Co $'000
Current liabilities		
Trade payables (note (iii))	17,600	13,000
Bank overdraft	–	9,100
Total equity and liabilities	92,200	46,100

The following information is relevant:

(i) At the date of acquisition, Strata Co produced a draft statement of profit or loss which showed it had made a net loss for the year of $2 million at that date. Paradigm Co accepted this figure as the basis for calculating the pre- and post-acquisition split of Strata Co's profit for the year ended 31 March 20X3.

Also at the date of acquisition, Paradigm Co conducted a fair value exercise on Strata Co's net assets which were equal to their carrying amounts (including Strata Co's financial asset equity investments) with the exception of an item of plant which had a fair value of $3 million below its carrying amount. The plant had a remaining estimated useful life of three years at 1 October 20X2.

Paradigm Co's policy is to value the non-controlling interest at fair value at the date of acquisition. For this purpose, a share price for Strata Co of $1.20 each is representative of the fair value of the shares held by the non-controlling interest.

(ii) Each month since acquisition, Paradigm Co's sales to Strata Co were consistently $4.6 million. Paradigm Co had marked these up by 15% on cost. Strata Co had one month's supply ($4.6 million) of these goods in inventory at 31 March 20X3. Paradigm Co's normal mark-up (to third party customers) is 40%.

(iii) Strata Co's current account balance with Paradigm Co at 31 March 20X3 was $2.8 million, which did not agree with Paradigm Co's equivalent receivable due to a payment of $900,000 made by Strata Co on 28 March 20X3, which was not received by Paradigm Co until 3 April 20X3.

(iv) The financial asset equity investments of Paradigm Co and Strata Co are carried at their fair values as at 1 April 20X2. As at 31 March 20X3, these had fair values of $7.1 million and $3.9 million respectively.

(v) There were no impairment losses within the group during the year ended 31 March 20X3.

Required

Prepare the consolidated statement of financial position for Paradigm Co as at 31 March 20X3.

(20 marks)

320 Boo Co and Goose Co   **36 mins**

Boo Co acquired 80% of Goose Co's equity shares for $300,000 on 1 January 20X8. At the date of acquisition Goose Co had retained earnings of $190,000.

On 31 December 20X8 Boo Co despatched goods which cost $80,000 to Goose Co, at an invoiced cost of $100,000. Goose Co received the goods on 2 January 20X9 and recorded the transaction then. The two companies' draft financial statements as at 31 December 20X8 are shown below.

The fair value of the non-controlling interest in Goose Co at the date of acquisition was $60,000.

STATEMENTS OF PROFIT OR LOSS AND OTHER COMPREHENSIVE INCOME FOR THE YEAR ENDED 31 DECEMBER 20X8

	Boo Co $'000	Goose Co $'000
Revenue	5,000	1,000
Cost of sales	2,900	600
Gross profit	2,100	400
Other expenses	1,700	320
Profit before tax	400	80
Income tax expense	130	30
Profit for the year	270	50
Other comprehensive income:		
Gain on revaluation of property	20	–
Total comprehensive income for the year	290	50

STATEMENTS OF FINANCIAL POSITION AT 31 DECEMBER 20X8

	$'000	$'000
Assets		
Non-current assets		
Property, plant and equipment	1,940	200
Investment in Goose Co	300	–
	2,240	200
Current assets		
Inventories	500	120
Trade receivables	650	40
Cash and cash equivalents	170	35
	1,320	195
Total assets	3,560	395
Equity and liabilities		
Equity		
Share capital	2,000	100
Retained earnings	500	240
Revaluation surplus	20	–
	2,520	340
Current liabilities		
Trade payables	910	30
Tax	130	25
	1,040	55
Total equity and liabilities	3,560	395

Required

Prepare a draft consolidated statement of profit or loss and other comprehensive income and statement of financial position. It is the group policy to value the non-controlling interest at acquisition at fair value.

(20 marks)

321 Viagem Co (Dec 2012 amended)   36 mins

On 1 January 20X2, Viagem Co acquired 90% of the equity share capital of Greca Co in a share exchange in which Viagem Co issued two new shares for every three shares it acquired in Greca Co. Additionally, on 31 December 20X2, Viagem Co will pay the shareholders of Greca Co $1.76 per share acquired. Viagem Co's cost of capital is 10% per annum.

At the date of acquisition, shares in Viagem Co and Greca Co had a market value of $6.50 and $2.50 each respectively.

STATEMENTS OF PROFIT OR LOSS FOR THE YEAR ENDED 30 SEPTEMBER 20X2

	Viagem Co	Greca Co
	$'000	$'000
Revenue	64,600	38,000
Cost of sales	(51,200)	(26,000)
Gross profit	13,400	12,000
Distribution costs	(1,600)	(1,800)
Administrative expenses	(3,800)	(2,400)
Investment income	500	–
Finance costs	(420)	–
Profit before tax	8,080	7,800
Income tax expense	(2,800)	(1,600)
Profit for the year	5,280	6,200
Equity as at 1 October 20X1		
Equity shares of $1 each	30,000	10,000
Retained earnings	54,000	35,000

The following information is relevant:

(i)   At the date of acquisition the fair values of Greca Co's assets were equal to their carrying amounts with the exception of two items:

   1   An item of plant had a fair value of $1.8 million above its carrying amount. The remaining life of the plant at the date of acquisition was three years. Depreciation is charged to cost of sales.

   2   Greca Co had a contingent liability which Viagem Co estimated to have a fair value of $450,000. This has not changed as at 30 September 20X2.

   Greca Co has not incorporated these fair value changes into its financial statements.

(ii)   Viagem Co's policy is to value the non-controlling interest at fair value at the date of acquisition. For this purpose, the market value of Greca Co's shares at that date can be deemed to be representative of the fair value of the shares held by the non-controlling interest.

(iii)   Sales from Viagem Co to Greca Co throughout the year ended 30 September 20X2 had consistently been $800,000 per month. Viagem Co made a mark-up on cost of 25% on these sales. Greca Co had $1.5 million of these goods in inventory as at 30 September 20X2.

(iv)   Viagem Co's investment income is a dividend received from its investment in a 40% owned associate which it has held for several years. The associate's profit for the year ended 30 September 20X2 was $2 million.

(v)   Although Greca Co has been profitable since its acquisition by Viagem Co, the market for Greca Co's products has been badly hit in recent months and Viagem Co has calculated that the goodwill has been impaired by $2 million as at 30 September 20X2.

Required

(a)   Calculate the goodwill arising on the acquisition of Greca Co.   (6 marks)

(b)   Prepare the consolidated statement of profit or loss for Viagem Co for the year ended 30 September 20X2.   (14 marks)

(Total = 20 marks)

322 McIlroy Co

At 1 October 20X7, McIlroy Co had an 80% holding in Spieth Co and a 65% holding in Clarke Co.

On 30 September 20X8, McIlroy sold all of its 65,000 $1 shares in Clarke Co for $582,000. No accounting entries have been made to record the disposal, other than to record the disposal proceeds in a suspense account. The disposal is the final part of a plan by McIlroy Co to dispose of Clarke Co's operations because it operates in separate business sector to the other companies in the group. Clarke Co's retained earnings at 1 October 20X7 were $286,000. McIlroy Co measures all non-controlling interests using the proportionate method.

The draft individual statements of profit or loss of the three companies are shown below:

DRAFT STATEMENTS OF PROFIT OR LOSS FOR THE YEAR ENDED 30 SEPTEMBER 20X8

	McIlroy Co $	Spieth Co $	Clarke Co $
Revenue	3,463,760	828,000	1,939,520
Cost of sales	(1,558,690)	(402,400)	(878,830)
Gross profit	1,905,070	425,600	1,060,690
Administrative expenses	(486,700)	(103,580)	(421,380)
Operating profit	1,418,370	322,020	639,310
Investment income	318,000)	–	–
Profit before tax	1,736,370	322,020	639,310
Income tax expense	(302,000)	(74,700)	(201,910)
Profit for the year	1,434,370	247,320	437,400

The draft individual statements of financial position at 30 September 20X8 for McIlroy Co and Spieth Co show:

	McIlroy Co $	Spieth Co $
Equity		
Ordinary share capital ($1)	500,000	200,000
Retained earnings	3,419,310	581,580

Additional information

(1)   McIlroy Co acquired its holding in Spieth Co on 1 October 20X4 when Spieth Co's retained earnings were $180,600. The fair values of Spieth Co's net assets at the date of acquisition were the same as their carrying amounts, with the exception of equipment which was estimated to have a fair value of $80,000 in excess of its carrying amount. The equipment had a remaining useful life of eight years at the date of acquisition. Depreciation is presented within administrative expenses. McIlroy Co had determined that the goodwill recognised on the acquisition of Spieth Co has been impaired by $30,000 in the current year.

(2)   McIlroy Co acquired its holding in Clarke Co several years ago for $268,000 when Clarke Co's retained earnings were $174,200. The fair values of Clarke Co's net assets at the date of acquisition were the same as their carrying amounts. The goodwill in Clarke Co was impaired by $25,000 in the year ended 30 September 20X7. No further impairment of the goodwill in Clarke Co is required in the current year.

(3)   During the year Spieth Co sold goods to McIlroy Co for $54,000 earning a gross margin of 20%. At the year-end McIlroy Co had half of these goods in inventory.

(4)   McIlroy paid a dividend of $2.10 per share in the current year. Spieth Co paid a dividend of $1.50 per share during the current year. Clarke Co did not pay a dividend.

(5)   Clarke Co is considered a discontinued operation of McIlroy Co in accordance with IFRS 5 *Non-current Assets Held for Sale and Discontinued Operations*.

Required

(a)   Explain why Clarke Co is considered a discontinued operation of McIlroy Co.

(3 marks)

(b)   Prepare the consolidated statement of profit of loss for McIlroy Co for the year ended 30 September 2014.
(13 marks)

(c)   Calculate the consolidated retained earnings balance as at 30 September 20X8. (4 marks)

(Total = 20 marks)

323 Plastik Co (Dec 2014 amended)   36 mins

On 1 January 20X4, Plastik Co acquired 80% of the equity share capital of Subtrak Co. The consideration was satisfied by a share exchange of two shares in Plastik Co for every three acquired shares in Subtrak Co. At the date of acquisition, shares in Plastik Co and Subtrak Co had a market value of $3 and $2.50 each respectively. Plastik Co will also pay cash consideration of 27.5 cents on 1 January 20X5 for each acquired share in Subtrak Co. Plastik Co has a cost of capital of 10% per annum. None of the consideration has been recorded by Plastik Co.

Below are the summarised draft financial statements of both companies.

STATEMENTS OF PROFIT OR LOSS AND OTHER COMPREHENSIVE INCOME FOR THE YEAR ENDED 30 SEPTEMBER 20X4

	Plastik Co	Subtrak Co
	$'000	$'000
Revenue	62,600	30,000
Cost of sales	(45,800)	(24,000)
Gross profit	16,800	6,000
Distribution costs	(2,000)	(1,200)
Administrative expenses	(3,500)	(1,800)
Finance costs	(200)	–
Profit before tax	11,100	3,000
Income tax expense	(3,100)	(1,000)
Profit for the year	8,000	2,000
Other comprehensive income:		
Gain on revaluation of property	1,500	–
Total comprehensive income	9,500	2,000

STATEMENTS OF FINANCIAL POSITION AS AT 30 SEPTEMBER 20X4

	Plastik Co	Subtrak Co
	$'000	$'000
ASSETS		
Non-current assets		
Property, plant and equipment	18,700	13,900
Current assets		
Inventories (note(ii))	4,300	1,200
Trade receivables	5,700	2,500
Cash and cash equivalents	–	300
	10,000	4,000
Total assets	28,700	17,900

	Plastik Co $'000	Subtrak Co $'000
EQUITY AND LIABILITIES		
Equity		
Equity shares of $1 each	10,000	9,000
Revaluation surplus (note(i))	2,000	–
Retained earnings	6,300	3,500
	18,300	12,500
Non-current liabilities		
10% loan notes (note(ii))	2,500	1,000
Current liabilities		
Trade payables (note(iv))	3,400	3,600
Bank	1,700	–
Current tax payable	2,800	800
	7,900	4,400
Total equity and liabilities	28,700	17,900

The following information is relevant:

(i)   At the date of acquisition, the fair values of Subtrak Co's assets and liabilities were equal to their carrying amounts with the exception of Subtrak Co's property which had a fair value of $4 million above its carrying amount. For consolidation purposes, this led to an increase in depreciation charges (in cost of sales) of $100,000 in the post-acquisition period to 30 September 20X4. Subtrak Co has not incorporated the fair value property increase into its entity financial statements.

The policy of the Plastik Co group is to revalue all properties to fair value at each year end. On 30 September 20X4, the increase in Plastik Co's property has already been recorded, however, a further increase of $600,000 in the value of Subtrak Co's property since its value at acquisition and 30 September 20X4 has not been recorded.

(ii)   Sales from Plastik Co to Subtrak Co throughout the year ended 30 September 20X4 had consistently been $300,000 per month. Plastik Co made a mark-up on cost of 25% on all these sales. $600,000 (at cost to Subtrak Co) of Subtrak Co's inventory at 30 September 20X4 had been supplied by Plastik Co in the post-acquisition period.

(iii) Plastik Co's policy is to value the non-controlling interest at fair value at the date of acquisition. For this purpose Subtrak Co's share price at that date can be deemed to be representative of the fair value of the shares held by the non-controlling interest.

(iv)   Due to recent adverse publicity concerning one of Subtrak Co's major product lines, the goodwill which arose on the acquisition of Subtrak Co has been impaired by $500,000 as at 30 September 20X4. Goodwill impairment should be treated as an administrative expense.

(v)   Assume, except where indicated otherwise, that all items of income and expenditure accrue evenly throughout the year.

Required

(a)   Calculate the goodwill arising on the acquisition of Subtrak Co on 1 January 20X4.

(4 marks)

(b)   Calculate the following amounts for presentation in the consolidated statement of financial position:

(i)   Group retained earnings
(ii)   Non-controlling interest

(6 marks)

(c)   Prepare the consolidated statement of profit or loss and other comprehensive income for Plastik Co for the year ended 30 September 20X4.

(10 marks)

(Total = 20 marks)

324 Laurel Co   36 mins

Laurel Co acquired 80% of the ordinary share capital of Hardy Co for $160 million and 40% of the ordinary share capital of Comic Co for $70 million on 1 January 20X7 when the retained earnings balances were $64 million in Hardy Co and $24 million in Comic Co. Laurel Co, Comic Co and Hardy Co are public limited companies.

The statements of financial position of the three companies at 31 December 20X9 are set out below:

	Laurel Co $m	Hardy Co $m	Comic Co $m
Non-current assets			
Property, plant and equipment	220	160	78
Investments	230	–	–
	450	160	78
Current assets			
Inventories	384	234	122
Trade receivables	275	166	67
Cash at bank	42	10	34
	701	410	223
	1,151	570	301
Equity			
Share capital – $1 ordinary shares	400	96	80
Share premium	16	3	–
Retained earnings	278	128	97
	694	227	177
Current liabilities			
Trade payables	457	343	124
	1,151	570	301

You are also given the following information:

1   On 30 November 20X9, Laurel Co sold some goods to Hardy Co for cash for $32 million. These goods had originally cost $22 million and none had been sold by the year end. On the same date Laurel Co also sold goods to Comic Co for cash for $22 million. These goods originally cost $10 million and Comic Co had sold half by the year end.

2   On 1 January 20X7, Hardy Co owned some items of equipment with a carrying amount of $45 million that had a fair value of $57 million. These assets were originally purchased by Hardy Co on 1 January 20X5 and are being depreciated over six years.

3   Group policy is to measure non-controlling interests at acquisition at fair value. The fair value of the non-controlling interests in Hardy Co on 1 January 20X7 was calculated as $39 million.

4   Cumulative impairment losses on recognised goodwill amounted to $15 million at 31 December 20X9. No impairment losses have been necessary to date relating to the investment in the associate.

Required

Prepare a consolidated statement of financial position for Laurel Co and its subsidiary as at 31 December 20X9, incorporating its associate in accordance with IAS 28 *Investments in Associates*.   (20 marks)

325 Paladin Co (Dec 2011 amended)   36 mins

On 1 October 20X0, Paladin Co secured a majority equity shareholding in Saracen Co on the following terms.

An immediate payment of $4 per share on 1 October 20X0; and a further amount deferred until 1 October 20X1 of $5.4 million.

The immediate payment has been recorded in Paladin Co's financial statements, but the deferred payment has not been recorded. Paladin Co's cost of capital is 8% per annum, giving the deferred payment a current cost at 1 October 20X0 of $5 million.

On 1 February 20X1, Paladin Co also acquired 25% of the equity shares of Augusta Co paying $10 million in cash.

The summarised statements of financial position of the three companies at 30 September 20X1 are:

	Paladin Co $'000	Saracen Co $'000	Augusta Co $'000
Assets			
Non-current assets			
Property, plant and equipment	40,000	31,000	30,000
Intangible assets	7,500	–	–
Investments – Saracen Co (8 million shares at $4 each)	32,000	–	–
– Augusta Co	10,000	–	–
	89,500	31,000	30,000
Current assets			
Inventories	11,200	8,400	10,000
Trade receivables	7,400	5,300	5,000
Cash and cash equivalents	3,400	–	2,000
Total assets	111,500	44,700	47,000

	Paladin Co $'000	Saracen Co $'000	Augusta Co $'000
Equity and liabilities			
Equity			
Equity shares of $1 each	50,000	10,000	10,000
Retained earnings – at 1 October 20X0	25,700	12,000	31,800
– for year ended 30 September 20X1	9,200	6,000	1,200
	84,900	28,000	43,000
Non-current liabilities			
Deferred tax	15,000	8,000	1,000
Current liabilities			
Bank	–	2,500	–
Trade payables	11,600	6,200	3,000
Total equity and liabilities	111,500	44,700	47,000

The following information is relevant:

(i)   Paladin Co's policy is to value the non-controlling interest at fair value at the date of acquisition. The directors of Paladin Co considered the fair value of the non-controlling interest in Saracen Co to be $7 million.

(ii)   At the date of acquisition, the fair values of Saracen Co's property, plant and equipment was equal to its carrying amount with the exception of Saracen Co's plant which had a fair value of $4 million above its carrying amount. At that date the plant had a remaining life of four years. Saracen Co uses straight-line depreciation for plant assuming a nil residual value.

Also at the date of acquisition, Paladin Co valued Saracen Co's customer relationships as a customer base intangible asset at fair value of $3 million. Saracen Co has not accounted for this asset. Trading relationships with Saracen Co's customers last on average for six years.

(iii) At 30 September 20X1, Saracen Co's inventory included goods bought from Paladin Co (at cost to Saracen Co) of $2.6 million. Paladin Co had marked up these goods by 30% on cost. Paladin Co's agreed current account balance owed by Saracen Co at 30 September 20X1 was $1.3 million.

(iv) Impairment tests were carried out on 30 September 20X1 which concluded that consolidated goodwill was not impaired, but, due to disappointing earnings, the value of the investment in Augusta Co was impaired by $2.5 million.

(v) Assume all profits accrue evenly through the year.

Required

Prepare the consolidated statement of financial position for Paladin Co as at 30 September 20X1.

(20 marks)

326 Dargent Co (Mar/Jun 2017)   36 mins

On 1 January 20X6, Dargent Co acquired 75% of Latree Co's equity shares by means of a share exchange of two shares in Dargent Co for every three Latree Co shares acquired. On that date, further consideration was also issued to the shareholders of Latree Co in the form of $100 8% loan notes for every 100 shares acquired in Latree Co. None of the purchase consideration, nor the outstanding interest on the loan notes at 31 March 20X6, has yet been recorded by Dargent Co. At the date of acquisition, the share price of Dargent Co and Latree Co is $3·20 and $1·80 respectively.

The summarised statements of financial position of the two companies as at 31 March 20X6 are:

	Dargent Co $'000	Latree Co $'000
Assets		
Non-current assets		
Property, plant and equipment (note (i))	75,200	31,500
Investment in Amery Co at 1 April 20X5 (note (iv))	4,500	–
	79,700	31,500
Current assets		
Inventory (note (iii))	19,400	18,800
Trade receivables (note (iii))	14,700	12,500
Bank	1,200	600
	35,300	31,900
Total assets	115,000	63,400
Equity and liabilities		
Equity		
Equity shares of $1 each	50,000	20,000
Retained earnings – at 1 April 20X5	20,000	19,000
– for year ended 31 March 20X6	16,000	8,000
	86,000	47,000
Non-current liabilities		
8% loan notes	5,000	–
Current liabilities (note (iii))	24,000	16,400
	29,000	16,400
Total equity and liabilities	115,000	63,400

The following information is relevant:

(i)   At the date of acquisition, the fair values of Latree Co's assets were equal to their carrying amounts. However, Latree Co operates a mine which requires to be decommissioned in five years' time. No provision has been made for these decommissioning costs by Latree Co. The present value (discounted at 8%) of the decommissioning is estimated at $4 million and will be paid five years from the date of acquisition (the end of the mine's life).

(ii)   Dargent Co's policy is to value the non-controlling interest at fair value at the date of acquisition. Latree Co's share price at that date can be deemed to be representative of the fair value of the shares held by the non-controlling interest.

(iii)   The inventory of Latree Co includes goods bought from Dargent Co for $2.1 million. Dargent Co applies a consistent mark-up on cost of 40% when arriving at its selling prices.

        On 28 March 20X6, Dargent Co despatched goods to Latree Co with a selling price of $700,000. These were not received by Latree Co until after the year end and so have not been included in the above inventory at 31 March 20X6.

        At 31 March 20X6, Dargent Co's records showed a receivable due from Latree Co of $3million, this differed to the equivalent payable in Latree Co's records due to the goods in transit.

        The intra-group reconciliation should be achieved by assuming that Latree Co had received the goods in transit before the year end.

(iv)   The investment in Amery Co represents 30% of its voting share capital and Dargent Co uses equity accounting to account for this investment. Amery Co's profit for the year ended 31 March 20X6 was $6 million and Amery Co paid total dividends during the year ended 31 March 20X6 of $2 million. Dargent Co has recorded its share of the dividend received from Amery Co in investment income (and cash).

(v)   All profits and losses accrued evenly throughout the year.

(vi)   There were no impairment losses within the group for the year ended 31 March 20X6.

Required

Prepare the consolidated statement of financial position for Dargent Co as at 31 March 20X6.

(20 marks)

327 Party Co (Sep/Dec 2017)   **36 mins**

The following are the draft statements of financial position of Party Co and Streamer Co as at 30 September 20X5:

	Party Co $'000	Streamer Co $'000
ASSETS		
Non-current assets		
Property, plant and equipment	392,000	84,000
Investments	120,000	–
	512,000	84,000
Current assets	94,700	44,650
Total assets	606,700	128,650
EQUITY AND LIABILITIES		
Equity		
Equity shares	190,000	60,000
Retained earnings	210,000	36,500
Revaluation surplus	41,400	4,000
	441,400	100,500

	Party Co $'000	Streamer Co $'000
Non-current liabilities		
Deferred consideration	28,000	–
Current liabilities	137,300	28,150
Total equity and liabilities	606,700	128,650

The following information is relevant:

(i)   On 1 October 20X4, Party Co acquired 80% of the share capital of Streamer Co. At this date the retained earnings of Streamer Co were $34 million and the revaluation surplus stood at $4 million. Party Co paid an initial cash amount of $92 million and agreed to pay the owners of Streamer Co a further $28 million on 1 October 20X6. The accountant has recorded the full amounts of both elements of the consideration in investments. Party Co has a cost of capital of 8%. The appropriate discount rate is 0.857.

(ii)   On 1 October 20X4, the fair values of Streamer Co's net assets were equal to their carrying amounts with the exception of some inventory which had cost $3 million but had a fair value of $3.6 million. On 30 September 20X5, 10% of these goods remained in the inventories of Streamer Co.

(iii) During the year, Party Co sold goods totalling $8 million to Streamer Co at a gross profit margin of 25%. At 30 September 20X5, Streamer Co still held $1 million of these goods in inventory. Party Co's normal margin (to third party customers) is 45%.

(iv)   The Party group uses the fair value method to value the non-controlling interest. At acquisition the non-controlling interest was valued at $15 million.

Required

(a)   Prepare the consolidated statement of financial position of the Party group as at 30 September 20X5.   **(15 marks)**

(b)   Party Co has a strategy of buying struggling businesses, reversing their decline and then selling them on at a profit within a short period of time. Party Co is hoping to do this with Streamer Co.

       As an adviser to a prospective purchaser of Streamer Co, explain any concerns you would raise about making an investment decision based on the information available in the Party Group's consolidated financial statements in comparison to that available in the individual financial statements of Streamer Co.   **(5 marks)**

                                                                                        (Total = 20 marks)

328 Fresco Co (Jun 2012 amended)   **36 mins**

The following trial balance relates to Fresco Co at 31 March 20X2:

	$'000	$'000
Equity shares of 50 cents each (note (i))		45,000
Share premium (note (i))		5,000
Retained earnings at 1 April 20X1		5,100
Freehold property (12 years) at cost (note (ii)))	48,000	
Plant and equipment – at cost (note (ii))	47,500	
Accumulated depreciation of freehold property at 1 April 20X1		16,000
Accumulated depreciation of plant and equipment at 1 April 20X1		33,500
Inventories at 31 March 20X2	25,200	
Trade receivables (note (iii))	28,500	
Cash and cash equivalents		1,400
Deferred tax (note (iv))		3,200
Trade payables		27,300
Revenue		350,000

	$'000	$'000
Cost of sales	298,700	
Lease payments (note (ii))	8,000	
Distribution costs	16,100	
Administrative expenses	26,900	
Bank interest	300	
Current tax (note (iv))	800	
Suspense account (note (i))		13,500
	500,000	500,000

The following notes are relevant:

(i) The suspense account represents the corresponding credit for cash received for a fully subscribed rights issue of equity shares made on 1 January 20X2. The terms of the share issue were one new share for every five held at a price of 75 cents each. The price of the company's equity shares immediately before the issue was $1.20 each.

(ii) Non-current assets:

Fresco Co decided to revalue its freehold property on 1 April 20X1. The directors accepted the report of an independent surveyor who valued the freehold property at $36 million on that date. Fresco Co has not yet recorded the revaluation. The remaining life of the freehold property is eight years at the date of the revaluation. Fresco Co makes an annual transfer to retained profits to reflect the realisation of the revaluation surplus. In Fresco Co's tax jurisdiction the revaluation does not give rise to a deferred tax liability.

On 1 April 20X1, Fresco Co acquired the right to use an item of plant under an agreement that meets the definition of a lease under IFRS 16 *Leases*. The rate of interest implicit in the lease agreement is 10% per annum. The lease payments in the trial balance represent an initial deposit of $2 million paid on 1 April 20X1 and the first annual rental of $6 million paid on 31 March 20X2. The lease agreement requires four further annual payments of $6 million on 31 March each year, starting 31 March 20X3. The present value of the future lease payments on inception of the lease is $23 million. The useful life of the plant is 6 years.

Plant and equipment (other than the leased plant) is depreciated at 20% per annum using the reducing balance method.

No depreciation has yet been charged on any non-current asset for the year ended 31 March 20X2. Depreciation is charged to cost of sales.

(iii) In March 20X2, Fresco Co's internal audit department discovered a fraud committed by the company's credit controller who did not return from a foreign business trip. The outcome of the fraud is that $4 million of the company's trade receivables have been stolen by the credit controller and are not recoverable. Of this amount, $1 million relates to the year ended 31 March 20X1 and the remainder to the current year. Fresco Co is not insured against this fraud.

(iv) Fresco Co's income tax calculation for the year ended 31 March 20X2 shows a tax refund of $2.4 million. The balance on current tax in the trial balance represents the under/over provision of the tax liability for the year ended 31 March 20X1. At 31 March 20X2, Fresco Co had taxable temporary differences of $12 million (requiring a deferred tax liability). The income tax rate of Fresco Co is 25%.

Required

(a) Prepare the statement of profit or loss and other comprehensive income for Fresco Co for the year ended 31 March 20X2. **(8 marks)**

(b) Prepare the statement of financial position of Fresco Co as at 31 March 20X2. **(12 marks)**

(Total = 20 marks)

329 Loudon Co (September/December 2020)   36 mins

Loudon Co has prepared a draft statement of profit or loss for the year ended 30 September 20X8 (before any adjustments required by notes (1) to (4) below). The draft profit has been added to retained earnings and the summarised trial balance of Loudon Co as at 30 September 20X8 is:

	$'000	$'000
Equity shares of $1 each		10,000
Retained earnings as at 30 September 20X8 (draft)		4,122
Office building at cost	20,000	
Factories cost 1 October 20X7 (note (2))	40,000	
Office building accumulated depreciation 1 October 20X7		4,000
Factories accumulated depreciation 1 October 20X7		11,100
Environmental provision 1 October 20X7 (note (3))		1,228
Current liabilities		34,500
Current assets	14,700	
Proceeds of 5% loan note (note (1))		5,000
Deferred Tax		1,500
Interest paid (note (1))	250	
Suspense account (note (2))		3,500
	74,950	74,950

The following notes are relevant:

(i) **Loan note**

A 5% loan note was issued on 1 October 20X7 at its face value of $5m. Direct costs of the issue amounted to $0.125m and were charged to profit or loss. The loan will be redeemed in five years' time at a substantial premium which gives an effective interest rate of 8%. The annual repayments of $250,000 ($5m at 5%) are paid on 30 September each year.

(ii) **Non-current assets**

Loudon Co acquired an office building for $20m on 1 October 20X2 with an estimated useful life of 25 years. Depreciation is charged on a pro-rata basis. On 1 April 20X8, the building was deemed to be impaired as its fair value was estimated to be $12m. At that date the estimated remaining life was revised to 12 years. Ignore the deferred tax consequences of this revaluation. Loudon Co had ten factories. On 1 October 20X7 Loudon Co sold one of its factories with a carrying amount of $3m (cost $5m and accumulated depreciation $2m) for $3.5m. The proceeds were credited to the suspense account.

No depreciation has yet been charged on any non-current asset for the year ended 30 September 20X8. The factories are depreciated at 15% per annum using the reducing balance method.

(iii) **Environmental provision**

Loudon Co has an obligation to clean-up environmental damage caused at one of its factory sites during 20X7. The clean-up is due to take place at the end of the factory's useful life. The liability has been accounted for appropriately and the balance at 1 October 20X7 represents the correct present value at that date. Loudon Co has a cost of capital of 5%.

(iv) **Deferred tax**

At 30 September 20X8, the tax written down value of property, plant and equipment was $25m. The income tax rate applicable to Loudon Co is 20%.

Required

(a) Prepare a schedule of adjustments required to the retained earnings of Loudon Co as at 30 September 20X8 as a result of the information in notes (i) to (iv). **(8 marks)**

(b) Prepare the statement of financial position of Loudon Co as at 30 September 20X8.

   Note. The notes to the statement of financial position are not required. All calculations should be rounded to the nearest $'000. **(12 marks)**

   (Total = 20 marks)

330 Dexon plc

36 mins

Below is the summarised draft statement of financial position of Dexon plc, a publicly listed company, as at 31 March 20X8.

	$'000	$'000
ASSETS		
Non-current assets		
Property at valuation (land $20m; buildings $165m (note (i))		185,000
Plant (note (i))		180,500
Investments (note (ii))		12,500
		378,000
Current assets		
Inventories	84,000	
Trade receivables (note (iii))	52,200	
Cash and cash equivalents	3,800	
		140,000
Total assets		518,000
EQUITY AND LIABILITIES		
Equity		
Ordinary shares of $1 each		250,000
Share premium		40,000
Revaluation surplus		18,000
Retained earnings – At 1 April 20X7	12,300	
– For the year ended 31 March 20X8	96,700	
		109,000
		417,000
Non-current liabilities		
Deferred tax – at 1 April 20X7 (note (iv))		19,200
Current liabilities		81,800
Total equity and liabilities		518,000

The following information is relevant:

(i) The non-current assets have not been depreciated for the year ended 31 March 20X8.

   Dexon plc has a policy of revaluing its land and buildings at the end of each accounting year. The values in the above statement of financial position are as at 1 April 20X7 when the buildings had a remaining life of 15 years. A qualified surveyor has valued the land and buildings at 31 March 20X8 at $180 million.

   Plant is depreciated at 20% on the reducing balance basis.

(ii) The investment is a fund whose value changes directly in proportion to a specified market index. The investment is measure at financial assets at fair value through profit and loss are held. At 1 April 20X7 the relevant index was 1,200 and at 31 March 20X8 it was 1,296.

(iii) In late March 20X8, the directors of Dexon plc discovered a material fraud perpetrated by the company's credit controller that had been continuing for some time. Investigations revealed that a total of $4 million of the trade receivables as shown in the statement of financial position at 31 March 20X8 had in fact been paid and the money had been stolen by the credit controller. An analysis revealed that $1.5 million had been stolen in the year to

31 March 20X7 with the rest being stolen in the current year. Dexon plc is not insured for this loss and it cannot be recovered from the credit controller, nor is it deductible for tax purposes.

(iv)   During the year, the company's taxable temporary differences increased by $10 million of which $6 million related to the revaluation of the property. The deferred tax relating to the remainder of the increase in the temporary differences should be taken to profit or loss. The applicable income tax rate is 20%.

(v)   The above figures do not include the estimated provision for income tax on the profit for the year ended 31 March 20X8. After allowing for any adjustments required in items (i) to (iii), the directors have estimated the provision at $11.4 million (this is in addition to the deferred tax effects of item (iv)).

(vi)   Dividends totalling $15.5 million were paid during the year.

Required

Taking into account any adjustments required by items (i) to (vi) above:

(a)   Prepare a statement showing the recalculation of Dexon plc's profit for the year ended 31 March 20X8.   (8 marks)

(b)   Redraft the statement of financial position of Dexon plc as at 31 March 20X8.   (12 marks)

Notes to the financial statements are not required.

(Total = 20 marks)

331 Xtol Co (Jun 2014 amended)   36 mins

The following trial balance relates to Xtol Co at 31 March 20X4:

	$'000	$'000
Revenue		490,000
Cost of sales	290,600	
Distribution costs	33,500	
Administrative expenses	36,800	
Loan note interest and dividends paid (notes(iv) and (v))	13,380	
Bank interest	900	
Freehold property at cost	100,000	
Plant and equipment at cost (note (ii))	155,500	
Accumulated amortisation/depreciation at 1 April 20X3:		
Right-of-use asset		25,000
Plant and equipment		43,500
Inventories at 31 March 20X4	61,000	
Trade receivables	63,000	
Trade payables		32,200
Bank		5,500
Equity shares of 25 cents each (note (iii))		56,000
Share premium		25,000
Retained earnings at 1 April 20X3		26,080
5% convertible loan note (note (iv))		50,000
Current tax (note (vi))	3,200	
Deferred tax (note (vi))		4,600
	757,880	757,880

The following notes are relevant:

(i)   Revenue includes an amount of $20 million for cash sales made through Xtol Co's retail outlets during the year on behalf of Francais. Xtol Co, acting as agent, is entitled to a commission of 10% of the selling price of these goods. By 31 March 20X4, Xtol Co had remitted to Francais $15 million (of the $20 million sales) and recorded this amount in cost of sales.

(ii)   Plant and equipment is depreciated at 12½% per annum on the reducing balance basis. All amortisation and depreciation of non-current assets is charged to cost of sales. Freehold property is depreciated over 20 years.

(iii)   On 1 August 20X3, Xtol Co made a fully subscribed rights issue of equity share capital based on two new shares at 60 cents each for every five shares held. The issue has been fully recorded in the trial balance figures.

(iv)   On 1 April 20X3, Xtol Co issued a 5% $50 million convertible loan note at par. Interest is payable annually in arrears on 31 March each year. The loan note is redeemable at par or convertible into equity shares at the option of the loan note holders on 31 March 20X6. The interest on an equivalent loan note without the conversion rights would be 8% per annum.

The present values of $1 receivable at the end of each year, based on discount rates of 5% and 8%, are:

		5%	8%
End of year	1	0.95	0.93
	2	0.91	0.86
	3	0.86	0.79

(v)   An equity dividend of 4 cents per share was paid on 30 May 20X3 and, after the rights issue, a further dividend of 2 cents per share was paid on 30 November 20X3.

(vi)   The balance on current tax represents the under/over provision of the tax liability for the year ended 31 March 20X3. A provision of $28 million is required for current tax for the year ended 31 March 20X4 and at this date the deferred tax liability was assessed at $8.3 million.

Required

(a)   Prepare the statement of profit or loss for Xtol Co for the year ended 31 March 20X4.

(8 marks)

(b)   Prepare the statement of financial position for Xtol Co for the year ended 31 March 20X4.

(12 marks)

(Total = 20 marks)

332 Atlas Co   36 mins

The following trial balance relates to Atlas Co at 31 March 20X3.

	$'000	$'000
Equity shares of 50 cents each		50,000
Share premium		20,000
Retained earnings at 1 April 20X2		11,200
Land and buildings – at cost (land $10 million) (note (i))	60,000	
Plant and equipment – at cost (note (i))	94,500	
Accumulated depreciation at 1 April 20X2: – buildings		20,000
– plant and equipment		24,500
Inventories at 31 March 20X3	43,700	
Trade receivables	42,200	
Bank		6,800
Deferred tax (note (ii))		6,200
Trade payables		35,100
Revenue		550,000
Cost of sales	411,500	
Distribution costs	21,500	
Administrative expenses	30,900	
Dividends paid	20,000	
Bank interest	700	
Current tax (note (ii))		1,200
	725,000	725,000

The following notes are relevant:

(i) Non-current assets:

On 1 April 20X2, the directors of Atlas Co decided that the financial statements would show an improved position if the land and buildings were revalued to market value. At that date, an independent valuer valued the land at $12 million and the buildings at $35 million and these valuations were accepted by the directors. The remaining life of the buildings at that date was 14 years. Atlas Co does not make a transfer to retained earnings for excess depreciation. Ignore deferred tax on the revaluation surplus.

Plant and equipment is depreciated at 20% per annum using the reducing balance method and time apportioned as appropriate. All depreciation is charged to cost of sales, but none has yet been charged on any non-current asset for the year ended 31 March 20X3.

(ii) Atlas Co estimates that an income tax provision of $27.2 million is required for the year ended 31 March 20X3 and at that date the liability to deferred tax is $9.4 million. The movement on deferred tax should be taken to profit or loss. The balance on current tax in the trial balance represents the under/over provision of the tax liability for the year ended 31 March 20X2.

Required

(a) Prepare the statement of profit or loss and other comprehensive income for Atlas Co for the year ended 31 March 20X3. **(8 marks)**

(b) Prepare the statement of financial position of Atlas Co as at 31 March 20X3.

(10 marks)

(c) Calculate basic earnings per share for the year ended 31 March 20X3. **(2 marks)**

(Total = 20 marks)

333 Moby Co (Dec 2013 amended) 36 mins

The following trial balance relates to Moby Co as at 30 September 20X3.

	$'000	$'000
Revenue		227,800
Cost of sales	164,500	
Distribution costs	13,500	
Administrative expenses	16,500	
Bank interest	900	
Dividend	2,000	
Lease rental paid on 30 September 20X3 (note (ii))	9,200	
Land ($12 million) and building ($48 million) at cost (note (ii))	60,000	
Owned plant and equipment at cost (note (ii))	65,700	
Right-of-use asset – leased plant at initial carrying amount (note (ii))	35,000	
Accumulated depreciation at 1 October 20X2:		
Building		10,000
Owned plant and equipment		17,700
Leased plant		7,000
Inventories at 30 September 20X3	26,600	
Trade receivables	38,500	
Balance on contract (note (i))	4,000	
Bank		5,300
Insurance provision (note (iii))		150
Deferred tax (note (iv))		8,000
Lease liability at 1 October 20X2 (note (ii))		29,300
Trade payables		21,300
Current tax (note (iv))		1,050
Equity shares of 20 cents each		45,800
Share premium		3,200
Loan note (note (v))		40,000
Retained earnings at 1 October 20X2	–	19,800
	436,400	436,400

The following notes are relevant:

(i)   The balance on the long-term contract is made up of the following items.

Cost incurred to date $8 million
Value of invoices issued (work certified) $10 million

The contract commenced on 1 October 20X2 and is for a fixed price of $25 million. Performance obligations are satisfied over time. Moby Co's policy is to recognise satisfaction of performance obligations on such contracts based on a stage of completion given by the work certified as a percentage of the contract price. Moby has invoiced work to the value of $4 million in the year and has not yet received any payments from the customer.

(ii)   Non-current assets:

Moby Co decided to revalue its land and buildings for the first time on 1 October 20X2. A qualified valuer determined the relevant revalued amounts to be $16 million for the land and $38.4 million for the building. The building's remaining life at the date of the revaluation was 16 years. This revaluation has not yet been reflected in the trial balance figures. Moby Co does not make a transfer from the revaluation surplus to retained earnings in respect of the realisation of the revaluation surplus. Deferred tax is applicable to the revaluation surplus at 25%.

The right-of-use asset relates to leased plant was acquired on 1 October 20X1 under a five-year agreement which meets the definition of a lease under IFRS 16 *Leases*. The carrying amount of the leased plant in the trial balance is equal to the present value of the future lease payments at the lease inception date. The rentals are $9.2 million per annum payable on 30 September each year. The rate of interest implicit in the lease is 10% per annum. The useful life of the leased plant was 7 years.

Owned plant and equipment is depreciated at 12.5% per annum using the reducing balance method.

No depreciation has yet been charged on any non-current asset for the year ended 30 September 20X3. All depreciation is charged to cost of sales.

(iii)   On 1 October 20X2, Moby Co received a renewal quote of $400,000 from the company's property insurer. The directors were surprised at how much it had increased and believed it would be less expensive for the company to 'self-insure'. Accordingly, they charged $400,000 to administrative expenses and credited the same amount to the insurance provision. During the year, the company incurred $250,000 of expenses relating to previously insured property damage which it has debited to the provision.

(iv)   A provision for income tax for the year ended 30 September 20X3 of $3.4 million is required. The balance on current tax represents the under/over provision of the tax liability for the year ended 30 September 20X2. At 30 September 20X3 the tax base of Moby Co's net assets was $24 million less than their carrying amounts. This does not include the effect of the revaluation in note 2 above. The income tax rate of Moby Co is 25%.

(v)   The $40 million loan note was issued at par on 1 October 20X2. No interest will be paid on the loan; however it will be redeemed on 30 September 20X5 for $53,240,000, which gives an effective finance cost of 10% per annum.

(vi)   A share issue was made on 31 December 20X2 of 4 million shares for $1 per share. It was correctly accounted for.

Required

(a)   Prepare the statement of profit or loss and other comprehensive income for Moby Co for the year ended 30 September 20X3.   **(13 marks)**

(b)   Prepare the statement of changes in equity for Moby Co for the year ended 30 September 20X3.   **(7 marks)**

(Total = 20 marks)

334 Haverford Co (Mar/Jun 2018)   36 mins

Below is the trial balance for Haverford Co at 31 December 20X7:

	$'000	$'000
Property – carrying amount 1 January 20X7 (note (iv))	18,000	
Ordinary shares $1 at 1 January 20X7 (note (iii))		20,000
Other components of equity (Share premium) at 1 January 20X7 (note (iii))		3,000
Revaluation surplus at 1 January 20X7 (note (iv))		800
Retained earnings at 1 January 20X7		6,270
Draft profit for the year ended 31 December 20X7		2,250
4% Convertible loan notes (note (i))		8,000
Dividends paid	3,620	
Cash received from contract customer (note (ii))		1,400
Cost incurred on contract to date (note (ii))	1,900	
Inventories (note (v))	4,310	
Trade receivables	5,510	
Cash	10,320	
Current liabilities		1,940
	43,660	43,660

The following notes are relevant:

(i)   On 1 January 20X7, Haverford Co issued 80,000 $100 4% convertible loan notes. The loan notes can be converted to equity shares on 31 December 20X9 or redeemed at par on the same date. An equivalent loan without the conversion rights would have required interest of 6%. Interest is payable annually in arrears on 31 December each year. The annual payment has been included in finance costs for the year. The present value of $1 receivable at the end of each year, based on discount rates of 4% and 6%, are:

	4%	6%
End of year 1	0.962	0.943
End of year 2	0.925	0.890
End of year 3	0.889	0.840

(ii)   During the year, Haverford Co entered into a contract to construct an asset for a customer. Control of the asset transfers to the customer as it is completed and Haverford Co does not have an alternative use for the asset. Haverford Co measures satisfaction of performance obligations over time by way of reference to certified work completed. The contract had a total price of $14 million. The costs to date of $1.9 million are included in the above trial balance. Costs to complete the contract are estimated at $7.1 million.

At 31 December 20X7, the contract is was independently certified as be 40% complete. To date, Haverford Co has invoiced $1.4 million to the customer and this is shown in the above trial balance.

(iii) Haverford Co made a 1 for 5 bonus issue on 31 December 20X7, which has not yet been recorded in the above trial balance. Haverford Co intends to utilise the share premium as far as possible in recording the bonus issue.

(iv)   Haverford Co's property had previously been revalued upwards, leading to the balance on the revaluation surplus at 1 January 20X7. The property had a remaining life of 25 years at 1 January 20X7.

At 31 December 20X7, the property was valued at $16 million.

No entries have yet been made to account for the current year's depreciation charge or the property valuation at 31 December 20X7. Haverford Co does not make an annual transfer from the revaluation surplus in respect of excess depreciation.

(v)   It has been discovered that inventory totalling $0.39 million had been omitted from the final inventory count in the above trial balance.

Required

(a)   Calculate the adjusted profit for Haverford Co for the year ended 31 December 20X7.

(6 marks)

(b)   Prepare the statement of changes in equity for Haverford Co for the year ended 31 December 20X7.

(6 marks)

(c)   Prepare the statement of financial position for Haverford Co as at 31 December 20X7.

(8 marks)

(Total = 20 marks)

335 Flamingo Co   36 mins

You are the assistant accountant at Flamingo Co responsible for preparing the statement of cash flows for the year ended 30 June 20X2.

The draft statement of cashflows has been extracted from the computerised accounting system, however there is a discrepancy between the cash and cash equivalents figure at 30 June 20X2 presented in the draft statement of cash flows and the cash and equivalents figure presented in the statement of financial position.

You have been provided with the following information:

EXTRACT FROM DRAFT STATEMENT OF CASH FLOWS FOR THE YEAR ENDED 30 JUNE 20X2

	$	$
Net cash from operating activities		1,697,785
Cash flows from investing activities		
Purchase of property, plant and equipment	(2,150,700)	
Net cash used in investing activities		(2,150,700)
Cash flows from financing activities		
Proceeds from issue of ordinary share capital	1,000,000	
Proceeds from issue of borrowings	300,000	
Net cash from financing activities		1,300,000
Net increase in cash and cash equivalents		847,085
Cash and cash equivalents at beginning of period		112,800
Cash and cash equivalents at end of period		959,885

EXTRACTS FROM THE STATEMENT OF FINANCIAL POSITION AS AT 30 JUNE 20X2

	20X2 $	20X1 $
Non-current assets		
Property, plant and equipment	7,979,100	5,828,400
Right of use assets	535,000	0
Current assets		
Cash and cash equivalents	346,885	112,800
Equity		
Ordinary share capital ($1 shares)	3,000,000	2,400,000
Share premium account	600,000	200,000
Retained earnings	2,522,905	1,917,560
Revaluation surplus	200,000	0
Non-current liabilities		
Lease obligations	446,000	0
Current liabilities		
Lease obligations	69,000	0

BPP
LEARNING
MEDIA

The statement of financial position extract above has been correctly prepared and does not need adjusting for the additional information below:

(1) A share issue at market price was made on 1 January 20X2. The statement of cash flows has been prepared assuming this was the only movement in share capital in the year, however a 1 for 6 bonus issue of ordinary shares was made out of retained earnings prior to the cash share issue.

(2) 'Purchase of property, plant and equipment' had been calculated by taking the movement between the opening and closing balances property, plant and equipment balances presented in the statement of financial position. Depreciation relating to property, plant and equipment of $260,000 was expensed to the statement of profit or loss in the year and the revaluation surplus in 20X2 relates to the revaluation of land. Depreciation has not been adjusted for in calculating net cash from operating activities. Flamingo Co disposed of property, plant and equipment which had a carrying amount of $782,000 for proceeds of $825,000 on 1 July 20X1. The profit on disposal has not been adjusted for in calculating net cash from operating activities.

(3) Flamingo Co entered into a lease agreement on 1 February 20X2. The right of use asset was initially measured correctly at $540,000 on commencement of the lease. Flamingo Co incurred expenses of $20,000 directly relating to the arrangement of the lease. The right of use asset was depreciated by $5,000 in the year which has not been adjusted for in calculating net cash from operating activities.

(4) The lease obligations relate solely to the right of use asset referred to in (3) above. Interest paid in respect of lease obligations has been correctly adjusted for in calculating net cash from operating activities.

(5) Flamingo Co reported a profit of $912,345 in the year.

Required

(a) Prepare a revised extract from Flamingo Co's statement of cash flows for the year ended 31 December 20X2. (14 marks)

(b) Explain whether the information in the statement of cash flows might be considered more useful than the information provided by the statement of profit or loss and the statement of financial position. (6 marks)
(Total = 20 marks)

336 Dickson Co   36 mins

Below are the statements of financial position of Dickson Co as at 31 March 20X8 and 31 March 20X7, together with the statement of profit or loss and other comprehensive income for the year ended 31 March 20X8.

	20X8 $'000	20X7 $'000
Non-current assets		
Property, plant and equipment	799	657
Right-of-use asset	126	80
Development expenditure	290	160
	1,215	897
Current assets		
Inventories	360	227
Trade receivables	274	324
Investments	143	46
Cash and cash equivalents	29	117
	806	714
Total assets	2,021	1,611

	20X8	20X7
	$'000	$'000
	$'000	$'000
Equity		
Share capital – $1 ordinary shares	500	400
Share premium	350	100
Revaluation surplus	160	60
Retained earnings	229	255
	1,239	815
Non-current liabilities		
6% debentures	150	100
Lease liabilities	100	80
Deferred tax	48	45
	298	225
Current liabilities		
Trade payables	274	352
Lease liabilities	17	12
Current tax	56	153
Debenture interest	5	–
Bank overdraft	132	54
	484	571
Total equity and liabilities	2,021	1,611

STATEMENT OF PROFIT OR LOSS AND OTHER COMPREHENSIVE INCOME

	$'000
Revenue	1,476
Cost of sales	(962)
Gross profit	514
Other expenses	(157)
Finance costs	(15)
Profit before tax	342
Income tax expense	(162)
Profit for the year	180
Other comprehensive income:	
Gain on revaluation of property, plant and equipment	100
Total comprehensive income for the year	280

Notes

1 During 20X8, amortisation of $60,000 was charged on development projects.

2 During 20X8, items of property, plant and equipment with a carrying amount of $103,000 were sold for $110,000. Profit on sale of these items was netted off against 'other expenses'.

   Depreciation charged in the year on property, plant and equipment totalled $47,000.

   Dickson Co acquired a new right-of-use asset which was initially measured equal to the initial amount of the lease liability of $56,000. Depreciation on right-of-use assets has been correctly calculated as $10,000 for the year. Lease payments are made in arrears on the last day of each accounting period.

3 During the year Dickson Co made a 1 for 8 bonus issue, capitalising its retained earnings, followed by a rights issue.

4 The current asset investments are government bonds and management has decided to classify them as cash equivalents.

5 The new debentures were issued on 1 April 20X7. Finance cost includes debenture interest and lease finance charges only.

6 Dickson Co has a net cash generated from operating activities of $40,000.

Required

(a)   Prepare an extract from the statement of cash flows for Dickson Co showing the net cash generated by or used from both investing activities and financing activities.   **(10 marks)**

(b)   Explain to the board of directors of Dickson Co what information is included in the statement of cash flows that cannot be obtained from reviewing the other primary financial statements.   **(3 marks)**

(c)   Discuss Dickson Co's performance for the year with reference to the profit for the year and the extract from the statement of cash flows prepared in (a).   **(7 marks)**

(Total = 20 marks)

Answers

Section A

Conceptual framework

1 The correct answer is: A present economic resource controlled by an entity as a result of past events. An economic resource is a right that has the potential to produce economic benefits

(*Conceptual Framework*, para.4.3–4.4).

2 The correct answer is: Carter has estimated the tax charge on its profits for the year just ended as $165,000

The licence payment could be avoided by ceasing manufacture.

The fall in value of the investment is a loss chargeable to profit or loss.

Planned expenditure does not constitute an obligation.

3 The correct answer is: The present value of the future cash flows obtainable from the continued use of the asset and its ultimate disposal.

4 The correct answer is: The underlying assumption is going concern.

5 The correct answer is: Consistency

Consistency is an important part of the qualitative characteristic of comparability, but it is not the same thing. Comparability of financial statements is aided by the consistency of policies and methods used, either between companies within the same industry or within the same company, between different years.

6 The correct answers are:

To assist preparers to develop consistent accounting policies when no IFRS Standard applies to a particular event.

To assist in determining the treatment of items not covered by an existing IFRS Standard.

It is not to be authoritative where a specific IFRS Standard conflicts with the *Conceptual Framework* as the Conceptual Framework will be overridden if there is a specific IFRS Standard. Whenever there is a conflict between an IFRS Standard and the *Conceptual Framework*, the IFRS Standard takes precedence. Nor is it to issue rules regarding the accounting treatment of elements in the financial statements, as the *Conceptual Framework* is a principles-based format, not a prescriptive, rules-based approach.

7 The correct answer is: (i) and (iv)

A secret formula for the manufacture of a best-selling sauce. The recipe is kept secure at the company premises and known only by the company directors.

A receivable from a customer which has been sold (factored) to a finance company. The finance company has full recourse to the company for any losses.

The receivable has been factored with recourse so should continue to be recognised as an asset. The company selling the receivable still retains control over that debt, not the factoring company.

8 The correct answer is: Neither 1 nor 2

The *Conceptual Framework* states that permitting alternative accounting treatments for the same economic phenomenon diminishes comparability (para.2.29) and it also states that comparability does not equal uniformity (para.2.27).

Regulatory framework

9   The correct answer is: Publication of an Exposure Draft

An Exposure Draft will be published following the review of Discussion Paper comments.

10 The correct answers are:

It would be easier for investors to compare the financial statements of companies with those of foreign competitors.

Cross-border listing would be facilitated.

Adopting IFRS Standards improves the comparability of the financial statements. Many territories now have either adopted or require listed companies to adopt IFRS Standards, this means a more consistent approach across the global listing exchanges, in theory, meaning that the company will not have to report in local GAAP removing one barrier to listing abroad if they are already adopting IFRS Standards.

Accountants and auditors may have **less** defence in case of litigation as they will not be able to demonstrate that they followed some precise rule, but will instead have to defend their application of judgement.

One potential downside of adopting IFRS Standards is that they are standardised and cannot be amended easily to reflect local industries. One way a country can do this is by converging their local national accounting standards with IFRS Standards, albeit with the ability to make amendments to reflect local industries.

11 The correct answers are:

A rules-based system will tend to give rise to a larger number of IFRS Standards than a principles-based system.

A principles-based system requires the exercise of more judgement in application than a rules-based system.

12 The correct answer is: In the early stages of the project, the IASB will consult with the Advisory Committee and IFRS Advisory Council to seek out the key issues.

The Advisory Committee and IFRS Advisory Council will review and decide upon the key issues prior to issuing a Discussion Paper which will seek out public comments. An Exposure Draft will pull together the key responses following the public comments and seek out additional clarification prior to any IFRS Standard being issued.

13 The correct answer is: It avoids the overstatement of profit which can arise during periods of inflation

Historical cost accounting does not avoid the overstatement of profit which arises during periods of inflation, which is why alternative models have been proposed.

14 The correct answer is: Value in use

Value in use is a current cost measurement basis for assets. Fulfilment value is the equivalent current cost measurement basis for liabilities.

15 The correct answer is: $320,000 Historical cost; $384,000 current cost

	Historical cost $'000	Current cost $'000
Cost/valuation	500	600
Depreciation ((500,000 × 90%) /5) × 2	(180)	
Depreciation ((600,000 × 90%) /5) × 2		(216)
Carrying amount	320	384

16 The correct answer is: The amount of consideration received to incur the liability, less transaction costs

The present value of the estimated cash flows needed to fulfil a liability.

Fulfilment value is the present value of the amount of cash, or other economic resources, that the entity expects to be obliged to transfer to settle the liability.

17 The correct answer is: It assists a user to assess the future prospects of the business

The others are benefits of historical cost accounting.

18 The correct answer is: Present value of future cash flows, less costs of disposal

Costs incurred at the time of acquisition is historical cost. Open market value of the asset is fair value. Open market value less the present value of the future cash outflows is not a measurement under the *Conceptual Framework*.

Section B

Lisbon Co case

19   The correct answer is: The accountant should classify, characterise and present the information clearly and precisely

      The *Conceptual Framework* requires information to be presented in a manner that is clear and understandable, but without omitting complex issues.

20   The correct answer is: Faithful representation.

      The substance of the transaction is that a sale and leaseback has taken place and the transaction should be accounted for as such rather than a sale being recognised.

21   The correct answer is: Relevance.

      The historical cost of the properties will be less relevant than their current value.

22   The correct answer is: The financial statements should be prepared on a different basis.

      The basis of valuation of assets will be affected.

23   The correct answer is: The financial statements for the prior period as shown at 31 March 20X6 should be restated using the weighted average basis

      This is a change of accounting policy so the information will be amended retrospectively. As such, the prior period financial statements should be restated.

Section A

Tangible non-current assets

24   The correct answer is: $6,950,000

	$'000
Land	1,200
Materials	2,400
Labour	3,000
Architect's fees	25
Surveyor's fees	15
Site overheads	300
Testing fire alarms	10
	6,950

Answer option A includes everything up to surveyor's fees but omits the site overheads and testing fire alarm costs.

Answer option C includes all costs including administrative overheads and business rates which are incorrect.

Answer option D wrongly includes the administrative overheads.

25   The correct answer is: $549,333

Weighted average capitalisation rate =

$(9\% \times 15 / 39) + (11\% \times 24 / 39) = 3.5\% + 6.8\% = 10.3\%$

		$
Borrowing costs =	$6m × 10.3% × 9/12	463,500
+	$2m × 10.3% × 5/12	85,833
		549,333

The second answer option uses the 9% interest rate instead of calculating the weight average cost of borrowing.

The third answer option does not pro-rate for 9 months and 5 months respectively.

The fourth answer option uses a simple average of 10% instead of the weighted average.

26   The correct answer is: $140,000

	$
Borrowing costs March – December ($2.4m × 8% × 10 / 12)	160,000
Less investment income ($1m × 6% × 4/12)	(20,000)
	140,000

27   The correct answer is: Both statements 1 and 2

Transfers should only be made when there is a change in use of the property. (IAS 40: para. 57)

Transfers from an IAS 40 investment property to an IAS 16 property must be made at the fair value of the investment property at the date of the transfer. (IAS 40: para. 60)

An entity should treat any difference at the transfer date from a capitalised property (treated under IAS 16) when transferred to an investment property as a revaluation under IAS 16. (IAS 40: para. 61)

BPP
LEARNING
MEDIA

28 The gain or loss arising from a change in the fair value of an investment property should be recognised in profit or loss not the revaluation surplus.

Following initial recognition, investment property can be held at either cost or fair value	True	
If an investment property is held at fair value, this must be applied to all of the entity's investment property	True	
An investment property is initially measured at cost, including transaction costs	True	
A gain or loss arising from a change in the fair value of an investment property should be recognised in the revaluation surplus		False

29 The correct answer is: $2,200,000

Weighted capitalisation rate =

(10% × 140 / 340) + (8% × 200 / 340) = 4.1% + 4.7% = 8.8%

$50 million × 8.8% × 6/ 12 = $2.2 million

The first option assumes the cheaper 8% borrowing rate.

The second option assumes a simple average of 9%.

The third option does not pro-rate for 6 months.

30 $37,250

	$'000
Machine ((500,000 – 20,000) / 10 × 9/12)	36,000
Safety guard ((25,000/5) × 3 / 12)	1,250
	37,250

31 $4,765

The machine has been owned for 2 years 3 months, so the remaining useful life at 31 March 20X9 was 12 years 9 months.

Prior to revaluation it was being depreciated at $4,000 pa (60,000 / 15), so the charge for the first three months of 20X9 was $1,000.

The machine will now be depreciated over the remaining 12 years 9 months = 153 months. So the charge for the remaining 9 months of 20X9 is $3,765 ((64,000 / 153) × 9).

So total depreciation for the year ended 31.12.X9 is (1,000 + 3,765) = $4,765

32 $203,000

Prior to 30 June 20X8, the building was classified as property, plant and equipment and was accounted for under IAS 16. When the building was let out to a third party, there was a change in usage and it was transferred to an investment property, and so is accounted for under IAS 40. IAS 40 requires that assets must be measured at fair value at the date of transfer ($950,000 in the question) and be accounted for as a revaluation gain, recognised as a revaluation surplus.

	$
Cost 1.1.X0	900,000
Depreciation to 30.6.X8 (900,000 × 8.5 / 50)	(153,000)
Carrying amount 30.6.X8	747,000
Revaluation surplus	203,000
Fair value 30.6.X8	950,000

The increase of ($1,200,000 – $950,000) = $250,000 arising between 30.6.X8 and 31.12.X8 will be credited to profit or loss in accordance with IAS 40.

Intangible non-current assets

33   The correct answer is: It has not been possible to reliably allocate costs to development of the product.

In order for capitalisation to be allowed it is not necessary for development to be completed, patents to be registered or sales contracts signed. However, an intangible asset can only be recognised if its cost can be reliably measured.

34   The correct answer is: $7,800,000

	$
Research costs	1,400,000
Expensed development Jan–Mar (800 × 3)	2,400,000
Depreciation on capitalised amount b/f (20m × 20%)	4,000,000
	7,800,000

The first option includes depreciation on the development costs capitalised in the current year. Note that no depreciation is charged on the new project as it is still in development.

The second option includes depreciation on the development costs capitalised in the current year and does not write off the research costs.

The fourth option does not include the depreciation costs.

35

A customer list built up over the last ten years of trading updated for the customer's current preferences		Ineligible
Specialised tooling for a new product developed by the business	Eligible	
A working version of a new machine that uses new technology used for testing of the prototype apparatus	Eligible	
The title heading, font and design of the front page of a major broadsheet newspaper		Ineligible

Per IAS 38, development costs allowable for capitalisation include 'the design, construction and operation of a pilot plant that is not of a scale economically feasible for commercial production' (the working version of the new machine) and 'the design of tools, jigs, moulds and dies involving new technology' (specialised tooling) (IAS 38: paras. 57–62). Mastheads (the heading across a newspaper) and customer lists cannot be recognised as the value is subjective (no money has been paid in exchange for the item) and cannot be measured reliably (IAS 38: paras. 48–50).

36   $12,500

	$'000
Recoverable amount – fair value less costs of disposal	15,000
Less depreciation 1.4.X9 – 30.9.X9 (15m / 3 × 6/12)	(2,500)
	12,500

37

Carrying amount of intangible asset at 30 September 20X5	Amount charged to profit/loss for period ending 30 September 20X5
$152,000	$88,000

Working

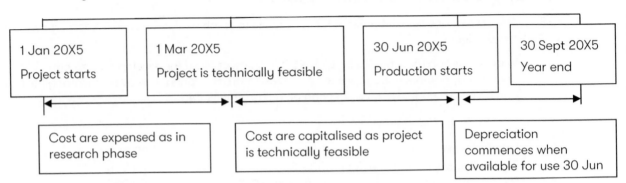

Capitalised as an intangible asset from1 March – 30 June 20X5 $40,000 × 4 = $160,000

Amortisation of asset from 1 June 20X5 $160,000/5 years × 3/12 = $8,000

Carrying amount of the asset at 30 September 20X5 = $160,000 – $8,000 = $152,000

Expenses for January and February 20X4 = 2 × $40,000 = $80,000

Amortisation expense for the period $8,000

Expenses taken to the statement of profit or loss = $80,000 + $8,000 = $88,000

Impairment of assets

38 The correct answer is: $594 (to the nearest '000)

	$'000
Total impairment (1,010 – 750)	260
Goodwill	(90)
Damaged plant	(40)
Balance to allocate	130

The remaining $130,000 will be allocated pro rata as follows:

	Building $'000	Plant $'000
	700	160
Impairment	(106)	(24)
	594	136

39 The **recoverable amount** of an asset of an asset is the higher of

| Fair value less costs of disposal | and | Value in use | under IAS 36 *Impairment*

of Assets.

40 $7,687

Fair value less costs of disposal (78,000 – 2,500) $75,500

Value in use:	$30,000 \times 1 / 1.08 = 27,778$
	$30,000 \times 1 / 1.08^2 = 25,720$
	$30,000 \times 1 / 1.08^3 = 23,815$
	$77,313

Recoverable amount is $77,313 and carrying amount is $85,000, so impairment is $7,687.

41 The correct answer is: An unusually significant fall in the market value of one or more assets.

An increase in the market interest rates used to calculate value in use of the assets.

The other options are internal indicators of impairment.

42 $350,000

	$
Fair value less costs of disposal (2.7m – 50,000)	2,650,000
Value in use	2,600,000
Carrying amount	3,000,000
Recoverable amount	2,650,000
Impairment loss	350,000

43 The correct answer is: $8 million

	$m	$m	$m
Goodwill	3	(3)	–
Patent	5	(3)	2
Property	10	(2)	8
Plant and equipment	15	(3)	12
Current assets	2	–	2
	35	(11)	24

The goodwill is written off, the patent is written down and the remaining $5m impairment is allocated pro rata to the property and the plant and equipment.

The second option does not allocate any of the impairment loss to the property.

The third option allocates the remaining $5m impairment equally to property and plant and equipment

The fourth option allocates all of the remaining impairment against property.

44 The correct answer is: $17,785

	$
Carrying amount (100,000 × 5/10)	50,000
Fair value less costs to sell	30,000
Value in use (8,500 × 3.79)	32,215

Recoverable amount is $32,215 and impairment loss = 50,000 − 32,215 = $17,785

The second option takes the recoverable amount to be the lower of the value in use and the fair value less costs to sell.

The third option takes the recoverable amount to be the lower of the value in use and the fair value less costs to sell and uses this as the amount of the impairment.

The fourth option assumes the recoverable amount to be the amount of impairment.

45 The correct answer is: $154,545

	Net assets prior to impairment $	Impairment $	Impaired net assets $
Property, plant and equipment	200,000	(45,455)	154,545
Goodwill	50,000	(50,000)	–
Product patent	20,000	(4,545)	15,455
Net current assets	30,000	–	30,000
	300,000	(100,000)	200,000

Goodwill is written off in full and the balance of the loss is pro-rated between PPE and the patent.

46

Advances in the technological environment in which an asset is employed has an adverse impact on its future use	Indicator of impairment	
An increase in interest rates which increases the discount rate an entity uses	Indicator of impairment	
The carrying amount of an entity's net assets is lower than the entity's number of shares in issue multiplied by its share price	Indicator of impairment	
The estimated net realisable value of inventory has been reduced due to fire damage although this value is greater than its carrying amount		Not an indicator of impairment

The estimated net realisable value of inventory that has been reduced due to fire damage but the value is greater than its carrying amount is **not** an indicator of impairment. If the NRV of inventory is **greater** than its carrying amount, then no impairment has arisen.

Section B

Plethora plc case

47    $314,000

Building transferred to investment property

	$'000
Original cost	600
Depreciation 1.1.X0 to 1.7.X9 ((600 / 50) × 9.5)	(114)
Carrying amount at 1.7.X9	486
Revaluation surplus	314
Fair value	800

48   The correct answer is: Credited to profit or loss

The increase in value in this case of $190,000 (740,000 – 550,000) will be credited to profit or loss in accordance with IAS 40.

49   The correct answer is: Recoverable amount

If the asset has been impaired, it must have been written down to its recoverable amount. This is the higher of fair value less costs of disposal and value in use.

50   The correct answer is: The reversal of impairment losses on revalued assets should be recognised in other comprehensive income.

An impairment loss can only be reversed if there is a change in the estimates used to determine the recoverable amount of the impaired assets.

Impairment losses in respect of goodwill cannot be subsequently reversed. Whilst IAS 36 does not apply to inventories, it does not scope out other current assets.

51   The correct answer is: $85,000

Impairment losses on assets, other than goodwill, can be reversed up to the maximum of what the asset would have been carried at had no impairment occurred.

Asset	Carrying amount at 31 December 20X8 before impairment	Impairment loss at 31 December 20X8	Carrying amount at 31 December 20X8 AFTER impairment	Carrying amount at 31 December 20X9 had no impairment occurred	Reversal of imp. Loss
	$'000	$'000	$'000	$'000	$'000
Building	900	100	800	875	75
Plant and equipment	300	20	280	290	10
Goodwill	40	40	Nil	40	Nil
Total					85

Linetti Co case

52   The correct answer is: $18.4m.

This is calculated as $10m + $0.5m + $1m + $6.6m less unused materials of $0.5m plus borrowing costs of $0.8m.

The second option does not include the borrowing costs which can be capitalised.

The third option includes the $0.5 million of unused materials.

The fourth option includes the unused materials but does not include the borrowing costs.

53 The correct answer is: Installation of new office fixtures and fittings

Insurance premiums are expensed as they form part of the normal costs of using the head office. Marketing costs are specifically disallowed by IAS 16. The maintenance costs of the computers are expensed as they are normal costs of operating the computers.

54 The correct answer is: The original head office building and the new extension are revalued separately

The extension is part of the original building, and therefore the building must be revalued as one asset.

55 The correct answer is: $1.8 million

The impairment loss for the CGU is $2.2m ($11.8m – $9.6m). The impairment loss is initially allocated to the goodwill balance of $1.4m. The unallocated impairment loss is $0.8m. This is allocated to the brand and PPE based on their carrying amounts:

	$m	Allocation of impairment $m
Brand	2	(0.2)
PPE	6	(0.6)
Total	8	(0.8)

The value of the brand is therefore $1.8m (2m – 0.2m).

56 The correct answer is: Both 1 and 2

Both of the actions are required on an annual basis (IAS 36: paras. 9 and 10).

Elite Leisure Co case

57 The correct answer is: $279m

	Cost $m	Dep'n period	Dep'n to date	Carrying amount
Ships fabric	300	8/25	(96)	204
Cabins etc	150	8/12	(100)	50
Propulsion	100	30/40 hrs	(75)	25
				279

58 $14m (140m × 5,000/50,000)

59 $45m (Repainting $20m + Loss on disposal $25m)

60 The correct answer is: Capitalise the cost when incurred and amortise over five years

IAS 16 paragraph 13–14 refers specifically to when assets may require substantial inspections and/or overhauls on a periodic basis' When each major inspection is performed, its cost is recognised in the **carrying amount** of the item of property, plant and equipment as a replacement' (IAS 16: para. 13).

61 $290,000

(250 + 40) At 55% losing the case is 'probable' so must be provided for.

Dexterity Co case

62

Patent for the new drug	Capitalise	
Licence for the new vaccine	Capitalise	
Specialist training courses undertaken by Dexterity staff		Expense
Temerity Co's patent on the existing drug currently licenced for use	Capitalise	

The patent for the new drug and the licence for the new vaccine will generate probable future economic benefits as they have been approved for clinical use. There is an existence of a market, management have ascertained reliably the costs and that the company can sell or control the assets.

Temerity Co's existing patent for a drug already in use should be capitalised as it meets the criteria under IAS 38 of an internally generated intangible asset.

Specialist training courses, although they will benefit the business (thus meeting the criteria of an expense from which benefits are expected to flow) they cannot be capitalised as the company does not control the staff (they can leave the company) so failing the control element of the definition of an intangible asset. IAS 38 states that training costs must be expensed as employees do not represent a resource controlled by the entity and therefore cannot recognise the training costs as an intangible asset (para. 15).

63

Required if Dexterity Co adopts the revaluation model

The entire class of intangible assets must be revalued at the same time

Valid active market for the asset

On initial recognition, the original cost of the item must be used, it cannot be used from initial recognition, regardless of whether there is an active market or not. The revaluation model may be used, provided the criteria have been met, at a later date.

Although prepaid marketing costs may be capitalised, training costs may not be capitalised as part of the intangible asset under IAS 38.

64   The correct answer is: The design of possible new or improved product or process alternatives

This activity is still at the research stage

65   The correct answer is: $9,375,000

($10m − (($10m/8) × 6/12))

66   The correct answer is: It should be capitalised and reviewed for impairment every year.

IAS 36 Impairment of Assets (para. 10) requires that goodwill be tested for impairment on an annual basis, regardless of whether there is any indication of impairment.

Advent Co case

67   The correct answer is: $256m

		$m
Land		85
Building	180 × 19/20	171
		256

The second option ignores the effect of depreciation in the current year.

The third option does not apply the revaluation in the current year.

The fourth option depreciates the building over the 25 years useful life at the date of the previous valuation.

68   The correct answer is: $35m

		$m
Existing plant	150 × 20%	30
New plant	50 × 20% × 6/12m	5
		35

69

The effective date of revaluation	Required	
Professional qualifications of the valuer		Not required
The basis used to revalue the assets	Required	
The carrying amount of assets if no revaluation had taken place	Required	

There is no requirement to disclose the professional qualifications of the valuer.

70    $140m

	$m
Balance 1.10.X8	270
Depreciation to 30.9.X9	(30)
	240
Impairment loss (β)	(140)
Recoverable amount	100

71   The **recoverable amount** of an asset of an asset is the higher of

Fair value less costs of disposal	and	Value in use

As stated in IAS 36 *Impairment of Assets*, para. 22. The other options are not in line with the accounting standard.

Systria Co case

72    $40,000

	Original	Impairment	
	$'000	$'000	
Goodwill	50	(50)	
Patent	10	(10)	
Land and buildings	100	(20)	*Remaining 30*
Plant and machinery	50	(10)	*pro rata*
Net current assets	10	–	
		(90)	

73   The correct answers are:

There are adverse changes to the use to which the asset is put.

The operating performance of the asset has declined.

Depreciation is irrelevant and the other options are an **external** indicator of impairment.

74    $1.5 million

Recoverable amount is $6 million, leaving an impairment loss of $4 million.

$2.5 million will be allocated to the destroyed assets and the remaining $1.5 million written off against goodwill.

$3 million – $1.5 million = $1.5 million.

75

	Debit	Credit
Accumulated depreciation	$20,000	
Property at cost	$30,000	
Revaluation surplus		$50,000

The depreciation is written off and the balance added to the cost of the property.

76 The correct answer is: $3,250

Depreciation to date of $20,000 means the property has 40 years of useful life left at the revaluation date. Depreciation will be $130,000/40.

Section A

Revenue

77   The correct answer is a contract asset of $180,000.

	$
Revenue recognised $2,800,000 × 35%	980,000
Less amounts invoiced to date	(800,000)
Contract asset	180,000

Contract asset	$180,000
Contract liability	$240,000

78   The correct answer is: $125,000

The $120,000 relating to the purchase of IT equipment can be recognised as income immediately as the terms of that portion of the grant have already been satisfied.

The remaining $600,000 should be initially deferred and then released to income on a monthly basis as the condition of the grant, being to provide training, are satisfied. The receipt date of the government grant is not relevant, the terms of the grant are being complied with from 1 April 20X5 and therefore grant income can be recognised from that date. At 31 October 20X5, the remaining term attached to the training grant is 17 months, of which 12 months are current and 5 months are non-current.

The non-current liability is therefore measured as $600,000 × 5/24 months = $125,000

The second option is based on the full amount of the grant of $720,000

The third option is the full amount of the liability

The fourth option is the current portion only

79   The correct answer is: $7,000,000

	$'000
Contract revenue recognised	22,000
Costs to date	(12,000)
Depreciation of specialist plant	(3,000)
Profit recognised at 31 March 20X3	7,000

The first option incorrectly calculates a proportion of the total profit on the contract.

The third option incorrectly reflects total expected profit.

The fourth option assumes that no profit or loss can be recognised to date.

80   The correct answer is: $9,600

	$
Revenue recognised ($120,000 × 50% (W))	60,000
Amounts invoiced	(50,400)
Contract asset	9,600

Working	
Costs to date	48,000
Costs to complete	48,000
Percentage completion	50%

The second option is the profit that can be recognised rather than the contract asset (50% × ($120,000 – $96,000)).

The third option is the trade receivables balance ($50,400 – $40,000).

The fourth option is the total amount invoiced.

81

DEBIT	Other income	1,425,000
CREDIT	Deferred income	1,425,000

	$
Grant received and recognised in other income 1.7.X5	1,500,000
Recognised year to 31.12.X5 (1,500,000 / 10yrs × 6/12m)	(75,000)
Amount to be deferred	1,425,000

82

	Debit	Credit
Other income		80,000
Deferred income	80,000	
Depreciation expense	155,000	
Accumulated depreciation		155,000

Workings

Grant is 50% of the asset, so the asset cost is $400,000 × 2 = $800,000

The depreciation is $800,000 – $25,000/5 years = $155,000

The grant is recognised as deferred income on the SOFP and released to the profit or loss in the same manner as the depreciation (over 5 years, therefore $400,000/5 years = $80,000).

83

	Value ($)
Revenue	nil
Current liability	90,000
Trade receivables	nil

No sale has taken place as control of the goods has not been transferred (so revenue will be nil), but Cambridge Co must show that it is holding $90,000 which belongs to Circus Co.

84 The correct answer is: Sales of $150,000 on 30 September 20X4. The amount invoiced to and received from the customer was $180,000, which included $30,000 for ongoing servicing work to be done by Repro Co over the next two years.

The amount to recognise in revenue is $150,000 as the servicing amount of $30,000 has not yet been earned. This would be recognised as deferred income.

85 The correct answer is: $160,000

Contract asset:

	$'000
Revenue recognised to date ($5m × 38%)	1,900
Less amounts invoiced	(1,740)
	160

The first option is incorrect as it refers to trade receivables rather than contract asset.

The third option is incorrect as it is the total profit for the contract.

The fourth option is incorrect as it is the profit that can be recognised at 30 September 20X4.

86 The correct answers are:

Manufacturer can require dealer to return the inventory

Manufacturer bears obsolescence risk

These both indicate that the manufacturer retains ownership of the inventory. The other options would indicate that the risks and rewards have been transferred to the dealer.

87 $400,000

An asset is defined as 'a present economic resource controlled by the entity as a result of past events' (Conceptual Framework). The staff training does not meet the definition of an asset because the employer does not control its employees; the employer cannot control whether or not an employee chooses to leave employment. If an employee leaves, the employer will not receive the full benefit of the staff training. If the staff training is not an asset, then $500,000 should be charged in full to profit or loss in the year in which it is incurred and cannot be spread across two years. As the second instalment of the government grant is virtually certain then the full $100,000 can be offset against the $500,000 staff training costs.

88 $24,920,000

	$'000
Revenue per draft profit or loss	27,000
Service and support costs (800 × 2 × 130%)	(2,080)
	24,920

89 The correct answer is: The inventories should be recorded in the statement of financial position at $450,000 and the $420,000 received should be reported as a liability. There is no profit or loss effect.

The transaction is entered into on the last day of the financial year and is, in substance, a financing transaction as AB can repurchase the inventories in two years later at a higher amount that includes interest for the two years.

Introduction to groups

90 The correct answer is: There is no basis on which a subsidiary may be excluded from consolidation.

91 The correct answer is: Credited to profit or loss

IFRS 3 requires a bargain purchase to be credited to profit or loss as it is an economic gain. If the consideration is higher than the net assets being purchased, that would constitute goodwill (not taking the debit to the profit and loss). By taking the bargain purchase to the profit and loss immediately, IFRS 3 aims to restrict any excess being carried forwards.

BPP LEARNING MEDIA

92 The correct answer is: Existence of significant influence.

The other options indicate control over a subsidiary as set out by IAS 27 *Consolidated and Separate Financial Statements*.

93 The correct answers are:

A subsidiary with a different reporting date may prepare additional statements up to the group reporting date for consolidation purposes.

Where a subsidiary's financial statements are drawn up to a different reporting date from those of the parent, adjustments should be made for significant transactions or events occurring between the two reporting dates.

The allowable gap between reporting dates is three months, not five. IAS 27 allows subsidiaries to have non-coterminous year ends, provided several criteria are met, including stating reasons why the financial year end is different to the parent.

94

The characteristics of the asset	Relevant	
The price paid to acquire the asset		Not relevant
The principal or most advantageous market for the asset	Relevant	
The highest and best use of the asset	Relevant	

The price paid to acquire the asset is the historical cost of the asset. Fair value looks at the future benefits which are expected to flow from the asset, as opposed to what was paid in the past.

IFRS 13 will take into account assumptions that market participants may use when establishing a fair value for the asset.

95 The correct answers are:

The ability to use its power over the investee to affect the amount of the investor's returns

Exposure to, or rights to, variable returns from its involvement with the investee

Power over the investee

In accordance with IFRS 10, paragraph 7.

IFRS 10 makes no reference to a holding of more than 50% of the equity shares of an investee company.

96 The correct answer is: Gamma Co is located in a country where a military coup has taken place and Petre Co has lost control of the investment for the foreseeable future.

Consolidation is not appropriate in this case as the parent has lost control.

Financial instruments

97 The correct answer is: $1,524,000

	$'000
Interest years 1–3 (30m × 8% × 2.49)	5,976
Repayment year 3 (30m × 0.75)	22,500
Debt component	28,476
Equity option (β)	1,524
	30,000

Answer option A is the present value of the future interest payments.

Answer option C is the debt component.

Answer option D is the total amount raised on the issue.

98   The correct answer is: $21,495,000

	$'000
Proceeds (20m – 0.5m)	19,500
Interest 10%	1,950
Interest paid (20m × 5%)	(1,000)
Balance 30 March 20X1	20,450
Interest 10%	2,045
Interest paid (20m × 5%)	(1,000)
	21,495

99

Fair value	with changes going through	profit or loss

Fair value through OCI would be correct if an election had been made to recognise changes in value through other comprehensive income. Amortised cost is used for debt instruments, not equity instruments.

100   The correct answer is: $514,560

	$
1 January 20X1	500,000
Interest 8%	40,000
Interest received (550,000 × 6%)	(33,000)
31 December 20X1	507,000
Interest 8%	40,560
Interest received	(33,000)
31 December 20X2	514,560

101   The correct answer is: Intangible assets

These do not give rise to a present right to receive cash or other financial assets. The other options are financial instruments.

102   $1,000,000

	$'000
$12,500 × 1,296 / 1,200	13,500
Carrying amount	(12,500)
Gain	1,000

103   $240,000

	$
40,000 shares @ $6	240,000

Transaction costs are added to the initial cost but omitted from subsequent measurement.

Lease Accounting

104   The correct answer is: $1,283,000 ($1,283,366 rounded)

	$
PV of future lease payments	1,871,100
Interest at 6% (6% × $1,871,100)	112,266
Balance of the lease liability at 31 Dec 20X6	1,983,366
Current	700,000
Non-current	1,283,366
	1,983,366

The first option is the current portion of the lease liability.

The second option does not account for interest in the year.

The fourth option is the opening balance.

105

The lessee obtains substantially all of the economic benefits from use of the asset	Indicates a lease	
Ownership in the asset is transferred at the end of the lease term	Indicates a lease	
The contract relates to an identified asset	Indicates a lease	
If it suits them to do so, the lessor can substitute an identical asset		Does not indicate a lease

The lessee does not have right of use of an identified asset as the lessor has substitution rights.

106   The correct answer is: $6,390,900

	$	Finance charge
Initial liability (PV of future cash flows)	15,462,000	
Interest 8% ($15.462m × 8%)	1,236,960	1,236,960
Payment	(6,000,000)	
Total lease liability at 31.3.X8	10,698,960	

Depreciation is charged based on the shorter of the lease term (three years) and the useful life (five years) as there is no option to purchase the asset the end of the lease period.

Initial measurement of right-of-use asset	15,462,000
Depreciation charge 15,462,000/3	(5,154,000)
Carrying amount	10,308,000

Charge to the profit and loss is $5,154,000 +$1,236,960 = $6,390,900

The first option only charges the finance cost.

The second option has depreciation charged over five years (instead of over the lease term).

The third option is just the payment made.

107   The correct answer is: Lease liability + other direct costs + amounts paid before or on commencement of the lease – incentives received

108   The correct answer is: $4,098,050

	$
Present value of the future lease payments at 1 October 20X3	22,745,000
Interest at 10%	2,274,500
Less payment in arrears	(6,000,000)
Lease liability as at 30 Sept 20X4	19,019,500

Extend the calculation to work out the lease liability at the end of the next period:

B/fwd	19,019,500
Interest at 10%	1,901,950
Payment in arrears	(6,000,000)
Lease liability at 30 Sept 20X5	14,921,450

Calculation of current liability (19,019,500 – 14,921,450)   4,098,050

The first option is only the interest charge for the next period.

The third option is just the cash payment to be made, not the liability.

The fourth option is the interest charge for the first period only.

109 The correct answers are:

The lessee has the right to substantially all the economic benefits from use of the asset.

The agreement concerns an identified asset which cannot be substituted.

The lease term does not have to be for substantially all of the estimated useful life of the asset. If the lessor has the right to direct the use of the asset, the lessee does not have right of use, so it is not a lease within the scope of IFRS 16.

110 $866,325

	$
Cost 1 July 20X4 ($4,657,500 + $37,500)	4,695,000
Depreciation to 30 June 20X5 ($4,695,000/8)	586,875

Lease liability at 1 July 20X4 6% interest = $4,657,500 × 6% = $279,450

Total charge to the SOPL (279,450 + 586,875) = $866,325

111 The correct answer is: Recognise proportion relating to right of use transferred.

112 $112,000

	$
Lease interest (250,000 × 16%)	40,000
Plant depreciation ((250,000 + 90,000) / 5)	68,000
Short-term lease (18,000 × 2/9)	4,000
Total charge to profit or loss	112,000

113 $270,356

Only the gain on the rights transferred to the financial institution can be recognised in profit or loss. As the accountant has recognised the total gain of $1,000,000 in other income, an adjustment is required to remove the gain on the rights retained.

	$
Total gain (8,000,000 – 7,000,000)	1,000,000
Gain on rights retained (1,000,000 × 2,162,850 / 8,000,000)	270,356
Gain on rights transferred (1,000,000 – 270,356) (P/L)	729,644

114 The correct answer is: $1,290,800

Only the gain in respect of the rights transferred to the financial institution can be recognised in profit or loss.

	$
Total gain (20,000,000 – 18,000,000)	2,000,000
Gain on rights retained $2,000,000 \times \dfrac{7,092,000}{20,000,000}$	709,200
Gain on rights transferred (2,000,000 – 709,200)	1,290,800

115 $13,588

		$
Depreciation for the year	100,650/10	10,065
Finance cost for the year	100,650 × 8%	8,052
Total charge for the year		18,702

Apportion for the year as acquired part way through the accounting period.

1 April – 31 December = 9 months so 9/12 × $18,702 = $13,588

Provisions and events after the reporting period

116 $100,000

Loss of the case is not 'probable', so no provision is made, but the legal costs will have to be paid so should be provided for.

117 The correct answer is: Provision $2 million and $2 million capitalised as part of cost of mine

$2 million should be provided for and capitalised as part of the cost of the mine. It will then be depreciated over the useful life.

118

Aston Co has a company policy of cleaning up any environmental contamination caused by its operations, even though it is not legally obliged to do so	Provision required	
Brum Co has a fixed price contract to supply widgets to Erdington Co. Brum Co has calculated that it will cost more to manufacture the widgets than budgeted, which is more than the revenue agreed from Erdington Co	Provision required	
Coleshill Co is closing down a division. The board has prepared detailed closure plans which have not yet been communicated to customers and employees		No provision required
Dudley Co has acquired a machine which requires a major overhaul every three years. The cost of the first overhaul is reliably estimated at $120,000		No provision required

Aston Co will create a provision for the present value of the environmental clear up cost – they have a probable outflow of costs (the decommissioning costs) and there is a present obligation (as they have a policy of cleaning up, it is a constructive obligation as opposed to a legal obligation).

Brum Co has discovered that the cost of supply exceeds the expected revenue from the contract. This is an example of an onerous contract. A provision should be recognised that is the unavoidable costs of meeting the contract with Erdington Co (the lower of the cost of fulfilling the contract or penalties from the failure to fulfil the contract). These costs are not stated in the question, but that would be the basis for the calculation of the provision.

Coleshill Co has not communicated the plans officially so the decision could still be reversed. Although no provision is required in the financial statements, it would be disclosed in a note to the accounts if material as it might affect the going concern of the company.

Dudley Co has acquired a machine which requires the staff to be retrained on its safe operation. The staff training will happen in the next financial period. Provisions as a result of the training of staff are forbidden by IAS 37 as the company does not have control over the staff (they can leave at any time).

119 The correct answer is: $2.21m

Provision at 1 July 20X8 = ($3m × 0.713) = $2,139,000

Interest to 31 Dec 20X8 = 7% × $2.139m × 6/12 = $74,865

Provision at 31 Dec 20X8 = $2,139,000 + $74,865 = $2,213,865 rounded to $2.21m

The first option is the initial carrying amount at 1 July 20X8.

The second option is based on unwinding the discount for 12 months instead of 6 months.

The third option is the undiscounted amount.

120

Provisions should be made for both constructive and legal obligations	True	
Discounting may be used when estimating the amount of a provision	True	
A restructuring provision must include the estimated costs of retraining or relocating continuing staff		False
A restructuring provision may only be made when a company has a detailed plan for the restructuring and has communicated to interested parties a firm intention to carry it out	True	

121 The correct answer is: Debit Provision $100,000, Debit Profit or loss $20,000; Credit Cash $120,000

The provision is a liability and therefore a credit balance. On settlement, the provision must be reversed with a debit. An expense of $100,000 was previously recognised in 20X4 when the original provision was created, so therefore only the extra $20,000 paid needs to be recognised as an expense in profit or loss in 20X5. Cash is an asset and therefore a debit balance. It is reduced by the amount paid with a credit entry.

122 $24,532,000

	$'000
Restoration of seabed (10,000 × 250)	2,500
Dismantling of equipment (30m × 0.68)	20,400
Unwinding of discount (20,400 × 8%)	1,632
	24,532

123 $0.6 million

	$m
$2 million × 15%	0.3
$6 million × 5%	0.3
	0.6

124 The correct answers are:

The discovery of a fraud which occurred during the year

The determination of the sale proceeds of an item of plant sold before the year end

These both provide evidence of conditions that existed at the end of the reporting period. The other options refer to conditions which arose after the reporting period and are therefore non-adjusting events according to IAS 10 *Events After the Reporting Period.*

125 The correct answers are:

Thomas Co, a customer of Coleridge Co, which owes the company $200,000 has gone into insolvency on 3 April 20X5

Inventory held in stock at 31 March which cost $200,000 was sold on 21 April 20X5 for $150,000

Both of these events give additional information about the value of assets which were included in the financial statements of Coleridge at 31 March 20X5. The inventory is required to be held at the lower of cost or net realisable value, and the receivable requires to be reduced by $200,000 as the amount will not be recovered.

The factory accident occurred after the year end, so is not an adjusting event.

The sale of the Wordsworth division, although it was decided prior to the year end, was not a commitment at the year end. However, it may be required to disclose these two events if they are material.

Inventories and biological assets

126 $95,100

Product	$
A 1,000 × 40	40,000
B 2,500 × 15	37,500
C 800 × 22	17,600
	95,100

127 The correct answer is: $14,900

	$
Cost	14,900
NRV (100 units × ($166 − $13) − ($166 × 2%)) = 100 × ($153 - $3.32)	14,968
Lower	14,900

128 The correct answer is: Fair value less estimated costs to sell

IAS 41 *Agriculture* requires biological assets to be measured on initial recognition at fair value less estimated costs to sell.

129 The correct answer is: Harvest

Harvest is an intervention, not a biological process. Growth, procreation and degeneration are natural biological processes.

130 The correct answer is: Included in profit or loss for the year

A gain or loss on a biological asset is included in profit or loss for the year.

131

Production overheads should be included in cost on the basis of a company's actual level of activity in the period		Incorrect
In arriving at the net realisable value of inventories, settlement discounts must be deducted from the expected selling price		Incorrect
In arriving at the cost of inventories, FIFO, LIFO and weighted average cost formulas are acceptable		Incorrect
It is permitted to value finished goods inventories at materials plus labour cost only, without adding production overheads		Incorrect

Production overheads are allocated on the basis of a company's **normal** level of activity. Settlement discounts are not deducted to arrive at NRV. The LIFO formula is not allowed under IAS 2 *Inventories*. Valuation of finished goods should include production overheads.

132 The correct answer is: IAS 10 *Events After the Reporting Period*

This may be relevant as agricultural produce is perishable and if prices have to be reduced after the year end, this will affect the year end valuation.

133 $39.3 million

	$m
Per inventory count	36.0
Received after year end	(2.7)
Sold after year end (7.8m / 1.3)	6.0
	39.3

134    $55,080   NRV − (12,000 × (5.4 × 85%)) = $55,080

The inventory at year end should be held at the lower of cost and net realisable value ($5.40 − ($5.40*15%) = $4.59 per unit, giving 12,000 × $4.59 = $55,080.

As information has come to light after the year end but before the approval of the financial statements and the inventory was held at the year end, the value should be restated to its net realisable value less selling costs.

Accounting for taxation

135   The correct answer is: $15.9 million

	$'000
Charge for year	16,200
Under-provision	2,100
P/L adjustment re: deferred tax (W)	(2,400)
Profit or loss charge	15,900

Working	
Provision needed (13m × 30%)	3,900
Provision b/f	(5,400)
Reduce provision	(1,500)
Amount to revaluation surplus (3m × 30%)	900
Amount to profit or loss	(2,400)

136   The correct answer is: $1.2 million

	$'000
Prior year under-provision	700
Current provision	4,500
Movement of deferred tax (8.4 − 5.6)	(2,800)
Deferred tax on revaluation surplus	(1,200)
Income tax expense	1,200

137   The correct answer is: $345,000

	$'000
B/f	850
Year to 31.12.X8 (500 − 450)	50
Revaluation surplus	250
	1,150
× 30%	345

138    $130 million

	$m
B/f (140 + 160)	300
Charge for year	270
C/f (310 + 130)	(440)
Tax paid	130

139    $19 million

	$'000
Current charge	19,400
Over-provision	(800)
Deferred tax (W)	400
	19,000
Working	
Required provision	6,750
Less revaluation	(3,750)
	3,000
Balance b/f	(2,600)
Charge to income tax	400

140   The correct answer is: $5,100 charge

As the tax base is less than the carrying amount for accounting purposes (more tax benefit has been taken), then a provision is required.

Carrying amount (accounting)

	$'000
Cost of asset	40,000
Depreciation charge (40,000 – 5,000)/5 years	(7,000)
Carrying amount at 31 August 20X2	33,000
Tax base	
Cost of asset	40,000
Less Y1 tax depreciation at 60% 40,000 × 0.6	(24,000)
	16,000
Difference $33,000 – $16,000	17,000
Tax provision 0.3 × $17,000	5,100

141

Asset/liability	Amount ($)
Liability	120,000

As the tax base is less than the accounting carrying amount (more tax benefit has been taken), then deferred tax liability is required:

	$'000
Carrying amount	
Cost of asset	1,000
Residual value	(200)
Depreciable value	800
Depreciation charge 800/8 years	(100)
Carrying amount at 31 December 20X5 (1,000 – 100)	900
Tax base	
Cost of asset	1,000
Less Y1 tax allowance at 50%	(500)
	500
Difference $900,000 – $500,000	400
Tax liability 30% × $400,000	120

Section B

Derringdo Co case

142   The correct answer is: $22,000

Operating expenses	$
Depreciation charge (800,000 × 85% × 10% × 6/12)	34,000
Release of grant (240,000 × 10% × 6/12)	(12,000)
	22,000

143   The correct answer is: $204,000

Deferred income	$
Grant received ($800,000 × 30%)	240,000
Release for this year ($240,000 × 10% × 6/12)	(12,000)
Total balance at year end	228,000

Presentation	
Current liability ($240,000 × 10%)	24,000
Non-current liability (balance)	204,000
	228,000

144 $439

Year 1	$
Laptop (W)	158
Broadband (562 (W) /2)	281
	439

Working			
Laptop	200	22%	158
Broadband (30 × 12 × 2)	720	78%	562
	920	100%	720

145   The correct answer is: Recognising revenue when a performance obligation is satisfied.

146   The correct answer is: Derringdo Co is not exposed to credit risk for the amount due from the customer

The other options would all suggest that Derringdo Co was the principal.

Campbell Co case

147

Revenue should be recognised as an entity satisfies a performance obligation	**CORRECT**	
Progress towards completion on a contract should be measured solely on an input basis		**INCORRECT**

148    $6.3m

	$m
Total revenue 31 December 20X8 ($9m × 90%)	8.1
Recognised in the period to 31 December 20X7 ($9m × 20%)	1.8
Amount recognised in the current year	6.3

149   The correct answer is: Contract liability $0.2m

Revenue will be recognised to the level of recoverable costs where the progress cannot be measured. Therefore $0.2 million should be recognised as Revenue and cost of sales. As no invoice has yet been issues a contract asset will be recognised for $0.2 million.

150   The correct answer is: $2.26m

The after sales support will be recognised over the 12-month period. As Campbell Co has already provided six months of support, $0.1 million can be recognised meaning that $2.26 million can be recognised overall ($2.36 million – $0.1 million).

151   The correct answer is: $1,500 should be recognised as revenue by Campbell Co when the accessory has been delivered and accepted by the customer

Campbell Co is acting as an agent as the equipment accessory is delivered directly to the customer from the manufacturer. Only the 3% commission should be recognised as revenue (3% × $50,000 = $1,500). As the customer has taken delivery and accepted the price of $50,000, the revenue can be recognised at that point.

Apex Co case

152   The correct answer is: An asset that takes a substantial period of time to get ready for its intended use or sale

(IAS 23: para. 5)

153   The correct answer is: Physical construction of the asset is nearing completion

IAS 23 has no requirements in respect of the stage of completion of the asset

154   The correct answer is: $625,000 (($10m 7.5%) × 10/12)

155   The correct answer is: 9.25%

	%
10% × 50/80	6.25
8% × 30/80	3.00
	9.25

156   The correct answer is: Recognised as investment income in the statement of profit or loss

The investment proceeds were earned before construction began, so are not deducted from the borrowing costs which are being capitalised.

Bertrand Co case

157   The correct answer is: As debt and equity

158   The correct answer is: $735,000

	$'000
Interest payable ($10m × 5% × 2.58*)	1,290
Capital repayable ($10m × 0.79)	7,900
Debt element	9,190
Finance costs for year = 9,190 × 8%	735

159   The correct answer is: $9,425,000

	$'000
1 October 20X0	9,190
Finance charge 8%	735
Interest paid (10,000 × 5%)	(500)
Balance 30 September 20X1	9,425

160   The correct answer is: Deducted from the proceeds of the loan notes.

The effective interest rate is then applied to the net amount.

161   As a financial | asset | at | amortised cost |

Fino Co case

162   The correct answer is: From the commencement of the lease to the shorter of the end of the lease term and the end of the useful life of the plant

163   The correct answer is: $286,500

	$
Present value of future lease payments	173,500
Payments made on the commencement of the lease	100,000
Initial direct costs	20,000
Less: Lease incentives	(7,000)
Initial cost of the right of use asset	286,500

164

Correct accounting treatment

The lease is for less than 12 months	Ownership is transferred at the end of the lease term

The leased asset has a low underlying value	

	The leased asset has been specially adapted for the use of the lessee

Where the agreement is for less than 12 months or the underlying asset is of low value, lease payments can be charged directly to profit or loss, in accordance with the optional recognition exemptions available in IFRS 16.

165    $190,850

	$
Present value of future cash flows at 1.4.X7	173,500
Interest accrued 1.4.X7 – 31.3.X8 ($173,500 × 10%)	17,350
Lease liability as at 31.3.X8	190,850

$173,500 does not factor in the interest charge, $200,000 is the future instalment payments. $90,850 takes the correct calculation of the interest but then deducts the payment which is not due until the following day (1 April 20X8).

166   The correct answer is: ((9,000/10) × 6) = $5,400

Jeffers Co case

167   The correct answer is: Neither 1 or 2

The reorganisation cannot be provided for because it has only gone as far as a feasibility study.

Staff training is not a valid provision as IAS 37 paragraph 81 specifically forbids costs relating to retraining or relocating staff to be provided for in restricting provisions.

168   The correct answers are:

The health and safety fine and the customer ceasing trading are both adjusting events

The health and safety fine resulted from an accident which had occurred by the financial year end

The customer's receivable was in existence had the financial year end, and the notice stating that the debt was unlikely to be recoverable was received after the year end, but prior to the financial statements being approved. Therefore it is an adjusting event.

Although it was likely that the competitor would be acquired by Jeffers Co, there was no certainty until the control was achieved after the year end. The control was not in existence at the year end.

Health and safety fine	Adjusting event	
Customer ceased trading	Adjusting event	
Acquisition of a competitor		Non-adjusting event

169   The correct answer is: $4.7 million

$5.2 million discounted at 0.909 = $4.7 million

170   The correct answer is: Nothing is recognised or disclosed in the financial statements

171   The correct answer is: The financial statements can no longer be prepared on a going concern basis

Julian Co case

172   The correct answer is: The amount attributed to an asset or liability for tax purposes

173

Property, plant and equipment   Development expenditure

$190,000	$60,000

PPE ($460,000 – $270,000). Development expenditure is in line with IAS 38 and is per the question.

174   The correct answer is: $63,000

The revaluation surplus is carried net of deferred tax.

	$
Revaluation	90,000
Deferred tax (90,000 × 30%)	(27,000)
Carrying amount of revaluation surplus	63,000

175   $45,000. The tax charge for the year.

176   The correct answer is: Accrued expenses which have already been deducted for tax purposes.

They will not give rise to a temporary difference.

Section A

Reporting financial performance

177 The correct answer is: A change in valuation of inventory from a weighted average to a FIFO basis.

A change of depreciation method is treated as a change of accounting estimate. Adoption of the revaluation method is dealt with under IAS 16. Application of a new accounting policy (such as capitalisation of borrowing costs) for transactions that did not previously occur is not a change in accounting policy according to IAS 8.

178 The correct answer is: A buyer must have been located for the asset.

It is not necessary for a buyer to have been located for the asset, only that the sale is 'highly probable' and a buyer is being actively sought by organisation (IFRS 5: para. 8).

179 Lower of | Carrying amount | and | Fair value less costs of disposal |

As the assets are to be sold, value in use is not relevant and recoverable amount will be fair value less costs of disposal.

180 The correct answer is: A change in reporting depreciation charges as cost of sales rather than as administrative expenses.

This is a change in presentation which will affect calculation of gross profit and will be retrospectively adjusted when presenting comparatives. A and D are simply adjustments made during preparation of the financial statements, C is a change of accounting estimate.

181 The correct answer is: Classifying commission earned as revenue in the statement of profit or loss, having previously classified it as other operating income.

This is a change in presentation so qualifies as a change in accounting policy.

182 The correct answer is: $36.8 million

Selling price × 90% minus selling costs.

183 $147,059   €125,000/0.85

184 Rate at the date of transaction

185 $98 loss

Date	Rate	$	€	Gain/(loss)
1/11	1.63	30,675	50,000	
1/12	1.61	(15,528)	(25,000)	(191)
31/12	1.64	15,244	25,000	93
				(98)

186 The correct answer is: $1.8 million

The factory is a held for sale asset from 1 December 20X6 and is therefore measured at the lower of its carrying amount and its fair value less costs to sell (IFRS 5: para. 15).

The fair value less costs to sell ($2.4 million − $0.3 million = $2.1 million) is greater than the carrying amount of $1.8 million and therefore no impairment is recognised on initial recognition of the held for sale asset on 1 December 20X6. As the information is the same at 31 December 20X6, no subsequent adjustment is required.

$1.6 million is the carrying amount less depreciation of $0.2 million, however, once the factory is classified as held for sale, depreciation is no longer charged and therefore the depreciation for December does not require to be accounted for.

$1.9 million is the value in use less costs of disposal, but this is not a valid measurement of the asset under IFRS 5.

187   The correct answer is: Changes in accounting estimates should be accounted for prospectively and errors accounted for retrospectively.

Changes in accounting estimates do not affect previous periods and are therefore not corrections of errors. IAS 8 does give examples on what constitutes changes in accounting policy and what is defined as an estimate. A change in the basis of measuring an asset, for example, such as inventory being measured on a FIFO basis instead of the weighted average cost, will be a change in accounting policy, not a change in estimate.

188

	31 Dec 20X6 $	31 Dec 20X7 $
Cost of sales	66,700	59,900

Working

Cost of sales	20X6 $'000	20X7 $'000
As stated in question	64,600	62,000
Inventory adjustment	2,100	(2,100)
	66,700	59,900

The $2.1 million was included in closing inventory at 31 December 20X6 in error. If the closing inventory decreases to remove the effect of the error, the cost of sales will increase by the same amount.

The opening inventory at 1 January 20X7 also included the $2.1 million in error. A decrease in opening inventory to remove the effect of the error will decrease cost of sales by the same amount.

Earnings per share

189   The correct answer is: $0.167

Earnings on dilution:	$'000
Basic	1,850
Add back interest (2,000 × 6% × 70%)	84
	1,934

Shares on dilution:	'000
Existing	10,000
Conversion (2m × 4/5)	1,600
	11,600

Basic EPS = 1,850 / 10,000 = $0.185

Diluted EPS = 1,934 / 11,600 = $0.167

190

	Share capital $'000	Share premium $'000

| $40,000 | $4,000 |

	Share capital $'000	Share premium $'000
Balance 30 September X2 (250m shares)	50,000	15,000
Rights issue:		
Share capital (50m × 20c)	(10,000)	
Share premium (50m × 22c)	–	(11,000)
Balance 30 September X1 (200m shares)	40,000	4,000

191　The correct answers are:

The issue during the year of a convertible (to equity shares) loan note

The granting during the year of directors' share options exercisable in three years' time

The convertible loan note and the share options should be taken into account when calculating diluted EPS.

192　The correct answer is: EPS takes into account the additional resources made available to earn profit when new shares are issued for cash, whereas net profit does not.

193　The correct answer is: $1.35

TERP

$5 \times 1.8 =$　9.0
$1 \times 1.5 =$　1.5
　　　　　　10.5 / 6 = $1.75

Shares	$'000
5,000 × 5/12 × 1.8 / 1.75	2,143
6,000 × 7/12	3,500
	5,643

EPS = 7,600 / 5,643 = $1.35

194　The correct answer is: 5.1 million

Calculate the shares that are treated as being issued for nil consideration:

No. of shares under option		500,000
No. of shares that would have been issued at the average market price	$\dfrac{500,000 \times \$2.80}{3.50}$	(400,000)
No. of shares treated as issued for nil consideration		100,000

Shares used in EPS calculation = 5,000,000 + 100,000 = 5.1m

195   EPS 20X8: $0.72

EPS 20X7: $0.56

Workings

1   Calculation of the effect of the bonus issue on the weighted average of shares

	Number of shares	Time apportioned	Bonus fraction	Weighted average
1/4/X7	4,000,000	6/12	5/4	2,500,000
30/09/X7 Bonus issue (1 for 4)	1,000,000			
	5,000,000			2,500,000
				5,000,000

2   Calculation of EPS for the year ended 31 March 20X8

$0.72 / $0.56	Shares $'000
B/f 1 April 20X7	4,000
Bonus issue (1 for 4)	1,000
C/f 31 March 20X8	5,000

EPS 20X8 = 3.6 / 5 = $0.72

3   Calculation of the (restated) EPS for the year ended 31 March 20X7

Restated EPS 20X7 = $0.70 × 4,000 / 5,000 = $0.56 (after taking into account the effect of the bonus issue of shares in September 20X7)

196   The correct answer is: $2.46

Workings

Additional shares resulting from conversion $100,000/$10 × 3 shares = 30,000 shares

Total dilutive number of shares	100,000 + 30,000 = 130,000
Revised earnings	$313,000 + (10% × $100,000 × 70%) = $320,000
Diluted earnings per share	$320,000/130,000 = $2.46

The first option ignores the interest saving after conversion ($313,000/130,000 = $2.41)

The third option ignores the tax effect on the interest saving after conversion ($323,000/130,000 = $2.48)

The fourth option ignores the increase in shares and calculates the basic earnings per share ($313,000/100,000 = $3.13)

Section B

Tunshill Co (Dec10) case

197 The correct answer is: Change of accounting estimate: Prospective application

This is a change of accounting estimate so does not need to be retrospectively applied.

198 $10,000,000

	$m
Original cost 1 October 20X0	20
Two years depreciation ((20/5) × 2)	(8)
Carrying amount at 1 October 20X2	12
Depreciation to 30 September 20X3 (12/6)	(2)
Carrying amount at 30 September 20X3	10

199 The correct answer is: Tunshill Co has reclassified development costs from other operating expenses to cost of sales.

This is a change in presentation so it is a change of accounting policy.

200 The correct answer is: Reduced by $400,000

	FIFO $m	AVCO $m	Current year profit $m
Year to 30 September 20X2	15	13.4	(1.6)
B/f 1 October 20X2			1.6
Year to 30 September 20X3	20	18	(2.0)
At 30 September 20X3			(0.4)

The net effect at 30 September 20X3 of this proposal will be to reduce current year profits by $400,000.

201

Debit	Cost of sales
Credit	Inventory

The credit entry reduces inventory.

Hemlock Co case

202 The correct answer is: $196,203

The receivable is a monetary asset and is therefore retranslated at the closing rate at year end $155,000/0.79.

203 The correct answer is: Hemlock Co has reclassified head office administration costs from cost of sales to other operating expenses.

This is a change in presentation, so it is a change in accounting policy.

204 The correct answer is: Reduce by $800,000.

In 20X2 closing inventory is $3.2 million lower ($30m – $26.8m), so cost of sales in 20X2 will be higher and the profit will therefore be lower. So in 20X2, profit, retained earnings and inventory would all be decreased by $3.2 million.

In 20X3 opening inventory is $3.2 million lower and closing inventory is $4 million lower. Cost of sales in 20X3 will therefore increase by $0.8 million and so profit will be reduced by $0.8 million.

205 The correct answer is: Both statements (1) and (2)

IAS 8 states that the nature and the amount of the error should be disclosed, detailing each of the lines affected by the adjustment and the error.

206 $4.23 per share

	Weighted average number of shares
Ordinary shares	2,000,000
Shares under option	1,000,000
Equivalent at fair value (1,000,000 × 10.00/12.00)	(833,333)
	2,166,667
DEPS (9,160,000 / 2,166,667)	$4.23 per share

Part C

Section A

Interpretation of accounting ratios and trends

207   The correct answer is: A manufacturer

The low asset turnover suggests a capital-intensive industry. The high percentage of depreciation supports this theory that the business has a large amount of non-current assets. This rules out the estate agency or architectural practice. Supermarkets can also be capital-intensive but tend to operate on low profit margins, and the cost of sales personnel costs would be included within administrative and sales costs, rather than the cost of manufacturing the product itself, as in a manufacturing industry.

208   Reducing the **payables payment period** will increase the length of a company's operating cycle.

This will reduce working capital and means that it will take longer to build up working capital needed for production. The other options will all speed up the operating cycle.

209   The correct answer is: 4.1%

Working: (Dividends (3.4 + 11.1) / Share price) × 100 = 14.5 / 350 × 100 = 4.1%

210   The correct answer is: 3.9%

Profit margin is a component of ROCE: Profit margin × Asset turnover = ROCE

Working: 16.3% / 4.19 = 3.9%

211   7.5

Working: EPS = 800 / 4,000 = $0.20. P/E ratio = 150 / 20 = 7.5

212   5.1%

	$'000
Profit before interest and tax	230
Capital employed (3,500 + 1,000)	4,500
	= 5.1%

Limitations of financial statements and interpretation techniques

213   The effect of this impairment will **increase** the ROCE ratio of Cyan Co, and **increase** its gearing ratio.

Capital employed (assets) would decrease, increasing ROCE. The impairment loss will reduce equity (revaluation surplus) and so increase gearing.

214   The correct answer is: Current ratio: Decrease. Quick ratio: Decrease

The value of the inventory will be added to both current assets and current liabilities. It will add proportionately more to liabilities and so reduce the current ratio. The effect on the quick ratio will be even greater as inventory is excluded from assets.

215

Operating profit margin	ROCE
Decrease	Increase

The new product will have an operating profit of 120 / 1,600 = 7.5%, so will reduce the current margin. It will have a ROCE of 120 / 500 = 24%, higher than the current 20%.

216 The correct answer is: Obsolete inventory lines

Obsolete goods can lead to a build-up of unsold inventory, thereby increasing the holding period. A reduction in selling price or an increase in demand could increase sales leading to a fall in the holding period. Seasonal fluctuations will change the holding period throughout the year, but should not affect the year on year picture.

217 The correct answer is: Overstatement of profits

The use of historical cost accounting during a period of inflation can lead to overstatement of profits. Non-current assets carried at historical cost may be presented at a value well below their fair value, leading to understated depreciation and consequently overstated profits. This can be compounded by the use of FIFO, if inventory is held at an original cost which is significantly below replacement cost. The charge to cost of sales will be understated and profit overstated.

The use of historical cost accounting will lead to understatement rather than overstatement of non-current asset values and will not affect interest costs. It is likely to lead to overstatement rather than understatement of ROCE.

218

Renegotiating a loan to secure a lower interest rate		No effect
Applying the options recognition exemption to a lease contract under IFRS 16 Leases	Reduce	
Repaying a loan just before the year end and taking it out again at the beginning of the next year.	Reduce	
'Selling' an asset under a sale and leaseback agreement	Reduce	

219 The correct answer is: Enter into a sale and short-term leaseback, the terms of which meet the requirements to use the optional recognition exemption under IFRS 16 Leases.

This would be an unlikely transaction as it would remove the asset from the statement of financial position.

The deferral method of accounting for government grants leaves the carrying amount of the asset intact, rather than deducting the amount of the grant from the asset amount.

Revaluing assets is the obvious way of increasing the carrying amount of assets.

Under the reducing balance method, more depreciation is charged in the earlier years of the life of an asset, so a change to 10% straight line would reduce the depreciation charge for the first few years. Of course, this effect is only temporary as the charge will catch up after a few years.

220 The correct answer is: Trent factors with recourse the receivable of its largest customer

A receivable factored with recourse will still be included in trade receivables at the year end. Seasonal trading will create particular distortion if the busiest period is just before the year end. Cash sales will need to be removed from the calculation and an adjustment will have to be made for sales tax.

Specialised, not-for-profit and public sector entities

221 The correct answer is: Shareholders

Charities do not usually have shareholders, in the commercial sense of the term.

222 The correct answer is: Accruals

Public sector accounting needs to move from cash-based accounting to application of the accruals concept.

223 The correct answers are:

Rent receipts outstanding

Interest cover

Financial actuals against budget

A local council would not pay dividends and would be unlikely to measure ROCE, which deals with return to investors.

224 The correct answers are:

Operating profit margin and earnings per share

Charities do not operate with a view to earning a profit and do not have shareholders.

Inventory holding period is relevant to a charity as the charity will generate funds based on the inventory it sells. The current ratio will also be relevant as to remain viable, the charity must be able to pay any liabilities as they fall due.

225 The correct answer is: Funded by government

Public sector bodies have a major advantage not generally enjoyed by charities – government funding.

226 The correct answer is: Disclosure of dividends per share

Not-for-profit entities do not have share capital so dividends per share is not relevant. The other requirements could be relevant to a not-for-profit entity.

227 The correct answers are:

There is no requirement to calculate an earnings per share figure as it is not likely to have shareholders who need to assess its earnings performance.

It is prioritising non-financial KPIs over financial targets.

The objectives of a not-for-profit entity do not include making a profit so it would not calculate earnings per share or report to shareholders. However, it is likely to have to account to the trustees of the Board of the charity or entity using non-financial KPIs. For example, a hospital may account for mortality rates, or a children's charity show the numbers of children assisted during the period.

228 The correct answers are:

Inventory holding period and payables payment period

Cyan holds inventory for resale and therefore the inventory holding period is relevant. It purchases inventory from suppliers and therefore the payables payment period is also relevant.

ROCE is not relevant for a charity and as sales are all in cash, there will be no receivables balance.

Section B

Sandbag plc case

229 The correct answer is: 1.29

Current ratio = current assets/current liabilities = 133/103 = 1.29

230 The correct answer is: Make a rights issue of ordinary shares

This would increase both cash and share capital, increasing current assets without incurring any additional liabilities.

Offering a settlement discount to customers would make cash received lower than receivables which would decrease the current ratio.

Making a bonus issue of shares would generate no cash at all and would not affect the current ratio.

Selling current asset investments would simply replace one current asset with another, at the same amount.

231 0.36

Acid test ratio = (current assets – inventories)/current liabilities = (133 – 96)/103 = 0.36

232

Proposal 1	Proposal 2
Decrease ratio	Increase ratio

Proposal 1 will cause the acid test ratio to fall because, although receivables will convert into cash more quickly, the amount of cash received will be less than the amount of the receivables. Current assets will fall without any change in current liabilities, so the acid test ratio will fall.

Proposal 2 will cause the acid test ratio to rise, by delaying the reduction in cash that would occur by paying suppliers. Since the acid test ratio is less than 1, anything that prevents an equal fall in current assets and current liabilities will boost the ratio.

233 The correct answer is: Non-current asset turnover

A manufacturing company will have high non-current assets (factory, plant and machinery), so this ratio will measure how efficiently it is using its non-current assets to generate revenue.

The P/E ratio is a measure of market confidence in the future of the entity. Gearing relates to long-term solvency and the current ratio relates to liquidity.

Section C

234 Woodbank Co (Jun 2014 amended)

> **Text reference.** Chapter 20.
>
> **Top tips.** The question makes it very clear where your analysis should be heading – the effect of the purchase of Shaw Co – so concentrate on this and review the information from this angle.
>
> **Easy marks.** The ratios were easy marks and a thorough reading of the question would have given you some obvious points to make.
>
> **Examining Team's comments.** Many candidates paid too little attention to the incremental effect of the acquisition of Shaw Co and few commented on the fact that profit or loss only included the results of Shaw Co for three months. This led a lot of candidates to conclude that the acquisition was not advantageous, which is not the conclusion borne out by taking into account the expected profits of Shaw over 12 months.

Marking scheme

	Marks
1 mark per valid point (including 8 for ratios)	20

(a) and (b)

Ratio	Woodbank Co 20X3	Working	Woodbank Co 20X4	Working	Woodbank Co 20X4 excluding Shaw
Return on capital employed	10.5%	(16,250 + 1,750) / (95,000 + 55,000)	12%	(18,000 – 5,000)/(150,000 – 50,000)	13%
Gross profit margin	22%	33,000/150,000	22%	(33,000 – 9,000)/(150,000 – 30,000)	20%
Profit before interest and tax margin	9.1%	(16,250 + 1,750) /150,000	12%	(18,000 – 5,000)/(150,000 – 30,000)	10.8%
Current ratio	1.7:1	27,000/25,000	1.08:1	N/A	N/A
Gearing (debt/(debt + equity))	5.3%	55,000 / (55,000 + 95,000)	36.7%	N/A	N/A

(c)   **Analysis of performance and position**

The acquisition of Shaw Co has materially affected the results of Woodbank Co for the year ended 31 March 20X4. In order to make a meaningful comparison of the performance of Woodbank Co during the year to 31 March 20X4 with its performance during the year to 31 March 20X3, it is necessary to isolate the effects of the acquisition and consider how Woodbank Co's performance would have looked without Shaw Co.

Profitability

Shaw Co has contributed positively to profitability with both the gross profit margin and profit before interest and tax margin both being higher after the acquisition. However, the $50 million of loan notes which financed the acquisition have increased capital employed and so exerted a downward pull on ROCE. With Shaw Co, ROCE is 12%. Without Shaw Co it would have been 13%. This is likely to be due to only three months profits of Shaw Co being included in PBIT. If 12 months' profits were used, we could expect the return to be correspondingly higher.

Woodbank Co's individual gross profit has declined by 2% since 20X3. While revenue has risen by 9%, cost of sales has increased by 11%. However, Woodbank Co has done well at keeping down expenses and its PBIT margin without Shaw Co (10.8%) would have been up on 20X3 (9.1%). It is important to remember that Shaw Co was only owned for the final three months of the financial year, not much time for the additional assets to show a return. It is likely that the acquisition will enhance profitability to a greater extent over the next 12 months.

Liquidity

The current ratio of Woodbank Co has fallen from 1.7:1 to 1.08:1. This is a steep drop. We can see immediately that cash reserves have declined by $4.5 million, which is likely to be due to using cash reserves to partly fund the acquisition of Shaw Co. Trade payables have increased by $8 million. This suggests that Woodbank Co is having trouble paying its suppliers on time or that Shaw had a large amount of trade payables which have now been consolidated within the group. The retained earnings balance shows that Woodbank Co paid a dividend of $5.5 million during 20X4. This was perhaps unwise when working capital was needed to finance expansion and pay the additional loan interest. Had the dividend not been paid the current ratio for 20X4 would be 1.3:1 – still a fall from 20X3, but less alarming.

Gearing

Gearing has risen from 5.3% to 36.7%, attributable to an additional $50 million loan notes issued to finance the acquisition of Shaw Co. The interest payments each year will be $5.5 million which is the same as the amount of the dividend paid in 20X4. Shareholders may expect to receive less in future years as the servicing of the debt will take priority, but had the acquisition been funded by a share issue their returns would have been diluted. Gearing of 36.7% is still within acceptable limits and future good returns from the acquisition will build up retained earnings and keep gearing in check.

Conclusion

Woodbank Co's performance would have been broadly comparable to the previous year had no acquisition taken place. The acquisition of Shaw Co has had a detrimental effect on liquidity and gearing for 20X4 but appears from three months results to have the capacity to significantly increase profits for Woodbank Co. It seems likely that over a longer period this will also improve liquidity and gearing, giving an overall positive result for shareholders.

ANSWERS

235 Hassle Co

(a)

ROCE	$(2,500 - 500 - 10)/(2,800 + 3,200 + 3,000 + 500) \times 100$	= 20.9%
Pre-tax ROE	$(1,400/2,800) \times 100$	= 50%
Net asset turnover	$20,500/(14,800 - 5,700)$	= 2.3 times
Gross profit margin	$(2,500/20,500) \times 100$	= 12.2%
Operating profit margin	$(2,000/20,500) \times 100$	= 9.8%
Current ratio	$7,300/5,700$	= 1.3 : 1
Closing inventory holding period	$(3,600/18,000) \times 365$	= 73 days
Trade receivables collection period	$(3,700/20,500) \times 365$	= 66 days
Trade payables payment period	$(3,800/18,000) \times 365$	= 77 days
Gearing	$(3,200 + 500 + 3,000)/9,500 \times 100$	= 71%
Interest cover	$2,000/600$	= 3.3 times
Dividend cover	$1,000/700$	= 1.4 times

(b) **Assessment of relative position and performance of Astral Co and Breakout Co**

Profitability

At first sight it appears that Hassle Co would see a much greater return on its investment if it acquired Breakout Co rather than Astral Co. A closer analysis of the figures suggests that this may not be the case.

Breakout Co has a ROCE over 40% higher than Astral Co's and a ROE more than double Astral Co's ROE. However, the difference is due more to the lower level of equity in Breakout Co than to the superiority of its profit. Breakout Co's equity ($2.8m) is only half that of Astral Co ($5.5m). This reduces the denominator for ROCE and doubles the ROE. In addition, only Astral Co has revalued its assets (evidenced by the existence of the revaluation surplus). Increases in asset value have a negative impact on ROCE but do not contribute to earnings, hence the ROCE measure may appear worse for Astral Co. A closer look at the profits of both companies shows that the operating profit margin of Astral Co is 10.5% and that of Breakout Co is 9.75%.

The net asset turnover of Breakout Co (2.3 times) suggests that it is running the more efficient operation. Breakout Co has certainly achieved a much greater turnover than Astral Co and with a lower level of net assets, though again, this could be due to the revaluation of Astral Co's assets. The problem is that, on a much higher level of turnover, its net profit is not much higher than Astral Co's.

Further analysis of net assets shows that Astral Co owns its factory, while Breakout Co's factory must be rented, partly accounting for the higher level of operating expenses. Astral Co's factory is carried at current value, as shown by the property revaluation surplus, which increases the negative impact on Astral Co's ROCE.

Gearing

Breakout Co has double the gearing of Astral Co, due to its lease obligations. At 7.5% Breakout Co is paying less on the lease than on its loan notes, but this still amounts to a doubling of its interest payments. Its interest cover is 3.4 times compared to 6 times for Astral Co, making its level of risk higher. In a bad year Breakout Co could have trouble servicing its debts and have nothing left to pay to shareholders. However, the fact that Breakout Co has chosen to operate with a higher level of gearing rather than raise funds from a share issue also increases the potential return to shareholders.

Liquidity

Astral Co and Breakout Co have broadly similar current ratios, but showing a slightly higher level of risk in the case of Breakout Co. Breakout Co is also running an overdraft while Astral Co has $1.2m in the bank. Astral Co is pursuing its receivables slightly less aggressively than Breakout Co, but taking significantly longer to pay its suppliers. As this does not appear to be due to shortage of cash, it must be due to Astral Co being able to negotiate more favourable terms than Breakout Co.

Summary

Breakout Co has a higher turnover than Astral Co and a policy of paying out most of its earnings to shareholders. This makes it an attractive proposition from a shareholder viewpoint. However, if its turnover were to fall, there would be little left to distribute. This is the risk and return of a highly geared company. Breakout Co is already running an overdraft and so has no cash to invest in any more plant and equipment. In the light of this, its dividend policy is not particularly wise. Astral Co has a lower turnover and a much more conservative dividend policy but may be a better long-term investment. Hassle Co's decision will probably depend upon its attitude to risk and the relative purchase prices of Astral Co and Breakout Co.

236 Funject Co

Text references. Chapters 20 and 21

Top tips. Clearly laying out the calculations, especially for the ratios was vital in this question. You should ensure you show your workings or underlying formula for all ratio calculations performed. Remember to state whether an adjustment makes an increase or decrease in profit (show decreases in brackets). Calculating the ratios in the correct way gained easy marks, but additional marks were given for adding comments relevant to the situation.

Easy marks. Calculation of ratios, remember to use the preformatted response area provided and show your workings (as the revised figures were used, it was imperative to show the workings or zero marks were given). A mark was given for stating a conclusion, which the markers encouraged.

Examining Team's comments. Most answers confined themselves to giving a textbook based explanation of what the ratio told users and whether the company's ratio was higher or lower than the industry average. Some answers went on to suggest whether the company ratios were better or worse than the industry averages, but very few provided any further analysis. Better answers referred to the differing performance of the division disposed of and its impact on the company's results.

		Marks
(a)	Adjustment to revenue and cost of sales	1	
	Disposal of non-core division	1	
	Management charge (remove old, add new)	1	
	Rent expense (remove current, add commercial)	1	
			4
(b)	Calculation of ratios		6
(c)	Profitability comments	5	
	Liquidity comments	3	
	Gearing comments	1	
	Conclusion	1	
			10
			20

(a) **Restated financial information**

Statement of profit or loss

	20X4
	$'000
Revenue (54,200 – 2,100 (note1))	52,100
Cost of sales (21,500 – 1,200 (note1)	(20,300)
Gross profit	31,800
Operating expenses (W1)	(12,212)
Profit before tax	19,588

W1 Restatement of operating expenses	
As per question	11,700
Less: expenses relating to non-core division	(700)
loss on disposal of non-core division	(1,500)
Gamilton Group management charge (54,200 × 1%)	(542)
Add: Funject management charge (31,800 × 10%)	3,180
Less: rent charged by Gamilton Group	(46)
Add: commercial rent	120
	12,212

(b) Profit has decreased from $21,000,000 to $19,588,000 and the resulting journal entry will be ($'000s):

Debit Retained earnings (21,000 – 19,588)	$1,412	
Credit Cash		$1,412

Ratio calculations

	Industry KPIs 20X4	Working	Aspect Co 20X4
Gross profit margin	45%	31,800/52,000 × 100	61%
Operating profit margin	28%	19,588/52,100 × 100	38%
Receivables collection period	41 days	(5,700/52,100) × 365	40
Current ratio	1.6:1	(12,900 – 1,412)/11,600	1:1

BPP LEARNING MEDIA

	Industry KPIs 20X4	Working	Aspect Co 20X4
Acid test (quick) ratio	1.4:1	(12,900 – 4,900 – 1,412)/(11,600)	0.57:1
Gearing (debt/equity)	240%	16,700 / (9,000 – 1,412)	220%

(c)   **Commentary on performance**

Profitability

The discontinued operation had a gross profit % (GP%) of 43% (900/2,100 × 100) and an operating profit % (OP%) of 10% (200/2,100 × 100). Before adjusting for the disposal, Aspect Co has a GP% of 60%. After an adjustment has been made to reflect the disposal, Aspect Co's GP% is 61% which is higher than the industry average of 45%. Thus, it would appear that the disposal of the non-core division has had a positive impact on the GP% of Aspect Co. Such a positive comparison of the GP% to the industry average would suggest that Aspect Co has negotiated a very good deal with its suppliers for the cost of goods in comparison to its competitors; the GP% is 16% (61 – 45) higher than the industry average.

However, when considering the OP%, the financial statements have been adjusted to reflect:

(i)   the disposal of the discontinued operation;
(ii)   a new management charge which would be imposed by Funject Co; and
(iii)   commercial rent charges.

These adjustments result in an OP% of 38%. So, although the OP% is still 10% (38 – 28) higher than the industry average, it would appear that some of the advantage of having such a good deal with its suppliers is lost when operating costs are incurred. The OP% does not outperform the industry average to the same extent that GP% did. Although the management charge will be eliminated as an intra-group transaction on consolidation, it will still have an impact in the individual financial statements of Aspect Co. However, there is no indication of what this charge is for and whether or not it represents a market value for these costs. The rent of $120,000 is deemed to be a fair market value which would indicate that the previous rent charge of $46,000 was artificially low. If Funject Co acquires Aspect Co, it may wish to capitalise on the relationship which Aspect Co has with its supplier of goods but it might also need to investigate the composition of operating costs other than those described above to see if any of these can be avoided/reduced.

Liquidity

Aspect Co's receivables collection period appears to be comparable with the KPIs provided (40 days in comparison to 41 days). Terms of trade of 30 days are quite reasonable (though this usually depends on the type of business) and so there are no causes for concern here.

Given that Aspect Co's receivables collection period is comparable to the industry average, the difference in the current ratio (1·1:1 in comparison to 1·6:1) can only be explained by either lower current assets other than receivables (for example, cash) or higher current liabilities. As Aspect Co's cash balance does not appear to be low ($2·3m), this suggests that its liabilities might be higher than average. Perhaps Aspect Co's favourable relationship with its suppliers also extends to longer than average credit terms. As Aspect Co's acid (quick) ratio (0·57:1) is much less than the industry average (1·4:1), this would also suggest that Aspect Co is holding a higher than average level of inventory. This may raise a concern about Aspect Co's ability to sell its inventory. There is also a current tax bill to consider. Indeed, if Aspect Co were asked to settle its current liabilities from merely its receivables and bank, it would be unable to do so. Perhaps Funject Co may wish to further investigate the procedures associated with the purchase and holding of Aspect Co's inventory prior to a takeover. As a parent company, Funject Co should be able to influence these procedures and have more control over the levels of inventory held.

BPP LEARNING MEDIA

Gearing

Aspect Co appears to be highly geared but perhaps this is not a huge cause for concern because it appears to be a highly geared industry (220% compared to 240%). It may be that the proceeds from the sale of the non-core division can be/were used to pay down loans. As the gearing for the industry is higher than that of Aspect Co, it may be that Aspect Co could still increase borrowings in future. If so, Aspect Co may need to increase working capital efficiency and reduce costs in order to generate enough cash to service higher borrowings.

Conclusion

Overall, Aspect's statement of financial position gives little cause for concern; the profitability margins appear to be healthy although further investigations of operating costs and working capital efficiency may be required. More information also needs to be obtained about the nature of the business and perhaps the financial statements of several years (as opposed to one) might also be beneficial.

237 Pastry Co

Text references. Chapters 20 and 21.

Top tips. You have been given the ratios before adjustment and are asked to recalculate them after making adjustments for consistent accounting policies. You need to find an efficient way to process any adjustments in respect of the accounting policies and calculating the ratios as the requirement is only worth six marks. The CBE version of the question available on the ACCA website (www.accaglobal.com) contains a pre-formatted response area which would help with your approach. You must ensure your analysis uses information provided in the question in order that your answer has sufficient depth. The Examiner's report for this question states that rote learned answers to ratio analysis will not score credit.

Easy marks. The calculation of ratios should be well practiced and should be relatively easy.

Examining Team's comments. Most candidates scored poorly on this question due to poor exam technique, either due to not addressing the requirements or not using the information in the scenario.

Marking scheme

	Marks
Adjustment of financial statements	3
Ratio calculations	3
Analysis – 1 mark per well explained point	14
	20

(a) Adjusted financial statement extracts and ratios for Dough Co

	As per question $'000	Adjustment $'000	Adjusted $'000
SOPL:			
Revenue	16,300		16,300
Cost of sales	(8,350)	(2,500)	(10,850)
Gross profit	7,950		5,450
Operating expenses	(4,725)	1,000	(1,225)
		2,500	

	As per question $'000	Adjustment $'000	Adjusted $'000
Profit from operations	3,225		4,225
SOFP:			
Property	68,500	(30,000) 1,000	39,500
Equity shares	1,000		1,000
Revaluation surplus	30,000	(30,000)	Nil
Retained earnings	2,600	1,000	3,600
Loan notes	5,200		5,200

	Cook Co	Dough Co (original)	Workings	Dough Co (restated)
Gross profit margin	32.3%	48.8%	5,450/16,300 × 100	33.4%
Operating profit margin	23.3%	19.8%	4,225/16,300 × 100	25.9%
ROCE	18.8%	8.3%	4,225/(4,600 + 5,200) × 100	43.1%

If Dough Co accounted for properties under the cost model:

- Depreciation would reduce by $1,000,000 ($30 million/30 years) making operating expenses $3,725,000, and profit from operations $4,225,000.

- Retained earnings would increase by $1,000,000 to $3,600,000.

- Revaluation surplus of $30 million would be removed.

- Property would decrease by $29 million ($30 million less extra depreciation).

If Dough Co accounted for amortisation in cost of sales:

- Cost of sales would increase by $2.5 million, making gross profit $5,450,000.

- Operating expenses would decrease by $2.5 million, but profit from operations would remain at $4,225,000

(b) Cook Co may be a slightly larger company, having made more sales and profits during the year. Initially, it appears that Dough Co makes a significantly higher margin than Cook Co (48.8% compared to 32.3%), which suggests that it is much more profitable to sell as a retailer rather than wholesale.

However, this is misleading as the higher gross profit margin is largely due to the accounting policy of where amortisation is charged. Once the figures are adjusted to make the two companies comparable, the two gross profit margins are much closer (33.4% and 32.3%).

Even with this adjustment, Dough Co still makes a higher gross profit margin, suggesting that the relatively high-cost properties are still producing a good return. Looking at the operating profit margin, it appears that Cook Co makes a significantly higher margin, suggesting a greater cost control (23.3% compared to 19.8%). Once the adjustments for the different accounting policies are taken into account, it can be seen that the margins are much more comparable (23.3% and 25.9%). Without further information on the operating expenses, it is difficult to draw too many conclusions about the cost management of the two companies. The one thing which can be noted is the higher payment of salaries in Dough Co compared to Cook Co. As both companies are owner managed, it may be that

Cook Co's management are taking a lower level of salaries in order to show increased profits.

Alternatively, it could be that the Dough Co management are taking salaries which are too high, at the expense of the growth of the business. The low level of retained earnings suggests that Dough Co's owners may not leave much money in the business for growing the company.

ROCE

When looking at the return on capital employed, the initial calculations show that Cook Co is making a much more impressive return from its long-term funding (18.8% compared to 8.3%). This is completely reversed when the revaluation surplus is removed from Dough Co's figures, as Dough Co makes a return of almost twice that of Cook Co (18.8% and 43.1%).

This return is not due to high operating profits, as the margins of the two companies are similar, with Dough Co actually making lower profits from operations.

The reason for the high return on capital employed is that Dough Co has a much better asset turnover than Cook Co. This is not because Dough Co is generating more sales, as these are lower than Cook Co. The reason is that Dough Co has a significantly lower equity balance, due to having extremely low retained earnings relative to Cook Co.

Difficulties

Without examining the market value of Cook Co's properties, it will be difficult to assess which company is likely to cost more to purchase. Basing any investment decision on a single year's financial statements is difficult, as the impact of different accounting policies is difficult to assess. From the information provided, it is unclear whether Cook Co's directors are taking an unrealistically low salary, or whether Dough Co's directors are taking vastly greater salaries than average.

Conclusion

Overall, both companies appear to be profitable and have performed well. Looking at previous years' financial statements of both entities will enable us to make a much clearer investment decision, as will looking at the notes to the accounts to assess the accounting policies applied by each company.

238 Quartile Co (Dec 2012 (amended))

Text references. Chapters 20 and 21.

Top tips. A bit of planning is useful for a question like this and the categories of profitability, liquidity and gearing give you a structure around which to base your analysis. Note that this is a retail business, so this will affect the ratios.

Easy marks. Analysis of the ratios is straightforward and some useful points on the limitations on usefulness of a sector average comparison could have earned four marks.

Marking scheme

		Marks
(a)	Ratios	8
(b)	1 mark per valid comment	12
Total for question		20

(a)

	Sector average	Working	Quartile Co
Return on year-end capital employed (ROCE)	16.8%	(3,400 + 800) / (26,600 + 8,000)	12.1%
Net asset turnover	1.4 times	56,000 (26,600 + 8,000)	1.6 times
Gross profit margin	35%	14,000 / 56,000	25%
Operating profit margin	12%	(14,000 − 9,800) / 56,000	7.5%
Current ratio	1.25:1	11,200/7,200	1.55:1
Average inventory turnover	3 times	42,000 / 10,200	4.1 times
Trade payables' payment period	64 days	5,400/42,000 × 365	47 days
Gearing	38%	8,000 / (26,600 + 8,000)	33%

(b) **Analysis of financial and operating performance of Quartile Co compared to sector average**

Profitability

Quartile Co has a ROCE **significantly lower** at 12.1% than the sector average of 16.8%. This is mainly due to the lower than average gross profit margin and consequent **low operating profit margin**. The operating expenses are actually lower (17.5%) as a percentage of revenue than the sector average of 23% (35% − 12%) so the problem lies between revenue and cost of sales. This is consistent with the fact the directors regularly hold 'all stock must go' sales, when inventory will be sold at a discount to its normal retail prices to encourage sales to be made. The inventory turnover is quite brisk (4.5 times compared to a sector average of 3 times) but Quartile Co's mark-up of 33.3% ((25 / 75) × 100) is significantly below the sector average of 54% ((35 / 65) × 100). Quartile Co is maintaining turnover **by keeping prices down**.

The other component of ROCE, net asset turnover, is slightly higher than the sector average. This is due to the buoyant turnover, as the ratio will have been depressed by the property revaluation and the capitalisation of the development expenditure, which have increased the asset base. It is to be hoped that the development expenditure will generate the expected revenue. If it had been necessary to expense it for the year ended 30 September 20X2 Quartile Co would have reported a loss before tax of $1.6 million.

Liquidity

Quartile Co has a current ratio of 1.55:1 compared to the sector average of 1.25:1. Both appear low, but satisfactory for the retail sector as the cash cycle is fairly rapid. Inventory can be turned into immediate cash and this is particularly true for Quartile Co with its high inventory turnover level. It has no trade receivables which is consistent with expectations for a retail company. The lower than average payables days (45 compared to 64) and the absence of an overdraft suggest that **Quartile Co is not suffering liquidity problems.**

Gearing

Quartile Co's debt to equity ratio is 30%, well below the sector average of 38% and the interest rate on the loan notes is below the ROCE of 12.1%, meaning that the **borrowings are earning a good return** for the business. The loan notes need to be repaid in two years' and the company does not currently have sufficient cash reserves to repay the loan. The company paid a large dividend of $1.5m in the year and it would be advisable not to make such large payments in the future in order to fund the loan repayments. The interest cover of 5.25 times (4,200 / 800) is satisfactory. Quartile Co is not having any problems servicing its loan and is unlikely to give lenders any particular concern.

Conclusion

There are no going concern worries for Quartile Co but it does have an issue with **low profitability**. It appears to be positioned at the bottom end of the jewellery market selling high volume cheap items rather than more valuable pieces on which there would be significantly higher profit margins. This may or may not be the most advantageous strategy in a period of recession.

239 Mowair Co (Sept/Dec 2017)

Text references. Chapters 20 and 21.

Top tips. Following calculation of the ratios, it is important to consider the narrative behind the scenario not just the financial information provided. This question gives suitable headings as part B asks for commentary on the 'performance' and 'position' of the business. As this is a discussion question, it is expected that the candidate can supply a suitable conclusion, even if only a short paragraph or couple of sentences as this shows an understanding of the whole question and that the candidate can pull their answer together.

Easy marks. Ensure workings (or underlying formula) are shown for the calculation of the ratios (which is generally performed well by candidates). Marks are awarded not just for the ratio answers, but also for the workings behind them.

Examining Team's comments. The Examining Team are looking for meaningful use of the scenario, not just stating that ratios have improved/worsened, there needs to be relevant suggested reasons why these changes may have occurred. Calculation of ratios was performed well, however, candidates are not using all the information provided in the question when answering the analysis question in part B.

Marking scheme

		Marks	
(a)	Ratio calculations	6	
			6
(b)	Performance	6	
	Position	4	
	Future issues of concern	3	
	Conclusion	1	
			14
			20

(a)

	20X7	Workings	20X6	Workings
Operating profit margin	8.0%	(12,300/154,000) × 100	11.7%	(18,600/159,000) × 100
Return on capital employed	3.6%	(12,300/(192,100 + 130,960 + 19,440)) × 100	8.7%	(18,600/(44,800 + 150,400 + 19,440)) × 100
Net asset turnover	0.45 times	154,000/(192,100 + 130,960 + 19,440)	0.74 times	159,000/(44,800 + 150,400 + 19,440)
Current ratio	0.53:1	15,980/29,920	1.22:1	28,890/23,690
Interest cover	1.3 times	12,300/9,200	1.8 times	18,600/10,200
Gearing (Debt/Equity)	78.3%	((130,960 + 19,440)/192,100) × 100	379.1%	((150,400 + 19,440)/44,800) × 100

(b)   **Performance**

Mowair Co's revenue has declined in the year. As Mowair Co has had exactly the same number of flights in the year, the decline must be due to either lower numbers of passengers or from Mowair Co reducing the price on certain flights. To substantiate this, it would be helpful to see the number of passengers who have flown on Mowair Co flights during the year.

In addition to the decline in revenue, there has been a decline in the operating profit margin in the year. As the number of flights operated by Mowair Co has remained the same, it would appear that a number of the costs incurred by Mowair Co on operating the airline will be relatively fixed and may not have changed significantly during the year. It has been noted that there has been an increase in cost of licences charged by airports during the year, which would again cause the operating profit margin to fall as amortisation would be higher. This only occurred in April 20X7, so the full impact will not actually be felt until next year.

In addition to this, it important to note that there are numerous contracts up for renewal in the next year. This could lead to higher prices for using the airports, and may even result in Mowair Co being unable to use those airports in future. If this was the case, it may have a significant impact on the revenue for the business, as these are described as major airports, which will have the higher levels of demand.

Return on capital employed has declined significantly in the year. There are two major reasons for this. First, there has been a decline in the profit from operations, as discussed above. In addition to this, Mowair Co has revalued its non-current assets in the year. This means that there is a large revaluation surplus in 20X7 which was not present in 20X6. This will have the effect of reducing the return on capital employed due to there being a much larger total balance in equity. If the return on capital employed is calculated without this, it would be 6·2%, which still represents a decline in performance.

Looking at the net asset turnover, this has declined dramatically from 0·74 times to 0·45 times. This will again be affected by the revaluation surplus, making the two years incomparable. If this is removed from the calculation, the net asset turnover increases to 0·78 times. This is a slight increase in performance. This increase has not come from increased revenue, as it can be seen that revenue has fallen by $5 million. Rather, this increase has come from the decrease in capital employed. This arises from the reduction in the loan notes, which appear to have a significant amount repaid annually.

Position

The value of non-current assets has risen sharply in the year, by $147 million. A large proportion of that will be due to the revaluation which has taken place, leading to an increase of $145 million. This suggests that Mowair Co has acquired some new assets in the year, but it is unclear what these are. They may be replacement components on aircraft, as it is unlikely to be significant enough to be an actual new aircraft itself.

The level of debt in the business is a concern, as this makes up a significant portion of the entity's financing, and appears to incur a large annual repayment. The reduction in the current ratio can be attributed to the large decrease in cash, which is likely to be due to the debt repayments made.

It is worth noting that Mowair Co is almost completely funded by debt, with a relatively small amount held in share capital. Therefore, there is an opportunity for a new investor to consider putting more money into the business in the form of shares and the company then repaying some of the loans held by Mowair Co. As Mowair Co is currently repaying $19 million a year on the loans, it may be more sensible to repay these if possible, freeing up a lot more cash for growing the business or to be returned annually in the form of dividends, also saving $9 million a year in interest.

Issues to consider in the future

There are a number of things to consider regarding the future performance of Mowair Co. The first of these is the ten major licences which are due for renegotiation with airports. If the price is raised on these, then this will lead to reduced profits being made by Mowair Co in future periods.

The debt appears to be being repaid in annual instalments of $19 million, meaning that Mowair Co needs to generate sufficient cash to repay that each year, before returning any profit to the owner. In addition to this, the $9 million interest means that the business appears currently unable to return any cash to investors.

Finally, Mowair Co's business model is heavily dependent on large, expensive items of non-current assets. It has been noted that there has been criticism of under-investment in these, so this could lead to large potential outlays in the near future to replace assets.

Conclusion

Mowair Co has not shown a weakened performance in the current year, but appears to be a profitable business at its core. The major issue with the business is the level of debt, which is resulting in $19 million annual repayments and $9 million annual interest. Any new investor who was able to reduce these amounts as part of any future purchase, would put the business in a much stronger cash position.

240 Perkins Co (Mar/Jun 2018)

Text references. Chapters 20 and 21.

Top tips. Start with the calculations in the order they are presented in the requirement. Ensure that the time apportionment is correctly calculated for the number of months that the subsidiary is owned. Use the headings given in the question when structuring the narrative answer, and consider what the calculated ratios represent (for example, liquidity) and so what those ratios have informed the user of the financial statements.

Easy marks. Ensure workings (or underlying formula) are shown for the calculation of the ratios (which is generally performed well by candidates). Marks are awarded not just for the ratio answers, but also for the workings behind them.

Examining Team's comments. Once again, the Examining Team have indicated that narrative analysis is brief or not relevant to the scenario, for example, omitting the disposal of the subsidiary. The loss on disposal is generally performed well, but be careful to ensure time-apportionment of the results on the subsidiary when completing the statement of profit or loss.

Marking scheme

			Marks
(a)	Proceeds	0.5	
	Goodwill	2.5	
	Net assets	0.5	
	NCI	1.5	
			5
(b)	Revenue and COS	2	
	Other costs	2	
			4
(c)	Ratios		2
(d)	Gross profit margin	2	
	Operating profit margin	5	
	Interest cover	1	
	Conclusion	1	
			9
			20

(a)   Gain on disposal in Perkins group consolidated statement of profit or loss

	$'000
Proceeds	28,640
Less: Goodwill (W1)	(4,300)
Less: Net assets at disposal	(26,100)
Add: NCI at disposal (W2)	6,160
	4,400

Workings

1   *Goodwill*

	$'000
Consideration	19,200
NCI at acquisition	4,900
Less: Net assets at acquisition	(19,800)
	4,300

2   *NCI at disposal*

	$'000
NCI at acquisition	4,900
20% × (26,100 − 19,800)	(1,260)
	6,160

(b)   Adjusted P/L extracts:

	$'000
Revenue (46,220 − 9,000 (S × 8/12) + 1,000 (intra-group))	38,220
Cost of sales (23,980 − 4,400 (S × 8/12)) [see note]	(19,580)
Gross profit	18,640
Operating expenses (3,300 − 1,673 (S × 8/12) + 9,440 profit on disposal)	(11,067)
Profit from operations	7,573
Finance costs (960 − 800 (S × 8/12))	(160)

Note: Originally, the intra-group sale resulted in $1 million turnover and $0.7 million costs of sales. These amounts were recorded in the individual financial statements of Perkins Co. On consolidation, the $1 million turnover was eliminated – this needs to be added back. The corresponding $1 million COS consolidation adjustment is technically made to Swanson Co's financial statements and so can be ignored here.

(c)   Ratios of Perkins Co, eliminating impact of Swanson Co and the disposal during the year

	20X7 recalculated	Working (see P/L above)	20X7 original	20X6
Gross profit margin	48.8%	18,640/38,220	48.1%	44.8%
Operating margin	19.8%	7,573/38,220	41%	16.8%
Interest cover	47.3 times	7,573/160	19.7 times	3.5 times

(d)   **Analysis of Perkins Co**

Gross profit margin

In looking at the gross margin of Perkins Co, the underlying margin made by Perkins Co is higher than in 20X6.

After the removal of Swanson Co's results, this continues to increase, despite Swanson Co having a gross margin of over 50%. It is possible that Swanson Co's gross profit margin was artificially inflated by obtaining cheap supplies from Perkins Co.

Perkins Co makes a margin of 48.8%, but only sold goods to Swanson at 30%.

Operating margin

The operating margin appears to have increased significantly on the prior year. It must be noted that this contains the profit on disposal of Swanson Co, which increases this significantly.

Removing the impact of the Swanson Co disposal still shows that the margin is improved on the prior year, but it is much more in line.

Swanson Co's operating margin is 32.6%, significantly higher than the margin earned by Perkins Co, again suggesting that a profitable business has been sold. This is likely to be due to the fact that Swanson Co was able to use Perkins Co's facilities with no charge, meaning its operating expenses were understated compared to the market prices.

It is likely that the rental income earned from the new tenant has helped to improve the operating margin, and this should increase further once the tenant has been in for a full year.

Interest cover

Initially, the interest cover has shown good improvement in 20X7 compared to 20X6, as there has been a significant increase in profits. Even with the profit on disposal stripped out, the interest cover would still be very healthy.

Following the removal of Swanson Co, the interest cover is improved further. This may be because the disposal of Swanson Co has allowed Perkins Co to repay debt and reduce the interest expense incurred.

Conclusion

Swanson Co seems to have been a profitable company, which raises questions over the disposal. However, some of these profits may have been derived from favourable terms with Perkins Co, such as cheap supplies and free rental. It is worth noting that Perkins Co now has rental income in the year. This should grow in future periods, as this is likely to be a full year's income in future periods.

241 Pirlo Co

(a) **Gain/loss on disposal**

(i) Individual financial statements of Pirlo Co

	$'000
Sales proceeds	300,000
Cost of investment	(210,000)
Gain on disposal	90,000

(ii)   Consolidated financial statements of the Pirlo group

	$'000
Sales proceeds	300,000
Less: goodwill	(70,000)
Less: net assets ($260m + $50m FV)	(310,000)
Add: NCI	66,000
Loss on disposal	(14,000)

(b)   **Key ratios**

	20X9	20X8
Gross profit margin	45.8%	44.9%
	(97,860/213,480) × 100%	(97,310/216,820) × 100%
Operating margin	11.9%	13.5%
	(25,500/213,480) × 100%	(29,170/216,820) × 100%
Interest cover	1.43	1.8
	(25,500/17,800)	(29,170/16,200)

(c)   The directors of Pirlo Co have determined that Samba Co is not a discontinued operation. In determining this outcome, the directors would have considered whether the operation:

- Represents either a separate major line of business or a geographical area of operations

- Is part of a single co-ordinated plan to dispose of a separate major line of business or geographical area of operations; or

- Is a subsidiary acquired exclusively with a view to resale and the disposal involves loss of control.

If Samba Co had been considered a discontinued operation, the net amount of the post-tax profit or loss of Samba Co and the loss on disposal of Samba Co would be presented separately on the face of the consolidated statement of profit or loss and other comprehensive income.

(d)   **Comment on the performance**

The revenue for the group for the year has actually declined in the year. The scenario states that the Samba Co revenue has remained the same in both years, so this decrease appears to represent a decline from the remaining companies in the group.

Whilst there has been an overall decline in revenue, the gross profit margin has improved in 20X9 (44.9% increased to 45.8%). Samba Co has a significantly higher gross profit margin (81%) in relation to the rest of the group, suggesting that the rest of the Pirlo group operates at a lower gross profit margin.

The operating profit margin of the group has deteriorated in 20X9 (13.5% has decreased to 11.9%). This is initially surprising due to the significant increase in the operating profit margin of Samba Co (41% has increased to 66%). However, the increase in Samba Co's operating profit margin may not represent a true increase in performance in Samba Co due to the following:

- Samba Co has recorded a $2m profit on disposal of its properties, which will inflate its profit from operations in 20X9.

- In addition to this, Samba Co has been charged a lower rate of rent by Pirlo Co, which may also have the impact of making the profit from operations in 20X9 higher than the previous period if the rent is lower than the depreciation Samba Co would have recorded.

This concern is further enhanced when the share of the profit of the associate is considered. This has contributed $4.6m to the profit for the year, which is nearly 40% of the overall profit of the group.

The combination of these factors raises concerns over the profitability of Pirlo Co and any other subsidiaries in the group, as it appears to be loss making. Some of these losses will have been made through the loss of rental income through the new arrangement.

The joining fee paid to Samba Co's previous directors is a one-off cost paid by Pirlo Co. Consequently, it is included in the consolidated statement of profit or loss for the year ended 31 December 20X9. A similar amount was paid by Samba Co in the form of an annual bonus in the year ended 20X8. Therefore, 20X8 and 20X9 are comparable but the joining fee represents a cost saving for Pirlo Co in future years.

The decline in interest cover appears to be driven by both the decrease in profit from operations and an increase in finance costs. As Samba Co has a large amount of debt, and much lower interest cover than the group, this should increase in future periods.

The disposal of Samba Co appears to be surprising, given that it generates the high margins compared to the rest of the group. The loss on disposal of Samba Co should be brought into the consolidated statement of profit or loss. This would reduce profit from operations by a further $14m and would reduce the operating profit margin further to 5.4%.

The sale of Samba Co at a loss is very surprising given that it appears to contribute good results and has a history of strong performance. Whilst selling Samba Co at a loss may be a strange move, Pirlo Co may believe that the real value of the Samba Co business has been secured by employing the two founding directors.

Conclusion

The disposal of Samba Co does not appear to be a good move, as the Pirlo group seems to be losing its most profitable element. The Pirlo Co directors seem to have made a risky decision to move into the software development industry as a competitor of Samba Co.

242 Karl Co

Marking scheme

			Marks
(a)	Disposal loss		4
(b)	Ratio calculations	5	
	Analysis	8	13
(c)	Comparability		3
			20

(a) **Loss on disposal**

The loss on disposal in the consolidated financial statements is:

	$m
Proceeds	20
Less: net assets	(29)
Less: carrying amount of goodwill (W1)	(2.1)
Loss on disposal	(11.1)

Working

Goodwill

	$m
FV/cost of investment	35
Less net assets at acquisition	(28)
Goodwill at acquisition	7
Goodwill impairment (70%)	(4.9)
Carrying amount of goodwill	2.1

(b) **Ratios and commentary**

	20X8	20X7
Profitability ratios		
Gross profit margin	42.9%	48.5%
	($124m / $289m × 100)	($132m / $272m × 100)
Operating profit margin	22.1%	35.3%
	($64m / $289m × 100)	($96m / $272m × 100)
ROCE	8.9%	13.2%
(operating profit / equity + NCL)	($64m / ($621m + $100m)	($96m / ($578m + $150m)
Liquidity ratios		
Current ratio	3.1:1	0.8:1
	$112m / $36m	$125m / $161m
Gearing (debt / debt + equity)	13.9%	20.6%
	100/100 + 621	150/150 + 578

Financial performance

Consolidated revenue has increased from 20X7 to 20X8, despite the loss of Sinker Co's significant customer contract three months into the financial year. This might suggest that an increase in the revenue of Karl (or its other subsidiary, or both) has more than compensated for Sinker Co's lost revenue. However, even though the group revenue has increased, the gross profit margin has fallen by 5.6% and the group cost of sales is higher than 20X7. This is likely to have been impacted by the poor financial performance of Sinker Co. Alternatively, it may be that the sales mix of the group has changed.

As sales of Sinker Co represent 14% of the total group sales, this poor performance will also have impacted on the group operating margin. Operating profit margin has dropped significantly from 35.3% to 22.1%. Administrative expenses have almost doubled from $23 million for the year ended 31 December 20X7 to $45 million for the year ended 31 December 20X8. Part of this increase will be due to the $11.1 million loss on disposal of Sinker Co. The administrative expenses will also have increased as a result of the $15 million staff redundancy costs and impairment of goodwill.

ROCE has fallen from 13.2% to 8.9%, but this figure is hard to interpret, as the return includes the results of Sinker Co (including the loss on disposal and impairment of goodwill) but the capital employed does not include the capital of Sinker Co due to the disposal at the year end. The operating loss made by Sinker Co of $17 million, plus the loss on disposal of $11.1 million and impairment of $4.9 million will have reduced operating profit. Although it is a simplification, removing these balances would result in a group ROCE of 12.9% ($64m + ($17m + $11m + $4.9m))/(($621m + $17m + $11.1m + $4.9m) + $100m) which is more in line with the 20X7 figure.

Financial position

The current ratio shows considerable improvement for the year ended 20X8, following the disposal of Sinker Co. The group was in a net current liability position at the end of 20X7. This would suggest that Sinker Co may have had a large bank overdraft balance or high levels of payables at 31 December 20X8. It would appear that the sale of Sinker Co has improved the liquidity of the group.

BPP
LEARNING
MEDIA

It should be noted that 20X8 group current assets of $112 million will include the $20 million consideration for Sinker Co. This could be used to settle some of the long-term debt. Bank loans have already decreased by at least $50 million. There is no information about the long-term loans of Sinker Co.

Gearing has been reduced during the year from 20.6% to 13.9% but, without further information on Sinker Co's non-current liabilities, it is very difficult to tell if this is a result of the disposal or whether Karl Co has simply repaid debt during the year.

Conclusion

The inclusion of Sinker Co in the consolidated statement of profit or loss does not appear to have had an adverse impact on revenue generation but, now that Karl Co has disposed of the poorly performing subsidiary, it might be able to better control costs, thereby improving gross and operating profit margins. Sinker Co appears to have been a drain on the liquidity of the group, and the position of the group appears to be much healthier following the disposal of Sinker Co.

(c)   The results of Karl Co and its two subsidiaries, including Sinker Co, will have been consolidated in the group financial statements for the year ended 31 December 20X7 but only in the consolidated statement of profit or loss for the year ended 31 December 20X8.

So, 20X8 will not be directly comparable to 20X7 because Karl Co sold its holding in Sinker Co on the last day of the year ended 31 December 20X8. This means that the consolidated statement of financial position at 31 December 20X8 will have been prepared on a different basis to that of 20X7. The results of Sinker Co for the year ended 31 December 20X8 will be included in the 20X8 consolidated statement of profit or loss (SOPL). Because Sinker Co was disposed on the last day of the financial year, its results for the full year will be included, and therefore, with the exception of the loss on disposal, the figures in the consolidated SOPL will be comparable to those of the previous year. The loss on disposal is included within administrative expenses in the consolidated SOPL for the year ended 31 December 20X8 which explains why this balance is significantly higher than in the previous year.

Operating profit of the group for the year ended 31 December 20X8 will be distorted by this loss. The consolidated statement of financial position as at 31 December 20X8 will not include the assets and liabilities of Sinker Co as the net assets are no longer controlled by Karl at that date.

Therefore, the consolidated assets and liabilities will not be directly comparable year on year.

243 Kostner Co

(Note. More points have been made to cover the type of answers which may be given, not all are required to make the maximum score of 15 marks. Marking allocation is 5 marks on profitability and 5 marks on liquidity with a further 5 marks commenting on overall performance, interactions and recommendations for management with any suitable conclusions).

(a)   **Performance**

Profitability

- Although revenue has increased year on year, management should review the individual revenue streams to assess whether there are any areas of concern.

- Membership and sundries have seen the largest decrease year on year in revenue, and as the information has stated that revenue from consumables has remained static, the fall must be attributed to membership subscriptions. As this is the core of the business, management need to assess why the income is dropping so drastically. From a strategic point, there may be an issue with the quality of the freelance trainers who are renting the studio rooms, and it is recommended that the members who are cancelling their subcriptions be asked for their reasoning to ascertain the issues.

- Membership revenue may also be affected as the revenue is not split between the non-refundable joining fee and the regular subscriptions. There may be a decrease in attracted new members hence the reduction in revenue.

- The new sports drink, ProBizz was bought at a heavily discounted rate by buying in bulk prior to the year end. Provided that Kostner can sell the product and it is attractive to the members, this may prove to be a profitable decision.

- Kostner have increased their cash using an issue of share capital $1,500,000 and increasing their gearing further by taking out a further loan of $1,100,000. Although this will have helped the liquidity of the company, there will be additional costs (and therefore reduced profitability) in interest charges.

- The provision in the accounts in respect of the legal claim against Kostner will have affected the profitability of the company in terms of the legal costs and any compensation which may be due to be paid out. Management should review their safety guidelines and ensure that such accidents are unlikely to be the cause of negligence on the part of Kostner. Management should also investigate whether the manufacturer of the equipment was negligent and whether a claim may be made regarding the fault.

- The operating profit of the business has significantly decreased from 35% in 20X7 to 17% in 20X8, with the biggest increase in operating costs (60% increase year on year). The information provided does not split down the costs, but as the cost of personal trainers is likely to be deemed a cost of sales, and other salaries in administration costs, it is expected that rental costs may be an issue here. They have sold property and are likely to be leasing gyms and properties, which may go some way to explaining the increase in rental costs. A service industry such as gyms, will have the bulk of their costs in premises and staff. Other costs, which may fall into this category include insurances, utilities and legal and professional costs. The impact of the legal claim may be greater than just the provision of $50,000 in the financial statements, but profitability may be affected by a subsequent increase in insurance and legal costs as a result. Management should review the operating costs and ensure that the costs are relevant to the income streams.

Liquidity

- Net increase in cash over the year of $5,918,000 is explained by:
  - Cash outflow from operating activities of $3,382,000
  - Cash inflow from investing activities of $9,140,000
  - Cash inflow from financing activities of $160,000

- Accounts receivable balance has increased by $722,000 year on year, this can be partly explained by two new revenue streams for the business, both of which are paid for in arrears by the consumers (the Fitness Festival receivable of $325,000 and the $300,000 from the studio hire). The remaining increase of $97,000 ($722,000 – $325,000 – $300,000) relates to the only remaining revenue invoiced with credit terms, that of the TotemPow licence. The absence of the credit controller has clearly had an impact on the recoverability of these debts, and management should address a temporary replacement to cover the collection of debts in her absence.

- By purchasing the ProBizz drinks in a high volume, and so close to the year-end, means that cash is tied up in the inventory and cannot be used to pay suppliers (which has seen an increase at year end).

- It looks like they are taking out long term finance to fund the short-term operations of the business. Normally long-term finance would be taken out to fund long term purchases of property, plant and equipment but there has been minimal purchase in the year (per the cash flow). Therefore, this seems a bit of a strange strategy and it is likely that the financing arrangement has been put in place to fund day to day operational costs rather than investing in future business.

Overall points to make

- The trade receivables, inventories and cash balances are all increased year on year, but this may be a timing issue due to when suppliers may be paid. It may also be a deliberate decision made by management to show a strong asset base at year end.

- Although the cash position at year end is positive, and shows a significant increase from an overdraft to a positive balance, the operating cash flow should be compared with the operating profit. Comparing the operating profit of $550,000 to the net operating cash outflow of $3,382,000 highlights a significant issue whereby the organisation cannot seem to cover its day to day costs. The further that the operating cash flow is from the operating profit, the greater the potential issue.

- The reasons for Kostner having an overall cash inflow are ones which are tricky to repeat on an ongoing basis, namely the issue of share capital ($1,500,000), the increase in the 10% loan ($1,100,000) and the sale of a significant non-current asset with proceeds of $9,900,000. Management need to address the issue of a negative operating cash flow position as a matter of urgency rather than relying on increasing their gearing (by increasing loans) and issuing new share capital to fund the shortfall.

- The issue of shares may be contentious with the shareholders as their previous holdings may have become diluted, and together with the fall in profits (and lack of dividends paid during the year) may potentially cause investors to sell their holdings, making the business an attractive one for a takeover by a competitor.

- Given the issues stated above, there may be a significant issue regarding the going concern of Kostner and management should take urgent action to address this.

(b)
- Liquidity and profitability can sometimes be at odds with each other. For example, profitability is increased by buying the ProBizz drink in bulk, however, the cash to purchase this will be tied up for longer (it cannot be used for other purposes within the business until the drinks are sold).

- The profit and loss statement may show no significant issues regarding the going concern of a company, however, a cash flow statement can show in more detail where the cash has been spent. An organisation should have an operating cash inflow of a similar size to the operating profit in order to prove that the business can cover its day to day expenses simply by operating in a normal manner. Kostner has seen a net cash inflow, but this is mainly because of non-trading conditions (share issue, loan increase, sale of a significant asset).

- Delays in paying suppliers may result in losing out on settlement discounts, therefore impacting profitability.

- Cash flows can also highlight where the cash is coming from, so if the trade payables are increasing year on year, with a operating cash outflow, it is a possible sign that the business is withholding payments in order to fund other areas of its business (payroll, taxes etc).

Section A

Consolidated statement of financial position

244 $195,000

	$
Fair value at acquisition (200,000 × 30% × $1.75)	105,000
Share of post-acquisition retained earnings ((750 – 450) × 30%)	90,000
	195,000

245 The correct answer is: $689,370

Consideration transferred:	$
Cash	250,000
Deferred consideration (400,000/1.08)	370,370
Shares (30,000 × $2.30)	69,000
	689,370

246 Increase $40,000

($1.2 million/8 × 4/12) × 80% = $40,000

The adjustment will reduce depreciation over the next eight years, so it will increase retained earnings.

247 The correct answer is: $105 million

	$'000
Shares (18m × 2/3 × $5.75)	69,000
Deferred consideration (18m × $2.42 × 1/1.1^2)	36,000
	105,000

248

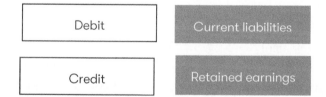

This adjustment reduces (debits) the liability and the credit is to retained earnings. The re-measurement relates to the post-acquisition period, so goodwill is not affected.

249 Fair value = $260,000; Share of net assets = $192,000

	Fair value		Share of net assets	
	$	$	$	$
Consideration transferred		800,000		800,000
Non-controlling interest at fair value		220,000		
Non-controlling interest at share of net assets				152,000
		1,020,000		952,000
Fair value of net assets:				
Shares	100,000		100,000	
Retained earnings	570,000		570,000	
FV adjustment – customer list	90,000		90,000	
		(760,000)		(760,000)
		260,000		192,000

BPP
LEARNING
MEDIA

250 The correct answer is: Record the net assets at the carrying amounts shown above and credit profit or loss with $1.2 million

This combination results in a bargain purchase of $1.2 million which should be credited to profit or loss.

251 The correct answer is: $16,800

	$
The additional depreciation charged as a result of the fair value adjustment is $5,000/5 =$1,000	1,000
Impairment of goodwill	20,000
	21,000
Restrict write off to the group share only (Pratt Co owns 80% of Sam Co) Therefore, 80% × $21,000	16,800

252 The correct answer is: Current assets $1.195 million and current liabilities $0.5 million

	$
Current assets (700,000 + 500,000)	1,200,000
Current assets	
Less: Unrealised profit on inventory ($100,000 × ¼) × 20%	(5,000)
Cash in transit	
No effect as asset in the subsidiary is exchanged for asset in the parent	-
	1,195,000
Current liabilities (300,000 + 200,000)	500,000

253 The correct answer is:

		$	$
Debit	Retained earnings	25,200	
Debit	Non-controlling interest	16,800	
Debit	Property, plant and equipment	28,000	
Credit	Goodwill		70,000

The increase due to the use of fair value is $70,000 ($160,000-$90,000) which should be adjusted by a credit to goodwill in its entirety.

		$	$
Debit	Property, plant and equipment	70,000	
Credit	Goodwill		70,000

An additional depreciation charge is required for 3 years (31 Dec 20X4, 20X5 and 20X6), therefore

$70,000/5 years × 3 years = $42,000. Therefore property, plant and equipment is increased by $28,000 ($70,000-42,000).

As the non-controlling interest is valued at fair value, the adjustment for the depreciation needs to be split between the group earnings ($42,000 × 60% = $25,200) and the NCI ($42,000 × 40% = $16,800). As Boat Co has acquired 60% of Anchor Co, the NCI share of this adjustment to earnings is 40% of the additional depreciation charge.

		$	$
Debit	Retained earnings	25,200	
Debit	NCI	16,800	
Credit	Property, plant and equipment		42,000

Therefore, to summarise

		$	$
Debit	Retained earnings	25,200	
Debit	NCI	16,800	
Debit	Property, plant and equipment	28,000	
Credit	Goodwill		70,000

254   The correct answer is: $15,000

	$
Subsidiary profits ($200,000 × 6/12)	100,000
Write off goodwill (per question, this is fully impaired)	(10,000)
Additional depreciation ($300,000/10 × 6/12)	(15,000)
	75,000
NCI at 20%	15,000

Remember to apportion the profits of the subsidiary as acquired part way through the accounting period.

Depreciation to be calculated on the fair value of the asset belonging to Sat Co. Time apportioned for the six months of investment by Pull Co in Sat Co.

255   The correct answers are:

It will be included at its fair value on acquisition plus share of post-acquisition earnings of Penguin Co.

It will be included as a separate component of equity.

25% of the impairment in the goodwill arising on acquisition will be debited to it.

If the proportionate method was used, non-controlling interest on acquisition would have been lower at $692,500 (25% × ($1,000,000 + $1,770,000)). Non-controlling interest is included in the equity of the Zebra group, not non-current liabilities.

256 $180,000

	$'000	$'000
Fair value of consideration transferred		
Cash consideration		β
Contingent consideration		250
Plus: Fair value of NCI at acquisition		100
Less: fair value of net assets acquired		
Shares	500	
Retained losses at acquisition (W)	(270)	
		230
Goodwill		300

Working: Retained losses at acquisition

	$'000
Retained losses at 1 January 20X0	(300)
Profit to the date of acquisition (120 × 3/12 months)	30
Retained losses at the date of acquisition	(270)

257

Where a parent company is satisfied that there has been a gain on a bargain purchase (negative goodwill), it should be recognised in the consolidated statement of profit or loss immediately	TRUE	
If the liabilities of the acquired entity are overstated, then goodwill will also be overstated	TRUE	

A gain on bargain purchase will be credited to the consolidated statement of profit or loss immediately. It is not recognised in the consolidated statement of financial position.

If liabilities are overstated, then the net assets would be understated. This would cause any goodwill recognised to be overstated.

Consolidated statement of profit or loss and other comprehensive income

258 The correct answer is: $144,000

	$
Consolidated cost of sales:	
Paprika	60,000
Salt	100,000
Additional depreciation for year (200,000 – 120,000)/8	10,000
Unrealised profit in inventory (32,000 × 25%) = $8,000 × 3/4	6,000
Less: Intragroup sales sold by Salt Co to Paprika Co	(32,000)
	144,000

$132,000 option deducts the unrealised profit instead of adding it on.

$176,000 omits to cancel the intragroup sales of $32,000.

$140,000 calculates the unrealised profit assuming ¾ of goods are sold to third parties, instead of ¾ goods remaining in inventory at year end.

259 The correct answer is: Decrease by $11.5 million

	$m
Decrease	12.0
Increase ($2m × 25% (profit margin))	0.5
Net decrease	11.5

260 The correct answer is: Group retained earnings will be reduced by $160,000

	$'000
Loss of investment income (Spider) (10m × 8% × 6/12)	(400)
Saving of interest payable (Fly) group share (400 × 60%)	240
Therefore the net impact is to reduce retained earnings by	160

261 The correct answer is: $50,000

	$
Profit to 30 June 20X8 (1.6m × 6/12)	800,000
Additional depreciation on FVA ((2m/20) × 6/12)	(50,000)
Goodwill impairment	(500,000)
	250,000
NCI share 20%	50,000

262 $717,463

	$
Basil Co	547,700
Parsley Co (206,900 × 10/12)	172,417
PURP ((46,000 × 30/130) × 25%)	(2,654)
	717,463

263 $80,000 $2m × 25/ 125 × 20% = $80,000

264 $264,000

		$'000
Profit for the year		1,300
Intragroup interest (5m × 8%)		(400)
Impairment (50,000 – 30,000)		(20)*
		880
× 30%		264

* The revaluation surplus is eliminated first and the remainder charged to profit or loss.

Disposals of subsidiaries

265   $145,000

	$	$
Sales proceeds		450,000
Share capital	100,000	
Retained earnings	185,000	
Goodwill	20,000	
		(305,000)
		145,000

266   $280,000 (680,000 – 400,000)

267   $245,000 profit

	$
Disposal proceeds	950,000
Goodwill on disposal (600,000 – (700,000 × 70%))	(110,000)
Share of net assets at disposal (850,000 × 70%)	(595,000)
	245,000

268   $80,000

	$'000
Consideration	580
Non-controlling interest at 20% share of net assets (640 × 25%)	160
Fair value of net assets	(640)
Goodwill at acquisition	100
Impairment at 20%	(20)
Carrying amount	80

Only the goodwill on the acquisition of Habanero Co will be included in the consolidated statement of financial position as Bonnet Co has been disposed of during the year.

269   $8m profit

	$m
Proceeds	50
Less: net assets at disposal	(39)
Less: carrying amount of goodwill (W)	3
Profit on disposal	8

Working: Goodwill at acquisition

	$m
Consideration	28
Less: net assets at acquisition	(22)
Goodwill at acquisition	6
Impairment	(3)
Carrying amount of goodwill at the date of disposal	3

Accounting for associates

270 The correct answer is: $144 million

	$m
Cost (75m × $1.60)	120
Share of post-acquisition retained earnings (100 − 20) × 30%	24
	144

271 The correct answer is: Credit group inventory $48,000.

The sale is an upstream transaction from the associate to the parent. The associate is the seller and therefore the unrealised profit of $48,000 ($2m × 25/125 × 40% × 30%) must be deducted from the share of profit of the associate. The parent is the buyer and will therefore hold the inventory at year end. The adjustment is therefore:

DEBIT   Share of profit of associate

CREDIT   Group inventory

272 The correct answer is: $5,230,000

	$'000
Cost of investment	5,000
Share of post-acquisition profit (8,500 − 7,400) × 25%	275
PURP (600 × 30% × 25%)	(45)
	5,230

273 $10,200,000

	$'000
Cost of investment	10,000
Share of post-acquisition profit (6,000 × 8/12) − 1,000) × 30%	900
Impairment	(700)
	10,200

274 $591,000

Share of profit of associate ($1,980,000 × 30%) = $594,000

Unrealised profit ($160,000/4) × 25% × 30% = $3,000

Amount recognised as share of profit of associate $591,000 ($594 − 3)

275 DR   Cost of sales

CR   Investment in associate

This is a downstream transaction as the parent sold goods to the associate. The parent was the seller and therefore earned the unrealised profit. An adjustment to cost of sales is needed to eliminate the unrealised profit. The associate holds the goods in inventories at year end. However, as the financial statements of the associate are not consolidated on a line by line basis, the unrealised profit is instead eliminated from the Investment in associate.

276 The correct answers are:

Acquisition of 50% of Castur Co. Zuckal Co has appointed two of the five board members.

Acquisition of 15% of Furnitt Co. Zuckal Co can appoint one of Furnitt Co's five board members. No party can appoint more than two.

The 50% owned in Castur Co will give significant influence as Zuckai Co will not have the power to direct operating decisions but will be able to participate in the financial and operating decisions.

The 15% owned in Fumitt Co will also give significant influence as no individual party will have control or the ability to appoint two board members. It is important that candidates understand the 20% holding is a rebuttable presumption and candidates need to read all of the information provided and not merely concentrate on the % holdings given.

Presentation of published financial statements

277   The correct answer is: The liability has arisen during the current accounting period

The fact that a liability has arisen during the current accounting period does not make it a current liability. The other options would all lead to classification as a current liability.

278   The correct answer is: A revaluation surplus of a factory building

The revaluation surplus on the factory will be presented under 'other comprehensive income'. Increases in the valuation of investment properties and profit on disposal of an investment go through profit or loss. The treatment of a government grant depends on the purpose of the grant, but ultimately it is included in profit or loss.

279   The correct answer is: Government grants

Inventories, provisions and intangible assets are shown separately. There is no such requirement for government grants.

280   The correct answer is: The time between acquisition of assets for processing and receipt of cash from customers.

281   The correct answer is: As a deduction from retained earnings in the statement of changes in equity

Statement of cash flows

282   The correct answer is: $160 million

	$m
Issue of shares	
Share capital and premium b/f (500 + 100)	600
Bonus issue (500/0.50 × 1/10)	100
Cash received (β)	400
Share capital and premium c/f (750 + 350)	1,100
Dividends paid	
Retained earnings b/f	1,740
Profit for the year	480
Dividend paid (β)	(240)
Retained earnings c/f	1,980
Cash inflow from financing activities (400 – 240)	160

283   The correct answer is: $1,440,000

	$'000
Balance b/f	1,860
Revaluation	100
Disposal	(240)
Depreciation	(280)
	1,440
Additions (β)	1,440
Balance c/f	2,880

284   The correct answer is: $8.5 million

	$'000
Carrying amount 20X3	14,400
Depreciation	(2,500)
Sale of plant	(3,000)
Revaluation	2,000
Environmental provision	4,000
	14,900
Purchases (β)	8,500
	23,400

285   $293m

	$m
B/f	410
Depreciation	(115)
Revaluation	80
Acquired under lease agreements (12 + 5 + 1)	18
Purchases (β)	287
C/f	680

In addition to the cash purchase of PPE of $287m, cash expenditure was also incurred on the direct costs of arranging the lease of $1m and the deposit paid of $6m therefore the total is $293m

286

$2,100,000	$'000
B/f (2,000 + 800)	2,800
Additions (6,500 – 2,500 – 50* + 1,800)	5,750
Payments made (β)	(2,050)
C/f (4,800 + 1,700)	6,500

*The direct costs of $50,000 incurred on arranging new lease contracts would be included in the initial measurement of the right-of-use asset but would **not** be included as part of the lease liability. An adjustment is therefore needed to remove the effect of the direct costs when calculating the lease payments made.

Section B

Root Co and Branch Co case

287   $268 million

	$m
Cash	210
Shares (116m × 100/200)	58
	268

288   $5.6 million

	Acquisition $m	Movement (2 years) $m
Property	20	(2)
Brand	25	(5)
		(7)

$7 million × 80% = $5.6 million

289   $16 million

$56m × 40/140

290   The correct answer is:

DR Cost of sales/CR Inventories

The unrealised profit is added to cost of sales and removed from inventories.

291   The correct answer is: Control of the subsidiary has been lost.

Exclusion from consolidation is only allowed when control has been lost.

Port Co and Alfred Co case

292   The correct answer is: Share capital $235,000/Share premium $1,115,000

Issue of shares

	Draft $'000	New issue $'000	Revised $'000
Share capital	200	35	235
Share premium	500	615	1,115
Fair value of proceeds		650	

293   $500,000

	$'000
Net assets at date of acquisition	
Share capital	100
Share premium	85
Retained earnings 331 − (96 × 2/12)	315
	500

294 The correct answers are:

The non-controlling interest share of profit is part of the consolidated statement of profit or loss.

If a subsidiary is acquired during the year, its results are apportioned over the year of acquisition.

The statement of financial position shows all non-current assets. Goodwill is not amortised, it is subject to an annual impairment review.

295 $404,000

Port Co $364,000 and Alfred Co ($240,000 × 2/12) = $404,000

296 The correct answer is: $2,912,000

	Port $'000	Alfred $'000
Port retained earnings	2,900	
Alfred post-acquisition (96,000 × 2/12)		16
Share of Alfred Co: (16 × 75%)	12	
	2,912	

Polestar Co case

297 $22.3 million

	$'000
Share capital	6,000
Retained earnings at 30.9.X3	14,300
Fair value adjustment on property	2,000
	22,300

298 The correct answer is: $130 million

(110m + (66m × 6/12) – 13m intragroup)

299

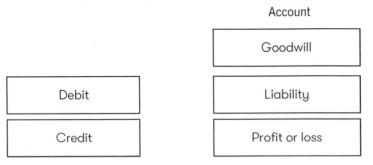

IFRS 3 *Business Combinations* states that changes to the contingent consideration should result in a remeasurement to fair value with any gain or loss taken to the profit or loss. The effect would adjust the goodwill figure if there arose new information regarding the position at acquisition date. However, if the contingent consideration, being cash in this instance which is dependent on a certain level of profit being achieved, then the adjustment is made to the statement of profit or loss. (IFRS 3: para. 58)

300 $150,000

Unrealised profit = 9m – 5.4m = 3.6m
Still in inventory = 3.6m × 1.5/9 = 600,000 × 25% = 150,000

301 The correct answer is: The non-controlling interest will be allocated its share of any goodwill impairment.

The other options are incorrect.

Plateau Co case

302 The correct answer is: $12,750,000 ((3m/2 × $6) + (3m × $1.25))

303 The correct answer is: Should be recognised at $1 million and not amortised

The contract is estimated to have an indefinite life.

304 The correct answer is: $3,900,000

	$'000
NCI at acquisition (1m shares @ $3.25)	3,250
NCI share of post-acquisition retained earnings ((W) 2,600 × 25%)	650
	3,900

Working	$'000
Retained earnings per draft	2,900
Less unrealised profit ($2.7m × 50/150 × 1/3)	(300)
	2,600

305 The correct answer is: $10,500,000

	$'000
Cost (4m × 30% × $7.50)	9,000
Share of post-acquisition retained earnings (5,000 × 30%)	1,500
	10,500

306 Plateau Co is the seller and therefore this is a downstream transaction. The unrealised profit is eliminated by decreasing cost of sales. The unrealised profit is within the inventory of the associate which is not presented in the consolidated statement of financial position and therefore an adjustment is made to the investment in associate.

	Account
Debit	Cost of sales
Credit	Investment in associate

Pinto Co case

307 The correct answer is: $10,000 received

	$
B/f current (asset)	–
B/f deferred tax	30,000
Charge for the year	160,000
Received (balance)	10,000
C/f (current + deferred)	200,000

308 $1,130,000

	$'000
Proceeds from sale of plant (240 – 90)	150
Purchase of plant (W)	(1,440)
Proceeds from sale of investment property	160
	1,130

Working

	$'000
B/f	1,860
Revaluation gain	100
Disposal	(240)
Depreciation	(280)
Purchases (β)	1,440
	2,880

309 The correct answer is: $150,000

Opening retained earnings	860
Add: profit for the year	280
Less: Dividend paid	β
Closing retained earning	990

310 The correct answers are:

Financing activities

Operating activities

Dividends paid can be presented under operating activities or financing activities.

311 The correct answer is: The proceeds from sale of plant

It is the profit on disposal of the plant that will be adjusted against profit before tax, not the proceeds of disposal.

Woolf Co case

312 The correct answer is: $1,100,000

	$'000
Bfwd (1,700+800)	2,500
Right-of-use asset acquired (1,540 – 40)	1,500
Cash movement (balancing figure)	(1,100)
Cfwd (2,000+900)	2,900

Option $400,000 is the movement between the two years ignoring the effect of the new lease. Option $1,500,000 is the actual lease amount rather than the cash movement. Option $1,900,000 uses the correct figures, but subtracts the new lease during the year which makes the cash movement now $1,900,000.

313 The correct answer is: Cash inflow of $1,860,000

	$'000
Profit before taxation	50
Adjustments for	
Depreciation (per the question)	2,200
Interest received (per the question)	(40)
Release of grant (working)	(250)
Working capital movement (per the question)	(100)
Cash inflow from operations	1,860

Government grant working

	$'000
Bfwd (400 + 900)	1,300
Grant received in the year	950
Cash movement (balancing figure)	(250)
Cfwd (600 + 1,400)	2,000

Option B of $2,110,000 ignores the cash movement of the grant ($250,000). Option C adds on the cash movement of the grant instead of subtracting it. Option D of $3,060,000 adds on the value of the government grant received ($950,000) instead of recognising the net movement in grants.

314 The correct answer is: Option (iii) only

Both of options (i) and (ii) will decrease the balances of working capital assets (trade receivables and inventory). This will result in a working capital inflow in both cases. Only option (iii) will result in an overall working capital outflow.

315 The correct answer is: Cash proceeds from the sale of a factory

This would be included within the movements of cash from investing activities. Investing activities represents payments made to invest in assets used by the company to generate profits and the proceeds from the sale of those assets, such as payments to acquire non-current assets, payments to acquire shares in other companies and the proceeds from the sale of non-current assets.

316 The correct answer is: Options (i) and (ii)

Recognise the income from the grant as deferred income; or

Deduct the grant in arriving at the carrying amount of the asset acquired

Presenting the whole grant as a separate item in the statement of profit or loss is acceptable for grants received relating to income for which the expenditure has already been incurred, but not for assets as the grant income should be recognised over the useful life of the asset purchased.

Section C

317 Pedantic Co (Dec 2008 amended)

> **Text references.** Chapters 8 and 9.
>
> **Top tips.** The first point to note here is that the subsidiary was acquired mid-year. Remember this when it comes to working out the depreciation on the fair value adjustment. This question had lots to do but no real problems. In the exam, you should set up your proforma, transfer the numbers as they are provided in the question, then start working through the adjustments. Transfer your adjustments to the proforma when you have completed each working.
>
> **Easy marks.** There were lots of easy marks here. There were lots of marks available in the statement of financial position even if you did not get the goodwill quite right. Correctly calculating the figures from the share exchange would have gained you marks on goodwill, share capital and share premium.

Marking scheme

			Marks
(a)	Statement of financial position:		
	Property, plant and equipment	2	
	Goodwill	5	
	Current assets	1½	
	Equity shares	1	
	Share premium	1	
	Retained earnings	2	
	Non-controlling interest	2	
	10% loan notes	½	
	Current liabilities	1	16
(b)	1 mark per valid point to maximum		4
			20

(a)   PEDANTIC CO – CONSOLIDATED STATEMENT OF FINANCIAL POSITION AT 30 SEPTEMBER 20X8

	$'000
Non-current assets	
Property, plant and equipment (40,600 + 12,600 + 1,800 (W6))	55,000
Goodwill (W2)	4,500
	59,500
Current assets (16,000 + 6,600 – 800 – 600 + 200) (or see (W9))	21,400
Total assets	80,900
Equity attributable to owners of the parent	
Share capital (10,000 + 1,600 (W5))	11,600
Share premium (W5)	8,000
Retained earnings (W3)	35,700
	55,300
Non-controlling interests (W4)	6,100
	61,400
Non-current liabilities	
10% loan notes (3,000 + 4,000)	7,000
Current liabilities (8,200 + 4,700 – 400 (W9))	12,500
	80,900

(b) Pedantic Co cannot take assurance from the Tradhat group financial statements that Trilby Co would be able to meet its liability in respect of the goods. The group financial statements will have aggregated the assets and liabilities of all the group companies and it will not be possible to use them to calculate liquidity ratios for any one company.

This is important, because Pedantic Co's contract would not be with the Tradhat group, it would be with Trilby Co. If Trilby Co defaulted on its obligations, the Tradhat group would be under no legal obligation to step in, so that the fact that the group has a strong financial position is not really relevant. It would only become relevant if Tradhat group were willing to offer a parent company guarantee.

In the absence of a parent company guarantee, Pedantic Co must base its decision on the financial position of Trilby Co as shown in its individual company financial statements. It should also obtain references from other suppliers of Trilby Co, specifically those who supply it with large orders on 90 day credit terms.

Workings

1 *Group structure*

Pedantic Co

1.4.X8   ↓   60%   Mid-year acquisition, six months before year end

Sophistic Co

2 *Goodwill*

	$'000	$'000
Consideration transferred (W5)		9,600
Fair value of non-controlling interests		5,900
Less: Fair value of net assets at acquisition:		
Share capital	4,000	
Retained earnings	5,000	
Fair value adjustment (W6)	2,000	
		(11,000)
Goodwill		4,500

3 *Retained earnings*

	Pedantic Co $'000	Sophistic Co $'000
Per question	35,400	6,500
Movement on FV adjustment (W6)		(200)
PUP (W7)		(800)
Pre-acquisition		(5,000)
		500
Group share (500 × 60%)	300	
	35,700	

4 *Non-controlling interests*

	$'000
NCI at acquisition	5,900
NCI share of post-acquisition retained earnings ((W3) 500 × 40%)	200
	6,100

5 *Share exchange*

	Debit $'000	Credit $'000
Consideration transferred (4,000 × 60% × 2/3 = 1,600 × $6)	9,600	
Share capital of Pedantic Co (1,600 × $1)		1,600
Share premium of Pedantic Co (1,600 × $5)		8,000

BPP
LEARNING
MEDIA

6 Fair value adjustments

	$'000 Acq'n 1.4.X8	$'000 Mov't 6/12	$'000 Year end 30.9.X8
Plant (*$2m/5 × 6/12)	2,000	(200)*	1,800

7 Intragroup trading

	$'000	$'000
Eliminate unrealised profit		
Cost of sales/retained earnings ((8,000 − 5,200) × 40/140)	800	
Inventories (SOFP)		800

8 Current assets (supplementary working)

	$'000
Pedantic Co	16,000
Sophistic Co	6,600
Unrealised profit in inventory (W7)	(800)
Intercompany receivables (per question)	(600)
Cash in transit (W9)	200
	21,400

9 Cash in transit

	Debit	Credit
Receivables		600
Payables	400	
Cash	200	

318 Gold Co

Text reference. Chapters 9 and 10

Top tips. Make sure that you read the requirement carefully before doing anything. You are asked to prepare the goodwill calculation and the consolidated statement of profit or loss. No other statement of financial position balances are required.

Easy marks. There are some standard adjustments for transactions such as dividends paid and intragroup trading that shouldn't cause you too many problems.

Examining Team's comments. This was a fairly straightforward consolidated financial statements question. The examining team reminded students of the importance of providing workings to support their calculations. Ensure you present workings or use formula in the spreadsheet response area.

Marking scheme

			Marks
(a)	Goodwill		6
(b)	Revenue / cost of sales	5.5	
	Other, inc NCI	8.5	
			14
	Maximum for question		20

BPP LEARNING MEDIA

(a) Goodwill

	$'000	$'000
Consideration transferred		
Deferred cash (90% × 16,000 × $2.42 × 0.9091)		31,680
Shares (90% × 16,000 × 3/5 × $8.40)		69,120
		100,800
Non-controlling interest (NCI) (10% × 16,000 × $3.50)		5,600
		106,400
Fair value of net assets at acquisition:		
Carrying amount of net assets at 1.4.20X4:		
Equity shares	16,000	
Retained earnings: at 1 Oct 20X1	56,000	
1 October 20X1–1 January 20X2 (9,920 × 3/12)	2,480	
Fair value adjustments: Plant	2,600	
Contingent liability	(850)	
		(76,230)
Carrying amount at 31 March 20X5		30,170

(b) Consolidated statement of profit or loss for the year ended 30 September 20X2

		$'000
Revenue	(103,360 + (60,800 × 9/12) – 5,400 (W1))	143,560
Cost of sales	(81,920 + (41,600 × 9/12) – 5,400 (W1) + 240 (W1) + 650 (W2))	(108,610)
Gross profit		34,950
Distribution costs	(2,560 + (2,980 × 9/12))	(4,795)
Administrative expenses	(6,080 + (3,740 × 9/12))	(8,885)
Share of profit of associate	(3,000 × 40%)	1,200
Finance costs	(672 + 136 (W3) + 2,376 (W4))	(3,184)
Profit before tax		19,286
Income tax expense	(4,480 + (2,560 × 9/12))	(6,400)
Profit for the year		12,886
Profit attributable to:		
Owners of the parent		12,207
Non-controlling interests (W5)		679
		12,886

Workings

1   Intercompany and PUP Post-acquisition sales = ($600 × 9) = $5,400; PUP = (1,200 × 25/125) = $240

2   FV depreciation on plant = ($2,600/3 × 9/12) = $650

3   Convertible loan – calculate liability component

		$'000	DF @ 8%	$'000
Interest	(10,000 × 6%)	600	3.993	2,396
Principal		10,000	0.681	6,810
Liability				9,206
Interest charge to profit or loss:	9,206 × 8%			736
Already charged				(600)
				136

4   Deferred cash consideration - unwinding of discount on deferred consideration (see goodwill calculation) = $31,680 × 10% × 9/12 = $2,376

5   NCI

		$'000
Silver's profit for the year	($9,920 × 9/12)	7,440
FV Depreciation (W2)		(650)
		6,790
NCI @ 10%		679

319 Paradigm Co

> **Text reference.** Chapter 9.
>
> **Top tips.** There are two important issues in this question – Strata Co showed a pre-acquisition loss and had a negative fair value adjustment. The question was otherwise straightforward.
>
> **Easy marks.** Five marks are allocated for the goodwill calculation and plenty of marks are available for standard consolidation issues.
>
> **Examining Team's comments.** The question included a fair value adjustment for plant which was below its carrying amount – which many candidates treated as a surplus. Most candidates correctly calculated and accounted for the value of the share exchange and the NCI but there were some errors in calculating the number of loan notes issued. Some candidates incorrectly calculated post-acquisition profit as $6 million.

Marking scheme

	Marks
Statement of financial position	
Property, plant and equipment	1½
Goodwill	5
Equity investments	1
Inventories	1
Trade receivables	1½
Cash and cash equivalents	1
Equity shares	1½
Share premium	½
Retained earnings	3
Non-controlling interest	1½
10% loan notes	1
Trade payables	1
Bank overdraft	½
	20

CONSOLIDATED STATEMENT OF FINANCIAL POSITION AS AT 31 MARCH 20X3

	$'000	$'000
ASSETS		
Non-current assets		
Property, plant and equipment (47,400 + 25,500 – 2,500 (W6))		70,400
Goodwill (W1)		8,500
Financial asset: equity investments (7,100 + 3,900)		11,000
		89,900
Current assets		
Inventories (17,400 + 8,400 – 600 (W2))	25,200	
Trade receivables (14,800 + 9,000 – 900 (W3) – 2,800 interco)	20,100	
Cash and cash equivalents (5,100 + 900 (W3))	6,000	
		51,300
Total assets		141,200
EQUITY AND LIABILITIES		
Equity attributable to owners of Paradigm Co		
Share capital (40,000 + 6,000 (W1))		46,000
Share premium (W1)		6,000
Retained earnings (W4)		34,000
		86,000
Non-controlling interest (W5)		8,800
		94,800
Non-current liabilities		
10% loan notes (8,000 + 1,500 (W1))		9,500
Current liabilities		
Trade payables (17,600 + 13,000 – 2,800 intercompany)	27,800	
Overdraft	9,100	
		36,900
Total equity and liabilities		141,200

Workings

1   *Goodwill*

	$'000	$'000
Consideration transferred:		
Shares (20m × 2/5 × 75% × $2)		12,000
Loan notes (15m × 100/1,000)		1,500
		13,500
Non-controlling interest (5m × $1.2)		6,000
		19,500
Net assets at acquisition;		
Share capital	20,000	
Retained earnings ((4,000) + (2,000))	(6,000)	
Fair value adjustment (W5)	(3,000)	
		(11,000)
Goodwill		8,500

2   *PURP*

Intercompany sales in inventory $4.6m
PURP = $4.6m × 15/115 = $600,000

3   *Intercompany cash in transit*

	$'000	$'000
Debit Cash	900	
Credit Receivables		900

4   Retained earnings

	Paradigm $'000	Strata $'000
Per draft	26,600	4,000
Add back pre-acquisition loss		6,000
		10,000
PURP (W2)	(600)	
Gain (loss) on equity investments*	(400)	700
Movement on fair value adjustment (W6)		500
		11,200
Group share of Strata Co – 75% × 11,200	8,400	
Group retained earnings	34,000	

*Loss on equity investments in Paradigm Co: (7,500 – 7,100)

5   Non-controlling interest

	$'000
Fair value at acquisition (W1)	6,000
Share of post-acquisition retained earnings (11,200 (W4) × 25%)	2,800
	8,800

6   PPE carrying amount

	$'000
FVA on plant (W1)	3,000
Depreciation (3,000/3 yrs × 6/12)	(500)
Carrying amount	2,500

320 Boo Co and Goose Co

BOO GROUP – CONSOLIDATED STATEMENT OF PROFIT OR LOSS AND OTHER COMPREHENSIVE INCOME

FOR THE YEAR ENDED 31 DECEMBER 20X8

	$'000
Revenue (5,000 + 1,000 – 100 (W5))	5,900
Cost of sales (2,900 + 600 – 100 + 20 (W5))	(3,420)
Gross profit	2,480
Other expenses (1,700 + 320)	(2,020)
Profit before tax	460
Tax (130 + 30)	(160)
Profit for the year	300
Other comprehensive income	
Gain on property revaluation	20
Total comprehensive income for the year	320
Profit attributable to	
Owners of the parent	290
Non-controlling interest (20% × 50)	10
	300
Total comprehensive income attributable to	
Owners of the parent (ß)	310
Non-controlling interest	10
	320

CONSOLIDATED STATEMENT OF FINANCIAL POSITION AS AT 31 DECEMBER 20X8

	$'000	$'000
Assets		
Non-current assets (1,940 + 200)		2,140
Goodwill (W2)		70
Current assets		
Inventories (500 + 120 + 80)	700	
Trade receivables (650 – 100 (W5) + 40)	590	
Cash and cash equivalents (170 + 35)	205	
		1,495
Total assets		3,705
Equity and liabilities		
Equity attributable to owners of the parent		
Share capital		2,000
Retained earnings (W3)		520
Revaluation surplus		20
		2,540
Non-controlling interest (W4)		70
Total equity		2,610
Current liabilities		
Trade payables (910 + 30)	940	
Tax (130 + 25)	155	
		1,095
Total equity and liabilities		3,705

Workings

1   Group structure

Boo Co

     80%

Goose Co

2   Goodwill

	$'000	$'000
Consideration transferred		300
Fair value of non-controlling interest		60
		360
Fair value of net assets:		
Share capital	100	
Retained earnings	190	(290)
Goodwill		70

3   Retained earnings

	Boo Co $'000	Goose Co $'000
Per question	500	240
Unrealised profit (W5)	(20)	
	480	
Less pre-acquisition		(190)
		50
Goose: 80% × 50	40	
Group total	520	

4 Non-controlling interest

	$'000
NCI at acquisition	60
NCI share of post-acquisition retained earnings (50 × 20%)	10
	70

5 Intragroup issues

Step 1: Record Goose Co's purchase

Debit Cost of sales	$100,000	
Credit Payables		$100,000
Debit Closing inventory (SFP)	$100,000	
Credit Cost of sales		$100,000

These transactions can be simplified to:

Debit Inventory	$100,000	
Credit Payables		$100,000

Step 2: Cancel unrealised profit

Debit COS (and retained earnings) in Boo	$20,000	
Credit Inventory (SFP)		$20,000

Step 3: Cancel intragroup transaction

Debit Revenue	$100,000	
Credit Cost of sales		$100,000

Step 4: Cancel intragroup balances

Debit Payables	$100,000	
Credit Receivables		$100,000

321 Viagem Co (Dec 2012 amended)

Text reference. Chapter 9.

Top tips. The goodwill impairment must be deducted from the consolidated profit or loss. The subsidiary has been owned for nine months so revenue and expenses must be apportioned. You have not been told that the parent has accounted for the unwinding of the discount on the deferred consideration, so you should assume that (as is normal for this exam) you have to make this adjustment.

Easy marks. There were plenty of marks available here for standard workings.

Marking scheme

		Marks
Goodwill		6
Consolidated statement of profit or loss:		
Revenue	2	
Cost of sales	2	
Distribution costs	1	
Administrative expenses	2	
Share of profit of associate	1½	
Finance costs	2	
Income tax	1	
Profit for year – attributable to parent	½	
– attributable to NCI	2	
		14
		20

(a)   Consolidated goodwill at acquisition

	$'000	$'000
Consideration transferred:		
Shares (9m × 2/3 × $6.50)		39,000
Deferred consideration ((9m × $1.76)/1.1)		14,400
		53,400
Non-controlling interest ((10m × $2.50) × 10%)		2,500
		55,900
Fair value of net assets:		
Share capital	10,000	
Retained earnings: b/f	35,000	
three months to 1 Jan 20X2 (6,200 × 3/12)	1,550	
FVA on plant	1,800	
Contingent liability	(450)	
		(47,900)
Goodwill		8,000

(b)   CONSOLIDATED STATEMENT OF PROFIT OR LOSS FOR THE YEAR ENDED 30 SEPTEMBER 20X2

	$'000
Revenue (64,600 + (38,000 × 9/12) – 7,200 (W2))	85,900
Cost of sales (51,200 + (26,000 × 9/12) – 7,200 + 300 (W2) + 450 (W3))	(64,250)
Gross profit	21,650
Distribution costs (1,600 + (1,800 × 9/12))	(2,950)
Administrative expenses (3,800 + (2,400 × 9/12) + 2,000 (goodwill impairment))	(7,600)
Finance costs (W4)	(1,500)
Share of profit of associate (2,000 × 40%)	800
Profit before tax	10,400
Income tax expense (2,800 + (1,600 × 9/12))	(4,000)
Profit for the year	6,400
Profit attributable to	
Owners of the parent (ß)	6,180
Non-controlling interest (W5)	220
	6,400

Workings

1   Group structure

Viagem Co

1 Jan 20X2 ↓ 90%   Mid-year acquisition, nine months before year end

Greca Co

2   Intragroup trading

	$'000	$'000
Intragroup trading (800 × 9 months)		
Debit Revenue	7,200	
Credit Cost of sales		7,200
PURP (1,500 × 25/125)		
Debit Cost of sales	300	
Credit Group inventory (SFP)		300

3   Fair value adjustment

	Acquisition $'000	Movement $'000	Year end $'000
Plant	1,800	(450)*	1,350

*(1,800/3) × 9/12

4   Finance costs

	$'000
Viagem Co per statement of profit or loss	420
Unwinding of discount on deferred consideration:	
((14,400 × 10%) × 9/12)	1,080
	1,500

5   Non-controlling interest

	$'000
Profit for the year (6,200 × 9/12)	4,650
Depreciation on fair value adjustment (W3)	(450)
Goodwill impairment	(2,000)
	2,200
Non-controlling share 10%	220

322 McIlroy Co

(a)   Clarke Co is considered as a discontinued operation as it has been disposed of in the year and it appears to satisfy the criteria of:

- Representing a separate major line of business; and
- Being part of a single coordinated plan to dispose of a separate line of business.

As Clarke Co is a discontinued operation, it's results for the period and any gain or loss on disposal will be presented on the face of the consolidated statement of profit or loss as a separate line item.

(b)   CONSOLIDATED STATEMENT OF PROFIT OR LOSS FOR THE YEAR ENDED 30 SEPTEMBER 20X8

	$
Continuing operations	
Revenue (W1)	4,237,760
Cost of sales (W1)	(1,912,490)
Gross profit	2,325,270
Administrative expenses (W1)	(630,280)
Operating profit (W1)	1,694,990
Investment income (W1)	78,000
Profit before tax	1,772,990
Income tax expense (W1)	(376,700)
Profit for the year from continuing operations	1,396,290
Discontinued operations	
Profit for the year from discontinued operations (437,200 − 17,980 (W4))	419,420
Profit for the year	1,815,710
Profit attributable to	
Owners of McIlroy Co	1,616,236
Non-controlling interest (W2)	199,474

(c)   Retained earnings as at 30 September 20x8

	Retained earnings $
Individual statements of financial position per question:	
McIlroy Co	3,419,310
Post-acquisition share of Spieth Co (80% × (581,580 − 180,600))	1,080
Adjustments:	
Impairment of goodwill in Spieth Co	(30,000)
Excess depreciation on fair value adjustments ($10,000 × 4yrs)	(40,000)
McIlroy Co gain on disposal of Clarke Co (582,000 − 268,000) (Note)	314,000
	3,984,094

Note. Because the only accounting that has taken place in respect of the disposal of Clarke Co is to record the disposal proceeds in the suspense account, the gain on disposal in the individual financial statements of McIlroy Co needs to be recorded in McIlroy Co's retained earnings. An alternative working using the group profit on disposal is as follows:

Individual statements of financial position per question:	
McIlroy Co	3,419,310
Post-acquisition share of Spieth Co (80% × (581,580 − 180,600))	320,784
Post-acquisition share of Clarke Co (65% × (286,000 − 174,200) + (65% × 437,400))	356,980
Adjustments:	
Impairment of goodwill in Spieth Co	(30,000)
Excess depreciation on fair value adjustments ($10,000 × 4yrs)	(40,000)
Impairment of goodwill in Clarke Co	25,000
Group loss on disposal of Clarke Co (W4)	17,980
	3,984,094

Workings

1   *Consolidation schedule*

	McIlroy Co $	Spieth Co $	Adj $	Consol $
Revenue	3,463,760	828,000	(54,000)	4,237,760
Cost of sales – per Q	(1,558,690)	(402,400)	54,000	(1,912,490)
– PURP (W5)		(5,400)		
Admin expenses – per Q	(486,700)	(103,580)		(630,280)
– FV depreciation (80,000/8yrs)		(10,000)		
– Impairment of goodwill	(30,000)			
Investment income	318,000		(240,000)	78,000
Income tax expense	(302,000)	(74,700)		(376,700)
	1,404,370	231,920		

2   *Non-controlling interest in year*

	$
Spieth Co (20% × 231,920 (W1))	46,384
Clarke Co (35% × 437,400)	153,090
	199,474

3 *Goodwill – Clarke Co*

		$
Consideration transferred		268,000
Non-controlling interest at acquisition (274,200 × 35%)		95,970
		363,970
Less Net assets at acquisition		
Share capital	100,000	
Retained earnings	174,200	
		(274,200)
Goodwill		89,770
Impairment loss		(25,000)
Goodwill at date of disposal		64,770

4 *Group profit/loss on disposal of Clarke Co*

	$	$
Sale proceeds		582,000
Less carrying amount of goodwill at disposal (W3)		(64,770)
Less carrying amount of net assets at disposal		
Share capital	100,000	
Retained earnings (286,000 + 437,400)	723,400	
		(823,400)
		288,190
Add back attributable to non-controlling interest (823,400 × 35%)		
Loss on disposal		(17,980)

5 *PURP*

	%	$
Selling price	100	54,000
Cost	(80)	(43,200)
Gross profit	20	10,800
× 1/2 in inventory		5,400

323 Plastik Co (Dec 2014 amended)

Text references. Chapters 3, 4 and 15.

Top tips. This is quite a time-pressured question so you need to work fast. Get the proforma down for the statement of profit or loss and then go methodically through the workings, showing your workings clearly.

Easy marks. There are some marks available for figures that can be lifted straight from the question and good, clear workings will help you to fill in several gaps.

Marking scheme

			Marks
(a)	Goodwill		4
(b)	Group retained earnings	4	
	Non-controlling interest	2	
			6
(c)	Consolidated statement of profit or loss and other comprehensive income		
	Revenue	1½	
	Cost of sales	2½	
	Distribution costs	½	
	Administrative expenses (including goodwill impairment)	1	

	Marks	
Finance costs	1	
Income tax expense	½	
Gain on revaluation of properties	1	
Non-controlling interest – profit for the year	1	
– total comprehensive income	1	
		10
Total for question		20

(a) *Goodwill*

	$'000	$'000
Consideration transferred – 4.8m shares @ $3		14,400
Deferred consideration (7.2m × $0.275 × 1/1.1)		1,800
		16,200
Fair value of NCI (1.8m shares @ $2.50)		4,500
		20,700
Fair value of net assets:		
Shares	9,000	
Retained earnings (3,500 – (2,000 × 9/12))	2,000	
Fair value adjustment – property	4,000	
		(15,000)
Goodwill at acquisition		5,700

(b) *Retained earnings*

	Plastik $'000	Subtrak $'000
Per question	6,300	3,500
Less pre-acquisition (1,500 + (2,000 × 3/12))		(2,000)
Goodwill impairment		(500)
Unwinding of discount on deferred consideration (1,800 (a) × 10% × 9/12)	(135)	
Depreciation on FVA		(100)
PURP (600,000 × 25/125)	(120)	
	6,045	900
Share of Subtrak Co (900 × 80%)	720	
	6,765	

Non-controlling interest

	$'000
NCI at acquisition (see goodwill)	4,500
Share of post-acquisition retained earnings (900 × 20%)	180
Share of property revaluation gain (600 × 20%)	120
	4,800

(c) CONSOLIDATED STATEMENT OF PROFIT OR LOSS AND OTHER COMPREHENSIVE INCOME
     FOR THE YEAR ENDED 30 SEPTEMBER 20X4

	$'000
Revenue (62,600 + (30,000 × 9/12) – 2,700 (W2))	82,400
Cost of sales (45,800 + (24,000 × 9/12) – 2,580 (W2) + 100 (b))	61,320
Gross profit	21,080
Distribution costs (2,000 + (1,200 × 9/12))	(2,900)
Administrative expenses (3,500 + (1,800 × 9/12) + 500 (goodwill))	(5,350)
Finance costs (200 + 135 (see retained earnings))	(335)
Profit before tax	12,495
Income tax (3,100 + (1,000 × 9/12))	(3,850)
	8,645
Other comprehensive income	
Gain on revaluation of property (1,500 + 600)	2,100
Total comprehensive income	10,745
Profit for the year attributable to:	
Owners of the parent (β)	8,465
Non-controlling interest (W1)	180
	8,645
Total comprehensive income attributable to:	
Owners of the parent (β)	10,445
Non-controlling interest (W1)	300
	10,745

Workings

1   *Non-controlling interests*

	Profit for year $'000	Total comprehensive income $'000
Per (b) above	900	900
Gain on property revaluation		600
	900	1,500
NCI 20%	180	300

2   *Intragroup trading*

		$'000	$'000
(1)	*Cancel intragroup sales/purchases*		
	Debit Group revenue (300,000 × 9)	2,700	
	Credit Group cost of sales		2,700
(2)	*Eliminate unrealised profit*		
	Debit Cost of sales (600,000 × 25/125)	120	
	Credit Group inventories		120

324 Laurel Co

STATEMENT OF FINANCIAL POSITION AS AT 31 DECEMBER 20X9

	$m
Non-current assets	
Property, plant and equipment (220 + 160 + (W7) 3)	383.0
Goodwill (W2)	9.0
Investment in associate (W3)	96.8
	488.8
Current assets	
Inventories (384 + 234 – (W6) 10)	608.0
Trade receivables (275 + 166)	441.0
Cash and cash equivalents (42 + 10)	52.0
	1,101.0
	1,589.8
Equity attributable to owners of the parent	
Share capital – $1 ordinary shares	400.0
Share premium	16.0
Retained earnings (W4)	326.8
	742.8
Non-controlling interests (W5)	47.0
	789.8
Current liabilities	
Trade payables (457 + 343)	800.0
	1,589.8

Workings

1   Group structure

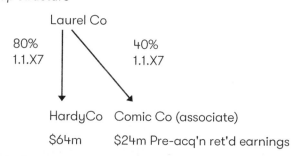

Laurel Co

80%
1.1.X7

40%
1.1.X7

HardyCo   Comic Co (associate)

$64m $24m Pre-acq'n ret'd earnings

2   Goodwill

	$m	$m
Consideration transferred		160
Non-controlling interests (at fair value)		39
Fair value of net assets at acq'n:		
Share capital	96	
Share premium	3	
Retained earnings	64	
Fair value adjustment (W7)	12	
		(175)
		24
Impairment losses		(15)
		9

3   *Investment in associate*

	$m
Cost of associate	70
Share of post-acquisition retained reserves (W4)	29.2
Unrealised profit (W6)	(2.4)
Impairment losses	(0)
	96.8

4   *Consolidated retained earnings*

	Laurel $m	Hardy $m	Comic $m
Per question	278	128	97
Less: PUP re Hardy Co (W6)	(10)		
PUP re Comic Co (W6)	(2.4)		
Fair value adjustment movement (W7)		(9)	
Less pre-acquisition retained earnings		(64)	(24)
		55	73
Group share of post-acquisition retained earnings:			
Hardy Co (55 × 80%)	44		
Comic Co (73 × 40%)	29.2		
Less group share of impairment losses (15 × 80%)	(12.0)		
	326.8		

5   *Non-controlling interests*

	$m
Non-controlling interests at acquisition (W2)	39
NCI share of post-acquisition retained earnings:	
Hardy Co (55 × 20%)	11
Less NCI share of impairment losses (15 × 20%)	(3)
	47

6   *Unrealised profit*

Laurel Co's sales to Hardy Co: $32m – $22m = $10m

| DR Retained earnings (Laurel Co) | $10m |
| CR Group inventories | $10m |

Laurel Co's sales to Comic Co (associate) ($22m – $10m) × ½ × 40% share = $2.4m.

| DR Retained earnings (Laurel Co) | $2.4m |
| CR Investment in associate | $2.4m |

7   *Fair value adjustments*

	At acquisition date $m	Movement $m	At year end $m
PPE (57 – 45)	+12	(9)*	+3
	↓	↓	↓
	Goodwill	Ret'd earnings	PPE

*Extra depreciation $12m × ¾

325 Paladin Co (Dec 2011 amended)

Marking scheme

	Marks
Consolidated statement of financial position	
Property, plant and equipment	2
Goodwill	4
Other intangibles	2
Investment in associate	2
Inventories	1
Trade receivables	1
Cash and cash equivalents	½
Equity shares	½
Retained earnings	4
Non-controlling interest	2
Deferred tax	½
Bank overdraft	½
Deferred consideration	1
Trade payables	1
	22
Maximum	20

CONSOLIDATED STATEMENT OF FINANCIAL POSITION AS AT 30 SEPTEMBER 20X1

ASSETS	$'000
Non-current assets	
Property, plant and equipment (40,000 + 31,000 + 3,000 (W6))	74,000
Goodwill (W2)	15,000
Intangible assets (7,500 + 2,500 (W6))	10,000
Investment in associate (W3)	7,700
	106,700

Current assets		
Inventories (11,200 + 8,400 − 600 (W7))		19,000
Trade receivables (7,400 + 5,300 − 1,300 (W7))		11,400
Cash and cash equivalents		3,400
		33,800
Total assets		140,500

EQUITY AND LIABILITIES
Equity attributable to owners of Paladin

Share capital		50,000
Retained earnings (W4)		35,200
		85,200
Non-controlling interests (W5)		7,900
		93,100

Non-current liabilities

Deferred tax (15,000 + 8,000)		23,000

Current liabilities

Overdraft		2,500
Trade payables (11,600 + 6,200 − 1,300 (W7))		16,500
Deferred consideration (5,000 + 400 (W2))		5,400
		24,400
Total equity and liabilities		140,500

Workings

1   *Group structure*

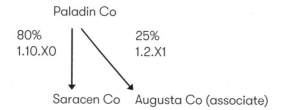

Paladin Co

80%
1.10.X0

25%
1.2.X1

Saracen Co   Augusta Co (associate)

2   *Goodwill*

	$'000	$'000
Consideration transferred:		
Cash		32,000
Deferred consideration		5,000
		37,000
Non-controlling interest		7,000
		44,000
Fair value of net assets:		
Share capital	10,000	
Retained earnings	12,000	
Fair value adjustment on plant	4,000	
Intangible asset	3,000	
		(29,000)
Goodwill		15,000

3   *Investment in associate*

	$'000
Cost of investment	10,000
Share of post-acquisition retained earnings (800 (W4) × 25%)	200
Impairment	(2,500)
	7,700

4 Retained earnings

	Paladin Co $'000	Saracen Co $'000	Augusta Co $'000
Per question – 1.10.20X0	25,700	12,000	31,800
– year to 30.9.20X1	9,200	6,000	1,200
		18,000	33,000
PURP (W7)	(600)		
Depreciation on fair value adjustments (W6)		(1,500)	
Unwinding of discount (5,400 – 5,000 (W2))	(400)		
Less pre-acquisition retained earnings to 1.10.20X0		(12,000)	(31,800)
Less pre-acquisition to 1.2.X1 (1,200 × 4/12)		–	(400)
		4,500	800
Saracen Co (4,500 × 80%)	3,600		
Augusta Co (800 × 25%)	200		
Impairment of investment in associate (W3)	(2,500)		
	35,200		

5 Non-controlling interests

	$'000
NCI at acquisition (W2)	7,000
Share of post-acquisition retained earnings (4,500 (W4) × 20%)	900
	7,900

6 Fair value adjustments

	Acquisition $'000		Movement $'000	Year end $'000
Plant	4,000	1/4	(1,000)	3,000
Intangible asset (customer relationships)	3,000	1/6	(500)	2,500
	7,000		(1,500)	5,500

7 Intragroup trading

Unrealised profit:

	$'000	$'000
Debit Cost of sales/retained earnings (2,600 × 30/130)	600	
Credit Inventories		600
Current account:		
Debit Group trade payables	1,300	
Credit Group trade receivables		1,300

at the year end, so this is the only option which would require adjustment. The others have all taken place after the year end.

326 Dargent Co

Text references. Chapters 7, 8 and 11.

Top tips. This question required good knowledge of accounting for groups including correctly accounting for intragroup trading, dividends and accounting for new acquisitions (including goodwill).

Easy marks. Calculating the plant and machinery and goodwill (including consideration) carried the most marks in this question. Lay out the consolidation workings clearly, ensuring accurate time apportionment of earnings, goods in transit, intra-group balances and dealing with the investment in the associate. Don't forget the easy marks regarding the loan and the interest. Trickier points were the calculation of the fair value adjustment for the decommissioning of the mine. Remember to only time apportion SPL and not SOFP balances!

Marking scheme

	Marks
Property, plant and equipment	2
Goodwill: consideration	2½
Goodwill: fair value net assets	2
Investments in associate	1
Inventory	1½
Receivables	1
Bank	½
Equity shares and share premium	1
Retained earnings: post-acquisition sub	2
Retained earnings: other	2
Non-controlling interests	1½
8% loan notes	½
Environmental provision	1½
Current liabilities	1
	20

DARGENT CO – CONSOLIDATED STATEMENT OF FINANCIAL POSITION AS AT 31 MARCH 20X6

	$'000	$'000
ASSETS		
Non-current assets		
Property, plant and equipment (75,200 + 31,500 + 4,000 re mine – 200 depreciation)		110,500
Goodwill (W1))		11,000
Investment in associate (4,500 + 1,200 (W3)		5,700
		127,200
Current assets		
Inventories (19,400 + 18,800 + 700 GIT – 800 URP (W2)	38,100	
Trade receivables (14,700 + 12,500 – 3,000)	24,200	
Cash and cash equivalents (1,200 + 600)	1,800	
		64,100
Total assets		191,300
EQUITY AND LIABILITIES		
Equity attributable to owners of the parent		
Equity shares of $1 each (50,000 + 10,000 (W1))		60,000
Other equity reserves (share premium) (W1)	22,000	
Retained earnings (W3)	37,390	59,390
		119,390

	$'000	$'000
Non-controlling interest (W4)		9,430
Total equity		128,820
Non-current liabilities		
8% loan notes (5,000 + 15,000 consideration)	20,000	
Accrued loan interest (W3)	300	
Environmental provision (4,000 + 80 interest (W3))	4,080	24,380
Current liabilities (24,000 + 16,400 − (3,000 −700 GIT) intra-group W2))		38,100
Total equity and liabilities		191,300

Workings (figures in brackets are in $'000)

1   *Goodwill in Latree Co*

	$'000	$'000
Controlling interest		
Share exchange (20,000 × 75% × 2/3 = 10,000 × $3.20)		32,000
8% loan notes (20,000 × 75% × $1,000/1,000)		15,000
Non-controlling interest (20,000 × 25% × $1.80)		9,000
		56,000
Equity shares	20,000	
Retained earnings at 1 April 20X5	19,000	
Earnings 1 April 20X5 to acquisition (8,000 × 9/12)	6,000	
Fair value adjustments − asset re mine	4,000	
− Provision re mine	(4,000)	(45,000)
Goodwill arising on acquisition		11,000

The share exchange of $32 million would be recorded as share capital of $10 million (10,000 × $1) and share premium of $22 million (10,000 × ($3.20 − $1.00)).

Applying the group policy to the environmental provision would mean adding $4 million to the carrying amount of the mine and the amount recorded as a provision at the date of acquisition. This has no overall effect on goodwill, but it does affect the consolidated statement of financial position and post-acquisition profit.

2   *Inventory*

The inventory of Latree Co includes unrealised profit (URP) of $600,000 (2,100 × 40/140). Similarly, the goods in transit sale of $700,000 includes URP of $200,000 (700 × 40/140).

3   *Consolidated retained earnings*

	$'000
Dargent Co's retained earnings	36,000
Latree Co's post-acquisition profit (1,720 × 75% see below)	1,290
Unrecorded share of Amery's retained profit ((6,000 − 2,000) × 30%)	1,200
Outstanding loan interest at 31 March 20X6 (15,000 × 8% × 3/12)	(300)
URP in inventory (W2)	(800)
	37,390
The adjusted post-acquisition profits of Latree Co are:	
As reported and time apportioned (8,000 × 3/12)	2,000
Interest on environmental provision (4,000 × 8% × 3/12)	(80)
Additional depreciation re: mine (4,000/5 years × 3/12)	(200)
	1,720

4   *Non-controlling interest*

	$'000
Fair value on acquisition (W1)	9,000
Post-acquisition profit (1,720 × 25% (W4))	430
	9,430

327 Party Co (Sep/Dec 2017)

> **Text reference.** Chapter 8.
>
> **Top tips.** This question required good knowledge of accounting for groups including correctly accounting for intragroup trading (and unrealised profit), deferred consideration (and use of discounting) and accounting for disposals of a subsidiary (including treatment of goodwill), Armstrong & Miller is a new question in the Workbook which will help candidates to practice the treatment of deferred consideration. Part B, the analysis of the group should ensure references to the scenario, taking figures from the financial statements and explaining the usefulness of consolidated accounts.
>
> **Easy marks.** It is important to show your workings clearly, as marks can be gained by showing where you have obtained the numbers in your consolidated statement of financial position.
>
> **Examining Team's comments.** Candidates struggled with the deferred consideration calculation, and mark up and margin continue to cause confusion. The goodwill calculation was generally done well, but ensure practice of how to treat fair value adjustments. Part B of the question neglected to mention the related parties impact of consolidated financial statements (ie the intragroup trading being removed from the calculations), and many candidates failed to mention the possible favourable trading conditions that group companies benefit from.

Marking scheme

		Marks	
(a)	Property plant and equipment	½	
	Goodwill	4	
	Current assets	2½	
	Share capital	½	
	Retained earnings	3½	
	Revaluation surplus	½	
	NCI	1½	
	Deferred consideration	1½	
	Current liabilities	½	
			15
(b)	Limitations of interpretation using consolidated financial statements	5	
			5
			20

(a)

		$'000
ASSETS		
Non-current assets		
Property, plant and equipment	(392,000 + 84,000)	476,000
Investments	(120,000 – 92,000 – 28,000)	0
Goodwill	(W3)	32,396
		508,396
Current assets	(94,700 + 44,650 + 60 FV – 250 URP)	139,160
Total assets		647,556
EQUITY AND LIABILITIES		
Equity		
Share capital		190,000
Retained earnings	(W5)	209,398
Revaluation surplus		41,400
		440,798

		$'000
Non-controlling interest	(W4)	15,392
Total equity		456,190
Non-current liabilities		
Deferred consideration	(23,996 + 1,920)	25,916
Current liabilities	(137,300 + 28,150)	165,450
Total equity and liabilities		647,556

Workings

1   Group structure

Party Co owns 80% of Streamer Co.
Party Co has owned Streamer Co for one year

2   Net assets

	Acquisition	SOFP date	Post acq
	$'000	$'000	$'000
Share capital	60,000	60,000	0
Retained earnings	34,000	36,500	2,500
Revaluation surplus	4,000	4,000	0
Fair value adj inventory	600	60	(540)
	98,600	100,560	1,960

3   Goodwill

	$'000
Cash	92,000
Deferred cash (28m × 0.857)	23,996
NCI at acquisition	15,000
Less: Net assets at acquisition	(98,600)
Goodwill at acquisition	32,396

4   Non-controlling interest

	$'000
NCI at acquisition	15,000
NCI % of Streamer post acquisition (1,960 × 20%)	392
	15,392

5   Retained earnings

	$'000
Party Co	210,000
P's % of Streamer post acquisition RE (1,960 × 80%)	1,568
Unwinding discount on deferred consideration (23,996 × 8%)	(1,920)
Unrealised profit (1,000 × 25%)	(250)
	209,398

(b)   The consolidated financial statements of the Party Group are of little value when trying to assess the performance and financial position of its subsidiary, Streamer Co. Therefore the main source of information on which to base any investment decision would be Streamer Co's individual financial statements. However, where a company is part of a group, there is the potential for the financial statements (of a subsidiary) to have been subject to the influence of related party transactions. In the case of Streamer Co, there has been a considerable amount of post-acquisition trading with Party Co and, because of the related party relationship, there is the possibility that this trading is not at arm's length (ie not at commercial rates). Indeed, from the information in the question, Party Co sells goods to Streamer Co at a much lower margin than it does to other third parties. This gives Streamer Co a benefit which is likely to lead to higher profits (compared to what they would have been if it had paid the market value for the goods purchased from Party Co). Had the sales of $8m been priced at Party Co's normal prices, they would have been sold to Streamer Co for $10.9 million (at a margin of 25% these goods cost $6m; if sold at a normal margin of 45% they would have been sold at $6m/55% × 100). This gives Streamer Co a trading 'advantage' of $4.9 million ($10.9 million – $6 million).

There may also be other aspects of the relationship where Party Co gives Streamer Co a benefit which may not have happened had Streamer Co not been part of the group, eg access to technology/research, cheap finance, etc.

The main concern is that any information about the 'benefits' Party Co may have passed on to Streamer Co through related party transactions is difficult to obtain from published sources. It may be that Party Co has deliberately 'flattered' Streamer Co's financial statements specifically in order to obtain a high sale price and a prospective purchaser would not necessarily be able to determine that this had happened from either the consolidated or entity financial statements.

328 Fresco Co (Jun 2012 amended)

Marking scheme

	Marks	
Statement of profit or loss and other comprehensive income:		
Revenue	½	
Cost of sales	3	
Distribution costs	½	
Administrative expenses	½	
Finance costs	1½	
Income tax	1	
Other comprehensive income	1	8
Statement of financial position:		
Property, plant and equipment	2½	
Inventory	½	
Trade receivables	½	
Share capital	1	
Share premium	1	
Revaluation surplus	1	
Retained earnings	2	

	Marks	
Current tax	½	
Non-current lease obligation	½	
Deferred tax	1	
Trade payables	½	
Current lease obligation	½	
Bank overdraft	½	12
		20

(a) STATEMENT OF PROFIT OR LOSS AND OTHER COMPREHENSIVE INCOME
FOR THE YEAR ENDED 31 MARCH 20X2

	$'000
Revenue	350,000
Cost of sales (W1)	(311,000)
Gross profit	39,000
Distribution costs (W1)	(16,100)
Administrative expenses (W1)	(29,900)
Finance costs (300 + 2,300 (W3))	(2,600)
Loss before tax	(9,600)
Income tax (W5)	1,800
Loss for the year	(7,800)
Other comprehensive income:	
Gain on revaluation of property (W2)	4,000
Total comprehensive loss for the year	(3,800)

(b) STATEMENT OF FINANCIAL POSITION AS AT 31 MARCH 20X2

	$'000
ASSETS	
Non-current assets	
Property, plant and equipment (W2)	62,700
Current assets	
Inventories	25,200
Trade receivables (28,500 – 4,000 (W4))	24,500
Tax asset (W5)	2,400
Total assets	114,800
EQUITY AND LIABILITIES	
Equity	
Share capital 50c shares (45,000 + 9,000 (W6))	54,000
Share premium (5,000 + 4,500 (W6))	9,500
Revaluation surplus (4,000 – 500 (W2))	3,500
Retained earnings (5,100 – 1,000 (W4) – 7,800 + 500 (W2))	(3,200)
	63,800
Non-current liabilities	
Deferred tax (W5)	3,000
Lease liability (W3)	15,230
Current liabilities	
Trade and other payables	27,300
Lease liability (19,300 – 15,230 (W3))	4,070
Bank overdraft	1,400
Total equity and liabilities	114,800

Workings

1   Expenses

	Cost of sales $'000	Distribution costs $'000	Administrative expenses $'000
Per trial balance	298,700	16,100	26,900
Depreciation (W2)	7,800	–	–
Amortisation (W2)	4,500	–	–
Fraud – current year cost (W4)	–	–	3,000
	311,000	16,100	29,900

2   Property, plant and equipment

	Freehold property $'000	Plant and equipment $'000	Right of use plant $'000	Total $'000
Cost	48,000	47,500		
Acc. amortisation/depreciation	(16,000)	(33,500)		
Balance 1 April 20X1 (FVFLP $23,000 + deposit $2,000)	32,000	14,000	25,000	
Revaluation surplus	4,000			
Revised carrying amount	36,000			
Depreciation: 36,000/8	(4,500)			
14,000 × 20%		(2,800)		
25,000/5 (shorter of lease term and useful life)			(5,000)	
	31,500	11,200	20,000	62,700

The transfer to retained earnings = 4,000/8 = 500

3   Lease liability

	$'000
Present value of future lease payments	23,000
Interest 10%	2,300
Instalment 31.3.X2	(6,000)
Balance 31.3.X2	19,300
Interest 10%	1,930
Instalment 31.3.X3	(6,000)
Balance 31.3.X3	15,230

4   Fraud

	Debit $'000	Credit $'000
Retained earnings – prior year	1,000	
Current year profit	3,000	
Receivables		4,000

5   Tax credit

	$'000
Underprovided in prior year	800
Tax refund due (asset in SFP)	(2,400)
Reduction in deferred tax provision (3,200 – (12,000 × 25%))	(200)
Current tax (credit to profit or loss)	(1,800)

6   *Share issue*

Shares issued = 13.5m/0.75 = 18m

			$'000
Share capital	18m × 50c		9,000
Share premium	18m × 25c		4,500
			13,500

329 Loudon Co

Text references. Chapters 3, 12, 14 and 16.

Top tips. Work methodically through the information performing relevant calculations and working out which parts of calculations result in an adjustment to profit.

Easy marks. Non-current assets is generally a well-liked topic and you should have been able to score well in that section.

Examining Team's comments. This is a typical example of a published financial statements exam question. Candidates do not need to deal with the adjustments in order and may be advised to address the areas they feel most comfortable with first. Read the requirements carefully before starting.

Marking scheme

		Marks
(a)	Adjust profit	8
(b)	SFP	12
		20

(a)   SCHEDULE OF ADJUSTED RETAINED EARNINGS OF LOUDON AS AT 30 SEPTEMBER 20X8

Workings

	$'000
Retained earnings per trial balance	4,122
Adjustments:	
Add back issue costs of loan	125
Loan finance costs (W1)	(390)
Building depreciation (W2)	(900)
Impairment (W2)	(3,600)
Factory depreciation (W2)	(3,885)
Disposal gain on factory (W2)	500
Unwinding of discount on environmental provision ($1,228 × 5%)	(61)
Deferred tax adjustment (W3)	(203)
Adjusted retained earnings	(4,292)

(b)   STATEMENT OF FINANCIAL POSITION AS AT 30 SEPTEMBER 20X8

	$'000
Assets	
Non-current assets	
Property, plant and equipment ($11,500 + $22,015) (W2)	33,515
Current assets (per TB)	14,700
Total assets	48,215

	$'000
Equity and liabilities	
Equity	
Equity shares $1 each (per TB)	10,000
Retained earnings (part (a))	(4,292)
	5,708
Non-current liabilities	
5% loan note (W1)	5,015
Environmental provision ($1,228 + $61 (part(a))	1,289
Deferred Taxation (W3)	1,703
	8,007
Current liabilities (per TB)	34,500
Total equity and liabilities	48,215

Workings

1   **Loan note**

The issue costs should be deducted from the proceeds of the loan note and not charged as an expense. This gives the loan note an opening carrying amount of $4,875,000 ($5,000,000 - $125,000). The finance cost of the loan note, at the effective interest rate of 8% applied to the carrying amount of the loan is $390,000. The actual interest paid is $250,000 (see TB) which leaves a closing carrying amount of $5,015,000 for inclusion as a non-current liability in the statement of financial position.

Opening balance 1 October 20X7	Finance costs 8% × opening balance	Interest paid 5% × principal	Closing balance 30 September 20X8
$'000	$'000	$'000	$'000
4,875	390	(250)	5,015

2   **Non-current assets**

	$'000
Office Building	
Carrying amount at 1 September 20X7 ($20,000 – $4,000)	16,000
Depreciation to 1 April 20X8 ($20,000/25 years × 6/12 months)	(400)
Carrying amount at 1 April 20X8	15,600
Impairment	(3,600)
Fair value at 1 April 20X8	12,000
Depreciation to 30 September 20X8 ($12,000/12 years × 6/12 months)	(500)
	11,500
Factories	
Carrying amount at 1 September 20X7 ($40,000 – $11,100)	28,900
Disposal at carrying amount	(3,000)
Carrying amount at 1 September 20X8	25,900
Depreciation for the year to 30 September 20X8 ($25,900 × 15%)	(3,885)
	22,015
Disposal of factory	
Proceeds	3,500
Carrying amount	(3,000)
Gain in disposal	500

3 Deferred Tax

	$'000
Tax written down value of PPE at 30 September 20X8	25,000
Carrying amount of PPE at 30 September 20X8 per SOFP	(33,515)
	8,515
Deferred tax provision required at 30 September 20X8 ($8,515 × 20%)	1,703
Deferred tax provision at 30 September 20X7 (per TB)	(1,500)
Deferred tax charge for year ended 30 September 20X8	203

330 Dexon plc

(a)

	$'000	$'000
Draft retained profit		96,700
Dividends paid		15,500
Draft profit for the year		112,200
Depreciation:		
Buildings (165,000/15)	11,000	
Plant (180,500 × 20%)	36,100	
		(47,100)
Gain on investment (W2)		1,000
Current year fraud loss		(2,500)
Increase in deferred tax provision (W4)		(800)
Income tax		(11,400)
		51,400

(b) DEXON CO – STATEMENT OF FINANCIAL POSITION AS AT 31 MARCH 20X8

	$'000	$'000
Non-current assets		
Property (W1)		180,000
Plant (W1)		144,400
Investments (W2)		13,500
		337,900
Current assets		
Inventories	84,000	
Trade receivables (W5)	48,200	
Cash and cash equivalents	3,800	
		136,000
Total assets		473,900
Equity and liabilities		
Share capital		250,000
Share premium		40,000
Revaluation surplus (W6)		22,800
Retained earnings (12,300 – 1,500(W3) + 51,400 – 15,500)		46,700
Total equity		359,500
Non-current liabilities		
Deferred tax (19,200 + 2,000 (W4))		21,200
Current liabilities		
As per draft SFP	81,800	
Tax payable	11,400	
		93,200
Total equity and liabilities		473,900

Workings

1   *Property, plant and equipment*

	Property $'000	Plant $'000	Total $'000
Per question	185,000	180,500	365,500
Depreciation (165,000/15)	(11,000)	(36,100)	(47,100)
	174,000	144,400	318,400
Revaluation	6,000	–	6,000
Balance c/d	180,000	144,400	324,400

2   *Financial assets at FV through profit or loss*

	$'000
FV at year end (12,500 × 1,296/1,200)	13,500
Per draft SOFP	(12,500)
Gain – to profit or loss	1,000

3   *Fraud*

	$'000	$'000
DR Retained earnings re prior year	1,500	
DR Current year profit	2,500	
CR Receivables		4,000

4   *Deferred tax*

	$'000	$'000
DR Revaluation surplus (6,000 × 20%)	1,200	
DR Income tax expense (4,000 × 20%)	800	
CR Deferred tax liability (10,000 × 20%)		2,000

5   *Trade receivables*

	$'000
Per draft SFP	52,200
Adjustment re fraud	(4,000)
	48,200

6   *Revaluation surplus*

	$'000
B/f	18,000
Surplus re land and buildings	6,000
	24,000
Deferred tax provision (6,000 × 20%)	(1,200)
Net surplus	24,800

331 Xtol Co (Jun 2014 amended)

Text references. Chapters 17, 18 and 19.

Top tips. You have two financial statements to produce here, so be very organised. Note that you will have to work out the effects of the rights issue to get the dividend payments.

Examining Team's comments. This question was generally well answered. Most of the errors that occurred involved the agency sale, the rights issue (such as failing to notice that the shares were 25c, not $1), the convertible loan note and the tax.

		Marks
(a)	Statement of profit or loss	
	Revenue	1
	Cost of sales	2
	Distribution costs	½
	Administrative expenses	½
	Agency sales	1
	Finance costs	1½
	Income tax	1½
		8
(b)	Statement of financial position	
	Property, plant and equipment	1½
	Inventory	½
	Trade receivables	½
	Share capital	½
	Share premium	½
	Equity option	1
	Retained earnings	2
	Deferred tax	1
	Loan note	1½
	Trade payables	1½
	Bank overdraft	½
	Current tax payable	1
		12
	Total for question	20

(a)   STATEMENT OF PROFIT OR LOSS FOR THE YEAR ENDED 31 MARCH 20X4

	$'000
Revenue (490,000 – 20,000 (W3))	470,000
Cost of sales (W1)	(294,600)
Gross profit	175,400
Distribution costs (W1)	(33,500)
Administrative expenses (W1)	(36,800)
Other operating income – agency sales (W3)	2,000
Finance costs (13,380 + 900 + 1,176 (W4) – 10,880 (W5))	(4,576)
Profit before tax	102,524
Income tax expense (28,000 + 3,200 + 3,700 (W6))	(34,900)
Profit for the year	67,624

(b)   STATEMENT OF FINANCIAL POSITION AS AT 31 MARCH 20X4

	$'000	$'000
ASSETS		
Non-current assets		
Property, plant and equipment (W2)		168,000
Current assets		
Inventories	61,000	
Trade receivables	63,000	
		124,000
Total assets		292,000

	$'000	$'000
EQUITY AND LIABILITIES		
Equity		
Equity shares 25c		56,000
Share premium		25,000
Other component of equity – equity option (W4)		4,050
Retained earnings (26,080 – 10,880 (W5) + 67,624)		82,824
		167,874
Non-current liabilities		
Deferred tax (4,600 + 3,700 (W6))	8,300	
5% convertible loan note (50,000 – 4,050 (W4) + 1,176)	47,126	
		55,426
Current liabilities		
Trade payables (32,200 + 3,000 (W3))	35,200	
Bank overdraft	5,500	
Current tax payable	28,000	
		68,700
Total equity and liabilities		292,000

Workings

1 Expenses

	Cost of sales $'000	Distribution costs $'000	Administrative expenses $'000
Per question	290,600	33,500	36,800
Agent not principal	(15,000)		
Depreciation – property (W2)	5,000		
Depreciation – plant and equipment (W2)	14,000		
	294,600	33,500	36,800

2 Property, plant and equipment

	Property $'000	Plant and equipment $'000	Total $'000
Cost per TB	100,000	155,500	255,500
Acc depreciation b/d per TB	(25,000)	(43,500)	(68,500)
	75,000	112,000	187,000
Depreciation property (100,000/20 years)	(5,000)		(5,000)
Depreciation P&E (112,000 × 12.5%)		(14,000)	(14,000)
	70,000	98,000	168,000

3 Agency transaction

Should have been:	$'000	*Did:*	$'000	*Correction:*	$'00
DR Cash	20,000	DR Cash	20,000	DR Revenue	20,00
CR Other income (10%)	2,000	CR Revenue	20,000	CR Cost of sales	15,00
CR Trade payables	18,000	DR Cost of sales	15,000	CR Other income	2,00
		CR Cash	15,000	CR Trade payables	3,00
DR Trade payables	15,000				
CR Cash	15,000				

4   *Loan notes*

		$'000	$'000
PV of principal	(50,000 × 0.79)		39,500
PV interest flows:			
20X4	50,000 × 5% = 2,500 × 0.93 =	2,325	
20X5	50,000 × 5% = 2,500 × 0.86 =	2,150	
20X6	50,000 × 5% = 2,500 × 0.79 =	1,975	
			6,450
Debt component			45,950
Equity component (β)			4,050
Cash received			50,000
Liability component b/d	1.4.20X3	45,950	
Effective interest	(45,950 × 8%)	3,676	
Cash coupon paid		(2,500)	
Liability component c/d	31.3.20X4	47,126	

Adjustment required:

	$'000	$'000
DR Loan notes	4,050	
CR Other components of equity		4,050
DR Finance costs (3,676 – 2,500)	1,176	
CR Loan notes		1,176

5   *Dividend paid*

	$'000	$'000
Before rights issue (56,000 × $1/25c × 5/7 = 160m × 4c)		6,400
After rights issue (56,000 × $1/25c × 2c)		4,480
		10,880
DR Retained earnings	10,880	
CR Loan note interest and dividends paid		10,880

6   *Tax*

	$'000	$'000
Current tax: DR Income tax (P/L)	28,000	
CR Current tax payable		28,000
Deferred tax:		
B/d (per TB)		4,600
To P/L		3,700
C/d		8,300

332 Atlas Co

Text references. Chapters 3, 4, 16 and 18.

Top tips. This is a standard question – preparation of financial statements from a trial balance.

Easy marks. While there were a few difficult bits, some marks were available for items which just needed to be brought across from the trial balance and dealing correctly with PPE and tax would have brought in five marks.

Marking scheme

		Marks	
(a)	Statement of profit or loss and OCI		
	Revenue	1	
	Cost of sales	2	
	Distribution costs	½	
	Administrative expenses	½	
	Finance costs	½	
	Income tax	2½	
	Other comprehensive income	1	
			8
(b)	Statement of financial position		
	Property, plant and equipment	3½	
	Inventory	½	
	Trade receivables	½	
	Retained earnings	2½	
	Deferred tax	1½	
	Trade payables	½	
	Current tax	½	
	Bank overdraft	½	
			10
(c)	Earnings per share		2
			20

(a) STATEMENT OF PROFIT OR LOSS AND OTHER COMPREHENSIVE INCOME FOR THE YEAR ENDED 31 MARCH 20X3

	$'000
Revenue	550,000
Cost of sales (W1)	(428,000)
Gross profit	122,000
Distribution costs	(21,500)
Administrative expenses	(30,900)
Finance costs	(700)
Profit before tax	68,900
Income tax expense ((27,200 – 1,200) + (9,400 – 6,200))	(29,200)
Profit for the year	39,700
Other comprehensive income:	
Gain on revaluation of property (W2)	7,000
Total comprehensive income for the year	46,700

(b)   STATEMENT OF FINANCIAL POSITION AS AT 31 MARCH 20X3

	$'000	$'000
ASSETS		
Non-current assets		
Property, plant and equipment (W2)		100,500
Current assets		
Inventories	43,700	
Trade receivables	42,200	
		85,900
Total assets		186,400
EQUITY AND LIABILITIES		
Equity		
Share capital		50,000
Share premium		20,000
Revaluation surplus		7,000
Retained earnings (11,200 + 39,700 – dividend 20,000)		30,900
		107,900
Non-current liabilities		
Deferred tax		9,400
Current liabilities		
Trade and other payables	35,100	
Tax payable	27,200	
Overdraft	6,800	
		69,100
		186,400

Workings

1   *Expenses*

	Cost of sales $'000	Distribution costs $'000	Administrative expenses $'000
Per TB	411,500	21,500	30,900
Depreciation (W2)	16,500	–	–
	428,000	21,500	30,900

2   *Property, plant and equipment*

	Land $'000	Buildings $'000	Plant $'000	Total $'000
Cost	10,000	50,000	94,500	
Accumulated depreciation	–	(20,000)	(24,500)	
Balance 1 April 20X3	10,000	30,000	70,000	110,000
Revaluation surplus	2,000	5,000		7,000
Revalued amount	12,000	35,000		
Depreciation (35/14)				
(70 × 20%)	–	(2,500)	(14,000)	(16,500)
	12,000	32,500	56,000	100,500

(c)   EPS = 39,700/100,000 = $0.40

333 Moby Co (Dec 2013 amended)

> **Top tips.** The issues to deal with here were the contract with performance obligations satisfied over time, the revaluation and the deferred tax. None of these were complicated, but make sure you know how to calculate contract assets/liabilities and how to deal with deferred tax on a revaluation.
>
> **Easy marks.** There were quite a few marks for items which only had to be lifted from the trial balance, so it was important to get workings down and collect those marks. The lease and the loan note were both simple and worth several marks.

Marking scheme

		Marks
(a)	Statement of profit or loss and other comprehensive income	
	Revenue	2
	Cost of sales	3½
	Distribution costs	½
	Administrative expenses	1
	Finance costs	2
	Income tax expense	2
	Gain on revaluation	1
	Deferred tax on gain	1
		13
(b)	Statement of changes in equity	
	Opening balances	1
	Share issue	2
	Dividend	1
	Total comprehensive income	2
	Closing balances	1
		7
		20

(a) STATEMENT OF PROFIT OR LOSS AND OTHER COMPREHENSIVE INCOME FOR THE YEAR ENDED 30 SEPTEMBER 20X3

	$'000
Revenue (227,800 + 10,000 (W3))	237,800
Cost of sales (W1)	(187,900)
Gross profit	49,900
Distribution costs	(13,500)
Administrative expenses (W1)	(16,350)
Finance costs (900 + 4,000 (W5) + 2,930 (W6))	(7,830)
Profit before tax	12,220
Income tax expense (W4)	(350)
Profit for the year	11,870
Other comprehensive income:	
Gain on revaluation of land and buildings (W2)	4,400
Deferred tax on gain (W4)	(1,100)
Total other comprehensive income	3,300
Total comprehensive income for the year	15,170

(b) STATEMENT OF CHANGES IN EQUITY FOR THE YEAR ENDED 30 SEPTEMBER 20X3

	Share capital $'000	Share premium $'000	Retained earnings $'000	Revaluation surplus $'000	Total $'000
Balance at 1 October 20X2	45,000	–	19,800	–	64,800
Share issue	800	3,200			4,000
Dividend paid			(2,000)		(2,000)
Total comprehensive income	–	–	11,870	3,300	15,170
Balance at 30 September 20X3	45,800	3,200	29,670	3,300	81,970

Workings

1 Expenses

	Cost of sales $'000	Distribution costs $'000	Administrative expenses $'000
Per question	164,500	13,500	16,500
Contract (W3)	8,000		
Depreciation (W2) – building	2,400		
– owned plant	6,000		
– leased plant	7,000		
Insurance provision reversal	–		(150)
	187,900	13,500	16,350

2 Property, plant and equipment

	Land $'000	Building $'000	Plant $'000	Leased plant $'000
Cost 1.10.X2	12,000	48,000	65,700	35,000
Depreciation b/f	–	(10,000)	(17,700)	(7,000)
	12,000	38,000	48,000	28,000
Revaluation	4,000	400	–	–
	16,000	38,400	48,000	28,000
Depreciation:				
Building (38,400/16)		(2,400)		
Plant (48,000 × 12.5%)			(6,000)	
Leased (35,000/5 (shorter of lease term and useful life)				(7,000)

3 Contract with performance obligations satisfied over time

	$'000
Revenue (work certified)	10,000
Costs incurred	(8,000)
Profit to date	2,000
Contract asset	
Revenue recognised	10,000
Amounts invoiced	(4,000)
Contract asset	6,000
Trade receivables	
Amounts invoiced	4,000
Amounts received from customers	Nil
Trade receivable	4,000

4   Income tax

	$'000
Deferred tax balance:	
On taxable temporary difference ($24m × 25%)	6,000
On revaluation (4,400 × 25%)	1,100
Liability at 30 September 20X3	7,100
Balance b/f at 1 October 20X2	8,000
Reduce balance by	900
Income tax charge:	
Provision for year	3,400
Prior year over-provision	(1,050)
Reduction in deferred tax balance	(900)
Deferred tax on revaluation debited to revaluation surplus	(1,100)
Charge for year	350

5   Loan note

	$'000
Proceeds	40,000
Interest 10%	4,000
Balance	44,000

6   Leased plant

	$'000
Present value of future lease payments	35,000
Interest 10%	3,500
Instalment paid	(9,200)
Balance 30.9.X2	29,300
Interest 10% 20X3	2,930

334 Haverford (Mar/Jun 2018)

Text reference. Chapters 5, 6, 12 & 16.

Top tips. Where adjustments to profit are requested, ensure that these are clearly stated, especially if the question asks for a schedule of adjustments, or wants a clear explanation of what the adjustments are made up of. Show your workings, the Examining Team frequently states that these are not clearly given (if at all) and this is vital for gaining maximum marks. You do not need to prepare a full statement or profit or loss.

Easy marks. Statement of changes in equity, using the already given details in the question regarding the dividend paid and the transfer of profit figures. Ensure the workings are shown clearly as marks are gained for showing method as well as a correct figure (credit is given where the final answer may be wrong but the method itself is correct).

Examining Team's comments. Candidates struggled with the treatment of a bonus issue of shares and that any impairment should not reduce a revaluation surplus to a negative reserve figure.

Marking scheme

			Marks
(a)	Convertible loan notes	1	
	Contract	2	
	Depreciation/impairment	2	
	Inventory	1	
			6
(b)	Opening balances	1	
	Convertible loan notes	1	
	Bonus issue	2	
	Profit/Dividend/revaluation	2	
			6
(c)	PPE	1	
	Contract	2	
	Other current assets	2	
	Equity	½	
	Convertible loan notes	2	
	Current liabilities	½	
			8
			20

(a) ADJUSTMENTS TO HAVERFORD CO'S PROFIT FOR THE YEAR ENDED 31 DECEMBER 20X7

	$'000
Draft profit	2,250
Convertible loan notes (W1)	(135)
Contract revenue (W2)	5,600
Contract cost of sales (W2)	(1,900)
Depreciation (W4)	(720)
Property impairment (W4)	(480)
Closing inventories	390
Revised profit	5,005

(b) STATEMENT OF CHANGES IN EQUITY FOR THE YEAR ENDED 31 DECEMBER 20X7

	Share capital $'000	OCE $'000	Retained earnings $'000	Revaluation surplus $'000	Option $'000
Balance as at 1 January 20X7	20,000	3,000	6,270	800	–
Profit – from (a)	–	–	5,005	–	–
Revaluation loss (W4)	–	–	–	(800)	–
Bonus issue (W3)	4,000	(3,000)	(1,000)	–	–
Convertible loan notes issued (W1)	–	–	–	–	424
Dividend paid	–	–	(3,620)	–	–
Balance as at 31 December 20X7	24,000	–	6,655	–	424

(c)   STATEMENT OF FINANCIAL POSITION FOR HAVERFORD CO AS AT 31 DECEMBER 20X7

	$'000
ASSETS	
Non-current assets	
Property (W3)	16,000
Current assets	
Inventory (W5)	4,700
Trade receivables	5,510
Contract asset (W2)	4,200
Cash	10,320
Total assets	40,730
EQUITY AND LIABILITIES	
Equity	
Share capital	24,000
Retained earnings	6,655
Convertible option	424
Total equity	31,079
Non-current liabilities	
Convertible loan notes (W1)	7,711
Current liabilities	1,940
Total equity and liabilities	40,730

Workings

1   Convertible loan notes

	Payment $'000	Discount rate $'000	Present value $'000
20X7	320	0.943	302
20X8	320	0.890	285
20X9	8,320	0.840	6,989
			7,576

As the full amount of $8m has been taken to liabilities, adjustment required is:

Debit Liability $424k
Credit Equity $424k

The liability should then be held at amortised cost, using the effective interest rate.

Balance b/f $000	Interest 6% $000	Payment $000	Balance c/f $000
7,576	455	(320)	7,711

As only $320k has been recorded in finance costs:

Debit Finance costs $135k
Credit Liability $135k

2   Contract with customer:

	$'000
Revenue recognised (14,000 × 40%)	5,600
Costs to date	(1,900)
Profit recognised to date	3,700

STATEMENT OF FINANCIAL POSITION

	$'000
Revenue recognised ($14,000 × 40%)	5,600
Less: amounts invoices	(1,400)
Contract asset	4,200

Amounts invoiced to date	1,400
Amounts received from customers	(1,400)
Adjustment to trade receivables	Nil

$5.6m should be recorded in revenue, and $1.9m in cost of sales, giving an overall increase to the draft profit of $3.7m. $4.2m should then be recorded in the statement of financial position as a current asset.

3 *Bonus issue*

The 1 for 5 bonus issue will lead to an increase in share capital of $4m ($20m × 1/5). Of this, $3m will be debited to other components of equity to take it to zero. The remaining $1m will be deducted from retained earnings.

Adjustment:

Debit Share premium	$3m	
Debit Retained earnings	$1m	
Credit Share capital		$4m

4 *Property*

The asset should first be depreciated. $18m/25 = $720k. This should be deducted from the draft profit and the asset, giving a carrying amount of $17,280k.

Debit Draft profit	$720k	
Credit Property		$720k

Then the asset should be revalued from $17,280k to $16,000k, giving a revaluation loss of $1,280k. As the revaluation surplus is only $800k, only $800k can be debited to this, with the remaining $480k being debited from the draft profit for the year.

Debit Revaluation surplus	$800k	
Debit Draft profit	$480k	
Credit Property		$1,280k

5 *Inventories*

Closing inventories should be adjusted from $4,310k to $4,700k.

Debit Inventories	$390k	
Credit Draft profit		$390k

335 Flamingo

(a) Flamingo Co

EXTRACT FROM DRAFT STATEMENT OF CASH FLOWS FOR THE YEAR ENDED 31 DECEMBER 2012

	$	$
Net cash from operating activities (W1)		1,919,785
Cash flows from investing activities		
Purchase of property, plant and equipment (W1)	(2,992,700)	
Proceeds from sales of property, plant and equipment	825,000	
Payments to acquire right of use assets	(20,000)	
Net cash used in investing activities		(2,187,700)

	$	$
Cash flows from financing activities		
Proceeds from issue of ordinary share capital (W3)	600,000	
Lease obligations paid (W4)	(5,000)	
Dividends paid (W5)	(93,000)	
Net cash from financing activities		502,000
Net increase in cash and cash equivalents		234,085
Cash and cash equivalents at beginning of period		112,800
Cash and cash equivalents at end of period		346,885

Workings

1   *Net cash from operating activities*

	$
Per question	1,697,785
Add: PPE depreciation	260,000
Add: RoU asset depreciation	5,000
Less: gain on sale of PPE (825,000 − 782,000)	(43,000)
Revised net cash from operating activities	1,919,785

2   *Purchase of PPE*

	$
Opening balance	5,828,400
Add: revaluation surplus	200,000
Less: depreciation	(260,000)
Less: disposal of PPE	(782,000)
Cash purchase (β)	2,992,700
Closing balance	7,979,100

3   *Share issue*

	$
Opening balance share capital	2,400,000
Opening balance share premium	200,000
1 for 6 bonus issue (2,400,000 × 1/6)	400,000
Issue for cash (β)	600,000
Closing balance share capital	3,000,000
Closing balance share premium	600,000

4   *Payment of lease obligations*

	$
Initial measurement of RoU asset	540,000
Less: direct costs	(20,000)
Initial measurement of lease liability	520,000
Repayments for cash (β)	5,000
Closing balance of lease liability	515,000

5   *Dividends paid*

	$
Retained earnings	1,917,560
Add: profit	912,345
Less: bonus issue	(400,000)
Dividends paid (β)	(93,000)
Closing balance	2,522,905

(b)   It is argued that the statement of cash flows contains information that is more useful to the users of financial statements than the statements of profit or loss and statements of financial position as the users are more likely to understand what a cash flow represents. Cash flows are not affected by, for example, accounting policy choices and accounting estimates and therefore a user would not require such a full understanding of accounting in order to understand the statement of cash flows compared with the other primary statements.

The focus on 'profit' can be misleading as it does not always give a useful or meaningful picture of a company's operations and the users may be unclear as to what a profit means for the business. Many users would see a company making a profit of, for example, $100,000 and assume that it could afford to pay its employees more or to make a dividend payment of the same amount, but they would need to look at the profit in conjunction with the cash flows to determine if it was affordable to the company.

It is often said that 'cash is king' and companies which use cash faster than they generate it will find it difficult to continue as a going concern. It is important to look not just at the total cash and cash equivalents, but at the movements in the period and the reasons for those movements in order to understand the true cash position of the company. A company may have an overall net increase in cash and equivalents, but if it has funded that by selling its assets and borrowings it will be looked on less favourably by users than a company that generates positive cash from its operations.

The statement of cash flows should be used in conjunction with the other primary financial statements in order to fully understand the performance and position of a company.

336 Dickson Co

(a)   STATEMENT OF CASH FLOWS FOR YEAR ENDED 31 MARCH 20X8

	$'000	$'000
Cash flows from investing activities		
Development expenditure (W1)	(190)	
Purchase of property, plant & equipment (W1)	(192)	
Proceeds from sale of property, plant & equipment	110	
Net cash used in investing activities		(272)
Cash flows from financing activities		
Proceeds from rights issue (W2)	300	
Proceeds from issue of debentures (W3)	50	
Payment of lease liabilities (W3)	(31)	
Dividends paid (W2)	(156)	
Net cash from financing activities		163

Workings

1   Assets

	Property, plant and equipment	Development expenditure	Right-of-use asset
	$'000	$'000	$'000
B/d	657	160	80
Disposals	(103)		
P/L	(47)		(10)
OCI	100		
Additions (β)		190	
Amortisation		(60)	
New right-of-use asset			56
Cash additions (β)	192	–	–
C/d	799	290	126

2   Equity

	Share capital and premium $'000	Revaluation surplus $'000	Retained earnings $'000
B/d	500	60	255
P/L			180
OCI		100	
Bonus issue (400/8)	50		(50)
Rights issue (β)	300		
Dividend paid (β)	–	–	(156)
C/d	850	160	229

3   Liabilities

	Debentures $'000	Leases $'000
B/d	100	92*
SPLOCI		
New lease		56
Cash received (paid) (β)	50	(31)
C/d	150	117

*Non-current + current

(b)   The statement of cash flows is one of the primary financial statements and should be used in conjunction with the other primary financial statements to help the users of financial statements to better understand how the activities of the company have generated or used cash in the period.

Users can gain further appreciation of the change in net assets, of the entity's financial position (liquidity and solvency) and the entity's ability to adapt to changing circumstances by affecting the amount and timing of cash flows. A statement of cash flows enhances comparability as cash flows are not affected by differing accounting policies used for the same type of transactions or events.

Cash flow information of a historical nature can be used as an indicator of the amount, timing and certainty of future cash flows. Past forecast cash flow information can be checked for accuracy as actual figures emerge. The relationship between profit and cash flows can be analysed as can changes in prices over time.

(c)   Dickson Co has reported a profit for the year of $180,000 and has made a cash inflow from operations of $40,000. This a positive factor which shows that the normal business of the company is generating sufficient cash for it to support itself. However, there are some issues to highlight:

- The operating profit for the year ended 31 March 20X8 was $357,000 (see appendix for calculation) which is significantly higher than the cash flow from operations ($40,000). This suggests that there may be issues over the working capital cycle (the time it takes to recover the money from operations).

- In particular, inventories have increased from $227,000 to $360,000 year on year (a 59% increase), with a notable decrease in trade receivables (a drop of 15%). We are not given the revenue figures for the prior year, but this information suggests that sales may be on the decline as more inventory is held and both cash and trade receivables have declined.

- With the increase in inventory, Dickson Co should review whether there is any risk of obsolescence. There is the potential that inventory is overstated at 31 March 20X8 which is over-inflating the gross profit.

- Investments have been classified as cash equivalents, however, it should be something to review as investments should only be classified as such if they are readily convertible to known amounts of cash.

Development expenditure of $190,000 was capitalised during the year. It is important that these expenses are genuine development expenditure (as opposed to research costs which must be expensed) and that future income will be generated from these projects. There is a risk that costs will not have been correctly capitalised in line with IAS 38 *Intangible Assets*, leading to understated expenses in the statement of profit and loss, and an overstated profit for the year ended 31 March 20X8.

- The new rights share issue has raised $300,000 and the debenture issue a further $50,000. Such financing of a company should be restricted to funding capital investments, and Dickson Co has spent $192,000 on new property, plant and equipment and a further $190,000 on development expenditure. However, this is partially offset by the proceeds of sale on property, plant and equipment of $110,000. This leaves a net outflow of $272,000 spent on capital purchases to support the future business of Dickson Co. This leaves $78,000 from the financing activities of 20X8 which Dickson Co has used to support the general funding of the business. This is not a sustainable option, especially as this financing has contributed to the large dividend payment of $156,000 during the year. The justification for this dividend is questionable given the cash position of the company.

Conclusion

The Board should carefully review the current inventory holding and the working capital cycle. Any future capital financing should be for specific long-term objectives. Also, all capitalised costs must meet the IAS 38 criteria and be amortised accordingly. It is recommended that the Board does not issue a sizeable dividend next year in order to support the working capital of the business.

Appendix

	$'000
Profit before tax	342
Add: finance costs	15
Operating profit	357

BPP
LEARNING
MEDIA

Mock exams

ACCA

Financial Reporting (FR)

Mock Examination 1 (ACCA CBE Practice Exam 1)

Questions	
Time allowed	3 hours
This mock exam is divided into three sections:	
Section A	ALL 15 questions are compulsory and MUST be attempted
Section B	ALL 15 questions are compulsory and MUST be attempted
Section C	BOTH questions are compulsory and MUST be attempted

DO NOT OPEN THIS EXAM UNTIL YOU ARE READY TO START UNDER EXAMINATION CONDITIONS

BPP LEARNING MEDIA

Section A – ALL 15 questions are compulsory and MUST be attempted

Each question is worth 2 marks.

1 **Identify, by selecting the relevant box in the table below, whether the following statements are true or false regarding the duties of the IFRS Interpretations Committee.**

To interpret the application of IFRS Standards	True	False
To work directly with national standard setters to bring about convergence with IFRS Standards	True	False
To provide guidance on financial reporting issues not specifically addressed in IFRS Standards	True	False
To publish draft interpretations for public comment	True	False

2 **For each of the following, identify whether the acquisition would or would not be treated as a subsidiary of Poulgo Co as at 31 December 20X7?**

The acquisition of 60% of Zakron Co's equity share capital on 1 March 20X7. Zakron Co's activities are significantly different from the rest of the Poulgo group of companies.	Subsidiary	Not a subsidiary
The offer to acquire 70% of Unto Co's equity share capital on 1 November 20X7. The negotiations were finally signed off during January 20X8.	Subsidiary	Not a subsidiary
The acquisition of 45% of Speeth Co's equity share capital on 31 December 20X7. Poulgo Co is able to appoint three of the ten members of Speeth Co's board.	Subsidiary	Not a subsidiary

3 On 1 January 20X6, Gardenbugs Co received a $30,000 government grant relating to equipment which cost $90,000 and had a useful life of six years. The grant was netted off against the cost of the equipment. On 1 January 20X7, when the equipment had a carrying amount of $50,000, its use was changed so that it was no longer being used in accordance with the grant. This meant that the grant needed to be repaid in full but by 31 December 20X7, this had not yet been done.

Using the drag and drop options in the table below, create the journal entry required to reflect the correct accounting treatment of the government grant and the equipment in the financial statements of Gardenbugs Co for the year ended 31 December 20X7?

	Debit	Credit
Depreciation expense		
Liability		
Property, plant and equipment		

$10,000

$15,000

$20,000

$30,000

---

4 The following two issues relate to Spiko Co's mining activities:

Issue 1: Spiko Co began operating a new mine in January 20X3 under a five-year government licence which required Spiko Co to landscape the area after mining ceased at an estimated cost of $100,000.

Issue 2: During 20X4, Spiko Co's mining activities caused environmental pollution on an adjoining piece of government land. There is no legislation which requires Spiko Co to rectify this damage, however, Spiko Co does have a published environmental policy which includes assurances that it will do so. The estimated cost of the rectification is $1,000,000.

In accordance with IAS 37 *Provisions, Contingent Liabilities and Contingent Assets*, which of the following statements is correct in respect of Spiko Co's financial statements for the year ended 31 December 20X4?

O A provision is required for the cost of both issues 1 and 2

O Both issues 1 and 2 require disclosure only

O A provision is required for the cost of issue 1 but issue 2 requires disclosure only

O Issue 1 requires disclosure only and issue 2 should be ignored

---

5   Parket Co acquired 60% of Suket Co on 1 January 20X7. The following extract has been
     taken from the individual statements of profit or loss for the year ended 31 March 20X7:

	Parket Co	Suket Co
	$'000	$'000
Cost of sales	710	480

Parket Co consistently made sales of $20,000 per month to Suket Co throughout the year.
At the year end, Suket Co held $20,000 of this in inventory. Parket Co made a mark-up on
cost of 25% on all sales to Suket Co.

What is Parket Co's consolidated cost of sales for the year ended 31 March 20X7?

$ [   ]

6   Quilo Co has decided to change its depreciation method to better reflect the pattern of use
     of its equipment.

**Which of the following correctly reflects what this change represents and how it should
be applied?**

O   It is a change of accounting policy and must be applied prospectively

O   It is a change of accounting policy and must be applied retrospectively

O   It is a change of accounting estimate and must be applied retrospectively

O   It is a change of accounting estimate and must be applied prospectively

7   Included within the financial assets of Zinet Co at 31 March 20X9 are the following two
     recently purchased investments in publicly traded equity shares:

Investment 1 – 10% of the issued share capital of Haruka Co. This shareholding was
acquired as a long-term investment as Zinet Co wishes to participate as an active
shareholder of Haruka Co.

Investment 2 – 10% of the issued share capital of Lukas Co. This shareholding was acquired
for speculative purposes and Zinet Co expects to sell these shares in the near future.

Neither of these shareholdings gives Zinet Co significant influence over the investee
companies.

Wherever possible, the directors of Zinet Co wish to avoid taking any fair value movements
to profit or loss, so as to minimise volatility in reported earnings.

**How should the fair value movements in these investments be reported in Zinet Co's
financial statements for the year ended 31 March 20X9?**

O   In profit or loss for both investments

O   In other comprehensive income for both investments

O   In profit or loss for investment 1 and in other comprehensive income for investment 2

O   In other comprehensive income for investment 1 and in profit or loss for investment 2

8   Shiba Co entered into lease for a right of use asset on 1 January 20X7. The lease contract
     is for four years and the useful life of the asset is six years. Information relating to the lease
     is as follows:

Initial lease liability	$48,000
Deposit paid on 1 January 20X7	$2,000
Direct costs incurred by Shiba Co	$5,000
Maintenance costs of $2,000 per annum	$8,000

BPP
LEARNING
MEDIA

What will be the carrying amount of the right of use asset at 31 December 20X8?

O $41,250

O $31,500

O $27,500

O $36,667

9   Trasten Co operates in an emerging market with a fast-growing economy where prices increase frequently.

Which TWO of the following statements are true when using historical cost accounting compared to current value accounting in this type of market?

☐   Capital employed which is calculated using historical costs is understated compared to current value capital employed

☐   Historical cost profits are overstated in comparison to current value profits

☐   Capital employed which is calculated using historical costs is overstated compared to current value capital employed

☐   Historical cost profits are understated in comparison to current value profits

10   Patula Co acquired 80% of Sanka Co on 1 October 20X5. At this date, some of Sanka Co's inventory had a carrying amount of $600,000 but a fair value of $800,000. By 31 December 20X5, 70% of this inventory had been sold by Sanka Co.

The individual statements of financial position at 31 December 20X5 for both companies show the following:

	Patula Co $'000	Sanka Co $'000
Inventories	3,250	1,940

What will be the total inventories figure in the consolidated statement of financial position of Patula Co as at 31 December 20X5?

O $5,250,000

O $5,330,000

O $5,130,000

O $5,238,000

11   Top Trades Co has been trading for a number of years and is currently going through a period of expansion.

An extract from the statement of cash flows for the year ended 31 December 20X7 for Top Trades Co is presented as follows:

	$'000
Net cash from operating activities	995
Net cash used in investing activities	(540)
Net cash used in financing activities	(200)
Net increase in cash and cash equivalents	255
Cash and cash equivalents at the beginning of the period	200
Cash and cash equivalents at the end of the period	455

Which of the following statements is correct according to the extract of Top Trades Co's statement of cash flows?

○ The company has good working capital management

○ Net cash generated from financing activities has been used to fund the additions to non-current assets

○ Net cash generated from operating activities has been used to fund the additions to non-current assets

○ Existing non-current assets have been sold to cover the cost of the additions to non-current assets

---

12 Rooney Co acquired 70% of the equity share capital of Marek Co, its only subsidiary, on 1 January 20X6. The fair value of the non-controlling interest in Marek Co at acquisition was $1.1 million. At that date the fair values of Marek Co's net assets were equal to their carrying amounts, except for a building which had a fair value of $1.5 million above its carrying amount and 30 years remaining useful life.

During the year to 31 December 20X6, Marek Co sold goods to Rooney Co, giving rise to an unrealised profit in inventory of $550,000 at the year end. Marek Co's profit after tax for the year ended 31 December 20X6 was $3.2 million.

What amount will be presented as the non-controlling interest in the consolidated statement of financial position of Rooney Co as at 31 December 20X6?

$ [   ]

---

13 When a gain on a bargain purchase (negative goodwill) arises, IFRS 3 *Business Combinations* requires an entity to first of all review the measurement of the assets, liabilities and consideration transferred in respect of the combination.

When a bargain purchase is confirmed, it should be [Accounting entry]

to [Financial statements]

Accounting entry

| debited |

| credited |

Financial statements

| retained earnings |

| profit or loss |

| positive goodwill |

---

14 On 1 October 20X5, Anita Co purchased 75,000 of Binita Co's 100,000 equity shares when Binita Co's retained earnings amounted to $90,000.

On 30 September 20X7, extracts from the statements of financial position of the two companies were:

	Anita Co $'000	Binita Co $'000
Equity shares of $1 each	125	100
Retained earnings	300	150
Total	425	250

What is the total equity which should appear in Anita Co's consolidated statement of financial position as at 30 September 20X7?

O $125,000

O $470,000

O $345,000

O $537,500

---

15 On 1 October 20X1, Bash Co borrowed $6 million for a term of one year, exclusively to finance the construction of a new piece of production equipment. The interest rate on the loan is 6% and is payable on maturity of the loan. The construction commenced on 1 November 20X1 but no construction took place between 1 December 20X1 and 31 January 20X2 due to employees taking industrial action. The asset was available for use on 30 September 20X2 having a construction cost of $6 million.

What is the carrying amount of the production equipment in Bash Co's statement of financial position as at 30 September 20X2?

$ _____

(30 marks)

Section B – ALL 15 questions are compulsory and MUST be attempted

Each question is worth 2 marks.

The following scenario relates to questions 16–20.

Aphrodite Co has a year end of 31 December and operates a factory which makes computer chips for mobile phones. It purchased a machine on 1 July 20X3 for $80,000 which had a useful life of ten years and is depreciated on the straight-line basis, time apportioned in the years of acquisition and disposal. The machine was revalued to $81,000 on 1 July 20X4. There was no change to its useful life at that date.

A fire at the factory on 1 October 20X6 damaged the machine leaving it with a lower operating capacity. The accountant considers that Aphrodite Co will need to recognise an impairment loss in relation to this damage. The accountant has ascertained the following information at 1 October 20X6:

(1)   The carrying amount of the machine is $60,750.

(2)   An equivalent new machine would cost $90,000.

(3)   The machine could be sold in its current condition for a gross amount of $45,000. Dismantling costs would amount to $2,000.

(4)   In its current condition, the machine could operate for three more years which gives it a value in use figure of $38,685.

16   **In accordance with IAS 16 *Property, Plant and Equipment*, what is the depreciation charged to Aphrodite Co's profit or loss in respect of the machine for the year ended 31 December 20X4?**

    O $9,000

    O $8,000

    O $8,263

    O $8,500

17   IAS 36 *Impairment of Assets* contains a number of examples of internal and external events which may indicate the impairment of an asset.

    In accordance with IAS 36, which of the following would definitely NOT be an indicator of the potential impairment of an asset (or group of assets)?

    O   An unexpected fall in the market value of one or more assets

    O   Adverse changes in the economic performance of one or more assets

    O   A significant change in the technological environment in which an asset is employed making its software effectively obsolete

    O   The carrying amount of an entity's net assets being below the entity's market capitalisation

18 **What is the total impairment loss associated with Aphrodite Co's machine at 1 October 20X6?**

    O $nil

    O $17,750

    O $22,065

    O $15,750

---

19 The accountant has decided that it is too difficult to reliably attribute cash flows to the damaged machine and that it would be more accurate to calculate the impairment on the basis of the factory as a cash generating unit.

In accordance with IAS 36, which of the following is TRUE regarding cash generating units?

    O   A cash generating unit to which goodwill has been allocated should be tested for impairment every five years

    O   A cash generating unit must be a subsidiary of the parent

    O   There is no need to consistently identify cash generating units based on the same types of asset from period to period

    O   A cash generating unit is the smallest identifiable group of assets for which independent cash flows can be identified

---

20 On 1 July 20X7, it is discovered that the damage to the machine is worse than originally thought. The machine is now considered to be worthless and the recoverable amount of the factory as a cash generating unit is estimated to be $950,000.

At 1 July 20X7, the cash generating unit comprises the following assets:

	$'000
Building	500
Plant and equipment (including the damaged machine at a carrying amount of $35,000)	335
Goodwill	85
Net current assets (at recoverable amount)	250
	1,170

In accordance with IAS 36, what will be the carrying amount of Aphrodite Co's plant and equipment when the impairment loss has been allocated to the cash generating unit?

    O $262,500

    O $300,000

    O $237,288

    O $280,838

The following scenario relates to questions 21–25.

On 1 January 20X5, Blocks Co entered into new agreements as follows:

Agreement one   This agreement meets the definition of a lease under IFRS 16 *Leases* and grants Blocks Co the right to use a piece of machinery. Under the terms of the agreement, Blocks Co must pay a deposit of $20,000 on inception of the lease on 1 January 20X5 followed by five equal annual instalments of $55,000, starting on 31 December 20X5. The present value of the future lease payments on 1 January 20X5 is $200,000. The interest rate implicit in the lease is 11.65%.

Agreement two   This agreement meets the definition of a lease under IFRS 16 *Leases* and grants Blocks Co the right to use a van for nine months. The fair value of the van is $120,000 and it has an estimated useful life of five years. The agreement requires Blocks Co to make no payment in month one and $4,800 per month in months 2–9. Blocks Co wishes to take advantage of any optional recognition exemptions available under IFRS 16.

Agreement three   This is a sale and leaseback relating to a cutting machine purchased by Blocks Co on 1 January 20X4 for $300,000. The carrying amount of the machine as at 31 December 20X4 was $250,000. On 1 January 20X5, it was sold to Cogs Co for $370,000 (being its fair value) and Blocks Co will lease the machine back for five years, the remainder of its useful life, at $80,000 per annum. The present value of the annual payments is $350,000 and the transaction satisfies the IFRS 15 criteria to be recognised as a sale.

21   **According to IFRS 16 *Leases*, which of the following gives the measurement of a right of use asset at the commencement of a lease?**

    ○   Sum of all rental payments to be paid to the lessor **less** any initial direct costs and dismantling costs

    ○   The amount of the initial measurement of the lease liability **plus** any initial direct costs and dismantling costs

    ○   The amount of the initial measurement of the lease liability **less** any initial direct costs and dismantling costs

    ○   Sum of all rental payments to be paid to the lessor **plus** any initial direct costs and dismantling costs

22   **For agreement two, what amount of asset should be initially recognised on commencement of the lease?**

    ○ $5,500

    ○ $10,000

    ○ $0

    ○ $11,000

23   The following calculations have been prepared for agreement one:

Year	Interest $	Annual payment $	Balance $
31 December 20X7	15,484	(55,000)	93,391
31 December 20X8	10,880	(55,000)	49,271
31 December 20X9	5,729	(55,000)	0

BPP
LEARNING
MEDIA

In respect of the lease obligation, match the values attributable to the non-current liability and current liability to in the statement of financial position as at 31 December 20X7?

Value

| $44,120 |

| $49,271 |

| $93,391 |

| $Nil |

Statement of financial position

| Non-current liability |

| Current liability |

24 For agreement one, what is the finance cost charged to profit or loss for the year ended 31 December 20X6?

$ _____

25 For agreement three, what profit should be recognised for the year ended 31 December 20X5 as a result of the sale and leaseback (to the nearest whole $)?

$ _____

The following scenario relates to questions 26–30.

Mighty IT Co provides hardware, software and IT services to small business customers.

Mighty IT Co has developed an accounting software package. The company offers a supply and installation service for $1,000 and a separate two-year technical support service for $500. Alternatively, it also offers a combined goods and services contract which includes both of these elements for $1,200. Payment for the combined contract is due one month after the date of installation.

In December 20X5, Mighty IT Co revalued its corporate headquarters. Prior to the revaluation, the carrying amount of the building was $2 million and it was revalued to $2.5 million.

Mighty IT Co also revalued a sales office on the same date. The office had been purchased for $500,000 earlier in the year, but subsequent discovery of defects reduced its value to $400,000. No depreciation had been charged on the sales office and any impairment loss is allowable for tax purposes.

Mighty IT Co's income tax rate is 30%.

26 In accordance with IFRS 15 *Revenue from Contracts with Customers*, when should Mighty IT Co recognise revenue from the combined goods and services contract?

- ○ Supply and install: on installation
  Technical support: over two years

- ○ Supply and install: when payment is made
  Technical support: over two years

- ○ Supply and install: on installation
  Technical support: on installation

- ○ Supply and install: when payment is made
  Technical support: when payment is made

27   For each combined contract sold, what is the amount of revenue which Mighty IT Co should recognise in respect of the supply and installation service in accordance with IFRS 15?

     O $700

     O $800

     O $1,000

     O $1,200

28   Mighty IT Co sells a combined contract on 1 January 20X6, the first day of its financial year. Mighty IT Co financial statements are prepared in accordance with IFRS 15.

What is the total amount for deferred income which will be reported in Mighty IT Co's statement of financial position as at 31 December 20X6?

$ [   ]

29   **In accordance with IAS 12 *Income Taxes*, what is the impact of the property revaluations on the income tax expense of Mighty IT Co for the year ended 31 December 20X5?**

     O   Income tax expense increases by $180,000

     O   Income tax expense increases by $120,000

     O   Income tax expense decreases by $30,000

     O   No impact on income tax expense

30   In January 20X6, the accountant at Mighty IT Co produced the company's draft financial statements for the year ended 31 December 20X5. He then realised that he had omitted to consider deferred tax on development costs. In 20X5, development costs of $200,000 had been incurred and capitalised. Development costs are deductible in full for tax purposes in the year they are incurred. The development is still in process at 31 December 20X5.

What adjustment is required to the income tax expense in Mighty IT Co's statement of profit or loss for the year ended 31 December 20X5 to account for deferred tax on the development costs?

     O   Increase of $200,000

     O   Increase of $60,000

     O   Decrease of $60,000

     O   Decrease of $200,000

(30 marks)

Section C – BOTH questions are compulsory and MUST be attempted

Question 31

After preparing a draft statement of profit or loss (before interest and tax) for the year ended 31 March 20X6 (before any adjustments which may be required by notes (i) to (iv) below), the summarised trial balance of Triage Co as at 31 March 20X6 is:

	$'000	$'000
Equity shares of $1 each		50,000
Retained earnings as at 1 April 20X5		3,500
Draft profit before interest and tax for year ended 31 March 20X6		30,000
6% convertible loan notes (note (i))		40,000
Freehold property (original life 25 years) – at cost (note (ii))	75,000	
Plant and equipment – at cost (note (ii))	72,100	
Accumulated /depreciation at 1 April 20X5: property		15,000
plant and equipment		28,100
Trade receivables (note (iii))	28,000	
Other current assets	9,300	
Current liabilities		17,700
Deferred tax (note (iv))		3,200
Interest payment (note (i))	2,400	
Current tax (note (iv))	700	
	187,500	187,500

The following notes are relevant:

(i)   Triage Co issued 400,000 $100 6% convertible loan notes on 1 April 20X5. Interest is payable annually in arrears on 31 March each year. The loans can be converted to equity shares on the basis of 20 shares for each $100 loan note on 31 March 20X8 or redeemed at par for cash on the same date. An equivalent loan without the conversion rights would have required an interest rate of 8%.

The present value of $1 receivable at the end of each year, based on discount rates of 6% and 8%, are:

		6%	8%
End of year:	1	0.94	0.93
	2	0.89	0.86
	3	0.84	0.79

(ii)   Non-current assets:

The directors decided to revalue the freehold property at $66.3 million on 1 October 20X5. Triage Co does not make an annual transfer from the revaluation surplus to retained earnings to reflect the realisation of the revaluation gain; however, the revaluation will give rise to a deferred tax liability at the company's tax rate of 20%.

The freehold property is depreciated on a straight-line basis and plant and equipment at 15% per annum using the reducing balance method.

No depreciation has yet been charged on any non-current assets for the year ended 31 March 20X6.

(iii)   In September 20X5, the directors of Triage Co discovered a fraud. In total, $700,000 which had been included as receivables in the above trial balance had been stolen by an employee. $450,000 of this related to the year ended 31 March 20X5, the rest to the current year. The directors are hopeful that 50% of the losses can be recovered from the company's insurers.

(iv) A provision of $2.7 million is required for current income tax on the profit of the year to 31 March 20X6. The balance on current tax in the trial balance is the under/over provision of tax for the previous year. In addition to the temporary differences relating to the information in note (ii), at 31 March 20X6, the carrying amounts of Triage Co's net assets are $12 million more than their tax base.

Required

(a) Prepare a schedule of adjustments required to the draft profit before interest and tax (in the above trial balance) to give the profit or loss of Triage Co for the year ended 31 March 20X6 as a result of the information in notes (i) to (iv) above. **(5 marks)**

(b) Prepare the statement of financial position of Triage Co as at 31 March 20X6. **(12 marks)**

(c) The issue of convertible loan notes can potentially dilute the basic earnings per share (EPS).

Calculate the diluted earnings per share for Triage Co for the year ended 31 March 20X6 (there is no need to calculate the basic EPS). **(3 marks)**

Note. A statement of changes in equity and the notes to the statement of financial position are not required.

(Total = 20 marks)

Question 32

Gregory Co is a listed company and, until 1 October 20X5, it had no subsidiaries. On that date, it acquired 75% of Tamsin Co's equity shares by means of a share exchange of two new shares in Gregory Co for every five acquired shares in Tamsin Co. These shares were recorded at the market price on the day of the acquisition and were the only shares issued by Gregory Co during the year ended 31 March 20X6.

The summarised financial statements of Gregory Co as a single entity at 31 March 20X5 and as a group at 31 March 20X6 are:

	Gregory group	Gregory Co single entity
STATEMENTS OF PROFIT OR LOSS FOR THE YEAR ENDED	31 March 20X6	31 March 20X5
	$'000	$'000
Revenue	46,500	28,000
Cost of sales	(37,200)	(20,800)
Gross profit	9,300	7,200
Operating expenses	(1,800)	(1,200)
Profit before tax (operating profit)	7,500	6,000
Income tax expense	(1,500)	(1,000)
Profit for the year	6,000	5,000
Profit for year attributable to:		
Equity holders of the parent	5,700	
Non-controlling interest	300	
	6,000	

STATEMENTS OF FINANCIAL POSITION AS AT	31 March 20X6 $'000	31 March 20X5 $'000
Assets		
Non-current assets		
Property, plant and equipment	54,600	41,500
Goodwill	3,000	–
	57,600	41,500
Current assets	44,000	36,000
Total assets	101,600	77,500
Equity and liabilities		
Equity		
Equity shares of $1 each	46,000	40,000
Other component of equity (share premium)	6,000	–
Retained earnings	18,700	13,000
Equity attributable to owners of the parent	70,700	53,000
Non-controlling interest	3,600	–
	74,300	53,000
Current liabilities	27,300	24,500
Total equity and liabilities	101,600	77,500

Other information:

(i) Each month since the acquisition, Gregory Co's sales to Tamsin Co were consistently $2 million. Gregory Co had chosen to only make a gross profit margin of 10% on these sales as Tamsin Co is part of the group.

(ii) The values of property, plant and equipment held by both companies have been rising for several years.

(iii) On reviewing the above financial statements, Gregory Co's chief executive officer (CEO) made the following observations:

(1) I see the profit for the year has increased by $1 million which is up 20% on last year, but I thought it would be more as Tamsin Co was supposed to be a very profitable company.

(2) I have calculated the earnings per share (EPS) for 20X6 at 13 cents (6,000/46,000 × 100) and for 20X5 at 12.5 cents (5,000/40,000 × 100) and, although the profit has increased 20%, our EPS has barely changed.

(3) I am worried that the low price at which we are selling goods to Tamsin Co is undermining our group's overall profitability.

(4) I note that our share price is now $2.30, how does this compare with our share price immediately before we bought Tamsin Co?

Required

(a) Reply to the four observations of the CEO.   **(8 marks)**

(b) Using the above financial statements, calculate the following ratios for Gregory Co for the years ended 31 March 20X6 and 20X5 and comment on the comparative performance:

(i) Return on capital employed (ROCE)
(ii) Net asset turnover
(iii) Gross profit margin
(iv) Operating profit margin

Four marks are available for the ratio calculations.   **(12 marks)**

Note. Your answers to (a) and (b) should reflect the impact of the consolidation of Tamsin Co during the year ended 31 March 20X6.

(Total = 20 marks)

Answers

DO NOT TURN THIS PAGE UNTIL YOU HAVE
COMPLETED THE MOCK EXAM

A plan of attack

Managing your nerves

As you start this mock exam a number of thoughts are likely to cross your mind. At best, examinations cause anxiety so it is important to stay focused on your task for the exam period! Developing an awareness of what is going on emotionally within you may help you manage your nerves. Remember, you are unlikely to banish the flow of adrenaline, but the key is to harness it to help you work steadily and quickly through your answers.

Working through this mock exam will help you develop the exam stamina you will need to keep going for three hours.

Managing your time

Planning and time management are two of the key skills which complement the technical knowledge you need to succeed. To keep yourself on time, do not be afraid to jot down your target completion times for each question, perhaps next to the title of the question on the exam. As all the questions are **compulsory**, you do not have to spend time wondering which question to answer!

Doing the exam

Actually doing the exam is a personal experience. There is not a single **right way**. As long as you submit complete answers to all questions after the three hours are up, then your approach obviously works.

Looking through the exam

Section A has 15 OTQs. This is the section of the exam where the examining team can test knowledge across the breadth of the syllabus. Make sure you read these questions carefully. The distractors are designed to present plausible, but incorrect, answers. Don't let them mislead you. If you really have no idea – guess. You may even be right.

Section B has 15 OTQs in total – questions 16–30. These are arranged as three scenarios with five questions each.

Scenario 1 is on impairment of assets.
Scenario 2 is on leasing.
Scenario 3 is on revenue recognition.

Section C has two 20-mark questions.

Question 31 is on accounting adjustments and the preparation of a statement of financial position.
Question 32 is on interpretation of financial statements.

Allocating your time

BPP's advice is to always allocate your time **according to the marks for the question**. However, **use common sense**. If you're doing a question but haven't a clue how to do part (b), you might be better off reallocating your time and getting more marks on another question, where you can add something you didn't have time for earlier on. Make sure you leave time to recheck the OTQs and make sure you have answered them all.

Section A

1

To interpret the application of IFRS Standards	True	
To work directly with national standard setters to bring about convergence with IFRS Standards		False
To provide guidance on financial reporting issues not specifically addressed in IFRS Standards	True	
To publish draft interpretations for public comment	True	

2

The acquisition of 60% of Zakron Co's equity share capital on 1 March 20X7. Zakron Co's activities are significantly different from the rest of the Poulgo group of companies.	Subsidiary	
The offer to acquire 70% of Unto Co's equity share capital on 1 November 20X7. The negotiations were finally signed off during January 20X8.		Not a subsidiary
The acquisition of 45% of Speeth Co's equity share capital on 31 December 20X7. Poulgo Co is able to appoint three of the ten members of Speeth Co's board.		Not a subsidiary

3

	Debit	Credit
Depreciation expense	$20,000	
Liability		$30,000
Property, plant and equipment	$10,000	

The repayment of the grant must be treated as a change in accounting estimate. The carrying amount of the asset must be increased as the netting off method has been used. The resulting extra depreciation must be charged immediately to profit or loss.

	Original $	As if no grant $	Adjustment $
Cost	90,000	90,000	
Grant	(30,000)		
	60,000		
Depreciation	(10,000) [1 yr]	(30,000) [2 yr]	Debit Dep'n exp 20,000
Carrying amount	50,000 [1/1/X7]	60,000 [31/12/X7]	Debit PPE 10,000
			Credit Liability 30,000

4   The correct answer is: A provision is required for the cost of both issues 1 and 2.

5   $774,000

   710,000 + (480,000 × 3/12) – (20,000 × 3) + (20,000 × 25/125) = $774,000

6   The correct answer is: It is a change of accounting estimate and must be applied prospectively.

7   The correct answer is: In other comprehensive income for investment 1 and in profit or loss for investment 2

Note. Investment 2 is held for trading.

8   The correct answer is: $27,500

The asset would be initially measured as $55,000 ($48,000 + $2,000 + $5,000). It is then depreciated over four years (the shorter of the lease term and its useful life) for two years from 1 January 20X7 to 31 December 20X8.

	$
Initial measurement	55,000
Depreciation ($55,000/4 × 2)	(27,500)
Carrying amount at 31 December 20X8	27,500

The maintenance costs are expensed over the length of the contract.

9   The correct answers are:

Capital employed which is calculated using historical costs is understated compared to current value capital employed.

Historical cost profits are overstated in comparison to current value profits.

This is the case in a period of inflation.

10   The correct answer is: $5,250,000

3,250 + 1,940 + (800 − 600 × 30%) = 5,250,000

11   The correct answer is: Net cash generated from operating activities has been used to fund the additions to non-current assets.

12    $1,880,000

FV of NCI at acquisition		1,100
Profit for year × 30%	3,200	
Dep'n on FVA (1.5m/30)	(50)	
Unrealised profit	(550)	
	2,600 × 30%	780
		1,880

13   When a bargain purchase is confirmed it should be **credited** to **profit or loss**.

14   The correct answer is: $470,000

Retained earnings = 300 + ((150 − 90) × 75%) = 345
Total equity = 125 + 345 = 470

15    $6,270,000

	$'000
Production cost of PPE	6,000
Capitalisation of borrowing costs:	
$6m × 6% × 9/12 =	270
Total cost capitalised (and carrying amount) at 30 September 20X2	6,270

Section B

16 The correct answer is: $8,500

Depreciation 1 January to 30 June 20X4 (80,000/10 × 6/12) = 4,000
Depreciation 1 July to 31 December 20X4 (81,000/9 × 6/12) = 4,500
Total depreciation = 8,500

17 The correct answer is: The carrying amount of an entity's net assets being below the entity's market capitalisation

This means that the share price is high, so the market has positive expectations of the entity.

18 The correct answer is: $17,750

VIU is lower than FV (less costs to sell), so impairment is 60,750 − 43,000 = $17,750

19 The correct answer is: A cash-generating unit is the smallest identifiable group of assets for which independent cash flows can be identified.

20 The correct answer is: $262,500

The impairment loss of $220m (1,170 − 950) is allocated: $35m to damaged plant and $85m to goodwill, the remaining $100m allocated proportionally to the building and the undamaged plant. The carrying amount of the plant will then be $262,500.

21 The correct answer is: The amount of the initial measurement of the lease liability **plus** any initial direct costs and dismantling costs

22 The correct answer is: $0

As the assets are of low value (less than $5,000) the rentals will be expensed to profit or loss on a straight-line basis over the period of the lease; no asset is recognised in the statement of financial position.

23 $49,271 as a non-current liability and $44,120 as a current liability

24 $19,607

Year 1 200,000 × 11.65% = 23,300
Year 2 (200,000 + 23,300 − 55,000) × 11.65% = $19,607

25 $6,486

Profit on sale = 120,000
Amount relating to rights retained = 120,000 × 350,000/370,000 = 113,514
Amount relating to rights transferred = 120,000 − 113,514 = 6,486

26 The correct answer is: Supply and install: on installation. Technical support: over two years

The performance obligation for the goods is satisfied when the package is supplied. The technical support obligation is satisfied over time.

27 The correct answer is: $800

1,000/1,500 × 1,200 = $800

28 $200

500/1,500 × 1,200 = 400/2 = $200

29 The correct answer is: Income tax expense decreases by $30,000

$30,000 (400 − 500 × 30%).
Revaluation and deferred tax of headquarters goes through OCI.

30 The correct answer is: Increase of $60,000

$60,000 (200 × 30%)
Debit Income tax expense Credit Deferred tax liability

Section C

Question 31

Marking scheme

			Marks
(a)	Schedule of adjustments		
	Profit before interest and tax	½	
	Loan finance costs	1	
	Depreciation charges	1½	
	Fraud loss	½	
	Income tax	1½	
			5
(b)	Statement of financial position		
	Property, plant and equipment	2½	
	Trade receivables	1	
	Other current assets	½	
	Equity shares	½	
	Equity option	1	
	Revaluation surplus	1	
	Retained earnings	1½	
	Deferred tax	1	
	Loan note	1½	
	Current liabilities	½	
	Current tax payable	1	
			12
Diluted EPS			3
	Total for question		20

(a)   Triage Co – Schedule of adjustments to profit for the year ended 31 March 20X6

	$'000
Draft profit before interest and tax per trial balance	30,000
Adjustments re:	
Note *(i)*	
Convertible loan note finance costs (w(i))	(3,023)
Note *(ii)*	
Depreciation of freehold property (1,500 + 1,700 (w(ii)))	(3,200)
Depreciation of plant and equipment (w(ii))	(6,600)
Note *(iii)*	
Current year loss on fraud (700 – 450 see below)	(250)
Note *(iv)*	
Income tax expense (2,700 + 700 – 800 (w(iii)))	(2,600)
Profit for the year	14,327

The $450,000 fraud loss in the previous year is a prior period adjustment (reported in the statement of changes in equity).

The possible insurance claim is a contingent asset and should not be recognised.

(b)   Triage Co – Statement of financial position as at 31 March 20X6

	$'000	$'000
Assets		
Non-current assets		
Property, plant and equipment (64,600 + 37,400 (w(ii)))		102,000
Current assets		
Trade receivables (28,000 – 700 fraud)	27,300	
Other current assets per trial balance	9,300	36,600
Total assets		138,600
Equity and liabilities		
Equity		
Equity shares of $1 each		50,000
Other component of equity (w(i))	2,208	
Revaluation surplus (7,800 – 1,560 (w(ii)))	6,240	
Retained earnings (w(iv))	17,377	25,825
		75,825
Non-current liabilities		
Deferred tax (w(iii))	3,960	
6% convertible loan notes (w(i))	38,415	42,375
Current liabilities		
Per trial balance	17,700	
Current tax payable	2,700	20,400
Total equity and liabilities		138,600

(c)   Diluted earnings per share (w(v))   29 cents

Workings (monetary figures in brackets in $'000)

(i)   *6% convertible loan notes*

The convertible loan notes are a compound financial instrument having a debt and an equity component which must both be quantified and accounted for separately:

BPP
LEARNING
MEDIA

Year ended 31 March	Outflow $'000	8%	Present value $'000
20X6	2,400	0.93	2,232
20X7	2,400	0.6	2,064
20X8	42,400	0.79	33,496
Debt component			37,792
Equity component (= balance)			2,208
Proceeds of issue			40,000

The finance cost will be $3,023,000 (37,792 × 8%) and the carrying amount of the loan notes at 31 March 20X6 will be $38,415,000 (37,792 + (3,023 – 2,400)).

(ii) *Non-current assets*

Freehold property
The gain on revaluation and carrying amount of the freehold property is:

	$'000
Carrying amount at 1 April 20X5 (75,000 – 15,000)	60,000
Depreciation to date of revaluation (1 October 20X5) (75,000/25 × 6/12)	(1,500)
Carrying amount at revaluation	58,500
Gain on revaluation = balance	7,800
Revaluation at 1 October 20X5	66,300
Depreciation to year ended 31 March 20X6 (66,300/19.5 years × 6/12)	(1,700)
Carrying amount at 31 March 20X6	64,600

Annual depreciation is $3m (75,000/25 years); therefore the accumulated depreciation at 1 April 20X5 of $15m represents five years' depreciation. At the date of revaluation (1 October 20X5), there will be a remaining life of 19.5 years.

Of the revaluation gain, $6.24m (80%) is credited to the revaluation surplus and $1.56m (20%) is credited to deferred tax.

Plant and equipment

	$'000
Carrying amount at 1 April 20X5 (72,100 – 28,100)	44,000
Depreciation for year ended 31 March 20X6 (15% reducing balance)	(6,600)
Carrying amount at 31 March 20X6	37,400

(iii) *Deferred tax*

Provision required at 31 March 20X6:

Revalued property and other assets (7,800 + 12,000) × 20%	3,960
Provision at 1 April 20X5	(3,200)
Increase in provision	760
Revaluation of land and buildings (7,800 × 20%)	(1,560)
Balance credited to profit or loss	(800)

(iv) *Retained earnings*

Balance at 1 April 20X5	3,500
Prior period adjustment (fraud)	(450)
Adjusted profit for year (from (a))	14,327
Balance at 31 March 20X6	17,377

(v) The maximum additional shares on conversion is 8 million (40,000 × 20/100), giving total shares of 58 million.

The loan interest 'saved' is $2.418m (3,023 (from (w(i)) above × 80% (ie after tax)), giving adjusted earnings of $16.745m (14,327 + 2,418)).

Therefore diluted EPS is $\dfrac{\$16,745,000 \times 100}{58 \text{ million shares}}$ = 29 cents

Question 32

Marking scheme

			Marks
(a)	2 marks for each reply to the CEO's observations	<u>8</u>	
			8
(b)	1 mark for each pair of ratios	4	
	1 mark per relevant comment up to	<u>8</u>	
			<u>12</u>
	Total for question		<u>20</u>

(a) **Note.** References to 20X6 and 20X5 are to the years ending 31 March 20X6 and 20X5 respectively.

Comment (1): I see the profit for the year has increased by $1m which is up 20% on last year, but I thought it would be more as Tamsin Co was supposed to be a very profitable company.

There are two issues with this statement. First, last year's profit is not comparable with the current year's profit because in 20X5 Gregory Co was a single entity and in 20X6 it is now a group with a subsidiary. A second issue is that the consolidated statement of profit or loss for the year ended 31 March 20X6 only includes six months of the results of Tamsin Co, and, assuming Tamsin Co is profitable, future results will include a full year's profit. This latter point may, at least in part, mitigate the CEO's disappointment.

Comment (2): I have calculated the EPS for 20X6 at 13 cents (6,000/46,000 × 100 shares) and at 12.5 cents for 20X5 (5,000/40,000 × 100) and, although the profit has increased 20%, our EPS has barely changed.

The stated EPS calculation for 20X6 is incorrect for two reasons. First, it is the profit attributable to only the equity shareholders of the parent which should be used and, second, the 6 million new shares were only in issue for six months and should be pro-rated by 6/12 months. Thus, the correct EPS for 20X6 is 13.3 cents (5,700/43,000 × 100). This gives an increase of 6% (13.3 − 12.5)/12.5) on 20X5 EPS which is still less than the increase in profit. The reason why the EPS may not have increased in line with reported profit is that the acquisition was financed by a share exchange which increased the number of shares in issue. Thus, the EPS takes account of the additional consideration used to generate profit, whereas the trend of absolute profit does not take additional consideration into account. This is why the EPS is often said to be a more accurate reflection of company performance than the trend of profits.

Comment (3): I am worried that the low price at which we are selling goods to Tamsin Co is undermining our group's overall profitability.

Assuming the consolidated financial statements have been correctly prepared, all intragroup trading has been eliminated, thus the pricing policy will have had no effect on these financial statements. The comment is incorrect and reflects a misunderstanding of the consolidation process.

Comment (4): I note that our share price is now $2.30, how does this compare with our share price immediately before we bought Tamsin Co?

The increase in share capital is 6 million shares, the increase in the share premium is $6m, thus the total proceeds for the 6 million shares was $12m giving a share price of $2.00 at the date of acquisition of Tamsin Co. The current price of $2.30 presumably reflects the market's favourable view of Gregory Co's current and future performance.

(b)

	20X6	20X5
Return on capital employed (ROCE) (7,500/74,300 × 100)	10.1%	11.3%
Net asset turnover (46,500/74,300)	0.63 times	0.53 times
Gross profit margin (9,300/46,500 × 100)	20.0%	25.7%
Operating profit margin (7,500/46,500 × 100)	16.1%	21.4%

Looking at the above ratios, it appears that the overall performance of Gregory Co has declined marginally; the ROCE has fallen from 11.3% to 10.1%. This has been caused by a substantial fall in the gross profit margin (down from 25.7% in 20X5 to 20% in 20X6); this is over a 22% (5.7%/25.7%) decrease. The group/company have relatively low operating expenses (at around 4% of revenue), so the poor gross profit margin feeds through to the operating profit margin. The overall decline in the ROCE, due to the weaker profit margins, has been mitigated by an improvement in net asset turnover, increasing from 0.53 times to 0.63 times. Despite the improvement in net asset turnover, it is still very low with only 63 cents of sales generated from every $1 invested in the business, although this will depend on the type of business Gregory Co and Tamsin Co are engaged in.

On this analysis, the effect of the acquisition of Tamsin Co seems to have had a detrimental effect on overall performance, but this may not necessarily be the case; there could be some distorting factors in the analysis. As mentioned above, the 20X6 results include only six months of Tamsin Co's results, but the statement of financial position includes the full amount of the consideration for Tamsin Co. (The consideration has been calculated [see comment (4) above] as $12m for the parent's 75% share plus $3.3m [3,600 – 300 share of post-acquisition profit] for the non-controlling interest's 25%, giving total consideration of $15.3m.) The above factors disproportionately increase the denominator of ROCE which has the effect of worsening the calculated ROCE. This distortion should be corrected in 20X7 when a full year's results for Tamsin Co will be included in group profit. Another factor is that it could take time to fully integrate the activities of the two companies and more savings and other synergies may be forthcoming such as bulk buying discounts.

The non-controlling interest share in the profit for the year in 20X6 of $300,000 allows a rough calculation of the full year's profit of Tamsin Co at $2.4m (300,000/25% × 12/6, ie the $300,000 represents 25% of 6/12 of the annual profit). This figure is subject to some uncertainty such as the effect of probable increased post-acquisition depreciation charges. However, a profit of $2.4m on the investment of $15.3m represents a return of 16% (and would be higher if the profit was adjusted to a pre-tax figure) which is much higher than the current year ROCE (at 10.1%) of the group. This implies that the performance of Tamsin Co is much better than that of Gregory Co (as a separate entity) and that Gregory Co's performance in 20X6 must have deteriorated considerably from that in 20X5 and this is the real cause of the deteriorating performance of the group.

Another issue potentially affecting the ROCE is that, as a result of the consolidation process, Tamsin Co's net assets, including goodwill, are included in the statement of financial position at fair value, whereas Gregory Co's net assets appear to be based on historical cost (as there is no revaluation surplus). As the values of property, plant and equipment have been rising, this in effect favourably flatters the 20X5 ratios. This is because the statement of financial position of 20X5 only contains Gregory Co's assets which, at historical cost, may considerably understate their fair value and, on a comparative basis, overstate 20X5 ROCE.

In summary, although on first impression the acquisition of Tamsin Co appears to have caused a marginal worsening of the group's performance, the distorting factors and imputation of the non-controlling interest's profit in 20X6 indicate the underlying performance may be better than the ratios portray and the contribution from Tamsin Co is a very significant positive. Future performance may be even better.

Without information on the separate financial statements of Tamsin Co, it is difficult to form a more definite view.

ACCA

Financial Reporting (FR)

Mock Examination 2

(ACCA Specimen CBE)

Questions	
Time allowed	3 hours
This mock exam is divided into three sections:	
Section A	ALL 15 questions are compulsory and MUST be attempted
Section B	ALL 15 questions are compulsory and MUST be attempted
Section C	BOTH questions are compulsory and MUST be attempted

DO NOT OPEN THIS EXAM UNTIL YOU ARE READY TO START
UNDER EXAMINATION CONDITIONS

Section A – ALL 15 questions are compulsory and MUST be attempted

Each question is worth 2 marks.

1 Consolidated financial statements are presented on the basis that the companies within the group are treated as if they are a single economic entity.

Which TWO of the following are requirements of preparing consolidated financial statements?

☐ All subsidiaries must adopt the accounting policies of the parent in their individual financial statements

☐ Subsidiaries with activities which are substantially different to the activities of other members of the group should not be consolidated

☐ All entity financial statements within a group should normally be prepared to the same accounting year end prior to consolidation

☐ Unrealised profits within the group must be eliminated from the consolidated financial statements

2 On 1 October 20X4, Flash Co acquired an item of plant under a five-year lease agreement. Under the terms of the agreement, an immediate deposit of $2 million is payable on inception of the lease and the present value of future lease payments at that date have been calculated as $22,745,000. Annual rentals of $6 million are payable on 30 September each year for five years. The agreement had an implicit rate of interest of 10% per annum.

What is the current liability for the leased plant in Flash Co's statement of financial position as at 30 September 20X5?

$ [   ]

3 Quartile Co is in the jewellery retail business which can be assumed to be highly seasonal. For the year ended 30 September 20X5, Quartile Co assessed its operating performance by comparing selected accounting ratios with those of its business sector average as provided by an agency. Assume that the business sector used by the agency is a meaningful representation of Quartile Co's business.

Which TWO of the following circumstances may invalidate the comparison of Quartile Co's ratios with those of the sector average?

☐ In the current year, Quartile Co has experienced significant rising costs for its purchases

☐ The sector average figures are compiled from companies whose year ends are between 1 July 20X5 and 30 September 20X5

☐ Quartile Co does not revalue its properties, but is aware that other entities in this sector do

☐ During the year, Quartile Co discovered an error relating to the inventory count at 30 September 20X4. This error was correctly accounted for in the financial statements for the current year ended 30 September 20X5

4   Financial statements represent transactions in words and numbers. To be useful, financial information must represent faithfully these transactions in terms of how they are reported.

Identify, by selecting the relevant box in the table below, whether the statement regarding faithful representation is true or false.

Charging the rental payments for an item of plant to the statement of profit or loss where the rental agreement meets the criteria for a lease and no recognition exemptions are available	True	False
Including a convertible loan note in equity on the basis that the holders are likely to choose the equity option on conversion	True	False
Treating redeemable preference shares as part of equity in the statement of financial position	True	False
Derecognising factored trade receivables sold without recourse to the seller	True	False

5   A parent sells goods to its 80% owned subsidiary during the financial year, some of which remains in inventory at the year end.

Using the drag and drop options below, select the correct adjustment required in the consolidated statement of financial position to eliminate any unrealised profit in inventory?

Credit		Group retained earnings
Debit		Inventory
		Non-controlling interest

6   **Which of the following criticisms does NOT apply to historical cost financial statements during a period of rising prices?**

- O   They are difficult to verify because transactions could have happened many years ago
- O   They contain mixed values; some items are at current values and some are at out of date values
- O   They understate assets and overstate profit
- O   They overstate gearing in the statement of financial position

7   On 1 October 20X4, Kalatra Co commenced drilling for oil from an undersea oilfield. Kalatra Co is required to dismantle the drilling equipment at the end of its five-year licence. This has an estimated cost of $30m on 30 September 20X9. Kalatra Co's cost of capital is 8% per annum and $1 in five years' time has a present value of 68 cents.

What is the provision which Kalatra Co would report in its statement of financial position as at 30 September 20X5 in respect of its oil operations?

- O $32,400,000
- O $22,032,000
- O $20,400,000
- O $1,632,000

8   When a parent is evaluating the assets of a potential subsidiary, certain intangible assets can be recognised separately from goodwill, even though they have not been recognised in the subsidiary's own statement of financial position.

Which of the following is an example of an intangible asset of the subsidiary which may be recognised separately from goodwill when preparing consolidated financial statements?

○   A new research project which the subsidiary has correctly expensed to profit or loss but the directors of the parent have reliably assessed to have a substantial fair value

○   A global advertising campaign which was concluded in the previous financial year and from which benefits are expected to flow in the future

○   A contingent asset of the subsidiary from which the parent believes a flow of future economic benefits is possible

○   A customer list which the directors are unable to value reliably

---

9   On 1 October 20X4, Pyramid Co acquired 80% of Square Co's 9 million equity shares. At the date of acquisition, Square Co had an item of plant which had a fair value of $3 million in excess of its carrying amount. At the date of acquisition it had a useful life of five years. Pyramid Co's policy is to value non-controlling interests at fair value at the date of acquisition. For this purpose, Square Co's shares had a value of $3.50 each at that date. In the year ended 30 September 20X5, Square Co reported a profit of $8million.

Using the pull-down list provided, identify the amount at which the non-controlling interests in Square Co should be valued in the consolidated statement of financial position of the Pyramid group as at 30 September 20X5?

Pull-down list:

$26,680,000
$7,900,000
$7,780,000
$12,220,000

---

10   Caddy Co acquired 240,000 of Ambel Co's 800,000 equity shares for $6 per share on 1 October 20X4. Ambel Co's profit for the year ended 30 September 20X5 was $400,000 and it paid an equity dividend on 20 September 20X5 of $150,000.

On the assumption that Ambel Co is an associate of Caddy Co, what would be the carrying amount of the investment in Ambel Co in the consolidated statement of financial position of Caddy Co as at 30 September 20X5?

○ $1,560,000

○ $1,395,000

○ $1,515,000

○ $1,690,000

11   Identify whether the following costs should or should not be capitalised in the initial carrying amount of an item of plant.

Cost of a three-year plant maintenance agreement	Cost of installing a new power supply required to operate the plant

Cost of transporting the plant to the factory	Cost of a three-week training course for staff to operate the plant

The initial carrying amount of plant should include:

The initial carrying amount of plant should NOT include:

---

12   When a single entity makes purchases or sales in a foreign currency, it will be necessary to translate the transactions into its functional currency before the transactions can be included in its financial records.

In accordance with IAS 21 *The Effect of Changes in Foreign Currency Exchange Rates*, which TWO of the following foreign currency exchange rates may be used to translate the foreign currency purchases and sales?

☐   The rate that existed on the day that the purchase or sale took place

☐   The rate that existed at the beginning of the accounting period

☐   An average rate for the year, provided there have been no significant fluctuations throughout the year

☐   The rate that existed at the end of the accounting period

---

13   Fork Co owns an 80% investment in Spoon Co which it purchased several years ago. The goodwill on acquisition was valued at $1,674,000 and there has been no impairment of that goodwill since the date of acquisition.

On 30 September 20X4, Fork Co disposed of its entire investment in Spoon Co, details of which are as follows:

	$'000
Sales proceeds of Fork Co's entire investment in Spoon Co	5,580
Cost of Fork Co's entire investment in Spoon Co	3,720

Immediately before the disposal, the consolidated financial statements of Fork Co included the following amounts in respect of Spoon Co:

	$'000
Carrying amount of the net assets (excluding goodwill)	4,464
Carrying amount of the non-controlling interests	900

What is the profit on disposal (before tax) which will be recorded in Fork Co's CONSOLIDATED statement of profit or loss for the year ended 30 September 20X4 (in whole $)?

$ [   ]

---

14 On 1 October 20X4, Hoy Co had $2.5 million of equity share capital (shares of 50 cents each) in issue.

No new shares were issued during the year ended 30 September 20X5, but on that date there were outstanding share options which had a dilutive effect equivalent to issuing 1.2 million shares for no consideration.

Hoy's profit after tax for the year ended 30 September 20X5 was $1,550,000.

In accordance with IAS 33 *Earnings per Share*, what is Hoy's diluted earnings per share for the year ended 30 September 20X5?

○ $0.25

○ $0.41

○ $0.31

○ $0.42

15 The following information has been taken or calculated from Fowler Co's financial statements for the year ended 30 September 20X5:

Cash cycle at 30 September 20X5	70 days
Inventory turnover	six times
Year-end trade payables at 30 September 20X5	$230,000
Credit purchases for the year ended 30 September 20X5	$2,000,000
Cost of sales for the year ended 30 September 20X5	$1,800,000

Complete the following table, using the tokens provided, in order to reflect Fowler Co's cash cycle at 30 September 20X5.

Tokens	Add/subtract		Days
add		Inventory turnover days	
subtract		Receivables collection period	
42 days		Trade payables period	
51 days		Fowler Co's cash cycle at 30 September 20X5	= 70 days
61 days			

(30 marks)

Section B – ALL 15 questions are compulsory and MUST be attempted

Each question is worth 2 marks.

The following scenario relates to questions 16–20.

Telepath Co has a year end of 30 September and owns an item of plant which it uses to produce and package pharmaceuticals. The plant cost $750,000 on 1 October 20X0, and at that date, had an estimated useful life of five years. A review of the plant on 1 April 20X3 concluded that the plant would last for a further three and a half years and that its fair value was $560,000.

Telepath Co adopts the policy of revaluing its non-current assets to their fair value but does not make an annual transfer from the revaluation surplus to retained earnings to represent the additional depreciation charged due to the revaluation.

On 30 September 20X3, Telepath Co was informed by a major customer that it would no longer be placing orders with Telepath Co. As a result, Telepath revised its estimates that net cash inflows earned from the plant for the next three years would be:

Year ended 30 September:	$
20X4	220,000
20X5	180,000
20X6	200,000

Telepath Co's cost of capital is 10% which results in the following discount factors:

Value of $1 at 30 September:	
20X4	0.91
20X5	0.83
20X6	0.75

Telepath Co also owns Rilda Co, a 100% subsidiary, which is treated as a cash-generating unit. On 30 September 20X3, there was an impairment to Rilda's assets of $3,500,000. The carrying amount of the assets of Rilda Co immediately before the impairment were:

	$
Goodwill	2,000,000
Factory building	4,000,000
Plant	3,500,000
Receivables and cash (at recoverable amount)	2,500,000
	12,000,000

16 Use the options below to complete the following definition in **accordance with IAS 36 *Impairment of Assets.***

An asset is impaired if its __________ is __________ than its recoverable amount. The recoverable amount of an asset is defined as the higher of its fair value less costs of disposal and its __________.

Options:

carrying amount	historical cost	less
replacement cost	greater	value in use

BPP LEARNING MEDIA

17   Prior to considering any impairment, what is the carrying amount of Telepath Co's plant and the balance on the revaluation surplus at 30 September 20X3?

	Plant carrying amount	Revaluation surplus
	$'000	$'000
○	480	nil
○	300	185
○	480	185
○	300	nil

18   Calculate the value in use of Telepath Co's plant as at 30 September 20X3 (in whole $).

$ [   ]

19   Which of the following are TRUE in accordance with IAS 36 *Impairment of Assets*?

(1)   A cash-generating unit is the smallest identifiable group of assets for which individual cash flows can be identified and measured

(2)   When considering the impairment of a cash-generating unit, the calculation of the carrying amount and the recoverable amount does not need to be based on exactly the same group of net assets

(3)   When it is not possible to calculate the recoverable amount of a single asset, then that of its cash-generating unit should be measured instead

○   (1) only

○   (2) and (3)

○   (3) only

○   (1) and (3)

20   Calculate the carrying amount of Rilda Co's plant at 30 September 20X3 after the impairment loss has been correctly allocated to its assets (in whole $).

$ [   ]

The following scenario relates to questions 21–25.

At a board meeting in June 20X3, Neutron Co's directors made the decision to close down one of its factories by 30 September 20X3 and market both the building and the plant for sale. The decision had been made public, was communicated to all affected parties and was fully implemented by 30 September 20X3.

The directors of Neutron Co have provided the following information relating to the closure:

(1)   Of the factory's 250 employees, 50 will be retrained and deployed to other subsidiaries within the Neutron group during the year ended 30 September 20X4 at a cost of $125,000. The remainder accepted redundancy at an average cost of $5,000 each.

(2)   The factory's plant had a carrying amount of $2.2 million, but is only expected to sell for $500,000, incurring $50,000 of selling costs. The factory itself is expected to sell for a profit of $1.2 million.

(3)   The company also rented a number of machines in the factory under short-term leases which have an average of three months to run after 30 September 20X3. The present value of these future lease payments at 30 September 20X3 was $1 million, however, the lessor has stated that they will accept $850,000 if paid on 30 October 20X3 as a full settlement.

(4)   Penalty payments, due to the non-completion of supply contracts, are estimated to be $200,000, 50% of which is expected to be recovered from Neutron Co's insurers.

21   **Which TWO of the following are required if an operation is to be classified as a discontinued operation in accordance with IFRS 5 *Non-current Assets Held for Sale and Discontinued Operations*?**

☐   The operation represents a separate major line of business or geographical area

☐   The operation is a subsidiary

☐   The operation has been sold or is held for sale

☐   The operation is considered not to be capable of making a future profit following a period of losses

22   IFRS 5 *Non-current Assets Held for Sale and Discontinued Operations* prescribes the recognition criteria for non-current assets held for sale. For an asset or a disposal group to be classified as held for sale, the sale must be highly probable.

Which TWO of the following must apply for the sale to be considered highly probable?

☐   A buyer must have been located

☐   The asset must be marketed at a reasonable price

☐   Management must be committed to a plan to sell the asset

☐   The sale must be expected to take place within the next six months

23   **Calculate the employee cost associated with the closure and sale of Neutron Co's factory which should be charged to profit or loss for the year ended 30 September 20X3 (in whole $).**

$ [   ]

24   **What is the profit or loss on discontinued operations relating to property, plant and equipment for the year ended 30 September 20X3?**

○ $1.75 million loss

○ $1.75 million profit

○ $550,000 loss

○ $550,000 profit

25   In respect of the leases and penalty payments, what provision is required in the statement
      of financial position of Neutron Co as at 30 September 20X3?

      O $950,000

      O $1,200,000

      O $1,050,000

      O $1,100,000

The following scenario relates to questions 26–30.

Speculate Co is preparing its financial statements for the year ended 30 September 20X3. The
following issues are relevant:

(1)   **Financial assets**

      Shareholding A – a long-term investment in 10,000 of the equity shares of another
      company. These shares were acquired on 1 October 20X2 at a cost of $3.50 each.
      Transaction costs of 1% of the purchase price were incurred. On 30 September 20X3 the
      fair value of these shares is $4.50 each.

      Shareholding B – a short-term speculative investment in 2,000 of the equity shares of
      another company. These shares were acquired on 1 December 20X2 at a cost of $2.50
      each. Transaction costs of 1% of the purchase price were incurred. On 30 September 20X3
      the fair value of these shares is $3.00 each.

      Where possible, Speculate Co makes an irrevocable election for the fair value movements
      on financial assets to be reported in other comprehensive income.

(2)   **Taxation**

      The existing debit balance on the current tax account of $2.4 million represents the
      over/under provision of the tax liability for the year ended 30 September 20X2. A provision
      of $28 million is required for income tax for the year ended 30 September 20X3. The
      existing credit balance on the deferred tax account is $2.5 million and the provision
      required at 30 September 20X3 is $4.4 million.

(3)   **Revenue**

      On 1 October 20X2, Speculate Co sold one of its products for $10 million. As part of the sale
      agreement, Speculate Co is committed to the ongoing servicing of the product until
      30 September 20X5 (ie three years after the sale). The sale value of this service has been
      included in the selling price of $10 million. The estimated cost to Speculate Co of the
      servicing is $600,000 per annum and Speculate Co's gross profit margin on this type of
      servicing is 25%. Ignore discounting.

26   Match the financial instrument to its appropriate classification in accordance with IFRS 9
      Financial Instruments

Financial instrument   Classification

A contract to exchange financial instruments with another entity under conditions that are potentially unfavourable

A contract that evidences the residual interest in the assets of an entity after deducting all of its liabilities

Cash

An equity instrument of another entity

A financial asset

A financial asset

An equity instrument

A financial liability

27   In respect of the financial assets of Speculate Co, what amount will be included in other
      comprehensive income for the year ended 30 September 20X3.

      ○   Nil

      ○ $9,650

      ○ $10,000

      ○ $10,650

28   Calculate the total amount which will be charged to the statement of profit or loss for the
      year ended 30 September 20X3 in respect of taxation.

      $ [   ]

29   What is the amount of deferred income which Speculate Co should recognise in its
      statement of financial position as at 30 September 20X3 relating to the contract for the
      supply and servicing of products?

      O $1.2 million

      O $1.6 million

      O $600,000

      O $1.5 million

30   **Which TWO of the following are TRUE in respect of the income which Speculate Co has
      deferred at 30 September 20X3?**

      ☐   The deferred income will be split evenly between the current and non-current
           liabilities in Speculate Co's statement of financial position as at 30 September 20X3

      ☐   The costs associated with the deferred income of Speculate Co should be recognised
           in the statement of profit or loss at the same time as the revenue is recognised

      ☐   The deferred income can only be recognised as revenue by Speculate Co when there
           is a signed written contract of service with its customer

      ☐   When recognising the revenue associated with the service contract of Speculate Co,
           the stage of its completion is irrelevant

      (30 marks)

Section C – Both questions are compulsory and MUST be attempted

Question 31

After preparing a draft statement of profit or loss for the year ended 30 September 20X5 and adding the current year's draft profit (before any adjustments required by notes (i) to (iii) below) to retained earnings, the summarised trial balance of Kandy Co as at 30 September 20X5 is:

	$'000	$'000
Equity shares of $1 each		20,000
Retained earnings as at 30 September 20X5		15,500
Proceeds of 6% loan note (note (i))		30,000
Investment properties at fair value (note (ii))	20,000	
Land ($5 million) and buildings – at cost (note (ii))	35,000	
Plant and equipment – at cost (note (ii))	58,500	
Accumulated depreciation at 1 October 20X4: buildings		20,000
plant and equipment		34,500
Current assets	68,700	
Current liabilities		43,400
Deferred tax (notes (ii) and (iii))		2,500
Interest paid (note (i))	1,800	
Current tax (note (iii))		1,100
Suspense account (note (ii))		17,000
	184,000	184,000

The following notes are relevant:

(i)   The loan note was issued on 1 October 20X4 and incurred issue costs of $1 million which were charged to profit or loss. Interest of $1.8 million ($30 million at 6%) was paid on 30 September 20X5. The loan is redeemable on 30 September 20X9 at a substantial premium which gives an effective interest rate of 9% per annum. No other repayments are due until 30 September 20X9.

(ii)   Non-current assets:

On 1 October 20X4, Kandy owned two investment properties. The first property had a carrying amount of $15 million and was sold on 1 December 20X4 for $17 million. The disposal proceeds have been credited to a suspense account in the trial balance above. On 31 December 20X4, the second property became owner occupied and so was transferred to land and buildings at its fair value of $6 million. Its remaining useful life on 31 December 20X4 was considered to be 20 years. Ignore any deferred tax implications of this fair value.

The price of property has increased significantly in recent years and so the directors decided to revalue the land and buildings. The directors accepted the report of an independent surveyor who, on 1 October 20X4, valued the land at $8 million and the buildings at $39 million on that date. This revaluation specifically excludes the transferred investment property described above. The remaining life of these buildings at 1 October 20X4 was 15 years. Kandy does not make an annual transfer to retained profits to reflect the realisation of the revaluation gain; however, the revaluation will give rise to a deferred tax liability. The income tax rate applicable to Kandy is 20%.

Plant and equipment is depreciated at 12.5% per annum using the reducing balance method.

No depreciation has yet been charged on any non-current asset for the year ended 30 September 20X5.

(iii) A provision of $2.4 million is required for income tax on the profit for the year to 30 September 20X5. The balance on current tax in the trial balance is the under/over provision of tax for the previous year. In addition to the temporary differences relating to the information in note (ii), Kandy has further taxable temporary differences of $10 million as at 30 September 20X5.

Required

(a) Prepare a schedule of adjustments required to the retained earnings of Kandy Co as at 30 September 20X5 as a result of the information in notes (i) to (iii) above.   **(8 marks)**

(b) Prepare the statement of financial position of Kandy Co as at 30 September 20X5.

   Note. The notes to the statement of financial position are not required.   **(9 marks)**

(c) Prepare the extracts from Kandy Co's statement of cash flows for operating and investing activities for the year ended 30 September 20X5 which relate to property, plant and equipment.   **(3 marks)**

(Total = 20 marks)

Question 32

The summarised consolidated financial statements for the year ended 30 September 20X5 (and the comparative figures) for the Tangier group are shown below.

Consolidated statements of profit or loss for the year ended 30 September:

	20X5 $m	20X4 $m
Revenue	2,700	1,820
Cost of sales	(1,890)	(1,092)
Gross profit	810	728
Administrative expense	(345)	(200)
Distribution costs	(230)	(130)
Finance costs	(40)	(5)
Profit before taxation	195	393
Income tax expense	(60)	(113)
Profit for the year	135	280

Consolidated statements of financial position as at 30 September:

	20X5 $m	20X5 $m	20X4 $m	20X4 $m
Non-current assets				
Property, plant and equipment		680		310
Intangible asset:		300		100
manufacturing licences				
Goodwill		230		200
		1,210		610
Current assets				
Inventory	200		110	
Trade receivables	195		75	
Bank	–	395	120	305
Total assets		1,605		915

	20X5 $m	20X5 $m	20X4 $m	20X4 $m
Equity shares of $1 each		330		250
Other components of equity		100		–
Retained earnings		375		295
		805		545
Non-current liabilities				
5% secured loan notes	100		100	
10% secured loan notes	300	400	–	100
Current liabilities				
Bank overdraft	110		–	
Trade payables	210		160	
Current tax payable	80	400	110	270
Total equity and liabilities		1,605		915

At 1 October 20X4, the Tangier group consisted of the parent, Tangier Co, and two wholly owned subsidiaries which had been owned for many years. On 1 January 20X5, Tangier Co purchased a third 100% owned investment in a subsidiary called Raremetal Co. The consideration paid for Raremetal Co was a combination of cash and shares. The cash payment was partly funded by the issue of 10% loan notes. On 1 January 20X5, Tangier Co also won a tender for a new contract to supply aircraft engines which Tangier Co manufactures under a recently acquired long-term licence. Raremetal Co was purchased with a view to securing the supply of specialised materials used in the manufacture of these engines. The bidding process had been very competitive and Tangier Co had to increase its manufacturing capacity to fulfil the contract.

Required

(a)   Comment on how the new contract and the purchase of Raremetal Co may have affected the comparability of the consolidated financial statements of Tangier Co for the years ended 30 September 20X4 and 20X5.   **(5 marks)**

(b)   Calculate appropriate ratios and comment on Tangier Co's profitability and gearing. Your analysis should identify instances where the new contract and the purchase of Raremetal Co have limited the usefulness of the ratios and your analysis.

Note. Your ratios should be based on the consolidated financial statements provided and you should not attempt to adjust for the effects of the new contract or the consolidation. Working capital and liquidity ratios are not required. There are up to 5 marks available for the ratio calculations.   **(12 marks)**

(c)   Explain what further information you might require to make your analysis more meaningful.   **(3 marks)**

(Total = 20 marks)

Answers

DO NOT TURN THIS PAGE UNTIL YOU HAVE
COMPLETED THE MOCK EXAM

A plan of attack

What's the worst thing you could be doing right now if this was the actual exam? Wondering how to celebrate the end of the exam in three hours' time? Panicking, flapping and generally getting in a right old state?

Well, they're all pretty bad, so turn back to the exam and let's sort out a **plan of attack**!

First things first

You have three hours for this exam. This exam is the examining team's specimen exam, so it is the best indication of what you will see in your exam. Read it carefully.

The Financial Reporting exam has 15 2-mark questions in Section A, 15 2-mark questions in Section B and two long-form questions in Section C. All questions are compulsory. Therefore, you do not have to spend time working out which questions to answer.

It's a good idea to just start with the Section A questions. Once you have them done, you will feel more relaxed. Leave any that you are unsure of and come back to them later but don't leave any unanswered.

Section B: Questions 16–20 are on non-current assets. Questions 21–25 are on discontinued operations. Questions 26–30 cover three issues – financial assets, taxation and revenue. For each of these Section B questions, make sure you read the scenario carefully.

Question 31 requires you to adjust retained earnings and prepare a statement of financial position and some cash flow extracts. There is nothing difficult here but you need to work methodically.

Question 32 is an interpretation question. Remember that you do not get marks for simply saying that a ratio went up or down. It is your job to look at why this happened.

You've got spare time at the end of the exam...?

If you have allocated your time properly, then you **shouldn't have time on your hands** at the end of the exam and you should start by checking the Section A questions to make sure you have left none unanswered. But if you find yourself with five or ten minutes to spare, check over your work to make sure that there are no silly arithmetical errors.

Forget about it!

And don't worry if you found the exam difficult. More than likely, other candidates will too. If this were the real thing, you would need to **forget** the exam the minute you leave the exam hall and **think about the next one**. Or, if it's the last one, **celebrate**!

Section A

1 The correct answers are:

All entity financial statements within a group should normally be prepared to the same accounting year end prior to consolidation.

Unrealised profits within the group must be eliminated from the consolidated financial statements.

Adjustments will be made on consolidation for different accounting policies. Subsidiaries with dissimilar activities are still consolidated.

2 $4,098,050

Year	Opening ($)	Interest @ 10% ($)	Payment ($)	Closing ($)
30 Sept X5	22,745,000	2,274,500	(6,000,000)	19,019,500
30 Sept X6	19,019,500	1,901,950	(6,000,000)	14,921,450
			Current	4,098,050

3 The correct answers are:

The sector average figures are compiled from companies whose year ends are between 1 July 20X5 and 30 September 20X5.

Quartile Co does not revalue its properties, but is aware that other entities in this sector do.

Rising costs will have affected all of the business sector and the inventory adjustment will have been corrected in the prior year, so no actual effect in 20X5.

4

Charging the rental payments for an item of plant to the statement of profit or loss where the rental agreement meets the criteria for a lease		False
Including a convertible loan note in equity on the basis that the holders are likely to choose the equity option on conversion		False
Treating redeemable preference shares as part of equity in the statement of financial position		False
Derecognising factored trade receivables sold without recourse to the seller	True	

Trade receivables factored without recourse are no longer an asset of the seller and therefore the statement is true. The other statements are all false.

5

Debit	Group retained earnings
Credit	Inventory

As the sale is made by the parent, there is no charge against non-controlling interest.

6 The correct answer is: They are difficult to verify because transactions could have happened many years ago

Historical cost transactions are easy to verify because there will be a record of the transaction.

7 The correct answer is: $22,032,000

Dismantling provision at 1 October 20X4 is $20.4 million (30,000 × 0.68) discounted

This will increase by an 8% finance cost by 30 September 20X5 = $22,032,000

8   The correct answer is: A new research project which the subsidiary has correctly expensed to profit or loss but the directors of the parent have reliably assessed to have a substantial fair value

The research project only as the customer list cannot be reliably valued. The advertising campaign cannot be capitalised and contingent assets are not recognised.

9    $7,780,000

	$'000
FV NCI at 1 October 14 (9000 × 20% × $3.50)	6,300
Post-acquisition profit (8000 – (3000/5)) = 7,400 at 20%	1,480
	7,780

10   The correct answer is: $1,515,000

	$'000
Cost (240,000 × $6)	1,440
Share of associate's profit (400 × 240/800)	120
Less dividend received (150 × 240/800)	(45)
	1,515

11

The initial carrying amount of plant should include:	
Cost of transporting the plant to the factory	Cost of installing a new power supply required to operate the plant

The initial carrying amount of plant should NOT include:	
Cost of a three-year plant maintenance agreement	Cost of a three-week training course for staff to operate the plant

12   The correct answers are:

The rate that existed on the day that the purchase or sale took place.

The rate that existed at the end of the accounting period.

13    $342,000

		$'000
Sales proceeds		5,580
Net assets at disposal	4,464	
Goodwill at disposal	1,674	
Less: carrying amount of NCI	(900)	(5,238)
		342

14   The correct answer is: $(1,550/(2,500 \times 2 + 1,200)) = \$0.25$

15

Add/subtract		Days
add	Inventory turnover days	61 days
subtract	Receivables collection period	51 days
	Trade payables period	42 days
	Fowler Co's cash cycle at 30 September 20X5	= 70 days

Inventory turnover is 61 days (365/6)

Trade payables period is 42 days (230,000 × 365/2)

Therefore, receivables collection period is 51 days (70 – 61 + 42)

BPP
LEARNING
MEDIA

Section B

16   An asset is impaired when its [carrying amount] is [greater] than its recoverable amount. The recoverable amount of an asset is defined as the higher of its fair value less costs of disposal and its [value in use].

17   The correct answer is: Plant carrying amount: 480. Revaluation surplus: 185

Annual depreciation prior to the revaluation is $150,000 (750/5).
At the date of revaluation (1 April 20X3), the carrying amount is $375,000 (750 – (150 × 2.5 yrs)). Revalued to $560,000 with a remaining life of 3.5 years results in a depreciation charge of $160,000 per annum which means $80,000 for six months. The carrying amount at 30 September 20X3 is therefore $480,000 (560 – 80).

Alternative calculation: $560,000 – ($560,000/3.5 × 6/12) = $480,000.

The revaluation surplus has a balance of $185,000 (560,000 – 375,000).

18   $499,600

	Cash flow $'000	Discount factor at 10%	Present value $'000
Year ended: 30 September 20X4	220	0.91	200.2
30 September 20X5	180	0.83	149.4
30 September 20X6	200	0.75	150.0
			499.6

19   The correct answer is: (1) and (3)

The assets of the CGU must remain the same when calculating impairment.

20   $2,800,000

	Carrying amount before $'000	Impairment loss $'000	Carrying amount after $'000
Goodwill	2,000	2,000	–
Property	4,000	800	3,200
Plant	3,500	700	2,800
Cash and receivables	2,500	–	2,500
	12,000	3,500	8,500

21   The correct answers are:

The operation represents a separate major line of business or geographical area

The operation has been sold or is held for sale.

The operation does not have to be a subsidiary. Future profit forecasts are not relevant.

22   The correct answers are:

A buyer does not need to have been specifically located

The sale must be expected to take place within the next 12 months.

23   $1,000,000

200 employees at $5,000 = $1,000,000 redundancy costs. The retraining costs are a future cost.

24   The correct answer is: $1.75 million loss

Impairment loss on plant is $1,750,000 (2,200,000 – (500,000 – 50,000)).

25   The correct answer is: Onerous contract $850,000 + penalty payments $200,000 = $1,050,000.

    The possible insurance receipt should be ignored as there is no certainty that it would be received and it would not be netted off against the provision anyway.

26

Financial instrument	Classification
A contract to exchange financial instruments with another entity under conditions that are potentially unfavourable	A financial liability
A contract that evidences the residual interest in the assets of an entity after deducting all of its liabilities	An equity instrument
Cash	A financial asset
An equity instrument of another entity	A financial asset

27   The correct answer is: $9,650

    Shareholding A is not held for trading as an election made – FVTOCI.

    Shareholding B is held for trading and so FVTPL (transaction costs are not included in carrying amount).

    Cost of shareholding A is 10,000 × $3.50 × 1.01 = $35,350.

    FV at 30 September 20X3 10,000 × $4.50 = $45,000.

    Gain = 45,000 − 35,350 = $9,650.

28    $32,300

	$'000
DT provision required at 30 September 20X3	4,400
DT Provision at 1 October 20X2	(2,500)
	1,900
Write off of the under provision for the year ended 30 September 20X2	2,400
Income tax for the year ended 30 September 20X3	28,000
Charge for the year ended 30 September 20X3	32,300

29   The correct answer is: At 30 September 20X3, there are two more years of servicing work, thus $1.6 million ((600,000 × 2) × 100/75) must be treated as deferred income.

30   The correct answers are:

    The deferred income will be split evenly between the current and non-current liabilities in Speculate Co's statement of financial position as at 30 September 20X3.

    The costs associated with the deferred income of Speculate Co should be recognised in the statement of profit or loss at the same time as the revenue is recognised.

    A written service contract is not needed, but the stage of completion is important in recognising revenue.

Section C

Question 31

		Marks
(a)	Schedule of retained earnings as at 30 September 20X4	
	Retained earnings per trial balance	½
	Issue costs	1
	Loan finance costs	1
	Gains on investment properties	1
	Depreciation charges	3
	Income tax expense	1½
		8
(b)	Statement of financial position	
	Property, plant and equipment	2
	Current assets	½
	Equity shares	½
	Revaluation surplus	2
	Deferred tax	1
	6% loan note	1½
	Current liabilities (per trial balance)	½
	Current tax payable	1
		9
(c)	Extracts from the statement of cash flows	
	Cash flows from operating activities:	
	Add back depreciation	1
	Less gain on revaluation of investment property	½
	Less gain on disposal of investment property	½
	Cash flows from investing activities:	
	Investment property disposal proceeds	1
		3
		20

(a)   Schedule of retained earnings of Kandy as at 30 September 20X5

	$'000
Retained earnings per trial balance	15,500
Adjustments re:	
Note (i)	
Add back issue costs of loan note (W1)	1,000
Loan finance costs (29,000 × 9%) (W1)	(2,610)
Note (ii)	
Gain on disposal of investment property (17,000 – 15,000)	2,000
Gain on revaluation of investment property prior to transfer	
(6,000 – 5,000)	1,000
Depreciation of buildings (W2)	(2,825)
Depreciation of plant and equipment (W2)	(3,000)
Note (iii)	
Income tax expense (W3)	(800)
Adjusted retained earnings	10,265

You would use the spreadsheet response option to answer this question in the CBE exam. When using the spreadsheet software, it is essential that you show your workings. You can do so by either using formula within the cells or by setting out your workings on the face of your answer. Below is an extract from the spreadsheet software showing how your answer may be presented:

Edit   Format

C6 : =-29000*0.09

	A	B	C	D	E	F	G	H	I
1	(a) Adjustment to retained earnings					Buildings depreciation			
2			$0			Depreciation on buildings pe		2600	
3	RE per TB		15500			Depreciation on IP transferre		225	
4	Adjustments:							2825	
5	Add issue costs of loa		1000						
6	Less Finance costs		-2610			P&E depreciation			
7	Add Gain on disposa		2000			CA per TB		24000	
8	Add Gain on FV adju		1000			Depreciation RB basis		3000	
9	Less Depreciation of		-2825						
10	Less Depreciation of		-3000			Income tax			
11	Less Income tax (W)		-800			Provision for current yr		2400	
12			10265			Less overprovision		-1100	
13						DT		-500	
14								800	

Sheet1

You should note the following:

- The answer is set out clearly with brief descriptions given to explain the adjustments made

- Simple calculations such as that shown in the highlighted cell C6 can be performed using formula within the cell.

- More complex calculations such as the income tax calculation should be set out as a separate calculation with the total included in the main answer by entering the formula =H14 in cell C1

- Subtotals and totals should be included using the sum function, for example in cell C12, the formula =SUM(C3:C11) should be used

(b)   STATEMENT OF FINANCIAL POSITION AS AT 30 SEPTEMBER 20X5

	$'000	$'000
Assets		
Non-current assets		
Property, plant and equipment (50,175 + 21,000 (W2))		71,175
Current assets (per trial balance)		68,700
Total assets		139,875
Equity and liabilities		
Equity		
Equity shares of $1 each		20,000
Revaluation surplus (32,000 – 6,400 (W2) and (W3))	25,600	
Retained earnings (from (a))	10,265	35,865
		55,865

	$'000	$'000
Non-current liabilities		
Deferred tax (W3)	8,400	
6% loan note (W1)	29,810	38,210
Current liabilities		
Per trial balance	43,400	
Current tax payable	2,400	45,800
Total equity and liabilities		139,875

Workings (monetary figures in brackets in $'000)

1   Loan note

The issue costs should be deducted from the proceeds of the loan note and not charged as an expense. The finance cost of the loan note, at the effective rate of 9% applied to the carrying amount of the loan note of $29 million (30,000 – 1,000), is $2,610,000. The interest actually paid is $1.8 million. The difference between these amounts of $810,000 (2,610 – 1,800) is added to the carrying amount of the loan note to give $29,810,000 (29,000 + 810) for inclusion as a non-current liability in the statement of financial position.

2   Non-current assets

Land and buildings

The gain on revaluation and carrying amount of the land and buildings will be:

	$'000
Carrying amount at 1 October 20X4 (35,000 – 20,000)	15,000
Revaluation at that date (8,000 + 39,000)	47,000
Gain on revaluation	32,000

	$'000
Buildings depreciation for the year ended 30 September 20X5:	
Land and buildings existing at 1 October 20X4 (39,000/15 years)	2,600
Transferred investment property (6,000/20 × 9/12)	225
	2,825
Carrying amount at 30 September 20X5 (47,000 + 6,000 – 2,825)	50,175

	$'000
Plant and equipment	
Carrying amount at 1 October 20X4 (58,500 – 34,500)	24,000
Depreciation for year ended 30 September 20X5 (12.5% reducing balance)	(3,000)
Carrying amount at 30 September 20X5	21,000

3   Taxation

	$'000
Income tax expense:	
Provision for year ended 30 September 20X5	2,400
Less over provision in previous year	(1,100)
Deferred tax (see below)	(500)
	800

	$'000
Deferred tax	
Provision required at 30 September 20X5 ((10,000 + 32,000) × 20%)	8,400
Provision at 1 October 20X4	(2,500)
Movement in provision	5,900
Charge to revaluation of land and buildings (32,000 × 20%)	(6,400)
Balance – credit to profit or loss	(500)

You would also use the spreadsheet response area to prepare the statement of financial position. The recommended way to do this is to create a proforma statement of financial position, such as that shown below, and then to enter your figures in the relevant cells as you complete your workings.

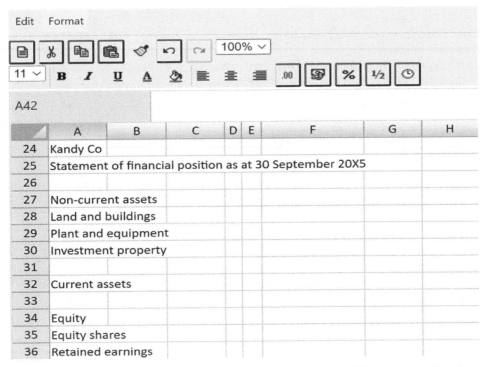

	A	B	C	D	E	F	G	H
24	Kandy Co							
25	Statement of financial position as at 30 September 20X5							
26								
27	Non-current assets							
28	Land and buildings							
29	Plant and equipment							
30	Investment property							
31								
32	Current assets							
33								
34	Equity							
35	Equity shares							
36	Retained earnings							

Remember that you can cross reference to any relevant workings undertaken to arrive at the answers for requirement (a) and do not need to recreate them for inclusion in the statement of financial position. For example, when calculating the carrying amount of plant and equipment, the depreciation for the year has already been calculated and therefore the depreciation can be included in the calculation by referring to the cell in which the depreciation calculation was presented. This can be seen in highlighted cell H30 which refers to another cell containing the calculation.

Highlighted cell C29 cross references to cell H31 which is the total of the plant and equipment working. Cell H31 itself uses the sum formula to arrive at the total.

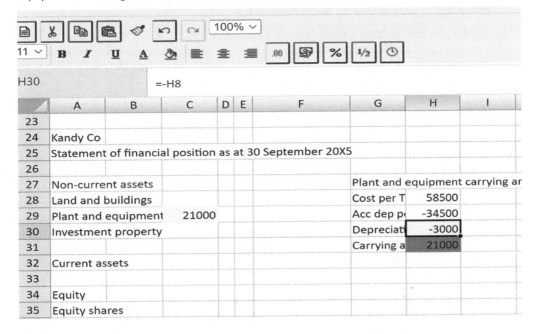

H30 : =-H8

	A	B	C	D	E	F	G	H	I
23									
24	Kandy Co								
25	Statement of financial position as at 30 September 20X5								
26									
27	Non-current assets					Plant and equipment carrying ar			
28	Land and buildings					Cost per T		58500	
29	Plant and equipment		21000			Acc dep pe		-34500	
30	Investment property					Depreciati		-3000	
31						Carrying a		21000	
32	Current assets								
33									
34	Equity								
35	Equity shares								

(c)

	$'000
Cash flows from operating activities:	
Add back depreciation	5,825
Deduct gain on revaluation of investment property	(1,000)
Deduct gain on disposal of investment property	(2,000)
Cash flows from investing activities:	
Investment property disposal proceeds	17,000

Question 32

			Marks
(a)	Analysis of results A like for like comparison taking account of the consolidation and the contract		5
(b)	Up to 5 marks for ratio calculations	5	
	Profitability	4½	
	Gearing and interest cover	2½	
			12
(c)	Additional information Any three of the six suggestions provided		3
			20

(a)   **Note.** References to '20X5' are in respect of the year ended 30 September 20X5 and '20X4' refers to the year ended 30 September 20X4.

The key matter to note is that the ratios for 20X4 and 20X5 will not be directly comparable because two significant events, the acquisition of Raremetal Co and securing the new contract, have occurred between these dates. This means that the underlying financial statements are not directly comparable. For example, the 20X4 statement of profit or loss (SOPL) will not include the results of Raremetal Co or the effect of the new contract. However, the 20X5 SOPL will contain nine months of the results of Raremetal Co (although intragroup transactions will have been eliminated) and nine months of the effects of the new contract (which may have resulted in either a net profit or loss). Likewise, the 20X4 statement of financial position does not contain any of Raremetal Co's assets and liabilities, whereas that of 20X5 contains all of the net assets of Raremetal Co and the cost of the new licence. This does not mean that comparisons between the two years are not worthwhile, just that they need to be treated with caution. For some ratios, it may be necessary to exclude all of the subsidiaries from the analysis and use the single entity financial statements of Tangier Co as a basis for comparison with the performance of previous years. Similarly, it may still be possible to compare some of the ratios of the Tangier group with those of other groups in the same sector although not all groups will have experienced similar acquisitions.

Assuming there has been no impairment of goodwill, the investment in Raremetal Co has resulted in additional goodwill of $30 million which means that the investment has cost more than the carrying amount of Raremetal Co's net assets. Although there is no indication of the precise cost, it is known to have been achieved by a combination of a share exchange (hence the $180 million new issue of shares) and a cash element (funded from the proceeds of the loan issue and the decrease in the bank balance). Any intragroup sales have been eliminated on consolidation and it is not possible to determine in which individual company any profit on these intragroup sales will be reported; it is therefore difficult to measure any benefits of the investment. Indeed, the benefit of the investment might not be a financial one but merely to secure the supply of raw materials. It would be useful to establish the cost of the investment and the profit (if any) contributed by Raremetal Co so that an assessment of the benefit of the investment might be made.

You would answer Requirement (a) using the word processing response area. You should arrange your answer in paragraphs and could consider using the bullet point list option if you consider it a better way to lay out your answer. Taking the first part of the full answer as an example, you could set out your answer in the word processing response area as follows:

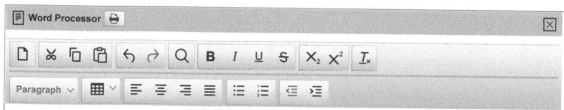

The ratios for 20X4 and 20X5 will not be directly comparable because two significant events: the acquisition of Raremetal Co and securing the new contract. This means that the underlying financial statements are not directly comparable.

For example:

- the 20X4 statement of profit or loss (SOPL) will not include the results of Raremetal Co or the effect of the new contract
- the 20X5 SOPL will contain nine months of the results of Raremetal Co (although intragroup transactions will have been eliminated) and nine months of the effects of the new contract (which may have resulted in either a net profit or loss)
- the 20X4 statement of financial position (SOFP) does not contain any of Raremetal Co's assets and liabilities
- the 20X5 SOFP contains all of the net assets of Raremetal Co and the cost of the new licence.

(b)

Relevant ratios:	20X5	20X4
Gross profit margin % (810/2,700 × 100)	30.0%	40.0%
Operating profit margin (235/2,700 × 100)	8.7%	21.9%
ROCE (235/(805 + 400))	19.5%	61.7%
Non-current asset turnover (2,700/1,210)	2.23 times	2.98 times
Debt/equity (400/805)	49.7%	18.3%
Interest cover (235/40)	5.9 times	79.6 times

Although the calculation of ratios is numerical, it is likely that the word processing response area will be provided in the exam to answer the interpretations question. You may be presented with a pre-formatted response area (a blank table), in which case you should use that to structure your answer. If you are not provided with a pre-formatted response area, you can use the table within the word processing response area to set out your calculations.

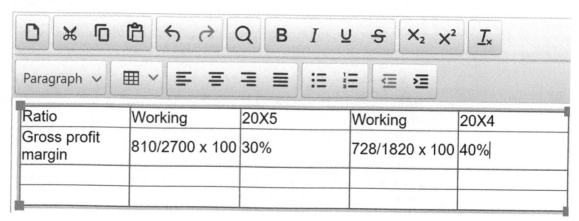

Ratio	Working	20X5	Working	20X4
Gross profit margin	810/2700 x 100	30%	728/1820 x 100	40%

All of the issues identified in part (a) make a comparison of ratios difficult and, if more information was available, then some adjustments may be required. For example, if it is established that the investment is not generating any benefits, then it might be argued that the inclusion of the goodwill in the ROCE and non-current asset turnover is unjustified (it may be impaired and should be written off). Goodwill has not been excluded from any of the following ratios.

The increase in revenues of 48.4% (880/1,820 × 100) in 20X5 will be partly due to the consolidation of Raremetal Co and the revenues associated with the new contract. Yet, despite these increased revenues, the company has suffered a dramatic fall in its profitability. This has been caused by a combination of a falling gross profit margin (from 40% in 20X4 to only 30% in 20X5) and markedly higher operating overheads (operating profit margin has fallen from 21.9% in 20X4 to 8.7% in 20X5). Again, it is important to note that some of these costs will be attributable to the consolidation of Raremetal Co and some to the new contract. It could be speculated that the 73% increase in administrative expenses may be due to one-off costs associated with the tendering process (consultancy fees, etc) and the acquisition of Raremetal Co and the 77% increase in higher distribution costs could be due to additional freight, packing and insurance cost of the engines, delivery distances may also be longer – even to foreign countries (although some of the increase in distribution costs may also be due to consolidation).

This is all reflected in the ROCE falling from an impressive 61.7% in 20X4 to only 19.5% in 20X5 (though even this figure is respectable). The fall in the ROCE is attributable to a dramatic fall in profit margin at operating level (from 21.9% in 20X4 to only 8.7% in 20X5) which has been compounded by a reduction in the non-current asset turnover, with only $2·23 being generated from every $1 invested in non-current assets in 20X5 (from $2.98 in 20X4).

The information in the question points strongly to the possibility (even probability) that the new contract may be responsible for much of the deterioration in Tangier Co's operating performance. For example, it is likely that the new contract may account for some of the increased revenue; however, the bidding process was 'very competitive' which may imply that Tangier Co had to cut its prices (and therefore its profit margin) in order to win the contract.

The costs of fulfilling the contract have also been heavy: investment in property, plant and equipment has increased by $370 million (at carrying amount), representing an increase of 61% (no doubt some of this increase will be due to the acquisition of Raremetal Co). The increase in licence costs to manufacture the new engines has cost $200 million plus any amortisation and there is also the additional goodwill of $30 million.

An eight-fold increase in finance cost caused by the increased borrowing at double the interest rate of the borrowing in 20X4 and (presumably) some overdraft interest has led to the dramatic fall in the company's interest cover (from 79.6 in 20X4 to only 5.9 in 20X5). The finance cost of the new $300 million 10% loan notes to partly fund the investment in Raremetal Co and other non-current assets has also increased debt/equity (one form of gearing measure) from 18.3% in 20X4 to 49.7% in 20X5 despite also issuing $180 million in new equity shares. At this level, particularly in view of its large increase from 20X4, it may give debt holders (and others) cause for concern as there is increased risk for all Tangier Co's lenders. If it could be demonstrated that the overdraft could not be cleared for some time, this would be an argument for including it in the calculation of debt/equity, making the 20X5 gearing level even worse. It is also apparent from the movement in the retained earnings that Tangier Co paid a dividend during 20X5 of $55 million (295,000 + 135,000 – 375,000) which may be a questionable policy when the company is raising additional finance through borrowings and contributes substantially to Tangier Co's overdraft.

Overall, the acquisition of Raremetal Co to secure supplies appears to have been an expensive strategy, perhaps a less expensive one might have been to enter into a long-term supply contract with Raremetal Co.

(c)   Further information which would be useful to obtain would therefore include:

   (i)   The cost of the investment in Raremetal Co, the carrying amount of the assets acquired and whether Tangier Co has carried out a goodwill impairment test as required under IFRS Standards.

(ii) The benefits generated from the investment; for example, Raremetal Co's individual financial statements and details of sales to external customers (not all of these benefits will be measurable in financial terms).

(iii) The above two pieces of information would demonstrate whether the investment in Raremetal Co had been worthwhile.

(iv) The amount of intragroup sales made during the year and those expected to be made in the short to medium term.

(v) The pricing strategy agreed with Raremetal Co so that the effects on the profits reported in the individual financial statements of Raremetal Co and Tangier Co can be more readily determined.

(vi) More information is needed to establish if the new contract has been detrimental to Tangier Co's performance. The contract was won sometime between 1 October 20X4 and 1 January 20X5 and there is no information of when production and sales started, but clearly there has not been a full year's revenue from the contract. Also there is no information on the length or total value of the contract.

Again, you would answer Requirement (b) using the word processing response area. You consider using the bullet point list option or the numbered list option to set out your answer.

ACCA

Financial Reporting (FR)

Mock Examination 3

(ACCA CBE Practice Exam 2)

Questions	
Time allowed	3 hours
This mock exam is divided into three sections:	
Section A	ALL 15 questions are compulsory and MUST be attempted
Section B	ALL 15 questions are compulsory and MUST be attempted
Section C	BOTH questions are compulsory and MUST be attempted

DO NOT OPEN THIS EXAM UNTIL YOU ARE READY TO START
UNDER EXAMINATION CONDITIONS

Section A – ALL 15 questions are compulsory and MUST be attempted

Each question is worth 2 marks.

1   **Which of the following is a possible advantage of a rules-based system of financial reporting?**

    ○   It encourages the exercise of professional judgement

    ○   It prevents a fire-fighting approach to the formulation of standards

    ○   It offers accountants more protection in the event of litigation

    ○   It ensures that no standards conflict with each other

2   IFRS 10 *Consolidated Financial Statements* states that 'A parent shall prepare consolidated financial statements using uniform accounting policies for like transactions and other events in similar circumstances'.

    Which of the following situations requires an adjustment because of this constraint?

    ○   A subsidiary has been acquired and its land is to be included in the consolidated financial statements at fair value

    ○   A subsidiary carries its assets at historical cost but the parent's assets are carried at revalued amounts

    ○   There have been intragroup transactions during the year which have resulted in unrealised profit in inventory at the year end

    ○   There has been intragroup trading which has resulted in intragroup balances for receivables and payables at the year end

3   The following trial balance extract relates to Topsy Co as at 30 April 20X6:

	$'000	$'000
Land at cost	800	
Building:		
Valuation at 1 May 20X2	1,500	
Accumulated depreciation at 30 April 20X5		90
Revaluation surplus at 30 April 20X5		705

On 1 May 20X2, when the carrying amount of the building was $750,000, it was revalued for the first time to $1.5m and its remaining useful life at that date was estimated to be 50 years. Topsy Co has correctly accounted for this revaluation in the above trial balance. However, Topsy Co has not yet charged depreciation for the year ended 30 April 20X6 or transferred the excess depreciation from the revaluation surplus to retained earnings at 30 April 20X6.

In February 20X6, the land, but not the building, was independently valued at $950,000. This adjustment has yet to be made for the year ended 30 April 20X6.

What is the balance on the revaluation surplus of Topsy Co as at 30 April 20X6 after the required adjustments have been made?

    ○ $555,000

    ○ $690,000

    ○ $840,000

    ○ $870,000

4   Plow Co purchased 3,500 of the 10,000 $1 equity shares of Styre Co on 1 August 20X4 for
     $6.50 per share.

     Styre Co's profit for the year ended 31 July 20X5 was $7,500. Styre Co paid a dividend of
     $0.50 per share on 31 December 20X4.

     **Calculate the carrying amount of the investment in Styre Co in the consolidated
     statement of financial position of Plow Co as at 31 July 20X5 (to the nearest whole $).**

     $ [   ]

5   **Identify, by selecting the relevant box in the table below, whether the following
     statements are correct or incorrect when calculating the impairment loss of an asset.**

Assets should be carried at the lower of their carrying amount and recoverable amount	Correct	Incorrect
The recoverable amount of an asset is the higher of value in use and fair value less costs of disposal	Correct	Incorrect

6   **Which of the following statements is NOT true?**

     ○   In some countries, accounting standards can be a detailed set of rules which
          companies must follow

     ○   Local accounting standards can be influenced by the tax regime within a country

     ○   Accounting standards on their own provide a complete system of regulation

     ○   Accounting standards are particularly important where a company's shares are
          publicly traded

7   A company had issued share capital on 1 January 20X9 of 2,000,000 equity $1 shares. On
     1 October 20X9, a rights issue was made on a one for four basis which was fully taken up.

     On 30 September 20X9, each share had a market value of $3.25, giving a theoretical ex-
     rights value of $2.84 per share.

     **In accordance with IAS 33 *Earnings per Share*, what is the weighted average number of
     shares in issue for the year ended 31 December 20X9?**

     ○   2,341,549

     ○   1,935,769

     ○   2,125,000

     ○   2,431,778

8   **Which TWO of the following would result in a credit to the deferred tax account?**

     ☐   Interest receivable, which will be taxed when the interest is received

     ☐   A loan, the repayment of which will have no tax consequences

     ☐   Interest payable, which will be allowable for tax when paid

     ☐   Prepaid expenses, which have been deducted to calculate the taxable profits of the
          previous year

9   IFRS 15 *Revenue from Contracts with Customers* states that, where performance obligations are satisfied over time, entities should apply an appropriate method of measuring progress.

Which TWO of the following are appropriate OUTPUT methods of measuring progress?

☐   Total costs to date of the contract as a percentage of total contract revenue

☐   Physical milestones reached as a percentage of physical completion

☐   Surveys of performance completed to date as a percentage of total contract revenue

☐   Labour hours expended as a percentage of total expected labour hours

---

10   Fifer Co has a current ratio of 1.2:1 which is below the industry average. Fifer Co wants to increase its current ratio by the year end.

Which of the following actions, taken before the year end, would lead to an increase in the current ratio?

○   Return some inventory which had been purchased for cash and obtain a full refund on the cost

○   Make a bulk purchase of inventory for cash to obtain a large discount

○   Make an early payment to suppliers, even though the amount is not due

○   Offer early payment discounts in order to collect receivables more quickly

---

11   On 1 October 20X8, Picture Co acquired 60% shares in Frame Co. At 1 April 20X8, the credit balances on the revaluation surpluses relating to Picture Co and Frame Co's equity financial asset investments stood at $6,400 and $4,400 respectively.

The following extract was taken from the financial statements for the year ended 31 March 20X9:

	Picture Co $	Frame Co $
Other comprehensive income: loss on fair value of equity financial asset investments	(1,400)	(800)

Assume the losses accrued evenly throughout the year.

What is the amount of the revaluation surplus in the consolidated statement of financial position of Picture Co as at 31 March 20X9?

○ $4,520

○ $4,760

○ $5,240

○ $9,160

---

12   A local authority department is responsible for waste collections. They have an annual budget to provide a regular collection service from households in the local area. The budget was increased to enable the department to increase the percentage of waste disposed of in an environmentally friendly manner.

Which of the following is the best measurement to justify the increase in the budget?

○   An increase in the number of collections made during the period

○   The percentage of waste recycled rather than being placed in landfill sites

○   The fair value of the machinery used in making the collections

○   A breakdown of expenditure between the cost of making collections and the cost of processing waste

---

BPP LEARNING MEDIA

13   Panther Co owns 80% of Tiger Co. An extract from the companies' individual statements of financial position as at 30 June 20X8 shows the following:

	Panther Co	Tiger Co
	$'000	$'000
Property, plant and equipment (carrying amount)	370	285

On 1 July 20X7, Panther Co sold a piece of equipment which had a carrying amount of $70,000 to Tiger Co for $150,000. The equipment had an estimated remaining life of five years when sold.

What is the carrying amount of property, plant and equipment in the consolidated statement of financial position of Panther Co as at 30 June 20X8?

$ [   ]

---

14   On 1 July 20X7, Lime Co acquired 90% of Soda Co's equity share capital. On this date, Soda Co had an internally generated customer list which was valued at $35m by an independent team of experts. At 1 July 20X7, Soda Co was also in negotiations with a potential new major customer. If the negotiations are successful, the new customer will sign the contract on 15 July 20X7 and the value of the total customer base would then be worth $45m.

What amount would be recognised for the customer list in the consolidated statement of financial position of Lime Co as at 1 July 20X7?

O $0

O $10m

O $35m

O $45m

---

15   **Identify whether the following statements relating to goodwill are correct or incorrect?**

Goodwill is amortised over its useful life with the charge expensed to profit or loss	CORRECT	INCORRECT
On the investment in an associate, any related goodwill should be separately identified in the consolidated financial statements	CORRECT	INCORRECT
The testing of goodwill for impairment is only required when circumstances exist which indicate potential impairment	CORRECT	INCORRECT
If the fair value of a subsidiary's contingent liabilities can be reliably measured at the date of acquisition, they should be included in consolidated net assets and will increase goodwill	CORRECT	INCORRECT

(30 marks)

Section B – ALL 15 questions are compulsory and MUST be attempted

Each question is worth 2 marks.

The following scenario relates to questions 16–20.

Artem Co prepares financial statements to 30 June each year.

During the year to 30 June 20X5, the company spent $550,000 on new plant as follows:

	$'000
Plant cost	525
Delivery to site	3
Building alterations to accommodate the plant	12
Costs of initial testing of the new plant	2
Plant operator training costs	8

Artem Co's fixtures and fittings were purchased on 1 July 20X2 at a cost of $50,000. The directors have depreciated them on a straight-line basis over an estimated useful life of eight years assuming a $5,000 residual value. At 1 July 20X4, the directors realise that the remaining useful life of the fixtures is five years. There is no change to the estimated residual value.

Artem Co began a research project in October 20X3 with the aim of developing a new type of machine. If successful, Artem Co will manufacture the machines and sell them to customers as well as using them in their own production processes. During the year ended 30 June 20X4, costs of $25,000 were incurred on conducting feasibility studies and some market research. During the year ended 30 June 20X5, a further $80,000 was incurred on constructing and testing a prototype of the machine.

16   In accordance with IAS 16 *Property, Plant and Equipment*, what is the value of additions to plant for Artem Co for the year ended 30 June 20X5?

$ _____

---

17   Which of the following is **TRUE** in relation to the change in the remaining useful life of the fixtures and fittings?

○   It is a change of accounting policy which should be retrospectively applied

○   It is a change of accounting policy which should be disclosed in the notes to the financial statements

○   It is a change of accounting estimate which should be retrospectively applied

○   It is a change of accounting estimate which should be prospectively applied

---

18   In accordance with IAS 16 *Property, Plant and Equipment*, what is the depreciation charge for the fixtures and fittings for Artem Co for the year ended 30 June 20X5?

○ $7,500

○ $9,000

○ $7,750

○ $6,750

---

19   Identify the correct accounting treatment for the $25,000 costs incurred on the research project during the year ended 30 June 20X4 and select the reason why it is correct in accordance with IAS 38 *Intangible Assets*.

In accordance with IAS 38 *Intangible Assets*, the $25,000 costs incurred on the research project during the year ended 30 June 20X4 should be:

Accounting treatment	Reason
Capitalised as PPE	As they are research costs at 30 June 20X4
Written off to profit or loss	As future economic benefits are expected from the use and sale of machinery
Provide for	
Capitalise as research	As machinery will be put into use once completed

20   In accordance with IAS 38, which of the following is true when Artem Co moves to the production and testing stage of the prototype during the year ended 30 June 20X5?

○   The project has moved to the development stage. If the IAS 38 development expenditure criteria are met, Artem Co can choose whether or not to recognise the $80,000 costs as an intangible non-current asset

○   The project is still in its research stage and the $80,000 costs incurred by Artem Co cannot be recognised as an intangible non-current asset until a product is ready for sale

○   The project has moved to the development stage. If the IAS 38 development expenditure criteria are met, Artem Co must recognise the $80,000 costs as an intangible non-current asset

○   The project is still in its research stage and so Artem Co must expense the $80,000 costs to profit or loss

The following scenario relates to questions 21–25.

Maykorn Co prepares its financial statements to 30 September each year. Maykorn Co's draft financial statements were finalised on 20 October 20X3. They were authorised for issue on 15 December 20X3 and the annual general meeting of shareholders took place on 23 December 20X3.

On 30 September 20X3, Maykorn Co moved out of one of its properties and put it up for sale. The property met the criteria as held for sale on 30 September 20X3. On 1 October 20X2, the property had a carrying amount of $2.6m and a remaining life of 20 years. The property is held under the revaluation model. The property was expected to sell for a gross amount of $2.5m with selling costs estimated at $50,000.

Maykorn Co decided to sell an item of plant during the year ended 30 September 20X3. On 1 October 20X2, the plant had a carrying amount of $490,000 and a remaining useful life of seven years. The plant met the held for sale criteria on 1 April 20X3. At 1 April 20X3, the plant had a fair value less costs to sell of $470,000, which had fallen to $465,000 at 30 September 20X3.

21   Identify, by selecting the relevant box in the table below, whether the following
        statements are true and in accordance with IAS 10 *Events After the Reporting Period*, for
        Maykorn Co?

All events which occur between 30 September 20X3 and 15 December 20X3 should be considered as events occurring after the reporting period	TRUE	FALSE
An event which occurs between 30 September 20X3 and 15 December 20X3 and which provides evidence of a condition which existed at 30 September 20X3 should be considered as an adjusting event	TRUE	FALSE

22   In accordance with IAS 10, identify whether the following events would be classed as
        adjusting or non-adjusting events in Maykorn Co's financial statements for the year
        ended 30 September 20X3?

During October 20X3, there was evidence of a permanent diminution in the carrying amount of a property held at 30 September 20X3	ADJUSTING	NON-ADJUSTING
On 1 December 20X3, the acquisition of a subsidiary was completed, following lengthy negotiations which began in September 20X3	ADJUSTING	NON-ADJUSTING
The sale of inventory during October 20X3 at a value less than its cost. This inventory was included in the financial statements at cost on 30 September 20X3	ADJUSTING	NON-ADJUSTING
The insolvency of a major customer during October 20X3, whose balance was included within receivables at 30 September 20X3	ADJUSTING	NON-ADJUSTING

23   What is the total amount charged to Maykorn Co's profit or loss in respect of the
        property for the year ended 30 September 20X3?

        O $130,000

        O $180,000

        O $150,000

        O $100,000

24   In accordance with IFRS 5 *Non-current Assets Held for Sale and Discontinued Operations*,
        what is the carrying amount of the plant in Maykorn Co's statement of financial position
        as at 30 September 20X3?

        O $420,000

        O $470,000

        O $455,000

        O $465,000

25   Which of the following items should be classed as an asset held for sale under IFRS 5?

  O   Maykorn Co's head office building is to be demolished, at which point the land will be put up for sale. A number of prospective bidders have declared an interest and the land is expected to sell within a few months of the demolition

  O   An item of plant was put up for sale at the start of the year for $500,000. Six parties have made a bid to Maykorn Co for the plant but none of these bids have been above $200,000

  O   A chain of retail outlets are currently advertised for sale. Maykorn Co has provisionally accepted a bid, subject to surveys being completed. The surveys are not expected to highlight any problems. The outlets are currently empty

  O   A brand name which Maykorn Co purchased in 20X2 is associated with the sale of potentially harmful products. Maykorn Co has decided to stop producing products under this brand, which is currently held within intangible assets

---

The following scenario relates to questions 26–30.

Vitrion Co issued $2m 6% convertible loan notes on 1 April 20X2. The convertible loan notes are redeemable on 31 March 20X5 at par for cash or can be exchanged for equity shares in Vitrion Co on that date. Similar loan notes without the conversion option carry an interest rate of 9%.

The following table provides information about discount rates:

	6%	9%
Year 1	0.943	0.917
Year 2	0.890	0.842
Year 3	0.840	0.772

On 1 April 20X3, Vitrion Co purchased 50,000 $1 equity shares in Gowhizzo Co at $4 per share, incurring transaction costs of $4,000. The intention is to hold the shares for trading. By 31 March 20X4 the shares are trading at $7 per share. In addition to the gain on investment, Vitrion Co also received a dividend from Gowhizzo Co during the year to 31 March 20X4.

26   In accordance with IAS 32 *Financial Instruments: Presentation*, which of the following describes an equity instrument?

  O   A contractual obligation to deliver cash or another financial asset to another entity

  O   A contract which is evidence of a residual interest in the assets of an entity after deducting all of its liabilities

  O   A contractual right to exchange financial instruments with another entity under potentially favourable conditions

  O   A contract which gives rise to both a financial asset of one entity and a financial liability of another

---

27   In accordance with IAS 32, how should the issue of the convertible loan notes be recognised in Vitrion Co's financial statements?

  O   As debt. Interest should be charged at 6% because it cannot be assumed that loan note holders will choose the equity option

  O   As equity because the loan notes are convertible to equity shares

  O   As debt and equity because the convertible loan notes contain elements of both

  O   As debt. Interest should be charged at 9% to allow for the conversion of the loan notes

28   What amount in respect of the loan notes will be shown under non-current liabilities in
        Vitrion Co's statement of financial position as at 1 April 20X2 (to the nearest $'000)?

        ○ $2,000,000

        ○ $1,848,000

        ○ $1,544,000

        ○ $2,701,000

29   In accordance with IFRS 9 *Financial Instruments*, at what amount will the Gowhizzo Co
        shares be shown under investments in equity instruments in Vitrion Co's statement of
        financial position as at 31 March 20X4?

        ○ $204,000

        ○ $354,000

        ○ $346,000

        ○ $350,000

30   Where should the gain on the investment in Gowhizzo Co and its dividend be
        recognised in Vitrion Co's financial statements for the year ended 31 March 20X4?

        ○   Both in profit or loss

        ○   Gain on investment in other comprehensive income and the dividend in profit or loss

        ○   Gain on investment in profit or loss and the dividend in other comprehensive income

        ○   Both in other comprehensive income

                                                                                    (30 marks)

Section C – BOTH questions are compulsory and MUST be attempted

Question 31

On 1 January 20X6, Laurel Co acquired 60% of the equity share capital of Rakewood Co in a share exchange in which Laurel Co issued three new shares for every five shares it acquired in Rakewood Co. The share issue has not yet been recorded by Laurel Co. Additionally, on 31 December 20X6, Laurel Co will pay to the shareholders of Rakewood Co $1.62 per share acquired. Laurel Co's cost of capital is 8% per annum.

At the date of acquisition, shares in Laurel Co and Rakewood Co had a market value of $7.00 and $2.00 each respectively.

STATEMENTS OF PROFIT OR LOSS FOR THE YEAR ENDED 30 SEPTEMBER 20X6

	Laurel Co	Rakewood Co
	$'000	$'000
Revenue	84,500	52,000
Cost of sales	(58,200)	(34,000)
Gross profit	26,300	18,000
Distribution costs	(2,000)	(1,600)
Administrative expenses	(4,100)	(2,800)
Investment income (note (iv))	500	400
Finance costs	(300)	–
Profit before tax	20,400	14,000
Income tax expense	(4,800)	(3,600)
Profit for the year	15,600	10,400

Equity as at 1 October 20X5

	Laurel Co	Rakewood Co
	$'000	$'000
Equity shares of $1 each	20,000	15,000
Retained earnings	72,000	25,000

The following information is relevant:

(i)   At the date of acquisition, Laurel Co conducted a fair value exercise on Rakewood Co's net assets which were equal to their carrying amounts with the following exceptions:

- An item of plant had a fair value of $4m above its carrying amount. At the date of acquisition it had a remaining life of two years.

- Inventory of $800,000 had a fair value of $1m. All of this inventory had been sold by 30 September 20X6.

(ii)   Laurel Co's policy is to value the non-controlling interest at fair value at the date of acquisition. For this purpose Rakewood Co's share price at 1 January 20X6 can be deemed to be representative of the fair value of the shares held by the non-controlling interest.

(iii)   Laurel Co had traded with Rakewood Co for many years before the acquisition. Sales from Rakewood Co to Laurel Co throughout the year ended 30 September 20X6 were consistently $1.2m per month. Rakewood Co made a mark-up on cost of 20% on these sales. Laurel Co had $1.8m of these goods in inventory as at 30 September 20X6.

(iv)   Laurel Co's investment income consists of:

- Its share of a dividend of $500,000 paid by Rakewood Co in August 20X6.

- A dividend of $200,000 received from Artic Co, a 25% owned associate which it has held for several years. The profit after tax of Artic Co for the year ended 30 September 20X6 was $2.4 million.

(v)   Assume, except where indicated otherwise, that all items of income and expense accrue evenly throughout the year.

(vi)   There were no impairment losses within the group during the year ended 30 September 20X6.

Required

(a)   Calculate the consolidated goodwill at the date of acquisition of Rakewood Co.

(7 marks)

(b)   Prepare the consolidated statement of profit or loss for Laurel Co for the year ended 30 September 20X6.

(13 marks)

(Total = 20 marks)

Question 32

Landing Co is considering the acquisition of Archway Co, a retail company. The summarised financial statements of Archway Co for the year ended 30 September 20X6 are:

STATEMENT OF PROFIT OR LOSS

	$'000
Revenue	94,000
Cost of sales	(73,000)
Gross profit	21,000
Distribution costs	(4,000)
Administrative expenses	(6,000)
Finance costs	(400)
Profit before tax	10,600
Income tax expense (at 20%)	(2,120)
Profit for the year	8,480

STATEMENT OF FINANCIAL POSITION

	$'000	$'000
ASSETS		
Non-current assets		
Property, plant and equipment		29,400
Current assets		
Inventory	10,500	
Bank	100	10,600
Total assets		40,000
EQUITY AND LIABILITIES		
Equity		
Equity shares of $1 each		10,000
Retained earnings		8,800
		18,800
Current liabilities		
4% loan notes (redeemable 1 November 20X6)	10,000	
Trade payables	9,200	
Current tax payable	2,000	21,200
Total equity and liabilities		40,000

From enquiries made, Landing Co has obtained the following information:

(i)   Archway Co pays an annual licence fee of $1m to Cardol Co (included in cost of sales) for the right to package and sell some goods under a well-known brand name owned by Cardol Co. If Archway Co is acquired, this arrangement would be discontinued. Landing Co estimates that this would not affect Archway Co's volume of sales, but without the use of the brand name packaging, overall sales revenue would be 5% lower than currently.

(ii)   Archway Co buys 50% of its purchases for resale from Cardol Co, one of Landing Co's rivals, and receives a bulk buying discount of 10% off normal prices (this discount does not apply to the annual licence fee referred to in note (i) above). This discount would not be available if Archway Co is acquired by Landing Co.

(iii) The 4% loan notes have been classified as a current liability due to their imminent redemption. As such, they should not be treated as long-term funding. However, they will be replaced immediately after redemption by 8% loan notes with the same nominal value, repayable in ten years' time.

(iv)   Landing Co has obtained some of Archway Co's retail sector average ratios for the year ended 30 September 20X6. It has then calculated the equivalent ratios for Archway Co as shown below:

	Sector average	Archway Co
Annual sales per square metre of floor space	$8,000	$7,833
Return on capital employed (ROCE)	18.0%	58.5%
Net asset (total assets less current liabilities) turnover	2.7 times	5.0 times
Gross profit margin	22.0%	22.3%
Operating profit (profit before interest and tax) margin	6.7%	11.7%
Gearing (debt/equity)	30.0%	Nil

A note accompanying the sector average ratios explains that it is the practice of the sector to carry retail property at market value. The market value of Archway Co's retail property is $3m more than its carrying amount (ignore the effect of any consequent additional depreciation) and gives 12,000 square metres of floor space.

Required

(a)   After making adjustments to the financial statements of Archway Co which you think may be appropriate for comparability purposes, restate:

(i)   Revenue;

(ii)   Cost of sales;

(iii) Finance costs;

(iv)   Equity (assume that your adjustments to profit or loss result in retained earnings of $2.3 million at 30 September 20X6); and

(v)   Non-current liabilities.   (5 marks)

(b)   Recalculate comparable sector average ratios for Archway Co based on your restated figures in (a) above.   (6 marks)

(c)   Comment on the performance and gearing of Archway Co compared to the retail sector average as a basis for advising Landing Co regarding the possible acquisition of Archway Co.   (9 marks)

(Total = 20 marks)

Answers

DO NOT TURN THIS PAGE UNTIL YOU HAVE
COMPLETED THE MOCK EXAM

A plan of attack

If this were the real Financial Reporting exam and you had been told to begin, what would be going through your mind?

Perhaps you're having a panic. You've spent most of your study time on groups and interpretation of accounts (because that's what your tutor/BPP Workbook told you to do), plus a selection of other topics, and you're really not sure that you know enough. So calm down. Spend the first few moments or so **looking at the examination**, and develop a **plan of attack**.

Looking through the examination

The first section is 15 2-mark questions. These will cover all sections of the syllabus. Some you may find easy and some more difficult. Don't spend a lot of time on anything you really don't know. You are not penalised for wrong answers, so you should answer all of them. If all else fails – guess!

Section B has 15 2-mark questions in total arranged around three scenarios.

- Scenario 1 is on non-current assets.
- Scenario 2 is on events after the reporting date and assets held for sale and discontinued operations.
- Scenario 3 deals with financial instruments.

Section C has two 20-mark questions.

Question 31 is a consolidated financial statements preparation question.

Question 32 deals with accounting adjustments and interpretation of financial statements.

All of these questions are compulsory.

This means that you do not have to waste time wondering which questions to answer.

Allocating your time

BPP's advice is always allocate your time **according to the marks for the question** in total and for the parts of the question. But **use common sense**. If you're confronted by a Section A question on a topic of which you know nothing, pick an answer and move on. Use the time to pick up marks elsewhere.

After the exam...forget about it!

And don't worry if you found the exam difficult. More than likely other candidates will too. If this were the real thing you would need to **forget** the exam the minute you left the exam hall and **think about the next one**. Or, if it's the last one, **celebrate!**

Section A

1   The correct answer is: It offers accountants more protection in the event of litigation

      The other options are advantages of a principles-based system.

2   The correct answer is: A subsidiary carries its assets at historical cost, but the parent's assets are carried at revalued amounts.

      This situation involves different accounting policies.

3   The correct answer is: $840,000

	$	$
At 30 April 20X5		705,000
Increase in value of land in the year ($900,000 – $750,000)		150,000
		855,000
Annual transfer to retained earnings		
Depreciation based on revalued amount ($1,500,000/50 years)	30,000	
Depreciation based on historic cost ($750,000/50 years)	(15,000)	
		(15,000)
At 30 April 20X6		840,000

4     $23,625

Cost of investment	3,500 × 6.50	22,750
Share of post-acq profit	35% × 7,000	2,625
Less dividend received	3,500 × $0.50	(1,750)
		23,625

5

Assets should be carried at the lower of their carrying amount and recoverable amount	Correct	
The recoverable amount of an asset is the higher of value in use and fair value less costs of disposal	Correct	

6   The correct answer is: Accounting standards on their own provide a complete system of regulation

      A system of regulation will also include tax rules and company legislation.

7   The correct answer is: 2,341,549 shares

1 January X9–30 September X9	2,000,000 × 3.25/2.84 × 9/12	1,716,549
1 October X9–31 December X9	2,500,000 × 3/12	625,000
		2,341,549

8   The correct answers are:

      Interest receivable, which will be taxed when the interest is received

      Prepaid expenses, which have been deducted to calculate the taxable profits of the previous year

9   The correct answers are:

      Physical milestones reached as a percentage of physical completion

      Surveys of performance completed to date as a percentage of total contract revenue

      The other options are input methods of measurement.

BPP LEARNING MEDIA

10   The correct answer is: Make an early payment to suppliers, even though the amount is not due

      This will reduce assets and liabilities by the same amount and so increase the ratio.

11   The correct answer is: (6,400 − 1,400 loss − (800 loss × 60% × 6/12)) = 4,760

12   The correct answer is: The percentage of waste recycled rather than being placed in landfill sites

      This measurement relates to the environmental impact.

13    $591,000

      Carrying amount 370,000 + 285,000 − 64,000 (see below) = 591,000

      The unrealised profit on the sale is 80,000 (150,000 − 70,000) of which 64,000 (80,000 × 4 years/5 years) is still unrealised at 30 June 20X8.

14   The correct answer is: $35m

      This is the valuation at acquisition.

15

Goodwill is amortised over its useful life with the charge expensed to profit or loss		INCORRECT
On the investment in an associate, any related goodwill should be separately identified in the consolidated financial statements		INCORRECT
The testing of goodwill for impairment is only required when circumstances exist which indicate potential impairment		INCORRECT
If the fair value of a subsidiary's contingent liabilities can be reliably measured at the date of acquisition, they should be included in consolidated net assets and will increase goodwill	CORRECT	

Section B

16    $542,000

	$'000
Plant cost	525
Delivery to site	3
Building alterations to accommodate the plant	12
Costs of initial testing of the new plant	2
	542

Training costs are not included within the capitalised amount of new plant.

17   The correct answer is: It is a change of accounting estimate and so is applied prospectively.

18   The correct answer is: $6,750

Carrying amount at date of revised remaining life is (50,000 – (50,000 – 5,000)/8 years ×
2 years) = 38,750

Depreciation year ended 30 June 20X5 is therefore 38,750 – 5,000/5 years = 6,750 pa

19   In accordance with IAS 38 *Intangible Assets*, the $25,000 costs incurred on the research
project during the year ended 30 June 20X4 should be

Written off to profit or loss	They are research costs at 30 June 20X4

20   The correct answer is: The project has moved to the development stage. If the IAS 38
development expenditure criteria are met, Artem Co must recognise the $80,000 costs as
an intangible non-current asset.

IAS 38 does not allow a choice regarding whether or not to capitalise development costs.

21

All events which occur between 30 September 20X3 and 15 December 20X3 should be considered as events occurring after the reporting period	TRUE	
An event which occurs between 30 September 20X3 and 15 December 20X3 and which provides evidence of a condition which existed at 30 September 20X3 should be considered as an adjusting event	TRUE	

22

During October 20X3, there was evidence of a permanent diminution in the carrying amount of a property held at 30 September 20X3	ADJUSTING	
On 1 December 20X3, the acquisition of a subsidiary was completed, following lengthy negotiations which began in September 20X3		NON-ADJUSTING
The sale of inventory during October 20X3 at a value less than its cost. This inventory was included in the financial statements at cost on 30 September 20X3	ADJUSTING	
The insolvency of a major customer during October 20X3, whose balance was included within receivables at 30 September 20X3	ADJUSTING	

23   The correct answer is: $180,000

Property is depreciated by $130,000 ($2,600,000/20) giving a carrying amount of
$2,470,000. When classed as held for sale, property is revalued to its fair value of
$2,500,000 (as it is carried under the revaluation model, $30,000 would go to revaluation
surplus). Held for sale assets are measured at the lower of carrying amount (now
$2,500,000) and fair value less costs to sell ($2,500,000 – $50,000 = $2,450,000), giving
an impairment of $50,000. Total charge to profit or loss is $130,000 + $50,000 = $180,000.

24   The correct answer is: $455,000

Carrying amount at 1 April is $455,000 (490 – (490/7 × 6/12)).

25   The correct answer is: A chain of retail outlets are currently advertised for sale. Maykorn Co
has provisionally accepted a bid, subject to surveys being completed. The surveys are not
expected to highlight any problems. The outlets are currently empty.

This is the only option where there is evidence of a 'highly probable' sale.

26   The correct answer is: A contract which is evidence of a residual interest in the assets of an
entity after deducting all of its liabilities

27   The correct answer is: As debt and equity because the convertible loan notes contain
elements of both

28   The correct answer is: $1,848,000

120,000 × 0.917	110,040	
120,000 × 0.842	101,040	
2,120,000 × 0.772	1,636,640	
	1,847,720	rounded to 1,848,000

29   The correct answer is: $350,000

50,000 shares at $7 each

30   The correct answer is: Both in profit or loss

The Gowhizzo shares are held for trading rather than long term investment purposes.

Section C

Question 31

Marking scheme

			Marks
(a)	Goodwill		
	Share exchange	1	
	Deferred consideration	1	
	NCI	1	
	Net assets: Equity shares	½	
	Retained earnings	1½	
	Fair value adjustments	2	
			7
(b)	Statement of profit or loss		
	Revenue	1½	
	Cost of sales	4 ½	
	Distribution costs	½	
	Administrative expenses	½	
	Investment income	1½	
	Finance costs	1 ½	
	Income tax	1	
	NCI	2	
			13
			20

(a) Laurel Co: Consolidated goodwill on acquisition of Rakewood Co

Investment at cost

	$'000	$'000
Shares (15,000 × 60% × 3/5 × $7.00)		37,800
Deferred consideration (9,000 × $1.62/1.08)		13,500
Non-controlling interest (15,000 × 40% × $2.00)		12,000
		63,300
Net assets (based on equity) of Rakewood Co as at 1 January 20X6		
Equity shares	15,000	
Retained earnings at 1 October 20X5	25,000	
Earnings 1 October 20X5 to acquisition (10,400 × 3/12)	2,600	
Fair value adjustments:		
plant	4,000	
inventory	200	
Net assets at date of acquisition		(46,800)
Consolidated goodwill		16,500

(b)   Laurel Co: Consolidated statement of profit or loss for the year ended 30 September 20X6

	$'000
Revenue (84,500 + (52,000 × 9/12) – (1,200 × 9 months) intragroup sales)	112,700
Cost of sales (working)	(74,900)
Gross profit	37,800
Distribution costs (2,000 + (1,600 × 9/12))	(3,200)
Administrative expenses (4,100 + (2,800 × 9/12))	(6,200)
Investment income (400 × 9/12)	300
Income from associate (2,400 × 25% based on underlying earnings)	600
Finance costs (300 + (13,500 × 8% × 9/12 re deferred consideration))	(1,110)
Profit before tax	28,190
Income tax expense (4,800 + (3,600 × 9/12))	(7,500)
Profit for the year	20,690

Profit for year attributable to:	
Owners of the parent	18,370
Non-controlling interest	
((10,400 × 9/12) – 200 re inventory – (1,500 depreciation – 300 URP) × 40%)	2,320
	20,690

Working in $'000

Cost of sales

	$'000
Laurel Co	58,200
Rakewood Co (34,000 × 9/12)	25,500
Intragroup purchases (1,200 × 9 months)	(10,800)
Fair value inventory adjustment	200
URP in inventory at 30 September 20X6 (1,800 × 20/120)	300
Additional depreciation (4,000/2 years × 9/12)	1,500
	74,900

Question 32

Text reference. Chapter 19.

Top tips. This is an interpretation question taking account of a prospective acquisition. As always with interpretation questions, most of the marks are not for ratios. You must take account of all the information and consider the group aspects. How would Archway's results look following its acquisition by Landing?

Easy marks. The ratios based on the amended figures are an easy five marks – but don't spend too long on them.

Marks

(a)
Revenue	½
Cost of sales	2
Loan interest	½
Equity	1½
Non-current liabilities	½

5

(b) 1 mark per ratio

6

(c) 1 mark per relevant comment

9

20

(a) Archway Co's restated figures

On the assumption that Landing Co purchases Archway Co, the following adjustments relate to the effects of notes (i) to (iii) in the question and the property revaluation:

	$'000
Revenue (94,000 × 95%)	89,300
Cost of sales (see below)	76,000
Loan interest (10,000 × 8%)	800
Equity (10,000 + 2,300 RE + 3,000 revaluation)	15,300
Non-current liabilities: 8% loan notes	10,000

The cost of sales should be first adjusted for the annual licence fee of $1m, reducing this to $72m. Half of these, $36m, are net of a discount of 10% which equates to $4m (36,000/90% − 36,000). Adjusted cost of sales is $76m (73,000 − 1,000 + 4,000).

(b) These figures would give the following ratios:

Annual sales per square metre of floor space	(89,300/12,000)	$7,442
ROCE	(13,300 − 10,000)/(15,300 + 10,000) × 100	13%
Net asset turnover	(89,300/(15,300 + 10,000))	3.5 times
Gross profit margin	((89,300 − 76,000)/89,300 × 100)	15%
Operating profit margin	((13,300 − 10,000)/89,300 × 100)	3.7%
Gearing (debt/equity)	(10,000/15,300)	65.4%

(c) **Performance**

	Archway Co As reported	Archway Co as adjusted	Sector average
Annual sales per square metre of floor space	$7,833	$7,442	$8,000
ROCE	58.5%	13%	18.0%
Net asset turnover	5.0 times	3.5 times	2.7 times
Gross profit margin	22.3%	15%	22.0%
Operating profit margin	11.7%	3.7%	6.7%
Gearing (debt/equity)	nil	65.4%	30.0%

A comparison of Archway Co's ratios based upon the reported results compares very favourably to the sector average ratios in almost every instance. ROCE is particularly impressive at 58.5% compared to a sector average of 18%; this represents a return of more than three times the sector average. The superior secondary ratios of profit margin and asset utilisation (net asset turnover) appear to confirm Archway Co's above average performance. It is only sales per square metre of floor space which is below the sector average. The unadjusted figure is very close to the sector average, as too is the gross profit margin, implying a comparable sales volume performance. However, the reduction in selling prices caused by the removal of the brand premium causes sales per square metre to fall marginally.

As indicated in the question, should Archway Co be acquired by Landing Co, many figures particularly related to the statement of profit or loss would be unfavourably impacted as shown above in the workings for Archway Co's adjusted ratios. When these effects are taken into account and the ratios are recalculated, a very different picture emerges. All the performance ratios, with the exception of net asset turnover, are significantly reduced due to the assumed cessation of the favourable trading arrangements. The most dramatic effect is on the ROCE, which, having been more than three times the sector average, would be 27.8% (18.0 – 13.0)/18.0 × 100) below the sector average (at 13.0% compared to 18.0%). Analysing the component parts of the ROCE (net asset turnover and profit margins), both aspects are lower when the reported figures are adjusted.

The net asset turnover (although adjusted to a lower multiple) is still considerably higher than the sector average. The fall in this ratio is due to a combination of lower revenues (caused by the loss of the branding) and the increase in capital employed (equal to net assets) due to classifying the loan notes as debt (non-current). Gross margin deteriorates from 22.3% to only 15.0% caused by a combination of lower revenues (referred to above) and the loss of the discount on purchases. The distribution costs and administrative expenses for Archway Co are less than those of its retail sector in terms of the percentage of sales revenue (at 11.3% compared to 15.3%), which mitigates (slightly) the dramatic reduction in the profit before interest and tax. The reduction in sales per square metre of floor space is caused only by the reduced (5%) volume from the removal of the branded sales.

Gearing

The gearing ratio of nil based on the unadjusted figures is not meaningful due to previous debt being classified as a current liability because of its imminent redemption. When this debt is replaced by the 8% loan notes and (more realistically) classified as a non-current liability, Archway Co's gearing is much higher than the sector average. There is no information as to how the increased interest payable at 8% (double the previous 4%) compares to the sector's average finance cost. If such a figure were available, it may give an indication of Archway Co's credit status although the doubling of the rate does imply a greater degree of risk in Archway Co seen by the lender.

Summary and advice

Based upon Archway Co's reported figures, its purchase by Landing Co would appear to be a good investment. However, when Archway Co's performance is assessed based on the results and financial position which might be expected under Landing Co's ownership, the recalculated ratios are generally inferior to Archway Co's retail sector averages. In an investment decision such as this, an important projected ratio would be the return on the investment (ROI) which Landing Co might expect. The expected net profit after tax can be calculated as $2m ((3,300 before interest and tax – 800 interest) × 80% post-tax), however, there is no information in the question as to what the purchase consideration of Archway Co would be. That said, at a (probable) minimum purchase price based on Archway Co's net asset value (with no goodwill premium), the ROI would only be 7.9% (2,000/25,300 × 100) which is very modest and should be compared to Landing Co's existing ROI. A purchase price exceeding $25.3m would obviously result in an even lower expected ROI. It is possible that under Landing Co's management, Archway Co's profit margins could be improved, perhaps coming to a similar arrangement regarding access to branded sales (or franchising) as currently exists with Cardol Co, but with a different company. If so, the purchase of Archway Co may still be a reasonable acquisition.

ACCA

Financial Reporting (FR)

Mock Examination 4

(Section C is the ACCA Sept/Dec 21 exam)

Questions	
Time allowed	3 hours
This mock exam is divided into three sections:	
Section A	ALL 15 questions are compulsory and MUST be attempted
Section B	ALL 15 questions are compulsory and MUST be attempted
Section C	BOTH questions are compulsory and MUST be attempted

DO NOT OPEN THIS EXAM UNTIL YOU ARE READY TO START
UNDER EXAMINATION CONDITIONS

Section A – ALL 15 questions are compulsory and MUST be attempted

Each question is worth 2 marks.

1   According to the *Conceptual Framework for Financial Reporting* of the International Accounting Standards Board (IASB), verifiability means that "different knowledgeable and independent observers could reach a consensus of faithful representation."

Which of the following procedures directly verifies that the relevant balances are faithfully represented?

O   Confirming the cash balance by conducting a physical count of cash

O   Confirming the inventory by reviewing the year-end list of inventory

O   Confirming a revaluation of land by agreeing the revaluation surplus to a minute of the board meeting where the directors agreed its estimate

O   Confirming the carrying amount of receivables by reviewing the year-end statements issued to customers at that date

(ACCA Examiner's report September 2019)

---

2   Cyanide Co had the following bank loans outstanding during the whole of 20X7 which form the company's general borrowings for the year:

	$m
9% loan repayable 20X9	30
11% loan repayable 20Y2	48

Cyanide Co began construction of a qualifying asset on 1 April 20X7 and $12 million of the loan funding was transferred to the construction project on that date to fund construction. On 1 August 20X7, an additional $4 million was transferred for the same purpose.

Calculate the borrowing costs which can be capitalised in respect of this project for the year ended 31 December 20X7. Round the capitalisation rate to one decimal place to calculate your answer.

O $1,098,667

O $823,998

O $1,500,000

O $700,000

---

3   Extracts from the statements of financial position of Polonium Co are as follows:

Statements of financial position as at 30 September:

	20X5	20X4
	$m	$m
Ordinary shares of $1 each	750	500
Share premium	350	100

On 1 October 20X4, a bonus issue of one new share for every ten held was made, financed from share premium. This was followed by a further issue for cash.

Using the pull-down list, what amount will appear under 'cash flows from financing activities' in the statement of cash flows of Polonium Co for the year ended 30 September 20X5 in respect of share issues?

Pull-down list:

$500 million
$450 million
$550 million
$250 million

4 Radium Co purchased a machine on 1 October 20X7 for $1,500,000. The machine has a useful life of 10 years with an estimated residual value of $75,000. It is Radium Co's policy to depreciate over the useful lives of non-current assets on a straight-line basis.

On 1 January 20X8, Radium Co purchased an upgraded motherboard to improve the capacity of the machine. This cost $30,000 and has a useful life of five years (no residual value).

Using the click and drag options below, select the correct depreciation expense for the year to 31 March 20X8.

Depreciation expense for the original machine	Depreciation expense for the motherboard

$71,250	$750
$72,250	$1,500
$75,000	$6,000

5 Muchmoo Co has a dairy farm with 100 head of cattle. Muchmoo Co produces milk and dairy produce, including butter and a specialist blue vein cheese for sale to the public and local farm shops. Once the dairy cows have ceased to produce milk, they are looked after by the farmer's daughter who runs an animal sanctuary, where they live out their days grazing on the fields in Snowdonia.

The financial accountant of Muchmoo Co is unsure of how to account for the different products and the herd of cattle.

Using the options provided, select the correct accounting standard to value the various assets of Muchmoo Co. Note that each option may be used more than once or not at all.

Dairy cows

Pasteurised milk, cheese, butter

Raw milk from the cows

Inventories (IAS 2)
Property, Plant and Equipment (IAS 16)
Agriculture (IAS 41)
Intangible Assets (IAS 38)

6   During the year ended 31 December 20X4, Bloop Co incurred expenditure on two projects:

- Project 1 costs relate to the evaluation of alternatives for improved production systems to be implemented during 20X5 and 20X6. The company spent $1m on related salaries and materials and $2m on design equipment (which had an expected life of four years).

- Project 2 involves the testing of a new product which will be introduced to the market in 20X5 and is expected to generate profits over a four-year period. The company spent $4m on salaries and materials. The policy is to charge a full year's depreciation on assets.

What is the TOTAL charge to profit or loss for the year ended 31 December 20X4?

○ $5.5 million

○ $3 million

○ $1.5 million

○ $1 million

(ACCA Examiner's report December 2019)

---

7   Pootle Co received a government grant on 1 September 20X4. The conditions of the grant state that Pootle Co must employ a local worker on a full-time contract over a five-year period. Pootle Co expects to meet the conditions of the grant.

The full amount of the grant received has been recorded as Other income for the year ended 31 December 20X4.

What is the adjustment required to correctly account for the grant as at 31 December 20X4?

Account name
Accrued income
Deferred income
Other income
Bank

	Account name	Value
Debit		
Credit		

Value

$4,000
$48,000
$56,000
$57,000

(ACCA Examiner's report March/June 2021)

8   **Which of the following meet(s) the recognition criteria for an asset and/or a liability?**

   (1)   Green Co spent $100,000 providing health and safety training to its staff

   (2)   Green Co has been told by a brand consultancy that the value of its internally created brands is $2,000,000

   (3)   Green Co is suing a supplier for $450,000 for losses that it suffered due to faulty goods. Green Co is likely, though not certain, to win the court case

   (4)   Green Co has sold goods subject to a five-year warranty on which it expects some claims will be made

   O   (1) and (2)

   O   (3) and (4)

   O   (2) only

   O   (4) only

(ACCA Examiner's report September 2018)

---

9   **Which of the following events taking place after the year end but before the financial statements were authorised for issue would require adjustment in accordance with IAS 10 Events After the Reporting Period?**

   O   Three lines of inventory held at the year-end were destroyed by flooding in the warehouse

   O   The directors announced a major restructuring

   O   Two lines of inventory held at the year-end were discovered to have faults rendering them unsaleable

   O   The value of the company's investments fell sharply

---

10   Root Co acquired 30% of the 100,000 equity shares in Branch Co for $7.50 per share on 1 January 20X7, when Branch Co had retained earnings of $460,000 and a balance on the revaluation surplus of $50,000. At the year-end date of 31 December 20X7, Branch Co had retained earnings of $370,000 and a balance of $70,000 on the revaluation surplus. Root Co considered that its investment in Branch Co had suffered an impairment loss of $40,000.

   Calculate the carrying amount of Root's investment in Branch.

   $ [   ]

(ACCA Examiner's report March 2020)

---

11   Tonton Co acquired 9,000 shares in Pogo Co on 1 August 20X3 at a cost of $6.40 per share. Tonton Co incurred transaction costs of $9,000 for this transaction. Tonton Co elected to hold these shares at fair value through other comprehensive income.

   At 31 December 20X3, the fair value of the Pogo Co shares was $7.25 per share and selling costs were expected to be 4%.

   What is the value of the Pogo Co shares in Tonton Co's individual financial statements at 31 December 20X3?

   O $65,250

   O $74,250

   O $62,640

   O $66,600

(ACCA Examiner's report March 2019)

12 Which of the following ratios are likely to DECREASE due to a significant revaluation gain on a depreciating asset at the start of the year?

(1)   Return on capital employed (ROCE)

(2)   Gearing (debt/equity)

(3)   Operating profit margin

(4)   Net asset turnover

○   1, 2, 3 and 4

○   1, 2 and 3 only

○   2, 3 and 4 only

○   1 and 4 only

(ACCA Examiner's report September/December 2020)

13 **Using the drag and drop options below, complete the statement to show how IAS 8 Accounting policies, Changes in Accounting Estimates and Errors require accounting policies to be adopted in the financial statements**

Each statement may be used more than once or not at all.

A company decides to change the accounting policy of the valuation of non-current assets. This change must be applied

A company discovers a fundamental error in the valuation of inventories. The correction should be made

prospectively

retrospectively

14 A company's statement of financial position at 31 December 20X4 included land at a cost of $200,000 and a deferred tax liability of $60,000. On 1 March 20X5, the land was professionally valued at $250,000. This valuation was incorporated into the financial statements for the year to 31 December 20X5. No other non-current assets have been revalued. Other taxable temporary differences increased during the year to 31 December 20X5 by $40,000. The relevant rate of tax is 20%.

What are the balances at 31 December 20X5 on the revaluation surplus and the deferred tax liability?

○   Revaluation surplus of $50,000 and deferred tax liability of $68,000

○   Revaluation surplus of $50,000 and deferred tax liability of $78,000

○   Revaluation surplus of $40,000 and deferred tax liability of $78,000

○   Revaluation surplus of $40,000 and deferred tax liability of $62,000

(ACCA Examiner's report December 2019)

15 A 60% owned subsidiary sold goods to its parent for $150,000 at a mark-up of 25% on cost during the year ended 30 June 20X5. One fifth of these goods remained unsold as at 30 June 20X5.

What is the debit adjustment to be made to group retained earnings to reflect the unrealised profit in inventory at 30 June 20X5?

○ $6,000

○ $3,600

○ $2,400

○ $4,500

(ACCA Examiner's report September 2018)

(30 marks)

Section B – ALL 15 questions are compulsory and MUST be attempted

Each question is worth 2 marks.

The following scenario relates to questions 16–20.

Rainbird Co decided to reorganise a manufacturing facility during November 20X1 and commissioned a consulting engineer to carry out a feasibility study. A provision for the reorganisation was created at 31 December 20X1.

Staff functions will change following the reorganisation, so in December 20X1 Rainbird Co contracted with a training company to provide retraining to take place in January 20X2. A provision for this expenditure was created at 31 December 20X1.

Rainbird Co hopes that reorganising its manufacturing facility will improve quality control. It gives a one-year warranty with all products and the rate of returns under warranty is 12%. 5% of the returned items can be repaired at a cost of $5 (free of charge to the customer). The other 95% are scrapped and a full refund of $30 is given. Rainbird Co sold 525,000 units during the year to 31 December 20X1.

In five years' time Rainbird Co will have to dismantle its factory and return the site to the local authority. A provision was set up for the present value of the dismantling costs when the factory was first acquired. The opening balance on the provision at 1 January 20X1 was $2.63 million. Rainbird Co has a cost of capital of 8%.

16   Rainbird Co's accountant is preparing the financial statements for the year to 31 December 20X1 and is not too sure about the provisions set up for the reorganisation of the facility and the staff training.

      Which of these is a correct provision under IAS 37 *Provisions, Contingent Liabilities and Contingent Assets*?

      O   The reorganisation

      O   The staff training

      O   The reorganisation and the staff training

      O   Neither the reorganisation nor the staff training

17   Rainbird Co's finance director is checking some of the financial estimates involved. In accordance with IAS 37, if the reporting entity is presently obliged to transfer economic benefit to another party, the occurrence is probable but the amount cannot be measured with sufficient reliability.

      Using the pull-down list below, select the correct option stating what this should give rise to in the financial statements

      Pull-down list:

      A provision
      A contingent liability
      A long-term liability
      A contingent asset

18   **What is the amount of the provision that should be created at 31 December 20X1 for returns under warranty?**

    ○ $1,890,000

    ○ $1,811,250

    ○ $1,795,500

    ○ $1,575,000

19   **What is the amount of the provision that should be carried forward at 31 December 20X1 for the dismantling of the factory?**

    ○ $2,630,000

    ○ $2,419,600

    ○ $2,435,185

    ○ $2,840,400

20   During January 20X2, before the financial statements of Rainbird Co for the year ended 31 December 20X1 had been finalised, a number of events took place.

Identify whether each of these events would require an adjustment to the financial statements as at 31 December 20X1 in accordance with IAS 10 *Events After the Reporting Period.*

Rainbird Co's board announced a plan to discontinue one of its operations and dispose of the plant. The loss on disposal is estimated at $2 million.	**Requires adjustment**	**Does not require adjustment**
The employees of the operation to be discontinued commenced a case against Rainbird Co for constructive dismissal. The total cost could be $3 million.	**Requires adjustment**	**Does not require adjustment**
A legal case for which Rainbird Co had provided $1.7 million at 31 December 20X1 to cover possible damages was unexpectedly settled in its favour.	**Requires adjustment**	**Does not require adjustment**
One of Rainbird Co's warehouses was destroyed by fire and half of the inventory on hand at 31 December 20X1, valued at $2.5 million, was destroyed.	**Requires adjustment**	**Does not require adjustment**

The following scenario relates to questions 21–25.

The following is an extract from Diaz Co's trial balance as at 31 December 20X8:

	Debit $m	Credit $m
Inventory at 31 December 20X8	8.6	
Trade receivables	6.2	
5% loan notes		9.0

The inventory count was completed on 31 December 20X8, but two issues have been noted. First, products with a sales value of $0.6m had been incorrectly excluded from the count. Second, items costing $0.2m which had been included in the count were damaged and could only be sold for 50% of the normal selling price. Diaz Co makes a mark-up of 50% on both of these items.

Diaz Co entered into a factoring agreement with Finaid Co on 31 December 20X8. In accordance with the agreement, Diaz Co sold trade receivables with a carrying amount of $6.2m to Finaid Co for $6m. Under the terms of the factoring agreement, after six months Finaid Co will return any unpaid receivables to Diaz Co for collection. Finaid Co will also charge Diaz Co a fee of 5% of any uncollected balances at the end of each month.

The 5% loan notes were issued for $9m on 1 July 20X8. Diaz Co incurred issue costs of $0.5m associated with this, which have been expensed within finance costs. The loan note interest is payable each 30 June and the loan note is repayable at a premium, giving them an effective interest rate of 8%.

21 **In accordance with IAS 32 *Financial Instruments: Presentation*, which of the items in the trial balance would be classified as financial instruments?**

○ Closing inventory and trade receivables only

○ 5% loan notes only

○ Trade receivables and 5% loan notes only

○ Closing inventory, trade receivables and 5% loan notes

---

22 **What is the correct carrying amount of inventory to be recognised in Diaz Co's financial statements as at 31 December 20X8?**

○ $8.95m

○ $9.0m

○ $8.9m

○ $9.15m

---

23 In an attempt to improve reported profit, the directors of Diaz Co want to change the valuation method of inventory from first in first out (FIFO) to an average cost method.

Which, if any, of the following statements regarding the potential change in inventory valuation is/are correct?

(1) The change will represent a change in accounting estimate
(2) The financial statements will be adjusted prospectively

○ 1 only

○ 2 only

○ Both 1 and 2

○ Neither 1 nor 2

---

24   Which of the following statements regarding the factoring arrangement is **NOT** true?

       O $6m received should be recorded in the liabilities of Diaz Co at 31 December 20X8

       O $0.2m should be expensed in Diaz Co's statement of profit or loss for the year ended 31 December 20X8

       O   A total of the 5% monthly fee should be expensed in Diaz Co's statement of profit or loss for the year ended 31 December 20X9

       O   The receivables will remain as an asset in the financial statements of Diaz Co at 31 December 20X8

---

25   In respect of the 5% loan notes, how much should be expensed within Diaz Co's statement of profit or loss for the year ended 31 December 20X8?

       O $0.68m

       O $0.45m

       O $0.72m

       O $0.34m

(ACCA Examiner's report Mar/Jun 2019)

Information relevant to questions 26–30.

Wilrob Co has the following research projects at 31 March 20X7:

Project 324 – The project commenced on 1 April 20X6 and incurred total costs of $15m during the period to 31 December 20X6 on a pro-rata basis. On 30 June 20X6, the directors were confident that the project met the capitalisation criteria of IAS 38 *Intangible Assets*. The project was completed and began to generate revenue from 1 January 20X7. It is estimated that the project will generate revenue for five years.

Project 325 – The project commenced on 1 September 20X6. Costs of $20,000 per month were incurred until 31 January 20X7 when the project was abandoned. The specialist equipment that had been purchased for Project 325 was transferred for use in another of Wilrob Co's research projects.

Project 326 – The project commenced on 1 January 20X7. Costs of $40,000 per month were incurred until 31 August 20X7 when the directors increased the spend to $60,000 to complete the project quickly as a potential buyer had been identified on 20 July 20X7. The directors had not been confident of the success of the project until this point.

26   Which **TWO** of the following are required by IAS 38 *Intangible Assets* in relation to the amortisation of intangible assets (excluding goodwill)?

       ☐   Intangible assets should be amortised over the expected useful life or not at all if the useful life is deemed to be indefinite

       ☐   Intangible assets should not be amortised but instead reviewed for impairment losses only

       ☐   Intangible assets should be amortised on the basis of the expected pattern of consumption of the expected future economic benefits

       ☐   Intangible assets should not be amortised or impaired and instead simply carried forward at their original cost until sold or scrapped

---

27　Which **TWO** of the following statements are true in relation to IAS 38 *Intangible Assets*?

☐　IAS 38 requires the revaluation of intangible assets where a company has chosen to revalue its tangible non-current assets

☐　IAS 38 does not permit the revaluation of any intangible assets in any circumstances

☐　IAS 38 permits the revaluation of intangible assets only if there is an active market for such assets

☐　IAS 38 requires that the initial recognition of intangibles must be at cost

28　In accordance with IAS 38 *Intangible Assets*, what is charged to the statement of profit or loss for the year ended 31 March 20X7 in respect of project 324?

○　$5.5m

○　$6.5m

○　$7m

○　$10m

29　In accordance with IAS 38 *Intangible Assets*, identify whether the following are true or false in respect of the accounting treatment of projects 325 and 326?

The cost for project 325 should be expensed in the statement of profit or loss for the year ended 31 March 20X7.	TRUE	FALSE
The specialist equipment which was purchased for project 325 should not be depreciated as it has only been used for abandoned or research projects.	TRUE	FALSE
The costs for project 326 should be included as an asset in the statement of financial position as at 31 March 20X7.	TRUE	FALSE

30   During the year ended 31 March 20X8, Wilrob Co incurred the following costs:

   (1) $400,000 in staff costs incurred in updating a computerised record of potential customers

   (2) $800,000 for the purchase of a domain name for the website of a company making substantial online sales

   (3) $4m for a patent purchased to improve the production process, with an expected useful life of three years

   Which of the above costs would be capitalised as intangible assets in accordance with IAS 38 *Intangible Assets*?

   ○   1 only

   ○   3 only

   ○   1 and 3 only

   ○   1, 2 and 3

   (ACCA, Examiners Report March/June 2021)

   (30 marks)

Section C – BOTH questions are compulsory and MUST be attempted

Question 31

This scenario relates to three requirements.

The following is an extract from the trial balance of Mims Co for the year ended 31 December 20X5:

	$'000	$'000
Revenue		24,300
Cost of sales	11,600	
Administrative expenses	10,900	
Distribution costs	7,300	
Income tax (note (3))	140	
Deferred tax liability 1 January 20X5 (note (3))		7,700
Provision at 1 January 20X5 (note (2))		4,600
Retained earnings 1 January 20X5		43,200
Equity share capital ($1) at 1 January 20X5		60,000
Intangible assets (note (6))	3,300	
Investment property (note (5))	19,000	
Finance costs	1,400	
Investment income		500
Suspense account		46,500

The following information is relevant:

(1) Mims Co noted there was an error in the inventory count at 31 December 20X4, meaning that the closing inventory balance in the 20X4 financial statements was overstated by $0.7m. No entries have yet been made to correct this error.

(2) The provision relates to a court case in existence since December 20X4. Mims Co settled this case on 31 December 20X5 for $6m. The full amount was credited correctly to cash, with a corresponding debit entry being made in the suspense account.

(3) The income tax figure in the trial balance relates to the under/over provision from the previous year. The current year tax is estimated to be a tax refund of $1.2m. In addition to this, the deferred tax liability at 31 December 20X5 is estimated to be $8.2m.

(4) On 30 September 20X5, Mims Co made a 1 for 4 rights issue. The exercise price was $3.50 per share. The proceeds were correctly accounted for in cash, with a corresponding credit entry being made in the suspense account.

(5) Mims Co acquired and investment property for $20m cash on 1 January 20X5 and decided to use the fair value model to account for investment properties. As the property is expected to have 20 year useful life, depreciation was recorded on this basis. The fair value of the property at 31 December 20X5 has been assessed at $22m but no accounting has taken place in relation to this. All depreciation and amortisation is charged on a pro-rata basis to administrative expenses. There were no other acquisitions or disposals of non-currents assets.

(6)   Mims Co incurred a number of expenses in relation to brands during the year and has capitalised the following costs as intangible assets:

- $1.3m cash was paid on 1 April 20X5 to promote one of its major brands which is deemed to have an indefinite life.

- $2m cash was paid on 1 October 20X5 to acquire a brand from one of its competitors. Mims Co expect the brand to have a useful life of five years. Mims Co intends to sell it after five years. At the point of sale, it is estimated that the value of the brand will have increased and so no amortisation has been accounted for in the current year.

(7)   Mims Co paid a dividend of $0.04 per share on all existing shares 31 December 20X5, recording the dividend paid in administrative expenses.

Required

(a)   Prepare the statement of profit or loss for Mims Co for the year ended 31 December 20X5.

(12 marks)

(b)   Prepare the statement of changes in equity for Mims Co for the year ended 31 December 20X5.

(5 marks)

(c)   Prepare the following extracts from the statement of cash flows for Mims Co for the year ended 31 December 20X5:

(i)   Cash flows from investing activities; and
(ii)   Cash flows from financing activities.

(3 marks)

(Total = 20 marks)

Question 32

This scenario relates to four requirements.

The Pinardi group operates in the fragrance and cosmetics industry. On 1 January 20X7 Pinardi Co disposed one of its subsidiaries, Silva Co, for cash of $42m. Silva Co manufactures jewellery and was sold because the Pinardi group wanted exit this particular sector.

Extracts from the consolidated financial statements of the Pinardi group for the years ended 31 December 20X6 and 20X7 are as follows:

Statement of profit or loss	20X7	20X6
	$'000	$'000
Revenue	98,300	122,400
Cost of sales	(47,600)	(71,800)
Gross profit	50,700	50,600
Operating expenses	(33,700)	(37,400)
Profit from operations	17,000	13,200
Finance costs	(3,200)	(5,500)
Profit before tax	13,800	7,700
Statement of financial position		
Inventories	13,300	22,400
Cash	31,400	14,600
Non-current liabilities	42,000	61,000

The following information is relevant:

(1) The accounting assistant has not accounted for Silva Co as a discontinued operation because the disposal occurred on 1 January 20X7. No figures from Silva Co have been included in the 20X7 financial statements extracts above. The proceeds from the disposal have been recorded in cash, with all net assets and goodwill derecognised. The balancing figure was held in a suspense account.

(2) Pinardi Co acquired 100% of Silva Co on 1 January 20X1 and goodwill was calculated as $6m. The goodwill has been impaired by 30% in 20X5. The net assets at 1 January 20X7 were $35m.

(3) As part of the sales agreement, Pinardi group will receive an annual fee of $2m for the use of the Silva Co brand. The 20X7 annual fee has been included in the Pinardi group revenue for the year ended 31 December 20X7.

(4) Results obtained from Silva Co's individual published financial statements show the following key information:

	20X7	20X6
	$'000	$'000
Revenue	39,000	36,000
Gross profit	18,800	12,600
Profit from operations	8,000	6,000

(5) Prior to the disposal Silva Co used to use some property belonging to the Pinardi group. Following the disposal, the Pinardi group moved its cosmetic division into this property.

Previously the cosmetic division had leased external facilities for $2.5m a year. At 1 January 20X7 the lease had ten years remaining. To exit the lease, the Pinardi group made a one-off payment of $3m to the lessor and recorded it as operating expenses.

(6) The Pinardi group acquires raw materials from overseas. In 20X6 the group recorded foreign exchange gains of $3m, and in 20X7 the group made a foreign exchange loss of $1m. Both items were recognised within operating expenses.

Required

(a) Calculate the gain on disposal of Silva Co that would need to be included in the consolidated statement of profit or loss for the Pinardi group for the year ended 31 December 20X7. (2 marks)

(b) Explain whether or not the disposal of Silva Co is likely to constitute a discontinued operation, and the correct accounting treatment for this. (3 marks)

(c) Calculate the following ratios, using the pre-formatted table, for the Pinardi group for 20X7 and 20X6:

- Gross profit margin;
- Operating profit margin;
- Interest cover; and
- Inventory turnover days. (4 marks)

Ratio	Working	20X7	Working	20X6
Gross profit margin				
Operating profit margin				
Interest cover				
Inventory turnover days				

(d) Analyse the performance and position for the Pinardi group for the year ended 31 December 20X7 compared to the year ended 31 December 20X6. (11 marks)

(Total = 20 marks)

Answers

DO NOT TURN THIS PAGE UNTIL YOU HAVE
COMPLETED THE MOCK EXAM

A plan of attack

Managing your nerves

As you start this mock exam a number of thoughts are likely to cross your mind. At best, examinations cause anxiety so it is important to stay focused on your task for the exam period! Developing an awareness of what is going on emotionally within you may help you manage your nerves. Remember, you are unlikely to banish the flow of adrenaline, but the key is to harness it to help you work steadily and quickly through your answers.

Working through this mock exam will help you develop the exam stamina you will need to keep going for three hours.

Managing your time

Planning and time management are two of the key skills which complement the technical knowledge you need to succeed. To keep yourself on time, do not be afraid to jot down your target completion times for each question, perhaps next to the title of the question on the exam. As all the questions are **compulsory**, you do not have to spend time wondering which question to answer!

Doing the exam

Actually doing the exam is a personal experience. There is not a single **right way**. As long as you submit complete answers to all questions after the three hours are up, then your approach obviously works.

Looking through the exam

Section A has 15 OTQs. This is the section of the exam where the examining team can test knowledge across the breadth of the syllabus. Make sure you read these questions carefully. The distractors are designed to present plausible, but incorrect, answers. Don't let them mislead you. If you really have no idea – guess. You may even be right.

Section B has 15 OTQs in total – questions 16–30. These are arranged as three scenarios with five questions each.

Scenario 1 is on provisions and events after the reporting period
Scenario 2 is on financial instruments and inventory
Scenario 3 is on intangible assets

Section C has two 20-mark questions.

Question 31 requires the preparation of a single entity statement of profit or loss, statement of changes in equity and extracts from the statement of cash flows. As you would expect in an accounts preparation question, you are presented with a draft trial balance and a number of notes which you must work through in order to prepare the financial statements and extracts. You need to work though the notes logically in order to determine their impact on the financial statements.

Question 32 requires the interpretation of group financial statements. You are required to calculate the gain or loss on disposal of a subsidiary, explain whether the subsidiary disposed of constitutes a discontinued operation and then calculate ratios and analyse the performance and position of the group. Ensure your analysis uses relevant information that is provided in the scenario.

Allocating your time

BPP's advice is to always allocate your time **according to the marks for the question**. However, **use common sense**. If you're doing a question but haven't a clue how to do part (b), you might be better off reallocating your time and getting more marks on another question, where you can add something you didn't have time for earlier on. Make sure you leave time to recheck the OTQs and make sure you have answered them all.

Section A

1   The correct answer is: Confirming the cash balance by conducting a physical count of cash

This is the only option that objectively verifies the existence of cash.

All other options verify the asset against an internal document; ie a 'list of inventory', a 'board minute' and a 'receivable statement'.

2   The correct answer is: $1,098,667

Weighted average capitalisation rate =

(9% × 30/78) + (11% × 48/78) = 3.5% + 6.8% = 10.3%

		$
Borrowing costs =	$12m × 10.3% × 9/12	927,000
+	$4m × 10.3% × 5/12	171,667
		1,098,667

3   $500 million

	$m
B/f (500 + 100)	600
Cash received (β)	500
C/f (750 + 350)	1,100

The bonus issue is irrelevant as no cash is received.

4   The correct answers are: $71,250 and $1,500.

Depreciation expense for the original machine	Depreciation expense for the motherboard
$71,250	$1,500

	$'000
Machine ((1,500,000 – 75,000)/10 × 6/12)	71,250
Motherboard ((30,000/5) × 3/12)	1,500
	72,750

5

Dairy cows	Agriculture (IAS 41)
Pasteurised milk, cheese, butter	Inventory (IAS 2)
Raw milk from the cows	Agriculture (IAS 41)

Dairy cows are classified as biological assets and therefore accounted for under IAS 41 as they are a living animal.

Raw milk from the cows is classified as agricultural produce at the point of harvest under IAS 41 as this is effectively the 'harvest' from the biological assets (the cows). It is not sold in this condition and must go through a process prior to being held as inventory (IAS 2) as pasteurised milk, butter or cheese.

6   The correct answer is: $1.5 million

Project 1 expenditure on the "evaluation of alternatives" could never be classified as an asset. Therefore the full $1m relating to salaries and materials should be charged to profit or loss. Also, the depreciation for the design equipment should be expensed ($2m/4); $1.5m in total. The project 2 costs associated with the testing of a new product which will be introduced to the market in 20X5 should be capitalised in 20X4 and written off from 20X5 for the next four years. Consequently, there will be no project 2 costs charged to profit or loss during 20X4.

The first option charges $1.5m for project 1 and $4m for project 2.

The second option writes off all costs associated with project 1 (including the design equipment).

The fourth option D charges the $1m for project 1 salaries and materials only.

	$
Fair value less costs of disposal (6.3m – 150,000)	6,150,000
Value in use	5,800,000
Recoverable amount is therefore:	6,150,000
Impairment loss (β)	850,000
Carrying amount	7,000,000

7   DEBIT   Other income $56,000

      CREDIT   Deferred income $56,000

$60,000 / (5 years × 12 months) = $1,000 per month

So, Pootle Co should have only recognised $4,000 ($1,000 × 4 months) of income in the statement of profit or loss for the year ended 31 December 20X4, with the remaining $56,000 recognised as deferred income in the statement of financial position.

8   The correct answer is: 4 only

Green Co has sold goods subject to a five-year warranty on which it expects some claims will be made.

This is because a legal obligation (the warranty) has been created as a result of the sales contract.

The $100,000 expenditure on the health and safety training does not meet the definition of an asset because Green Co does not control their staff (ie they could leave their jobs at any time) and it is not certain that the health and safety training will produce economic benefits.

As the brand has been internally generated, it cannot be reliably measured and so it does not meet the definition of an asset.

The court case against the supplier cannot be recognised as an asset because the economic benefits are not sufficiently certain. It may, however, be a contingent asset and disclosed in the notes to the financial statements.

9   The correct answer is: Two lines of inventory held at the year-end were discovered to have faults rendering them unsaleable.

We can assume that these faults also existed at the year end, so this is the only option which would require adjustment. The others have all taken place after the year end.

10    $164,000

	$
Cost of investment (30,000 × $7.50)	225,000
Post-acquisition loss in retained earnings (($370,000 – $460,000) × 30%)	(27,000)
Post-acquisition increase in revaluation surplus (($70,000-$50,000) × 30%)	6,000
Impairment	(40,000)
	164,000

11   The correct answer is: $65,250

9,000 shares × $7.25 = $65,250

Question is testing the knowledge of IFRS 13 which states that 'the fair value of an asset shall not be adjusted for transaction costs'.

12   The correct answer is: 1, 2, 3 and 4

The revaluation is at the beginning of the year and will affect the depreciation for the year and therefore operating profit:

ROCE – increased depreciation will reduce profit and capital employed will increase due to the revaluation surplus but the denominator (including the revaluation surplus) will increase more.

Gearing – increase in equity due to the revaluation surplus will decrease the ratio as debt will not be affected.

Operating profit margin – reduction in profit due to increased depreciation.

Asset turnover – increase in assets (PPE) due to revaluation even if the asset has one year's worth of depreciation.

13

A company decides to change the accounting policy of the valuation of non-current assets. This change must be applied	retrospectively
A company discovers a fundamental error in the valuation of inventories. The correction should be made	retrospectively

14   The correct answer is: Revaluation surplus of $40,000 and deferred tax liability of $78,000

The gain on the land revaluation is $50,000 and the associated deferred tax is $10,000 (20%). The journal entries for the land revaluation and its associated deferred tax are:

Debit Land	$50,000	
Debit Revaluation Surplus	$10,000	
Credit Revaluation Surplus		$50,000
Credit Deferred tax		$10,000

The closing balance on the revaluation surplus should then be $40,000 The opening balance on deferred tax is $60,000 which will be increased by the adjustment of $10,000 (above) for the land revaluation and $8,000 for the increase in taxable temporary differences ($40,000 × 20% per question). The closing balance on deferred tax should then be $78,000.

The first and second options do not take account of the deferred tax on the land revaluation.

The fourth option deducts the deferred tax on the taxable temporary differences instead of adding it on.

15   The correct answer is: $3,600

$150,000 × 25/125 × 1/5 × 60% = $3,600

Option A calculates the adjustment as if the sale was made by the parent

$150,000 × 25/125 × 1/5 = $6,000

Option C calculates using the NCI percentage as opposed to the group share

$150,000 × 25/125 × 1/5 × 40%= $2,400

Option D calculates using a margin as opposed to a mark-up

$150,000 × 25% × 1/5 × 60% = $4,500

Section B

16 The correct answer is: Neither the reorganisation nor the staff training

The reorganisation cannot be provided for because it has only gone as far as a feasibility study.

Staff training is not a valid provision as IAS 37 paragraph 81 specifically forbids costs relating to retraining or relocating staff to be provided for in restricting provisions.

17 The correct answers are:

A contingent liability.

The outcome is probable but cannot be reliably measured.

18 The correct answer is: $1,811,250

Total returns = 525,000 × 12% = 63,000

Expected cost:

	$
63,000 × 95% × 30	1,795,500
63,000 × 5% × 5	15,750
	1,811,250

19 The correct answer is: $2,840,400

$2.63 million × 108% = $2,840,400. This is the unwinding of the discount.

20

Rainbird Co's board announced a plan to discontinue one of its operations and dispose of the plant. The loss on disposal is estimated at $2 million.		Does not require adjustment
The employees of the operation to be discontinued commenced a case against Rainbird Co for constructive dismissal. The total cost could be $3 million.		Does not require adjustment
A legal case for which Rainbird Co had provided $1.7 million at 31 December 20X1 to cover possible damages was unexpectedly settled in its favour.	Requires adjustment	
One of Rainbird Co's warehouses was destroyed by fire and half of the inventory on hand at 31 December 20X1, valued at $2.5 million, was destroyed.		Does not require adjustment

Only the legal case requires adjustment because it provides evidence regarding conditions that existed at the end of the reporting period ie, the legal case that was ongoing.

The other events have all taken place after the reporting period.

21 The correct answer is: Trade receivables and 5% loan notes only

Trade receivables have been factored, but Diaz Co still retains the risks and rewards of the receivables (as Finaid Co can seek redress from Diaz Co on the unpaid balances). Therefore, a financial liability under IFRS 9 should be recognised.

The loan notes are an obligation to transfer economic benefit on the part of Diaz Co. This is a debenture loan, which is a financial instrument under IAS 32.

Closing inventory is classified as an asset of Diaz Co and IAS 32 does not recognise physical assets as financial instruments.

22 The correct answer is: $8.95m

The correct answer is $8.95m. This is the $8.6m plus the $0.4m missing items ($0.6m × 100/150) less the write down of $0.05m ($200,000 − $150,000 NRV. The items would normally be sold for $300,000 but actually being sold at $150,000).

23 The correct answer is: Neither 1 nor 2

Change in the basis of valuation of inventory is a change of accounting policy (not accounting estimate). The financial statements will be adjusted retrospectively.

24 The correct answer is: $0.2m should be expensed in Diaz Co's statement of profit or loss for the year ended 31 December 20X8

As Diaz Co still retains the risks and rewards of the receivables, this is an example of factoring with recourse. The receivables are still an asset of the company (so the fourth statement is correct that the receivables remain as an asset in the financial statements). Diaz Co is required to pay amounts received from the factor in respect of any losses (the first statement showing the liability of $6m remaining outstanding). The finance cost of the factoring (the monthly charge) is to be expensed as incurred (the third statement).

The $6m received from Finaid is in effect a loan, and will be recorded as such. The receivable is not derecognised and so there is no 'loss on derecognition' expense to be recorded in the statement of profit or loss (second statement).

25 The correct answer is: $0.34m.

The loan notes should initially be recorded at the net proceeds of $8.5m. The effective interest rate of 8% would then be expensed in relation to this, being $0.68m. As the loan notes were only issued on 1 July 20X8, the expense for the year would be $0.34m ($0.68m × 6/12).

26 The correct answers are:

Intangible assets should be amortised over the expected useful life or not at all if the useful life is deemed to be indefinite.

Intangible assets should be amortised on the basis of the expected pattern of consumption of the expected future economic benefits.

27 The correct answers are:

IAS 38 permits the revaluation of intangible assets only if there is an active market for such assets.

IAS 38 requires that the initial recognition of intangibles must be at cost.

28 The correct answer is: $5.5m

The $15m of project costs incurred between 1 April 20X6 and 31 December 20X6 cover a nine-month period. As the project did not meet the capitalisation criteria of IAS 38 until 30 June 20X6, this means that any costs related to the first three months of the year (1 April 20X6 − 30 June 20X6) were research expenditure which should be charged to the statement of profit or loss: $15m × 3/9 months = $5m.

Therefore, the remaining $10m ($15m × 6/9 months) would be capitalised as development expenditure. As the project was completed and began to generate revenue from 1 January 20X7, the capitalised development expenditure should then be amortised from that date over its useful life of five years. This requires an amortisation expense for three months

(1 January 20X7 – 31 March 20X7) which should be charged to the statement of profit or loss: $10m / 5 years × 3/12 months = $0.5m.

Therefore, the total charge to the statement of profit or loss in respect of project 324 for the year ended 31 March 20X7 is $5.5m.

Research $5m + amortisation $0.5m = $5.5m

29

The cost for project 325 should be expensed in the statement of profit or loss for the year ended 31 March 20X7.	**TRUE**	
The specialist equipment which was purchased for project 325 should not be depreciated as it has only been used for abandoned or research projects.		**FALSE**
The costs for project 326 should be included as an asset in the statement of financial position as at 31 March 20X7.		**FALSE**

30 The correct answer is: 1 and 3 only

An intangible asset can be recognised when it meets: 1. the definition of an intangible asset; and 2. the recognition criteria.

Both the domain name and the patent meet the definition of being intangible assets and the cost of each can clearly be measured reliably. Based on the information available, it appears that economic benefits will flow to the entity through revenue from online sales (domain name) and production cost savings (patent). Internally generated customer lists are specifically excluded by IAS 38 from being recognised as intangible assets (along with other items such as internally generated brands). This is because any expenditure incurred on such items cannot be distinguished from the cost of developing the business as a whole.

Section C

Question 31

		Marks
(a)	Statement of profit or loss	12
(b)	Statement of changes in equity	5
(c)	Extracts from statement of cash flows	3
		20

(a)   **Statement of profit or loss for the year ended 31 December 20X5**

	$'000
Revenue	24,300
Cost of sales (11,600 – 700 inventory)	(10,900)
Gross profit	**13,400**
Administrative expenses (10,900 + 1,400 provision + 1,300 promoting brand + 100 amortisation – 1,000 investment property depreciation – 3,000 dividend)	(9,700)
Distribution costs	(7,300)
Loss from operations	**(3,600)**
Finance costs	(1,400)
Investment income (500 + 2,000 investment property gain)	2,500
Loss before taxation	**(2,500)**
Taxation (140 – 1,200 current + 500 movement in deferred tax)	560
Loss for the year	**1,940**

(b)   **Statement of changes in equity for the year ended 31 December 20X5**

	Share capital $'000	Share premium $'000	Retained earnings $'000
Balance at 1 January 20X5	60,000	–	43,200
Prior period error	–	–	(700)
Restated balance 1 January 20X5	60,000		42,500
Share issue	15,000	37,500	–
Profit of the year	–	–	(1,940)
Dividends paid (75,000 × $0.04)	–	–	(3,000)
Balance 31 December 20X5	75,000	37,500	37,560

Extracts from statement of cash flows for the year ended 31 December 20X5

	$'000
Cash flows from investing activities	
Purchase of brand	(2,000)
Purchase of investment property	(20,000)
Net cash used investing activities	(22,000)
Cash flows from financing activities	
Proceeds from issue of share capital	52,500
Dividends paid	(3,000)
Net cash from financing activities	49,500

Question 32

		Marks
(a)	Calculations	2
(b)	Explanation	3
(c)	Ratios	4
(d)	Analysis	11
		20

(a) Gain on disposal:

	$'000
Proceeds	42,000
Less: Net assets at disposal	(35,000)
Less: Goodwill at disposal (W1)	(4,200)
Gain on disposal	2,800

Workings

1 *Goodwill at disposal*

	$'000
Goodwill at acquisition	6,000
Less: Impairment (6,000 × 30%)	(1,800)
Unimpaired goodwill at disposal	4,200

(b) Explanation of Silva Co disposal

Silva Co is likely to meet the criteria as it is a separate major line of operations which has been disposed of during the year.

As a discontinued operation, the results would be removed and presented separately on the face of the statement of profit or loss together with the gain (post-tax) on disposal of $2.8m.

As Silva Co was sold on 1 January 20X7, there are no results to incorporate for the current year. However, the results of 20X6 should be shown as a discontinued operation for comparative purposes.

(c)   Ratio calculations:

Ratio	Working	20X7	Working	20X6
Gross profit margin	(50,000/98,300) × 100	51.6%	(50,600/122,400) × 100	41.3%
Operating profit margin	(17,000/98,300) × 100	17.3%	(13,200/122,400) × 100	10.8%
Interest cover	(17,000/3,200)	5.3 times	(13,200/5,500)	2.4 times
Inventory turnover days	(13,300/47,600) × 365	102 days	(22,400/71,800) × 365	114 days

(d)   Analysis

Performance

The overall revenue is down by $24m, which may be largely due to the disposal of Silva Co which is in the 20X6 results but contributed no revenue in 20X7.

Last year, Silva Co contributed $36m in revenue. Removing this from the 20X6 results shows that there has been a like-for-like increase of $11.9m (($122.4m – $36) – $98.3m) from the fragrance and cosmetics divisions.

The gross profit margin is up significantly from 20X6 to 20X7, from 41% to 52%. We can see that the gross profit margin of Silva Co in 20X6 was only 35% ($12.6m/$36m), so the other parts of the group were able to generate higher gross profit margins historically.

The operating profit margin has increased, although not quite as dramatically as the increase in gross profit margin. In fact, the operating expenses have only decreased by $3.7m, despite the $24.1m decrease in revenue. There are some factors to consider within the operating expenses for 20X7. The is a one-off exit fee of $3m for the cosmetics division to exit the lease. While this is expensive, the division would have been paying $25m over 10 years so will ultimately save a significant amount of money.

In addition to this, the effects of foreign exchange gains and losses are included in the operating expenses line. In 20X6, there was a gain $3m but in 20X7 there was a loss of $1m which will have reduced operating profit. This shows that the Pinardi group has quite large exposure to foreign currency risk.

The interest cover has increased from 2.4 to 5.3 during the year, which is a combination of both an increase in operating profits and a decrease in finance costs. The finance costs are likely to have decreased due to the exit from the lease.

Position

The decrease in non-current liabilities is likely to be partly due to the removal of the lease liability for the cosmetics division, which had 10 years remaining.

Some of the non-current liabilities may also have been paid off from the proceeds from the sale of Silva Co. Silva Co was sold for $42m, but cash has only increased by around $17m. Therefore, the Pinardi group may have used some of the cash to reduce the non-current liabilities in the group.

It is also worth noting that in 20X6 the assets and liabilities would have included the Silva Co figures. It may have been that Silva Co had significant non-current liabilities which were removed when it was sold.

The inventory turnover figure shows that the Pinardi group is able to turn over inventory more quickly than previously. The inventory days are high, but the nature of the Pinardi group products will mean that they are not immediately perishable so this is unlikely to be a significant concern.

In 20X6, the Pinardi group inventory turnover period would have included the figures relating to Silva Co. The removal of this seems to show that the inventory turnover period relating to cosmetics and fragrance is lower than that of the jewellery sector.

Conclusion (marks awarded for sensible conclusion)

Whilst Silva Co does generate profits, the disposal seems to have been a good move. Silva Co's results have actually improved since disposal, showing it is not a struggling business. The additional focus on the remaining divisions has generated more profits for the Pinardi group, particularly now the cosmetics division is utilising the group property and no longer requiring leased premises.

Other comments which candidates may produce which could be given credit

It should be noted that there is now $2m revenue relating to the use of the Silva Co name which will be there each year. Removing this for comparability shows that the like-for-like increase in revenue is $10m.

The inclusion of the $2m income from Silva Co with no cost of sales will have increased the gross profit margin. Even removing this reduces it to 50.6% so has not accounted for a significant movement.

Whilst cash has only increased by $17m despite the $42m sale, it may have been that Silva Co had a significant amount of cash in the bank, which was removed from the group when Silva Co was disposed of.

The exclusion of the $36m revenue and $6.6m operating expenses of Silva Co from the 'continuing operations' consolidated statement of profit or loss for 20X6 suggests that operating expenses as a % of revenue in 20X6 were 35.6% (30,800 [37,400 – 6,600]/86,400 [122,400 – 36,000]), which is actually higher than that for 20X7 (34.2%). On a like-for-like basis this, along with the improvement in the gross profit margin, suggests a better financial performance for the Pinardi group without Silva Co.

Tell us what you think

Got comments or feedback on this book? Let us know.

Use your QR code reader:

Or, visit:

https://bppgroup.fra1.qualtrics.com/jfe/form/SV_cuphESF344D68Mm